DISCARDED

TRENDS IN YOUTH DEVELOPMENT
Visions, Realities and Challenges

OUTREACH SCHOLARSHIP

Editor:

Richard M. Lerner
Tufts University
Medford, Massachusetts, U.S.A.

SERVING CHILDREN AND FAMILIES THROUGH COMMUNITY-UNIVERSITY PARTNERSHIPS: Success Stories
Vol. 1   ISBN 0-7923-8540-3   T.R. Chibucos, R.M. Lerner

FAMILY DIVERSITY AND FAMILY POLICY: Strengthening Families for America's Children
Vol. 2   ISBN 0-7923-8612-4   R.M. Lerner, E.E. Sparks, L.D. McCubbin

SOCIAL CHANGE, PUBLIC POLICY AND COMMUNITY COLLABORATION: Training Human Development Professionals for the 21st Century
Vol. 3   ISBN 0-7923-8659-0   P.A. Ralston, R.M. Lerner, A.K. Mullis,
                              C.B. Simerly, J.P. Murray

TRANSFORMING SOCIAL INQUIRY, TRANSFORMING SOCIAL ACTION: New Paradigms for Crossing the Theory/Practice Divide in Universities and Communities
Vol. 4   ISBN 0-7923-7787-7   F.T. Sherman, W.R. Torbert

THE JUVENILE OFFENDER: Theory, Research and Applications
Vol. 5   ISBN 0-7923-7222-0   R.D. Hoge

TRENDS IN YOUTH DEVELOPMENT
Visions, Realities and Challenges

edited by

Peter L. Benson
Search Institute

Karen Johnson Pittman
Forum for Youth Investment

KLUWER ACADEMIC PUBLISHERS
Boston / Dordrecht / London

Distributors for North, Central and South America:
Kluwer Academic Publishers
101 Philip Drive
Assinippi Park
Norwell, Massachusetts 02061 USA
Telephone (781) 871-6600
Fax (781) 681-9045
E-Mail <kluwer@wkap.com>

Distributors for all other countries:
Kluwer Academic Publishers Group
Distribution Centre
Post Office Box 322
3300 AH Dordrecht, THE NETHERLANDS
Telephone 31 78 6392 392
Fax 31 78 6546 474
E-Mail <services@wkap.nl>

 Electronic Services <http://www.wkap.nl>

Library of Congress Cataloging-in-Publication Data

Trends in youth development: visions, realities, and challenges / edited by Peter L.Benson, Karen Johnson Pittman.
　p. cm. – (Outreach Scholarship; 6)
　Includes bibliographical references and index.
　ISBN 0-7923-7451-7 (alk. paper)
　1. Youth—Services for United States. 2. Social work with youth—United States. I. Benson, Peter L. II. Pittman, Karen Johnson III Series

HV1431 .T74 2001
362.7'083'0973—dc21   2001037588

Copyright　2001 by Kluwer Academic Publishers

All rights reserved. No part of this publication may be reproduced, stored in a retrieval system or transmitted in any form or by any means, mechanical, photo-copying, recording, or otherwise, without the prior written permission of the publisher, Kluwer Academic Publishers, 101 Philip Drive, Assinippi Park, Norwell, Massachusetts 02061

Printed on acid-free paper. Printed in the United States of America

The Editors gratefully acknowledge financial assistance provided by Public/Private Ventures towards the preparation of this volume.
Chapter 4 is reprinted with permission of the Center for Youth Development and Policy Research, Academy for Educational Development, Washington, D.C.

The Publisher offers discounts on this book for course use and bulk purchases. For further information, send email to <michael.williams@wkap.com>.

CONTENTS

Introduction
  MOVING THE YOUTH DEVELOPMENT MESSAGE:
  TURNING A VAGUE IDEA INTO A MORAL IMPERATIVE
  Peter L. Benson and Karen Pittman vii

Part I. Framing Youth Development 1
  1. UNFINISHED BUSINESS: FURTHER REFLECTIONS
     ON A DECADE OF PROMOTING YOUTH DEVELOPMENT
     Karen Pittman, Merita Irby, and Thaddeus Ferber 3

Part II. Arenas of Action That Drive Youth Development 51
  2. PERCEPTUAL BARRIERS TO VALUING AND
     SUPPORTING YOUTH
     Susan Nall Bales 55

  3. THE POLICY CLIMATE FOR EARLY ADOLESCENT
     INITIATIVES
     Gary Walker 77

  4. A MATTER OF MONEY: THE COST AND FINANCING
     OF YOUTH DEVELOPMENT
     Robert P. Newman, Stephanie M. Smith, and Richard Murphy 91

  5. THE SCIENTIFIC FOUNDATIONS OF YOUTH
     DEVELOPMENT
     Peter L. Benson and Rebecca N. Saito 135

  6. MEASURING DEFICITS AND ASSETS:
     HOW WE TRACK YOUTH DEVELOPMENT NOW,
     AND HOW WE SHOULD TRACK IT
     Gary B. MacDonald and Rafael Valdivieso 155

Part III. Locating Youth Development on the Ground:
  Systems and Settings 187
  7. HOW HISTORY, IDEOLOGY, AND STRUCTURE SHAPE
     THE ORGANIZATIONS THAT SHAPE YOUTH
     Joan Costello, Mark Toles, Julie Spielberger, and Joan Wynn 191

  8. JUVENILE JUSTICE AND POSITIVE YOUTH DEVELOPMENT
     Robert G. Schwartz 231

9. THE MORE THINGS CHANGE, THE MORE THEY STAY THE SAME: THE EVOLUTION AND DEVOLUTION OF YOUTH EMPLOYMENT PROGRAMS
   Alan Zuckerman   269

10. YOUTH DEVELOPMENT IN COMMUNITY SETTINGS: CHALLENGES TO OUR FIELD AND OUR APPROACH
    James P. Connell, Michelle Alberti Gambone, and Thomas J. Smith   291

Index   309

Introduction
MOVING THE YOUTH DEVELOPMENT MESSAGE: TURNING A VAGUE IDEA INTO A MORAL IMPERATIVE

Peter L. Benson and Karen Pittman

THE CONTAGION OF AN IDEA

In the past fifteen years, countless programs, agencies, funding initiatives, professionals, and volunteers have embraced the term "youth development." Linked more by shared passion than by formal membership or credentials, these people and places have contributed to a wave of energy and activity not unlike that of a social movement, with a multitude of people "on the ground" connecting to a set of ideas that give sustenance, support, and value to increasingly innovative efforts to build competent, successful, and healthy youth.

There are several particularly interesting dimensions to this movement. First, the youth development idea has the potential to draw people and organizations together across many sectors. Conferences and initiatives using youth development language attract increasingly eclectic audiences, bringing together national youth organizations, schools, city, county, and state agencies, police and juvenile justice workers, clergy, and committed citizens. Perhaps embedded in the youth development idea is a philosophy or a "way" that has created an intellectual and/or spiritual home for actors across many settings. However this happens, it is clear that one of the powerful social consequences of the youth development idea is a connecting of the dots—the weaving within and across city, county, state, and sometimes national lines, of a tapestry of new relationships. This uniting function has been critical in the creation of collaborative, community-wide initiatives in literally thousands of American cities and towns.

It also appears to be the case that the youth development idea brings to the surface a kind of work that, for a variety of reasons, has historically been diminished and marginalized. There have always been, of course, people and places attending to the developmental journey of children and adolescents; youth developers existed long before the label youth development was applied to a particular approach or field. But we suspect there is a mixture of cultural and social forces at work today that increases the need to place one's work in a broader context, advancing the social good in a time of rapid social change.

The crafting of youth development as a necessary and powerful idea does come at a time of heightened concern about American youth. Youth are on the national radar screen. And this awareness—as well as fear and worry—is fed by many dynamics. We've invented the concept of at-risk youth, for example, to mark the persistent presence of vulnerable, marginalized (and in the public mind, dangerous) youth. We've created professions and trained professionals to address this population. Employers worry about the vitality of the next generation of workers. School achievement data are worrisome. Running parallel to these phenomena are two additional social concerns: that many of the core elements necessary for shaping healthy human beings—parental presence, sustained relationships with caring adults, and access to social programs—are growing increasingly fragile, and a general sense that connectedness to major socializing institutions, such as schools, neighborhoods, families, and congregations, is evaporating.

The idea of youth development enters the world, then, at a time of greater social need. At the highest level, we suggest that the contagion associated with the idea is an attempt to make manifest a formula for cultivating healthy human beings in a society that is forgetting what has heretofore been a natural and instinctive knowledge. There is also evidence that efforts to capture and state this formula are of growing international interest, with youth development concepts, conferences, and networks thriving in a larger world in which social, economic, and technological changes threaten successful socialization.

Perhaps the most surprising dimension to this movement, then, is the enthusiasm with which countless individuals and institutions have embraced an idea that, in both practical and conceptual terms, remains vague, if not confusing. A funder once noted that attempting to promote youth development was akin to "shoveling fog." (See Chapter 1.) While the term youth development has made its way into the language of diverse service providers across an array of sectors and settings, the public at large and policy makers will be unlikely to embrace and fully support something that fails to conjure up an immediate image and a set of accompanying assumptions.

People understand what we mean when we talk about health services. People recognize the cluster of institutions we're referring to when we talk about schools. If we continue to use the term youth development to simultaneously denote a call to action, a mobilization of people and places, a body of knowledge, a set of organizations, a philosophy, and a life stage, without qualifying it accordingly, we run the risk of squandering the remarkable momentum of the past fifteen years.

FROM A VAGUE IDEA TO SPECIFIC CONCEPTS

We need to do a better job of saying what we mean and meaning what we say when we talk about youth development. Those of us who work in this area know

Introduction   ix

that our shared difficulty in defining the territory and its official canon is something of an Achilles' heel. But we need not be too apologetic, because our fuzziness is also a strength. Youth development as an arena of ideas, actions, and practices did not begin as an academic exercise grounded in theory and research. Had it done so, it would be easier at this moment to define the term, but it would likely have slowed the growth and innovation of the movement. We seem to be at a place now where the movement—to be sustained and strengthened—needs to circle back and focus energy on identifying principles, strategies, and evidence (i.e., a knowledge base) worthy of academic and policy attention.

Paying close attention to *how* we use the term "youth development" is as important as clarifying *what we mean* when we use the term. Let us acknowledge that there is indeed a handful of nouns (e.g., field, approach, program, professional, movement) that, when placed after the term youth development, point to several distinct concepts. In addition to clarifying one's intended meaning, qualifying the term by appending some "thing" to it also distinguishes these now common uses of the term from its literal meaning—namely, the development of youth. Youth development is, in the most basic sense, synonymous with child and adolescent development, concepts that, alone, have nothing to do with any particular flavor of intervention, approach, or philosophy. The simple act of disciplining ourselves to qualify the term this way could get us a long way toward communicating more clearly, with one another and with critical stakeholders whose attention we seek.

The youth development field, as we envision it, encompasses a vast territory. It is *comprehensive,* calling forth a host of inputs (e.g., relationships, programs, opportunities), in a variety of contexts (individuals, families, neighborhoods, communities), necessary to address a range of developmental targets (e.g., competence, belonging, connection, interdependence, contribution). Its organizing principle is *promotion,* by which we mean both mobilizing energy to enhance and increase access to strength-building inputs and building the personal strengths needed to thrive. It is, as the term denotes, *developmental,* recognizing the growth process and stages in the journey as well as the role that individual young people play in navigating themselves through those stages. And it is *symbiotic,* drawing into its orbit ideas, strategies, and practices from many disciplines and lines of inquiry (e.g., resiliency, prevention, public health, developmental psychology).

The youth development approach now benefits from high face validity in many arenas. Decision makers and practitioners can easily speak the language of promoting positive development, and as they do, heads nod knowingly and affirmatively. In response to this strong initial appeal has come an array of tough and important questions, many of which the authors of this volume begin to tackle in the chapters that follow. How do we really do this? Where's the hard evidence that sells this to decision makers wedded to accountability? Is our target vulnerable kids or all kids? What works?

Clearly, the youth development field is onto something big, something that touches both head and heart. Youth development has evolved from a vague but captivating idea into a substantial set of concepts that continues to mature. But could it be something more?

FROM SPECIFIC CONCEPTS TO A MORAL IMPERATIVE

The field is at a critical crossroads. For fifteen years, we've been in a storming phase, spreading this comprehensive, strength-based, symbiotic, developmental, high-social-purpose agenda. And by so doing, we've coalesced an impressive number of advocates and actors, providing impetus and courage for generating positive innovations in countless communities and programs. In the context of a public that is historically reluctant to dedicate significant portions of public budgets to developmental activities, and which, in response to piecemeal solutions to complex problems, has grown increasingly skeptical about government-funded social programs in general, we have witnessed significant leadership at the federal level for both after-school programs and mentoring (see Chapter 3). While the youth development approach has made substantial inroads with youth-focused nonprofit organizations, it has been much slower to take hold within larger public systems such as education and juvenile justice (Chapter 7).

If the idea of youth development is to add up not only to a legitimate set of concepts but also to a clear and compelling vision of what it takes for a nation to support young people, we need to move beyond showcasing examples of successful programs and focus on addressing the basic questions of effectiveness, scale, and sustainability. It is time to enter a formative stage, with more deliberate attention to creating and communicating a body of knowledge, evidence, principles, and strategies to undergird, direct, sustain, and strengthen the field into a recognized and valued paradigm. This volume is one step toward charting the issues we must address if youth development is to continue in its evolution from a vague idea of what young people need to a compelling moral imperative to provide every young person with a core set of services, supports, and opportunities.

THE YOUTH DEVELOPMENT DIRECTIONS PROJECT

This volume is grounded in a process launched in the spring of 1998. The Youth Development Directions Project (YDDP) was conceived by the Youth Development Funders Group at a meeting held at the Ewing Marian Kauffman Foundation in Kansas City in the summer of 1997. The project's stated purpose was to examine the state of the youth field, lay out the key challenges it faces, and suggest directions in which to advance its growth and effectiveness. YDDP brought together key youth development funders and national intermediary organizations to write and discuss a series of papers on the field. Public/Private Ventures president Gary Walker hosted and facilitated the process.

The project's structure was simple. The group met for a day and a half in late May 1998 to discuss the major issues confronting the field, and to determine the topics for and contributors to this volume. The authors wrote drafts over the remainder of 1998 and early 1999, meeting again for a day and a half in late 1998 to continue the May discussion and to critique the draft papers. Editing and further discussions took place during the remainder of 1999. The discussions, and the

Introduction   xi

chapters in this volume, focus on the political and social context for youth development as a guiding principle in youth policy, the state of scientific evidence supporting this work, and critical institutional challenges to the field. Chapter 1 uses the broadest of lenses to present a brief history of the youth development approach along with the importance of issue framing. The lens narrows in Part II, focusing on how youth development plays out in particular "arenas of action" such as policy, public opinion, and research. In the third and final section of the volume, the critical "systems and settings" where youth development becomes a concrete reality come into focus—communities, youth-serving organizations, the employment sector, juvenile justice.

This volume includes all of the papers generated by the Youth Development Directions Project. In addition, we've provided an introduction to each section as well as solicited one new chapter, Susan Nall Bales's "Perceptual Barriers to Valuing and Supporting Youth," which contributes crucial insights for the "taking stock" process and the strategic positioning of youth development.

TAKING STOCK OF TAKING STOCK

As the editors reflect on the Youth Development Directions Project and the preparation of this volume, several concluding thoughts come to mind.

First and foremost, there are several critically important themes that are only superficially touched on by this volume. In its efforts to push key conversations forward, the YDD Project neither intended to be nor included broad enough representation to provide a comprehensive picture of the many complex forces at play in influencing young people's development.

Academy for Educational Development
1825 Connecticut Avenue, N.W.
Washington, DC 20009
202-884-8000
www.aed.org

Center for Youth Development
 and Policy Research
Academy for Educational Development
1825 Connecticut Avenue, N.W.
Washington, DC 20009
202-884-8267
www.aed.org/us/youth.html

Chapin Hall Center for Children
University of Chicago
1313 East 60th Street
Chicago, IL 60637
773-753-5900
www.chapin.uchicago.edu

Community Action for Youth Project
308 Glendale Drive
Toms River, NJ 08753
732-288-2737
www.cayp.org

The Forum for Youth Investment,
International Youth Foundation
7014 Westmoreland Avenue
Takoma Park, MD 20912
301-270-6250
www.forumforyouthinvestment.org

Juvenile Law Center
1315 Walnut Street, 4th Floor
Philadelphia, PA 19107
215-625-0551
www.jlc.org

National Youth Employment Coalition
1836 Jefferson Place, N.W.
Washington, DC 20036
202-659-1064
www.nyec.org

Public/Private Ventures
2005 Market Street, Suite 900
Philadelphia, PA 19103
215-557-4400
www.ppv.org

Search Institute
700 South Third Street
Suite 210
Minneapolis, MN 55415-1138
612-376-8955
www.search-institute.org

Critical perspectives that require further exploration are, among others, the centrality of families in supporting the development process, advances made by advocacy organizations over the past two decades, and the role that recreation, faith-based organizations, and other sectors do and could play in the future. In addition, unpacking the complex potential of the intersection of education reform and youth development principles, and more concretely the intersection of schools and community-based organizations, is another key topic that this volume refers to but hardly tackles.

In thinking about the rich discussions that led up to this volume, we are once again struck by the tendency in our field to begin critical conversations but rarely to come to closure. Whether the reasons are logistical (time pressures, lack of funds) or more complicated (competition, ideological tensions), it is clear that our inability to conclusively answer such questions as "what is youth development?" and "what are critical inputs and outcomes?" has proved frustrating, not only to many of us and our constituencies, but to funders as well. It is now time to move forward—to articulate a clearer vision of what should be, better tools for assessing what is, and bolder strategies for closing the gaps.

Finally, the vision of youth development that is explored in these chapters, while in need of clarification, has led to a dramatic change in the way individuals, organizations, and communities conceptualize their work with and on behalf of young people. An incredible amount of information and effort is being generated at the national and local levels to support this vision. It is our hope that this volume, in celebrating that progress, will trigger intentional, collaborative efforts to direct, strengthen, grow, and sustain this vision, one that is crucial for advancing the well-being of our nation as a whole.

Part I. FRAMING YOUTH DEVELOPMENT

Each of the chapters in this volume evolved out of a common vision—a vision of youth development. While the vision lacks complete clarity, as discussed in the introduction, and while there is no consensus as to what it entails, the vision *has* led to dramatic changes in the way individuals, organizations, and policy makers conceptualize their work with and on behalf of youth.

The power of issue framing has gained increased prominence in recent years, led in part by the work of former secretary of labor Robert Reich, who has advanced the concept through several books, articles, and op-ed pieces. Writes Reich: "The way a debate is framed and choices are posed is often more important than which option is chosen."

The increasing recognition of the importance of issue framing is timely to the release of this volume, since the efforts of youth advocates to systematically shift the prevailing frameworks and language surrounding youth are considered a significant accomplishment, if not the hallmark, of the youth development movement.

The authors in this volume provide a testament both to the importance of issue framing in general, and to the power of the youth development framework in particular. Susan Nall Bales writes that "when the facts don't fit the frame, the facts are rejected, not the frame." James P. Connell, Michelle Alberti Gambone, and Thomas J. Smith assert that the youth development field needs "an overarching structure within which all of us can find our place—within which we can each articulate what we can contribute to making meaningful change and learning from it, on the ground, in diverse communities."

Because of the power associated with perspective, we begin this book with an introduction that explicitly places youth development in the context of issue framing. This chapter presents a brief history of the youth development approach, discusses the importance of issue framing, reflects on some of the emerging and recurring barriers to advancing the youth development framework, and proposes an agenda for moving forward.

CONTENTS OF PART I WITH ORGANIZATIONAL SKETCH OF CONTRIBUTING AUTHORS

1. Unfinished Business: Further Reflections on a Decade of Promoting Youth Development

Karen Pittman, Merita Irby, and Thaddeus Ferber

The Forum for Youth Investment is an initiative of the International Youth Foundation. The Forum is committed to increasing the quality and quantity of youth investments and involvement, by promoting a big-picture approach to planning and policy development among the broad range of national organizations that help constituents and communities invest in children, youth, and families. The Forum's work revolves around the need for clearer statements about who young people are, what they can do, and what should be available to support their development; stronger commitments to deliver what is needed; and better alignment among the various policies, systems, and professionals working for and with young people.

1 UNFINISHED BUSINESS: FURTHER REFLECTIONS ON A DECADE OF PROMOTING YOUTH DEVELOPMENT[1]

Karen Pittman, Merita Irby, and Thaddeus Ferber

THE CALL FOR A COHESIVE STRATEGY FOR PREPARING YOUNG PEOPLE FOR ADULTHOOD

Within the span of a year, two commissions, the Grant Foundation Commission on Work, Family and Citizenship, and the Carnegie Council on Adolescent Development, issued reports that framed challenges for the next decades.

The Carnegie Commission's *Turning Points* (Task Force on Education of Young Adolescents, 1989) asked:

> What qualities do we envision in the 15-year-old who has been well served in the middle years of schooling? What do we want every young adolescent to know, to feel, to be able to do upon emerging from that educational and school-related experience?
>
> Our answer is embodied in the five characteristics associated with being an effective human being. Our 15-year-old will be an intellectually reflective person, a person en route to a lifetime of meaningful work, a good citizen, a caring and ethical individual, and a healthy person.
>
> ... The challenge of the 1990s is to define and create the structures of teaching and learning for young adolescents 10 to 15 years old that will yield mature young people of competence, compassion and promise. (p. 15)

The Grant Commission's *The Forgotten Half* (1988) stated:

> Young people's experiences at home, at school, in the community, and at work are strongly interconnected, and our response to

problems that arise in any of these domains must be equally well integrated.... All young people need:

- More constructive contact with adults who can help them guide their talents into useful and satisfying paths;
- Opportunities to participate in community activities that they and adults value, especially giving service to others;
- Special help with particularly difficult problems ranging from learning disabilities to substance addiction; and
- Initial jobs, no matter how modest, that offer a path to accomplishment and to career opportunity. (p. 3)

These commissions focused on different age groups and to some extent on different systems. *The Forgotten Half* helped focus the country's attention on a vulnerable population—non-college-bound youth—simultaneously pushing age boundaries for support and challenging the adequacy of social, economic, and vocational supports for those not in trouble but not in college. The Carnegie Commission's report focused on a younger age group and the systems that serve those youth—schools, health-care institutions, and community-based organizations. Both commissions offered lists of desired youth outcomes and critical community resources that spanned systems and levels. Both offered broad agendas calling for systemic and social reforms. And, most important, both focused on preparing young people for successful adulthood rather than solely preventing or ameliorating their problems. Important reports preceded these volumes, and other reports have followed. But these reports captured public attention and set the stage for a decade of work focused on building on youth potential.

There have been significant wins since the publication of those two reports. With the assistance of funding from the U.S. Department of Housing and Urban Development (HUD), YouthBuild—a training and leadership program employing out-of-school young adults in housing rehabilitation—has been replicated nationally, and Boys & Girls Clubs have developed a foothold in low-income housing projects. Dedicated youth development taxes or youth authorities have been established in a number of cities from San Francisco to Savannah. The Youth Development Community Block Grant—a bill reallocating existing federal prevention funding into a dedicated funding stream—was introduced in Congress. Most recently, $454 million in federal funding has been earmarked for afterschool programming through the 21st Century Learning Centers. And at the state and local levels, one would be hard-pressed to count the many programs, policies, and initiatives addressing the challenges that have been proposed, started, or expanded since the release of those two reports.

But there have also been significant losses. Although the Youth Development Block Grant was introduced in Congress, it did not pass. Federal support for postsecondary education declined, reopening the gap that had been closed between minority and white college enrollment in the 1980s. Young people's rights to access reproductive health services continue to be challenged. And the last half of the 1990s saw the enactment of "get-tough" juvenile justice legislation that runs counter to theories of youth development or young offender rehabilitation.

The phrase "youth development" is now fairly well ingrained in the U.S. policy lexicon, undergirded by the bumper-sticker phrase "problem-free is not fully prepared." But the overall impact of this language shift is uneven—its importance challenged by such stories as youth corrections programs that have been renamed "youth development programs" with no concomitant changes in philosophy, programming, or staff practices. So, when all is tallied, what has really been accomplished in the past decade? What has not? What is needed in the next decade to make youth development not just a buzzword but a powerful public idea?

Making no claims of definitive historical accuracy (hence the word *reflections* in our title), we use the concept of creating a public idea as a lens through which to examine the successes and failures of efforts to promote youth development as an approach, a policy agenda, and a field. We do three things in this chapter. First, we summarize the paradigm shift associated with the phrase "youth development," and offer reflections on the successes and shortfalls of efforts to promote the concept as a public idea. Next, we summarize and reflect on the range of emerging and recurring issues that need to be addressed by the field. Finally, we offer an agenda for forging a strong public idea about the value of investing in and involving young people, including a concrete example of where this work has been done successfully.

THE PARADIGM SHIFT: YOUTH DEVELOPMENT AS A PUBLIC IDEA

The Paradigm Shift

"Paradigm shift" has become one of the many overused phrases of the 1990s. In this case, however, it is the appropriate term. The decade spawned the development of a number of frameworks put forth as either descriptive or predictive youth development models. Behind them all are an unflinching commitment to *broaden the goals* to promote not only problem reduction but preparation for adulthood; *increase the options* for instruction and involvement by improving the quality and availability of supports, services, and opportunities offered; and *redefine the strategies* in order to ensure a broad scale of supports and opportunities for young people that reach far beyond the existing status quo.

Broadening the Goals

What should young people accomplish? Since the Carnegie and Grant reports were issued, there have been numerous efforts to further specify a research-based list of desired youth outcomes that go beyond problem prevention to describe the types of attitudes, skills, knowledge, and behaviors society should expect of young people and young people should want for themselves. Indeed, the number and diversity of lists have prompted funders and end users to call for either a consensus list or a translation guide. Confusion notwithstanding, the outcomes lists share a few underlying themes:[2]

- **Problem-free is not fully prepared.** There is something fundamentally limiting about defining everything in terms of a problem. In the final analysis, we assess people not in terms of problems (or lack thereof) but *potential*. "Problem-free" does not represent the full range of goals most parents have for their children. And it does not reflect what young people want for themselves.
- **Academic competence, while critical, is not enough.** Success in adolescence and adulthood requires a range of skills. It includes intellectual competence, but it does not stop there. Numerous commissions, organizations, and reports, including the SCANS report (Secretary's Commission on Achieving Necessary Skills, 1991) on employability skills, have defined a generic set of competencies that go beyond academic or cognitive competence to include vocational, physical, emotional, civic, social, and cultural competencies.
- **Competence alone, while critical, is not enough.** Skills may go unused or be used in unproductive, antisocial ways if not anchored by confidence, character, and connections. Gang members, for example, are often extraordinarily competent, confident, and well connected. Their character, however, is seriously questioned by adults and youth with a strong sense of social responsibility.

These three assertions are not meant in any way to trivialize the importance of problem prevention or academic preparation. Nor are they presented as "stiffer" selection criteria, suggesting that, because society needs young adults who are more than problem-free and literate, investments should be made only in those young people who have the most potential. On the contrary, the power of the paradigm shift, to the extent that it is fully understood, is that it reaffirms the need to help *all youth* achieve the goals parents set for their children and young people set for themselves.

We have collapsed a complex list of behavioral and psychosocial outcomes into the "4 Cs" rubric used for close to a decade by the International Youth Foundation to define the broad tasks of adolescence: developing competence, confidence, character, and connections (Pittman and Irby, 1996). We have recently added a fifth C, contributions, to underscore the fact that fully prepared is not enough—young people need to find ways to become fully engaged. This requires access to pathways to full participation in the community, the workplace, and the broader society.

James Connell, Michelle Alberti Gambone, and Thomas J. Smith, in "Youth Development in Community Settings: Challenges to Our Field and Our Approach" (Chapter 10 in this volume), have updated the literature reviews done at the beginning of the decade (e.g., Pittman and Wright, 1991), and they propose that the short-term outcomes expected of adolescents can be summed up as three broad tasks: learning to be productive, learning to connect, and learning to navigate. They emphasize the importance of prioritizing "outcomes shown to predict success in adulthood," while avoiding "personality characteristics and other internal traits."

These two summary lists reflect the variations being circulated by youth development "experts." They are different but not dissimilar. For example, developing competence and learning how to contribute can translate into learning to be productive; developing connections translates into learning to connect; developing confidence and character translates into learning to navigate. Both reflect a desire to limit lists and to link them to outcomes that can be observed and measured. The utility is in the definition of clear behaviors and indicators.

Some of the most concrete work to date has been done not by researchers but by practitioners brought together by the Youth Development Institute of the Fund for the City of New York. Starting with the assorted research-based lists, practitioners engaged in a structured process to develop observable indicators for short-term outcomes that can be linked to longer-term goals. For example, under the category of civic competency,[3] they identified potential indicators, including:

- Voter registration;
- Knowledge of civil and human rights embodied in the Bill of Rights and elsewhere;
- Knowledge of how to interface with and access government systems (police, fire, emergency medical services);
- Contributing to the community and believing you can make a difference;
- Bringing a group of people together; and
- Understanding specific codes of conduct within organizations and consequences for failure to abide by them. (Networks for Youth Development, 1998, p. 6)

In the end, it is this kind of work that has pushed the paradigm shift into practical use. And these are the kinds of outcomes that parents and policy makers could look for as evidence of effective programming.

Increasing the Options

What do young people need? What must communities provide in order to expect fully prepared youth? The lists of recommended resources, inputs, and supports for youth are as numerous and varied as the lists of outcomes. America's Promise broke through the public awareness barrier with its pronouncement of five "fundamental resources" for youth: safe places, caring adults, healthy starts, education for marketable skills, and opportunities to serve. These are similar to those offered by the Center for Youth Development, the International Youth Foundation, and others (e.g., safe, stable places; caring, competent adults; basic health, human, and infrastructure services; role models; high-quality instruction and training; opportunities to participate and contribute; navigating resources and networks; high expectations and standards).[4] While there are many lists, the translations here are obvious.

Again, the Youth Development Institute demonstrates the importance of moving beyond abstract concepts to name concrete indicators of high-quality youth development organizations. For example, the following potential indicators are listed under "create safe environment":[5]

- Client rules, including the prohibition of violence, drug and alcohol use, and carrying weapons, are developed and established with input from the young people;
- Rules are published, distributed, and periodically reviewed by staff and participants of the organization on a regular basis;
- Rules are enforced in a manner consistent with the philosophy of the organization;
- There is a security plan;
- Conflict resolution and mediation training is available to young people and staff;
- New staff must attend training; and
- Staff are trained in emergency procedures.

In the end, these lists of inputs needed to promote overall development are surprisingly similar to the lists of inputs found effective in preventing problems.[6] The conceptual work advanced throughout the past decade on developmental domains, key inputs, and desired outcomes that underlie youth development are summarized in Figure 1.

Redefining the Strategies

What should communities and policy makers do? Much of the power of the youth development argument lies in the simple statement, "How we define goals deter-

FIGURE 1

Broadening the Goals and Increasing the Options for Youth

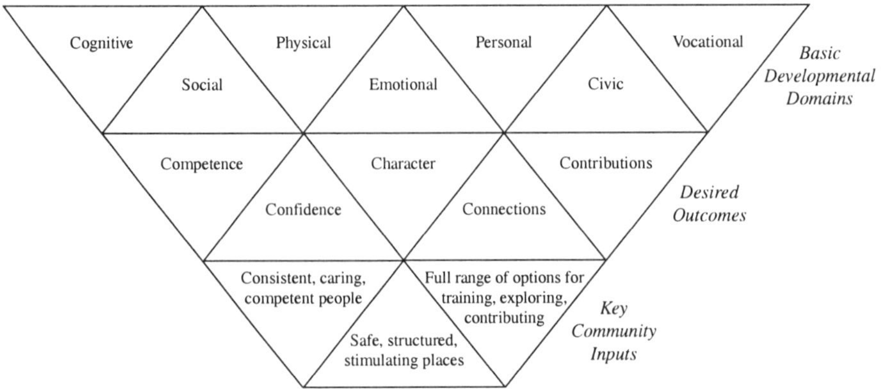

Unfinished Business

mines how we design strategies." The impetus for promoting development was, in large part, a desire to redefine the way services were conceived, funded, and implemented. Many strategies were proposed over the decade. Stepping back, however, our collective answer seemed to be, "Do things differently." The shift from thinking in terms of deficit reduction to thinking in terms of full preparation forced acknowledgment of the reality that "programs"—the intentional interventions designed to change youth's *behavior*—had to be recast as intentional interventions to change youth's *environments*. Building upon the basic things we know about youth development, a series of challenges were laid out over the past decade—challenges that were, for the most part, presented as lists of things that must be done to move beyond the status quo. Succinctly stated, they were challenges to push:

- **Beyond prevention.** Again, problem-free is not fully prepared. Addressing youth problems is critical, but defining goals exclusively in terms of problem prevention is limiting. We should be as articulate about the attitudes, skills, behaviors, and values we want young people to have as we are about those we hope they avoid. Academic competence is important but not sufficient. Social competence, health (emotional and physical), vocational and civic competence are all needed to be fully prepared. Competence in and of itself is not sufficient. Young people need skills, but they also need confidence, character, and connection to family, peers, and community, and they must contribute to those around them.
- **Beyond quick fixes.** Development does not occur in a vacuum, and it does not stop because program funds run out. Targeted, time-limited interventions may be needed. But, at a minimum, they should be offered with the full knowledge that young people are attached to programs or environments that are not time limited and not targeted solely to a specific population of young people with problems. There is a general need to foster investment in long-term, sustained growth services, opportunities, and supports. Having these as a base decreases the chances that short-term, targeted strategies will be needed and increases the chances that, when delivered, they will be effective.
- **Beyond basic services.** Young people need affordable, accessible care and services (e.g., health and transportation), safe and stable environments, and high-quality instruction and training. But they also need supports—relationships and networks that provide nurturing, standards, and guidance—and opportunities to try new roles, master challenges, and contribute to family and community.
- **Beyond schools and school buildings.** Schools are pivotal institutions in most young people's lives. But they are just one of many that affect youth development. Young people grow up in families, in neighborhoods, and with community-based organizations, service agencies, businesses and employers, as well as schools. All of these are *settings* for interactions that can contribute to or undermine development. Equally important, all of these are real or potential *coordinators* of interactions.
- **Beyond the school day.** Adolescence is a time of significantly expanded

interests and mobility. Young people want to (and have the mobility and skills to) seek relationships and experiences beyond the family and school. The nonschool hours (evenings, weekends, summers) can be times of opportunity, risk, or stagnation. Young people may be offered a range of attractive opportunities. They can venture out on their own and encounter significant risks, or, faced with the risks but not the opportunities, they can stagnate at home because of parental concerns for their safety.

- **Beyond youth professionals.** Adolescence is a time of relationship building. The work of youth professionals is important but not sufficient. Moreover, their numbers are not sufficient, and the relationships they offer, while critically important, are often insufficient unless they can demonstrate that they are involved, not just because they are being paid, but because they truly care (i.e., go beyond the job description). Parents, neighbors, relatives, business owners, non-youth-focused professionals, and older youth in the community who know local youth by name must be seen and cultivated as resources. Nonschool and, ultimately, non-youth-work professionals must be encouraged to view the preparation and involvement of young people as a part of their responsibility.
- **Beyond recipients.** Young people need services, supports, and training. But they also need opportunities to contribute. The best preparation for tomorrow is participation today. Further, young people's participation should not be seen only as contributing to *their own* development. Youth can and do play critical roles as change agents in their families, peer groups, and communities.
- **Beyond labeling.** One way or another, all young people develop. Most need additional support in navigating choices and assessing options. A growing number are disadvantaged by a lack of services, supports, and opportunities. All may be at risk, but the risks are not equal, and those risks do not define their potential. Targeting is fine; labeling is not. There must be ways to ensure that those who need extra resources receive them without being labeled "resource poor."
- **Beyond pilots.** All young people need the services, opportunities, and supports described. No one program or organization can or should be expected to deliver all supports to all youth in a neighborhood or even in a school or housing complex. Yet, to have a significant impact, these supports must be available to a critical mass of young people in a school or neighborhood. Too many programs remain at the pilot level, offering services and supports to a small fraction of those who need help. And too few neighborhoods weave these small efforts together to make a web of supports that are available to 70 or 80 percent of the youth population.

The "beyonds" language was effective in focusing attention on the need for new ways of framing the goals, presenting the options, and defining the strategies. But it was sometimes interpreted as a call for abandonment or vilification of the existing responses rather than a challenge to build on them. When taken not as "instead of" but as "in addition to," it is clear that the underlying themes of the calls for change were solid, combining to define what loosely could be

Unfinished Business

considered the "above and beyond" principles for youth preparation and development. Restated, "beyond prevention" is really a call for problem reduction and full preparation for adult roles and responsibilities. This is a laudable and logical goal. Similarly, "beyond quick fixes" is a call for a balanced focus on deficit remediation, crisis response, problem prevention, and ongoing attention to development. To summarize, each of the "beyonds" has been redrafted accordingly in Figure 2.

The paradigm shift took hold in programs and organizations, as practitioners and planners worked to address the "beyonds." But the most important implication of the paradigm shift was that the desired goals of overall youth development are difficult, if not impossible, to achieve within the bounds of a single intervention, unless that intervention is, in reality, not a single program (even a comprehensive one) but a reasonably complex strategy to change young people's environments and opportunity structures.

FIGURE 2

Above and Beyond:
Nine Principles of Full Investment and Full Involvement

THE GOAL:	Problem reduction *and* full preparation for adult roles and responsibilities.	**BEYOND PREVENTION**
THE FOCUS:	Deficit remediation, crisis response, problem prevention, *and* long-term attention to development.	**BEYOND QUICK FIXES**
THE INPUTS:	Basic services (human, health, housing, economic) *and* a full range of ongoing supports and opportunities.	**BEYOND BASIC SERVICES**
THE SETTINGS:	Schools *and* homes and a full range of community settings, including community centers, youth organizations, libraries, parks, malls, faith organizations, and businesses.	**BEYOND THE SCHOOL BUILDING**
THE TIMES:	24-7. During the school day *and* before and after school, including nights, holidays, weekends, and summers.	**BEYOND THE SCHOOL DAY**
THE ACTORS:	Teachers, youth workers, *and* families, community members, volunteers, young people, and non-youth-focused professionals.	**BEYOND PROFESSIONALS**
YOUTH ROLES:	Young people as recipients *and* as active agents in their own development and that of their communities and society.	**BEYOND RECIPIENTS**
THE TARGET:	Nonstigmatizing efforts for all youth, those living in high-risk areas, *and* those with specific challenges and problems (e.g., dropouts, young parents, court-involved youth).	**BEYOND LABELING**
THE NUMBERS:	Pilot programs *and* an array of services, supports, and opportunities that are affordable, accessible, and attractive enough that at least 80 percent of youth ages 10-22 are connected to something for at least 80 percent of their second decade of life and beyond.	**BEYOND PILOTS**

Public Ideas—What They Are and Why They're Important

Like the Grant and Carnegie Commission reports, the preceding section dealt at length with the framing of our approaches to (and with) youth—focusing on the call to think in terms of the preparation of young people rather than solely on the prevention or amelioration of their problems. Is this distinction merely academic, or does it have real implications for policy making and practice? Does it really matter how these reports and others frame our approaches to and with youth? Is changing the way an issue is framed a goal worthy of long-term, strategic effort?

In *The Power of Public Ideas,* Robert Reich (1988) writes:

> The core responsibility of those who deal in public policy—elected officials, administrators, policy analysts—is not simply to discover as objectively as possible what people want for themselves and then to determine and implement the best means of satisfying these wants. It is also to provide the public with alternative visions of what is desirable and possible, to stimulate deliberation about them, provoke a reexamination of premises and values, and thus to broaden the range of potential responses and deepen society's understanding of itself. (pp. 3-4)

By reframing the goals in terms of development and by articulating a vision of what it takes to support youth, the Grant and Carnegie reports were, in essence, calling for a new public idea. At the time, many youth advocates were becoming acutely aware of the disconnect between policy approaches to youth and the opinions of the people who actually spent their days directly interacting with youth—youth workers and parents. While policy makers maintained a "problem fixation" mentality, focusing on defining and eliminating deficits, those on the ground focused on young people's current strengths and future potential. Policy makers focused on isolated problems to be "solved" by programs staffed by professionals, while any parent could tell you that children are complex beings raised in families and communities—by parents, relatives, and neighbors. Policy makers spoke of services, while those on the ground began to speak about opportunities and supports. And the only public institution devoted to development (schools) did so within a narrow frame that limited them to promoting academic competence—yet those on the ground (including employers) know intuitively that academic competence in and of itself is not enough.

This disconnect coincided with several research syntheses and policy analyses that in many ways confirmed what parents and youth workers already knew. Indeed, much of the early work of advocates of the youth development approach could be characterized as "footnoting common sense." Research documented that problems covary (youth at risk of teen pregnancy are also at risk of substance abuse, dropping out, etc.), reinforcing a call for more comprehensive programs that address root causes.[7] Evidence that targeted educational and service interventions had at best a weak impact, which further underscored this call. Most important, research showed that problem behaviors are associated not only with each other but also with poor skills, poor motivation, poor connections, and poor options or perceived options (Berlin and Sum, 1988). These developments gave credibility to calls for a focus on improving options as a prevention strategy such as Marian Wright Edelman's famous quote: "Hope is the best contraceptive."

These analyses, coupled with the disconnect, made it clear that the time was ripe for a new public idea that would, as Reich suggests:

- **Provide an alternative vision of what is desirable and possible**—a positive and affirming vision that seems to more closely reflect young people's aspirations for themselves, and parents' aspirations for their children;
- **Stimulate deliberation about the visions**—the outcomes we hope our children will achieve, and what it will take to help them get there;
- **Provoke a reexamination of premises and values**—for example, whether our core value is problem-free youth or fully prepared youth; whether it is appropriate to "fix" youth and to "deter" them from specific behaviors, but not to help them develop; and
- **Broaden the responses**—the range of options that policy makers, practitioners, communities, families, and youth consider.

Reich argues that providing new public ideas such as this one can have powerful effects on our world, producing real, tangible change. We agree. Without a doubt, the past ten years have given rise to more programs—federally funded, nationally affiliated, and locally grown—that have adopted the language and principles of youth development. But numbers are not really the issue. There were plenty of high-quality youth programs in the late 1980s. In our opinion, the most significant change since then has not been in the quality or quantity of programs or policies that promote youth development, although there have been improvements in both. Rather, *the most significant change has been in the increased acceptance of youth preparation and development—not just problem prevention and deterrence—as broad goals requiring intentional monitoring and strategic action.*

As youth advocates, we could lower our sights as we look toward the next decade and focus only on the expansion of promising programs. But a decade ago, we embarked on a journey to create not only more and better programs but also an alternative vision. Progress has been made, but there have been wrong turns and missed opportunities. We need a plan. To create that plan we must look back objectively at what we have done—at both successes and failures. Systematic analysis is difficult—there is no central repository. But without attempting to be definitive or comprehensive, it is possible to offer some broad reflections on the advancement of youth development as a public idea, and on the shifts, drifts, and gaps in action that may have affected the uptake.

Promoting Youth Development as a Public Idea—Successes and Shortfalls

Also in *The Power of Public Ideas,* Mark Moore (1998) delineates the range of ways public ideas can have an impact:

> When ideas become dominant in public policy debates, when an organization develops a strong sense of mission, or when a social norm mobilizes private actions on behalf of public purposes and suppresses other possible approaches, ideas demonstrate their power to provide a context for public debate and action. (p. 75)

This "context for debate and action" is most robust when ideas have permeated the consciousness of policy makers, public and private actors and institutions, and the general populace. With youth development, a great deal of thought has gone into packaging and marketing the key concepts and basic approach within the sphere of philanthropy and among the nonprofit organizations that serve youth in the after-school hours. Many nonprofits, especially the large national organizations, have a renewed sense of mission. Comparatively few resources, however, have been used to nurture this idea within the broader public. (Case in point: Although the authors often refer to "problem-free is not fully prepared" as a "bumper-sticker phrase," it has yet to have actually been put on a bumper sticker.) Further, because efforts to affect public policy have not been built on broad consensus, they have been neither strong nor strategic. And, although some attempts have been made to infuse a youth development approach into such public systems as schools and juvenile justice, the results and responses have been mixed. While there have been successes, it is clear that the overarching vision of the youth development approach—the public idea—has not been sufficiently honed and promoted.

Moore indirectly offers some insight into how our efforts could be strengthened. The passage quoted above was preceded by the following statement:

> ... ideas simultaneously establish the *assumptions, justifications, purposes, and means* of public action. In doing so, they simultaneously authorize and instruct different sectors of the society to take actions on behalf of public purposes. ... In this way ideas both motivate and direct action. (p. 75, emphasis added)

In all likelihood, Moore did not intend the four points on this list to be taken as nonnegotiables. But they are useful. If the above summary of the major drifts is roughly accurate, then to some extent the youth development "public idea" missed the mark on all four of Moore's criteria:

- **Our assumptions were too vague.** We argued for too long that everything could be done for every young person. Having gained credence for a universal list of youth outcomes and needs, we were reluctant to argue for targeted efforts. Youth development experts offered insufficient guidance to communities, program planners, and policy makers who agreed with the vision but wanted assistance in prioritizing the work. Some were left feeling guilty that they could not deliver "the works," while others felt that they had made a significant impact by haphazardly picking only one or two things from the list.

- **Our justifications were weak.** We confused logic with evidence. In part because the early youth development arguments were so well received, there was insufficient attention paid to fortifying the evidence base. Many individual programs and organizations declared themselves too complex to evaluate, and balked (as did funders) at the cost and difficulty of good evaluation. Community-planning efforts were often built on insufficient data about demand or supply and were started without baseline data on reasonable youth indicators. And the early work that began to "footnote common sense"—to develop the research arguments for the connections being made between proposed outputs and desired outcomes—declined rather than accelerated.

- **The stated purposes were not compelling.** We eschewed problem-reduction goals, losing public interest and drifting away from the youth who needed the paradigm shift the most. Again, we allowed the "beyond" arguments to be cast too heavily as "instead of" rather than "in addition to." Without solid anchors to the things we want our children to avoid, youth development messages often failed to excite the public and policy makers. To sell, investments in such areas as after-school programming have to be tied to goals people are prepared to invest in—academic achievement, safety, substance abuse, and pregnancy prevention. Equally important, they must be seen as credible responses to the challenges faced and posed by young people who already have several strikes against them. As marketed, youth development programming was seen as either irrelevant or too insignificant to benefit the youth, families, and neighborhoods most in need. This is ironic since much of the impetus for broader youth development messages stemmed from a specific concern about the options-limiting strategies being used with these populations.

- **The chosen means were viewed as insufficient.** We allowed the focus to drift from developing youth to developing youth-serving organizations, thereby overemphasizing one delivery system. Strengthening the capacity of the national and local nonprofits that have the preparation and development of young people as their primary if not sole mission is a critical part of the equation. But it is by no means the only part. To succeed, the youth development movement must be linked to the dollars, facilities, and professional and administrative services associated with public institutions. Subtly but steadily, the youth development movement had less to do with promoting broad, critical use of the paradigm as a way to align the efforts of the wide range of public and private actors engaged in improving the lives of young people. Instead, it became more about promoting nonprofit youth-serving organizations and their issues and strategies.

While the past decade has seen clear progress in promoting youth development as a public idea, the coherence of that idea and the momentum behind it have suffered as a result of the drifting priorities described above. These drifts are not surprising, and they are far from fatal. As noted, many good things have happened over the past decade. But the failure to fully correct these drifts slowed progress and, frankly, left room for others with somewhat different ideas to fill the void. Over the decade, unconverted policy makers, planners, practitioners, advocates, and funders challenged our claims. We began to lose ground. But the good news is that each of these drifts has increasingly been addressed by planners, intermediaries, funders, and advocates within our ranks. We turn to their reflections and recommendations in the following section.

EMERGING AND RECURRING ISSUES

As the 1990s came to a close, the authors spent several months asking those most deeply involved in promoting youth development to identify critical issues for the next decade. Those interviewed suggested a range of things that need to be done to strengthen the overall case for increased investments in youth. We have clustered these into 10 larger categories that range from the message to monitoring, from evidence to infrastructure (see Figure 3). Combined, their recommendations reaffirm our conclusion that we might have avoided at least some of these shortfalls if we had kept our focus on the primary goal: to secure youth development as a powerful public idea.

1. Clarify the Message

In the conversations we have held (or been a part of) over the past six months, there has been unanimous agreement that the messages used to articulate the youth development approach have been fuzzy. One funder commented that promoting youth development is like "shoveling fog." Failure to clarify what is needed sparked a range of unproductive reactions. Responses to the argument that all young people need the full menu of services, supports, and opportunities consistently fell into one of several categories: "They don't need everything," "We can't afford to provide everything," and "Providing everything wouldn't make a difference." Each of these responses and, equally important, their implications need to be addressed. Doing so requires that advocates get much better at specifying what should be offered, why it should be offered, how it should be offered, and to whom it should be offered.

What

In Chapter 10, Connell, Gambone, and Smith note: "We have allowed youth development as an *approach* to remain far too broad. . . . The inclusionary impulse

Unfinished Business 17

has produced a mind-boggling mélange of principles, outcomes, assets, inputs, supports, opportunities, risks, and competencies . . . only loosely tied to what actually happens in the daily lives of youth." We agree. The public's hunger for

---
FIGURE 3
Emerging and Recurring Issues
---

1. **Clarify the Message**
   What: Getting to the specifics of youth development.
   Why: The necessity of a publicly understandable message.
   How: Engaging the public systems to help the majority of youth consistently.
   For Whom: The populations served by youth development efforts.
2. **Counter Negative Public Perceptions of Youth and of the Core Youth Development Messages**
   Understand and accommodate public opinion.
   Correct public misconceptions.
   Engage the communication professionals.
3. **Build Vocal Constituencies**
   Support youth organizing, governance, and leadership.
   Create grassroots citizen constituencies.
   Expand professional associations and unions.
   Nurture unlikely supporters.
4. **Connect to Popular Issues, Institutions, and Strategies**
   Link with established "development" efforts.
   Link with hot issues.
   Link with emerging change and reform efforts.
   Close the loop between prevention and development.
5. **Strengthen and Interpret the Evidence Base**
   Conduct strategic evaluations.
   Foster university-based research and teaching.
   Engage the established research disciplines.
   Create an interdisciplinary cadre of "translation" professionals.
6. **Encourage Monitoring and Assessment**
   Improve national indicators.
   Strengthen and diversify local monitoring and assessment tools.
7. **Define the Full Range of Roles and Actors**
   Define the actors.
   Specify their responsibilities.
8. **Strengthen and Link Public and Private Support Systems for Youth**
   Strengthen the nonprofit youth development sector.
   Engage the "remedial" public systems in promoting youth development.
   Link to schools, museums, libraries, primary health care, and recreation.
9. **Build Sustainable Local and Regional Infrastructures for Funding, Planning, Training, Advocacy, and Network Development**
   Build the capacity of local capacity-building intermediaries.
   Support regional advocacy and coalition building.
   Create and strengthen institutions that do cross-system planning and funding.
10. **Saturate Neighborhoods with Solid Supports**
    Effectiveness: Youth are provided with high-quality services, supports, and opportunities.
    Scale/Saturation: Opportunities and supports are available for youth that need and want them.
    Sustainability: Services are available from year to year and sibling to sibling.

specificity can be seen in its enthusiastic responses to sound but modest attempts to push beyond concepts to specify concrete deliverables, such as the five fundamental resources proposed at the President's Summit for America's Future and promoted now by America's Promise.[8]

Why

The if-then purpose statements needed to fuel public action are largely missing from arguments to invest in youth development. Many youth development enthusiasts decided early on not to yoke the calls for investment in primary supports[9] for youth to promised reductions in crime, pregnancy, and substance abuse, or increases in academic performance, supervision, and safety. While this decision was intentional and strategic, it left us without a clear, publicly understandable purpose for our proposals. The "your children have these" arguments helped people understand what we were talking about, but they did not convince them about what was necessary for all children.

How

Even when the proposed deliverables are clear, youth development advocates have tended to leave vague the hard questions of cost and funding and to be too specific about the important questions of implementation and settings. In Chapter 4, Robert Newman, Stephanie Smith, and Richard Murphy note that we discuss the need for infrastructure and outcomes at length but "do not spend equal time on the dollars needed to help achieve the desired outcomes." We simply have not done a good job of demonstrating that we have adequate funding to deliver a partial but useful subset of the supports that affluent youth have. Nor have we built confidence that we have adequate systems. And as Connell, Gambone, and Smith note in Chapter 10, "As applied in practice, youth development is defined so narrowly that it excludes key settings in which youth develop." Many nonprofit youth organizations have stellar track records in helping individual young people beat the odds. But most do not have the wherewithal—financial, political, and human resources—to help the majority of youth consistently. Engaging the public systems is critical.

For Whom

As noted, the youth development arguments were in many ways developed as a response to growing concerns that large segments of young people were being locked out of long-term options because they were being funneled into short-term solutions supported by an implicit double standard: fix those in trouble, develop those who are not. But the lessons of the past decade suggest that youth populations at the high ends of the age-and-risk continua—older youth (especially those

18 to early 20s, but even 14- to 17-year-olds) and "high-risk" youth (those young people already out of school, engaged in high-risk behaviors, or involved with the courts)—were not as well served by the paradigm shift.[10] By advancing normalizing language ("all youth are at risk, all youth need supports") to gain broader appeal, we may have had the least impact on those we were trying to help the most. Recent data, for example, confirm the risks associated with disconnected youth.[11] Long-term disconnection (during three or more of the transitional young adult years) can lead to high poverty rates for both men and women, and higher incarceration rates for men. Data like this help make the case for interventions in high school with marginal youth. But this will not happen unless we intentionally prioritize this population. It is critically important that we find ways to target without trapping.

2. Counter Negative Public Perceptions of Youth and of the Core Youth Development Messages

Running parallel to the belief that the messages were fuzzy was the conviction that the response to them was poor. That people did not receive the messages or did not receive them clearly was not the only issue; they did not like what they heard. The messages did not coincide with their perceptions, and that paved the way for the "prevention is pork" arguments that were flung freely during key congressional debates. Clarifying the message and boosting their power may help those who were unreached or reached but confused. The tougher task, however, is reaching those who are skeptics. Those interviewed suggested three immediate options:

Understand and Accommodate Public Opinion

Too many youth investment campaigns are based on the reality of the organizers. They define the issues and determine the strategies. But the broader public also has opinions that are based on a reality. The Public Agenda polling done in 1997 (Farkas et al., 1997), for example, found that adults of all backgrounds agree that youth today are "undisciplined, disrespectful and unfriendly." Two-thirds of Americans (67%) immediately reached for negative adjectives, such as "rude," "irresponsible," and "wild," while only 12 percent used positive terms, such as "smart" or "helpful." They believe this about teens and about younger children. They recognize that it is tougher today raising or being a teen, but they blame parents for abdicating responsibility. They think that the issues are more about discipline, morals, and community organizations than about government programs that address health or poverty. And they believe that young people can be turned around but are not sure how they as individuals can help. This information does not change our bottom-line beliefs, but each nugget of understanding clearly should influence how our messages are delivered and whom we ask to deliver them.

Correct Public Misconceptions

As disheartening as the Public Agenda findings are, they contain a fundamental truth that cannot be ignored. Many of the things that youth development advocates would argue young people must have (e.g., relationships and guidance) and must build (e.g., character and connections) are supported by the general public. But there are long-standing misconceptions about what young people and their families want, need, and can do that must be addressed. Some of these misconceptions are tied directly to race, ethnicity, and gender. Others reflect long-standing biases in media reporting on youth and their families that highlight the negative and underreport the positive—painting young people as problems or recipients more than as resources and stakeholders, and portraying parents as incompetent or insignificant. Focused efforts must be undertaken to counter these myths, misconceptions, and misrepresentations.

Engage the Communication Professionals

One of the loudest messages was that communication is serious business, and that youth development advocates have simply gone too long without strategic advice on message, positioning, and polling. The sophistication and success of such initiatives as the Benton Foundation's Campaign for Kids (recently renamed Connect for Kids) are evidence of the benefits of intentional development of messages, messengers, and mechanisms.

3. Build Vocal Constituencies

Public opinion is the sibling of public will. Vocal constituencies can change public opinion, increase public will (especially when organized at all levels), and, ultimately, change public and private policies. Ongoing efforts to build four key constituent bases must be strengthened.

Support Youth Organizing, Governance, and Leadership

Young people must have vehicles for organizing and speaking for themselves about issues that affect them directly and issues that affect the larger community and society.[12] Many organizations, governments, and initiatives have focused on the goal of getting young people into decision-making positions. But these positions are often only as powerful as the constituencies behind them.

Create Grassroots Citizen Constituencies

Organize "a Sierra Club for Youth," as Richard Murphy, director of the Center for Youth Development, often suggests. Make it clear that young people are a valuable resource to be protected and promoted as much as the environment. Such a broad-based constituency could include those who are actively involved in youth work, as well as those who are simply interested in the well-being of youth. Just as the Sierra Club includes many members who are not actively working to protect the environment in their day-to-day lives, a "Sierra Club for Youth" could involve everyone from a concerned grandmother to a local business owner. Organizations like Baltimore's Safe and Sound Campaign,[13] the Center for Youth Development, Search Institute, the Benton Foundation, and the National Network for Youth are already making progress in this area. Much more, however, needs to be done.

Expand Professional Associations and Unions

Some issues cannot be addressed by professional associations without the risk of appearing self-serving, and other issues may not be addressed because they are controversial. But many issues will remain untouched or unchallenged unless the people and organizations that work with youth organize within and across professional boundaries. The National Collaboration for Youth, for example, has demonstrated strategic successes. It still has a long way to go, however, to establish the level of clout claimed by other well-known collaborations and associations.

Nurture Unlikely Supporters

Sometimes the message is most powerful when it comes from an unexpected but respected source. Fight Crime: Invest in Kids—a national anticrime organization led by police chiefs, police officer organizations, sheriffs, prosecutors, and crime survivors—has a focused and positive mission: to encourage those in the justice system (and victims of injustice) to speak out on behalf of early and sustained investments in development and prevention. As their brochure states: "No weapons in the war on crime are more important than the investments that keep kids from becoming criminals in the first place—investments which help all children get the right start they need to become responsible adults." Such messages may go further to convince nonbelievers than our own advocacy work. These types of "unlikely" constituencies must be intentionally developed and strengthened.

4. Connect to Popular Issues, Institutions, and Strategies

The youth development movement is in some ways like a tractor trailer full of furniture with no truck. We keep waiting for the driver to show up to pull the whole trailer across the country, all the while missing opportunities to get pieces shipped for free on other folks' runs. In articulating the challenge as all things for all kids, we unnecessarily distanced ourselves from the systems, programs, professionals, policy makers, and even funders who controlled most of the traffic. We also failed to link with established development efforts, hot issues, and ongoing reform efforts.

Link with Established "Development" Efforts

As we refocus on the approach, we need to aggressively seek ways to learn from and link with efforts to strengthen and engage families, residents, citizens, and communities. To advance, the youth development movement has to find its way into a broader set of movements and efforts to support families and rebuild communities. Four such efforts come to mind:

- **Community development.** Experts in community-building strategies—community development, community organizing, neighborhood revitalization, and family support—are steadily increasing their interest in and commitment to providing youth services and engaging youth leaders. Community organizers, especially in immigrant neighborhoods, are increasingly engaging young people as valuable partners.[14]
- **Economic development.** Many experts are wooing young people as the next wave of entrepreneurs. And there are a growing number of efforts to rekindle civic pride and community ownership by engaging the younger generations.
- **Family support and development.** Family support efforts have grown stronger over the years, but have kept their primary emphasis on families with young children. Conversations at the beginning of the decade focused on how these efforts could be linked with youth development efforts. Many are now saying once again that it is time to connect efforts to support youth with efforts to support the families that raise them.
- **Early childhood care and development.** Now ten years older than the youth development movement, with a focus on young people ten years younger, the early childhood movement stands as an important model of what needs to happen in the youth development movement. As the early childhood field pushes its age boundaries up from five to eight, there is an opportunity to link and join forces.

Link with Hot Issues

The same advice given for linking with other development efforts applies to youth development advocates' connection to popular issues and strategies prominent on federal, state, and local agendas. Advocates need to be prepared to "hitch their trailers" to issues that address positively stated needs and opportunities (e.g., mentoring, after-school programming, and community service) as well as issues

Unfinished Business 23

that address risky behaviors (e.g., teen pregnancy, smoking, and violence prevention). Linking with hot issues has obvious risks. Advocates may contribute to the drift rather than reduce it if they are not absolutely clear about the goals and the strategies being proposed. Links with hot issues must be forged both opportunistically and responsibly. In Chapter 3 in this volume, Gary Walker says:

> Tight as the restrictions are, they do not deny any opportunity for action at the national level; they simply define a narrow avenue for successful strategy. That avenue requires that we view public interest in activities like mentoring and after-school programming not as narrow, modest items that are too limited and oriented to negative behavior to warrant an all-out effort, but as-good-as-they-come opportunities to gain public support for the very basic developmental supports that all youth need.

Link with Emerging Change and Reform Efforts

Perhaps the area in which the lack of linkages is most apparent is in reform efforts that engage adults to change the status quo. Young people grow up in communities and spend enormous amounts of time in school. Clearly, these two settings have a profound effect on youth development. Yet neither basic youth development tenets nor young people themselves are often represented "at the table" as decision makers in school or community reform efforts. More damning is the fact that their presence is seldom missed. At best, young people are seen as service recipients or valued customers, but they are rarely viewed as key informants, and they are often considered as part of the problem. In fact, the tenets of youth development (e.g., the importance of relationships and safe and stimulating places) are often left outside the boardroom, even by those who have been through the trainings.

Close the Loop between Prevention and Development

The statement that prevention and preparation are two sides of the same coin seems almost too obvious to make, especially in light of a host of programmatic examples that illustrate the power of this combined approach. But more than 10 years after arguments were made for investments in youth development (not just problem prevention), tensions still divide the researchers, policy advocates, and practitioners who promote youth development and those who promote problem prevention. These tensions persist, in part, for three reasons:

- **Unmet needs.** The youth-serving organizations and efforts that have capitalized most on the "youth development paradigm shift" have not consistently addressed the needs of young people who are dealing with or are most at risk for poverty, school failure, family crises, and problem behaviors.
- **Weak links.** The organizations and efforts that were strongest in attending to

the overlooked components of developmentally sound youth programming—relationship building, personal and social skills development, program and community participation, arts and recreation—were, in fact, often weak in the areas most closely associated with problem prevention and poverty reduction. They often failed to make strong links to health services, education, and employment.
- **The community tightrope.** The tensions were often exacerbated at the community level. Community-wide initiatives found it difficult to strike a balance between the "all youth" and "the high-risk youth" targets as well as between the "youth development" efforts (which tend to be focused on the softer components of a sound youth development package) and the prevention and remediation efforts.

These tensions are ironic because, as noted, "all youth are at risk" arguments were crafted specifically to combat the compartmentalizing and "dumbing down" of programs offered to youth deemed "high risk." Nonetheless, the tensions still exist. Closing the loop between prevention and development—in policy, program, practice, and basic premises and philosophy—must be a priority. The public still resonates to the prevention of problems.

5. Strengthen and Interpret the Evidence Base

The evidence base necessary to counter misconceptions and to advocate for the youth development approach remains weak. The youth development movement had neither solid program evaluations nor compelling scientific models to support interventions like Midnight Basketball for populations such as gang-involved youth. Many have suggested ways to best address this void. We note the following four themes.

Conduct Strategic Evaluations

A decade of investment in youth development programming has yielded an unusually small number of evaluations. The marketing value of good, objective evaluations with robust results is clear.[15] While every program cannot and probably should not be evaluated, a critical mass of strategically funded program evaluations could bring enormous credibility to broader efforts. Unfortunately, good evaluations are few and far between. A recently completed meta-analysis of more than 400 highly recommended programs, commissioned by the Department of Health and Human Services, yielded only a handful of programs that demonstrated significant results using rigorous evaluation methods (Catalano et al., 1999). The situation is only slightly better for demonstration projects and initiatives. Evaluation percentages are higher, but the outcomes and the lessons are long in coming and are not always as instructive as we would like.

Foster University-Based Research and Teaching

Research on youth problems, academic achievement, and recognized youth institutions such as schools is thriving in academia. But as Peter Benson and Rebecca Saito note in Chapter 5, "a disproportionate ratio of the scientific work [related to youth development] (research and evaluation) is conducted by intermediary nonprofits (e.g., Search Institute, P/PV, Academy for Educational Development [AED]) or university-affiliated centers of applied research (e.g., Chapin Hall Center for Children)." They correctly conclude that there is "little evidence of the kind of systematic inquiry necessary to guide, shape, refine and fuel the [youth development] approach. The potential power of the youth development paradigm is not matched by a like commitment to and investment in research."

Engage the Established Research Disciplines

As Joan Costello, Mark Toles, Julie Spielberger, and Joan Wynn note in Chapter 7, it is important to get those working in existing fields (e.g., education, social work, public health, and psychology) to engage in understanding and applying the youth development approach. These professionals have to be able to explain where their work fits into our overall picture of what it means to be an adolescent, and what services, opportunities, and supports young people need to become fully prepared adults. This kind of uptake is often propelled by research that links currently accepted definitions of goals and practices to new ones. Ironically, some of the strongest evidentiary arguments for investing in the types of high-quality supports and opportunities that have come to be associated with youth development have been made by researchers tracking problems. On this front, it would be wise to mend fences with the preventionists, a ready bridge into academic research, professional training, and public funding. As Benson and Saito note, "This work claims [arguably] a deeper research base than does youth development" and consequently "takes the scientific and moral high road in policy discussions of what works."

Create an Interdisciplinary Cadre of "Translation" Professionals

Creating a new academic discipline called "youth development" may not be necessary. In fact, it might well be disastrous to try to do so. The basic concepts that anchor both the goals and the approaches associated with youth development (prevention and preparation, academic and broader social education, formal classroom instruction, and supportive guidance and opportunities, classrooms, and neighborhoods) have been and still are tenets of education, social work, public health, juvenile justice, and urban planning. But it is absolutely critical that we nurture an interdisciplinary cadre of action researchers, practitioners, and policy advocates who not only can speak across topics (e.g., education, housing) but who also can influence the full range of strands that define a mature field (e.g., direct service, planning, research, advocacy and monitoring, policy development and administration). These "ambassadors" need to learn the language and logic of the youth development approach so that they can naturally take it into the broadest range of conversations.

6. Encourage Monitoring and Assessment

Throughout the decade, advocates have lamented that the lack of data on positive indicators has made their jobs especially difficult. They have had difficulty both defining the goals and specifying the unmet need. In Chapter 6, Gary MacDonald and Rafael Valdivieso conclude that our current data on young people "are at best inadequate and often misleading; that, in fact, our dominant approach to data collection—learning what is wrong with young people—is fundamentally flawed because it fails to investigate the factors in a young person's life that we know lead to healthy development." Their assessment and others suggest two parallel tracks for action.

Improve National Indicators

Whatever the quality of indicators, the youth development cause would be served if the public could catch on to the idea that, in every basic category (e.g., education, health, economic well-being), resources (e.g., available college scholarships, clinics, dentists) connect to status conditions (e.g., enrollment, poverty, immunization) that connect to behaviors (e.g., test scores, pregnancies). In the long run, new indicators will be needed. In the short run, better use of existing national survey data could, for example, make it more obvious that there is a relationship between poor children, lousy schools, and poor academic achievement. Creative use of data could begin to suggest similar relationships between poor children; insufficient spaces and places for physical, creative, and vocational activity; and poor overall preparation for adult responsibilities, including, but not limited to, involvement in dangerous and damaging activities.[16]

Strengthen and Diversify Local Monitoring and Assessment Tools

The Annie E. Casey Foundation's 10-year investment in the Kids Count databooks has given states, counties, and large cities a powerful tool to track and compare progress against common goals. But its reliance on nationally collected, publicly available data limits its utility for tracking progress in positive youth outcomes (beyond academic attainment) and primary community supports. In the long run, we need to advocate for the development of common indicators or at least common categories that can be used across neighborhoods, communities, and jurisdictions. In the short run, however, we must encourage jurisdictions to use as many forms as possible to amass the information needed to paint a local picture of resources, status conditions, environments, interventions, and behaviors.[17]

7. Define the Full Range of Roles and Actors

There are still many persistent questions about which individuals, which professionals, and which organizations are engaged in youth development or are included in the term. Families? Schools? Only nonprofits? Only those working to improve youth's personal, social, or civic outcomes? Only those directly involved with youth? And these are not either-or options. We must refine and translate what is known about youth development into the basic philosophy and practices of the full range of people, programs, and organizations that touch the lives of young people—ranging from those who have only occasional interactions with them to those who have formal, public responsibility for their well-being. We must find ways to promote the youth development approach among the full complement of individuals, professionals, programs, and organizations that interact with youth and their families while continuing to strengthen the nonschool, voluntary programs, and organizations that have traditionally addressed young people's nonacademic, nonhealth needs. We suggest the following two.

Define the Actors

One way to break the logjam is to group players not only by their attributes (hours of operation, public or private status) or their focus (academics vs. recreation vs. health) but also by the intensity and intentionality of their efforts:

- **"Steady hand" actors:** organizations, programs, and individuals that have the mission, mandate, and (ideally) resources to have an impact on some aspect of young people's development in an intentional, intensive, and ongoing fashion (e.g., families, schools, nonprofit youth-serving organizations, faith-based organizations).[18]
- **"Light touch" actors:** organizations, programs, and individuals that have intentional contact with or responsibility for youth, but whose relationships are relatively infrequent, low intensity, or short term (e.g., distant relatives and soccer coaches).
- **"Peripheral" actors:** organizations, programs, and individuals that have unstructured or infrequent interactions with or responsibilities for young people (e.g., businesses).

Specify Their Responsibilities

Expectations for action and results could then be defined accordingly. Collectively, our challenges could be defined as:

- **Influencing** public and private "steady hand" institutions and organizations—those with enough presence to have a significant impact—to broaden their goals and strengthen their practices so that they are doing maximum good.
- **Supporting and training** "light touch" professionals, organizations, and programs in the basics of youth development so that they can do more good.
- **Convincing** "peripheral actors," including planners, policy makers, and the general public, of the importance and relative ease of working with youth in ways that do no harm and do some good.

8. Strengthen and Link Public and Private Support Systems for Youth

The proposed $454 million in federal funding for after-school programming has once again put the spotlight on the tension between public and private supports for youth (in this case, school- and community-based organizations). Nonprofit youth organizations insist that at least some of these new dollars should flow directly to them, not through the schools. Their administrative infrastructure is arguably much weaker, but their track record in delivering high-quality after-school activities far outstrips that of the schools. This debate is important, but it needs to be part of broader discussions about who is responsible for improving youth outcomes, who is involved (regardless of whether they assume responsibility), and, equally important, how these actors can work together.

Strengthen the Nonprofit Youth Development Sector

At present, the youth development field is generally defined as those organizations, programs, and professionals that operate primarily in nonschool settings, in the nonschool hours, and with a focus on building nonacademic competencies and connections. While not true of every individual organization or network (e.g., the Scouts, the Ys), as a group, these organizations are in desperate need of funding, accountability, visibility, and marketing. The same is true of the professionals and volunteers who work within them. The distinction between "light touch" and "steady hand" programs, organizations, and individuals is critical within the self-named youth development field, which includes the full range of "touch" within its ranks and often within an individual organization. This broad range of programs and organizations faces two challenges. First, they must begin to self-regulate—to find ways to ensure that those in the field do no harm, to define the type of "good" they are trying to do, and to declare how, and if, they want to be held accountable. Second, they have to continue efforts to build organizational and professional capacity.

Engage the "Remedial" Public Systems in Promoting Youth Development

Strong elements of the youth development message are present in many of the juvenile justice, child welfare, and youth employment initiatives and policies developed over the past decade.[19] But as both Robert Schwartz and Alan Zuckerman note (Chapters 8 and 9, respectively), these highlights are often on the periphery. Costello, Toles, Spielberger, and Wynn note in Chapter 7 that "few child welfare or juvenile justice organizations involve young people in program development, planning, or implementation. Young people in these sectors are much more likely to be viewed as individuals whose behavior needs to be controlled than individuals whose input could be valuable in developing intervention strategies." Everyone, including those on the inside, acknowledges that these systems are slow to change. But the systems are where the young people and the resources are. We need to reinvigorate early efforts to tailor the presentation and language of the youth development framework to these institutions and work with them as they engage in their own reform efforts. Youth development advocates should bear the costs and responsibility of translation. Otherwise, when these systems and professionals pick up the youth development gauntlet, they may do so in ways that do not fully reflect the basic tenets.

Link to Schools, Museums, Libraries, Primary Health Care, and Recreation

The youth development tenets are admittedly hard to sell to the systems that are offering second and third chances to young people who are not in school, not employed, on drugs, or involved with the law. But it should not be such a stretch to imagine a well-stitched, if not seamless, web across the public and private institutions that offer primary supports to youth in education, health, and recreation. Creating such a web requires a sense of shared (if not equal) accountability for improving youth outcomes and youth environments and a sense of shared risk when trying new strategies.

9. Build Sustainable Local and Regional Infrastructures for Funding, Planning, Training, Advocacy, and Network Development

While there is a long-term need for a vibrant infrastructure at all levels, in the end, much of the paradigm shift must to be orchestrated locally and regionally, where the bulk of the energy and the need is. A successful paradigm shift requires stronger local and regional capacity to repeatedly unbundle and rebundle a seemingly endless set of tasks—from advocating for school buildings to remain open to educating the public about the comparative costs of early and sustained investments to building a network of local nonprofits that have the capacity to meet the increased demand for more supports, during more hours, offered in more places and in more neighborhoods.

Build the Capability of Local Capacity-Building Intermediaries

Local intermediaries for youth development often juggle a number of roles as catalysts and facilitators of positive change on behalf of (and often with) local youth.[20] They often focus efforts on a number of levels, seeking to support youth workers, programs, organizations, and communities. They take on a number of tasks, including creating networks for professional development, providing training and technical assistance, conducting policy advocacy, and providing analysis and research.[21] One of the key strengths of these organizations has been in translating theory into practice, or as Community Networks for Youth Development (San Francisco) writes, "bridging between people talking about theory and agencies working in practice with youth" (Needle, 1994, p. 3). In several places they have played an important role in community change initiatives. We need to understand this layer of functioning better (e.g., which roles are compatible within a single organization, which require separation, what type of supports intermediaries need) and to support its growth within cities and counties. Measured growth will come primarily when public and private funders help organizations and communities define and evaluate the roles that intermediaries play, create stable funding mechanisms, and help intermediaries determine effective geographic and functional divisions of labor.

Support Regional Advocacy and Coalition Building

Networks and coalitions that support service providers (public or private) play a key role in strengthening the base of community supports and opportunities for youth. But we also need organizations or coalitions that focus primarily on issues, not on providers. These could (and probably should) be independent advocacy groups that come together to define and advocate for changes within their ranks and beyond. Intermediary networks can have difficulty being tough advocates for change when they are, or are perceived to be, part of the problem or, even worse, part of the pool of organizations that might benefit from change.

Create and Strengthen Institutions That Do Cross-System Planning and Funding

Nonprofit or public-private intermediaries can build networks, address training and capacity-building needs, improve public education, and in some cases disperse funds. But in the end, they are not the institutions that have the clout or the positioning to do the type of cross-system monitoring, planning, policy development, and financing needed. New York continues to be the only state with an established (albeit chronically underfunded) system of youth bureaus designed to play this role at the county level.

10. Saturate Neighborhoods with Solid Supports

Perhaps the most important concern raised was that of institutionalization. Without good monitoring tools; clear definitions of what, why, how, and for whom; stable infrastructures for funding, planning, and capacity building; and healthy doses of evidence, opinion, and advocacy, effectiveness, innovation, and activity garnered more attention than systematic planning to saturate places. Little was done to ensure that in the end more young people in more neighborhoods have more and better supports and opportunities more of the time. We normally eschew "disease" analogies, but youth development advocates and researchers might want to consider the public health concept of thresholds. Contagious diseases are not contained until at least 80 percent of the population is inoculated. And they are not controlled unless the inoculations are sustained at the same level of implementation quality. Three critical goals have to be balanced:

- **Effectiveness**—*ensuring that those youth reached are provided with relevant, high-quality services, supports, and opportunities.* Effectiveness is obviously important, but too many programs and initiatives are held hostage to this challenge. A program's sustainability and reach capacity become so tied to annual measures of effectiveness that organizers cannot plan for growth or improvement.
- **Scale and saturation**—*ensuring that the opportunities, services, and supports offered are available for a critical mass of those young people who want or need them (building on the public health idea of thresholds).* There is nothing about the saturation goal that suggests that individual programs must get larger. In fact, setting this goal for a neighborhood forces the recognition that meeting the goal will require far more than expanding selected "brand name" organizations, of which there are far too few to approach the goal of serving 80 percent of youth.
- **Sustainability**—*ensuring that the opportunities created are sustained from year to year and from sibling to sibling.* Sustainability is by far the most pressing problem in expanding programming and opportunities that support young people's nonacademic development, whether the funding or implementation is public or private.

Framing the Emerging and Recurring Issues

Clearly, there is work to be done, and work being done, by a full range of actors at all levels, to define and address obstacles to increasing youth investments and youth involvement. The daunting agenda laid out above clusters specific concerns into ten large areas to focus on, but the more we review and discuss the list, the more it becomes clear that there is a pattern in these ten larger issues as well. They are symptomatic of our failure to think strategically to (1) saturate neighborhoods with effective and sustainable services, supports, and opportunities for youth; (2) strengthen infrastructures for coordinating, managing, delivering, monitoring, and sustaining efforts; and (3) address the underlying perceptions, messages, interests, evidence, and commitments that combine to create climates conducive for action (see Figure 4).

SHAPING AN AGENDA FOR ACTION—PROMOTING YOUTH DEVELOPMENT AS A PUBLIC IDEA

"Youth development is not a happenstance matter." This simple statement, made more than a decade ago by the Youth Committee of the Lilly Endowment, sums up the progress that has been made in the past decade in focusing attention on the need to promote healthy youth development. If the youth development approach is going to take hold as a powerful public idea, however, it has to land in a full range of places, as Mark Moore discussed, from the general public to organizations to public policy.

Cementing the paradigm shift begun in the late 1980s will require attention to far more than training nonprofit professionals and building nonprofits' organizational capacities. We believe that a major reason we continue to struggle with the issues raised in the previous section is that we let our efforts become too narrowly

FIGURE 4

Emerging and Recurring Issues

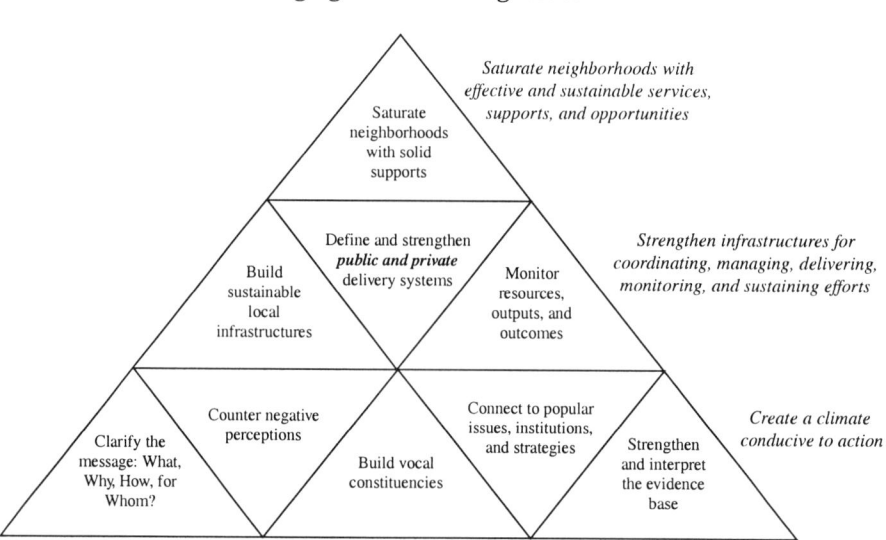

Unfinished Business 33

focused. We targeted most of our energy and resources on strengthening one delivery system instead of taking into account the full range of actors needed to shape and move a public idea. While there is not a clear one-to-one match, by surrounding each of the nagging issues with the institutions or organizations best suited to address it, a broad range of actors emerges (see Figure 5): youth and families; professionals and volunteers; public and private delivery systems and organizations; partnerships and collaboratives; capacity builders; advocacy organizations; movers, shapers, and monitors of public opinion; philanthropic organizations; public policy makers; and researchers and evaluators.

To advance youth development as a public idea, we must consider the full range of actors. But, in addition to being *intentional* about engaging the full range of actors, we must also be *strategic* in choosing where to focus our efforts, and we must *monitor* progress on each of these fronts.

The specific issues, plus the key actors, organizations, and institutions, combine to create an agenda for action. They give us specific tasks to accomplish and suggest that the agenda must be built by and with a full range of players from pollsters and funders, to advocates and practitioners, to youth and families. Further, we must recognize and link to expertise we don't possess. For example, rather than attempting to address public opinion solely by ourselves, we must build links to the pollsters and communications experts who have been specifically trained to do this.

The agenda for action is clearly too large for any one organization to tackle, regardless of its resources. Therefore, the key is to begin with the complete picture, monitor progress along all fronts, and base decisions intentionally and strategically along these lines. In other words, we cannot build toward a large-scale effort haphazardly.

FIGURE 5

Agenda for Shaping and Moving the Youth Development Approach as a Public Idea

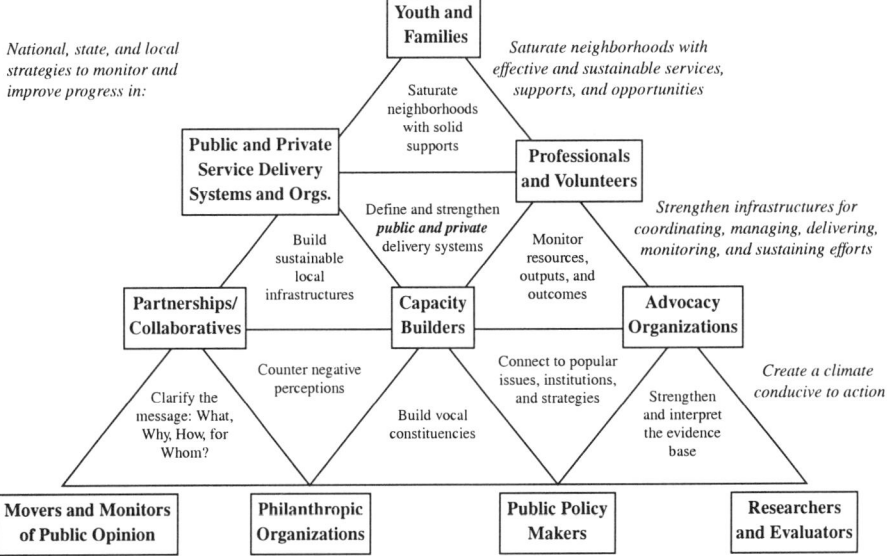

While the agenda appears daunting, it may help to realize that in a sense, it mirrors the role of parents, who, concerned about their children's development across the domains, exemplify the need to monitor the big picture. Parents need to be supported in this ongoing process by communities that share a similarly broad-based vision of what young people need. Communities, however, often struggle to advance a coherent picture of positive youth development in the midst of fragmented policy, resources, and opportunities. One concept that might help parents, communities, and the full range of actors discussed, is a focus on *pathways* rather than *programs*. We turn now to these points.

Learning from the Practicality of Parents

"Youth development is what you'd do for your own kid on a good day. We don't need a fancy definition to know what to do." This statement, made by Hugh Price, president and CEO of the National Urban League, sums up what we all intuitively know. Parents never provide all the services, supports, and opportunities that youth need. On a good day, however, they do monitor the full range of developmental domains (see Figure 1) and—intentionally and strategically—attempt to connect their children to the things they need.

A good portion of what we know about early childhood care and development was in fact learned by observing parents—good parents and troubled parents. The centrality and intuition of parents in the early development of their children are not debatable. But how often are the parents of adolescents consulted or observed? There is relatively little appreciation of the wisdom and centrality of parents, even though year after year polls show that a majority of young people either talk or want to talk with their parents as key advisers and look to their parents as role models. While it is true that early childhood is developmentally the time for bonding, and adolescence is (in some ways) the time for separation, we should not let the superficial differences in parent-child relationships (early adoration vs. adolescent antagonism) lead us to the conclusion that the parents of adolescents and young adults are clueless. We could learn much from observing and reflecting on the parents' balancing act—the ways in which parents attempt to monitor the development of their children and the environments in which they spend time, and the ways parents make intentional and strategic choices with limited resources.

Raising fully prepared youth is not as simple as A + B = C, but it is not rocket science either. As few as one in 20 parents might be able to label the steps they take, and perhaps only two in 1,000 would label them the same way. But it is quite likely that parents would quickly develop a common list if interviewed. There are six steps most parents or guardians take to support their children and, in fact, that most young people take to protect, prepare, and promote themselves:

- ✓ **Reality check.** Where are they developmentally—cognitively, emotionally, socially physically, spiritually?
- ✓ **Goals check.** Where are they aiming? What knowledge, attitudes, skills, and behaviors do parents and children want to achieve? Avoid?

- ✓ **Progress check.** Where are they now? What progress has been made? Are the goals still realistic targets?
- ✓ **Inputs check.** Are they getting what they need? Is the fuel supply adequate? Is the fuel mix correct?
- ✓ **Settings check.** What are the possible sources of needed fuels? Are they adequate? Marginal? Dangerous?
- ✓ **Overall community check.** Is the overall settings mix right? Is it easy to piece together a steady diet of needed inputs, or is it necessary to bypass or compensate for major settings (like schools, neighborhood blocks) that are not functioning well?

These six "checks" that parents do are not interchangeable, they are interlinked. While policy makers and programmers may arbitrarily select among them, parents view them together more organically in an ongoing assessment of their child's needs. But even when parents have a strong sense of what is needed, they often cannot find (or afford) the supports they seek. Community supports must be developed to help parents help their kids. This is an area in which youth development advocates have misjudged public opinion. As Gary Walker discusses in Chapter 3 and as Public Agenda research confirms,[22] there is a strong, long-standing belief in this country that youth development starts with families, not programs or initiatives. The public consistently pulls back when programs seem to be less interested in helping families help their children than in helping young people help themselves (especially, but not exclusively, around issues of reproductive health).[23]

Parents and young people intuitively use an algebra for youth development—one that we have yet to translate into powerful, policy-adaptable equations. If young people are to get the services, opportunities, and supports they need, policy planners, organizers, and researchers will have to find ways to assess the fuel mix as it is supplied by the full range of sources in a community (families, schools, community-based organizations, peer groups, faith organizations, gangs, etc.). Parents do this every day. Poor fuel mixes are one of the primary reasons parents move when they can afford to.

Why push for formulas? Because youth development requires multiple inputs from multiple sources over a sustained period of time. Formulas are the way to show concrete relationships among multiple variables. Lists (of desired outcomes, essential inputs, etc.) inform, but they do not instruct. More important, lists give funders, practitioners, and policy makers a false sense that they can choose to support their favorite outputs, inputs, or settings at whatever levels they feel comfortable.

The first lesson learned by youth development advocates was that it is unproductive to insist that everything be done simultaneously. The more recent lesson is that it is equally unproductive to insinuate that anything can be done in any order or at any level of scale and consistency. There is a logic to the list of "beyonds" (see Figure 2). And there is an internal logic to how the outcomes, inputs, and settings fit together. We may never get to formulas (and probably should only try in rhetorical ways), but we should be able to craft rough lenses that help communities assess their strengths and weaknesses (or force them to confront them), and push them to prioritize responsibly.

Prioritizing Community Agendas for and with Youth

One thing we know is that today, it is harder than ever to be a parent. Families need an engaged community—one that embraces a vision of youth development, taking into account the full range of relevant issues and actors. Looking back, it is regrettable that we failed to offer sufficient guidance to communities, program planners, and policy makers who agreed with the vision but wanted assistance in prioritizing the work. Unfortunately, once we realized that everything could not be done at once, we allowed the task lists to be presented as options. Our failure to develop a clear framework for strategic planning of action allowed these lists to be used as the basis for selections that reflected personal preferences or opportunistic use of available funding rather than strategic analysis.

On the surface, the questions "What do youth need?" and "What should communities do?" seem much more difficult to answer when the goal is overall preparation and full participation than when the goal is, say, prevention of violence or substance abuse. This is, in large part, because when the charge is specific (for example, substance abuse prevention), the solution is expected to be specific (a targeted, time-limited substance abuse prevention program). The program may (and should) contain elements that address basic needs, but it is the program as a whole, not the elements, that are sold as a package. The opposite needs to be true. Like parents, planners need to read the ingredients, not just the product name. To use a nutrition analogy, for many prevention programs the marketing was equivalent to that of a healthy snack. Planners were not encouraged to read the ingredients list on the packaging, much less to compare labels and think about total calories or daily requirements. Our approach was often analogous to searching for the perfect "snack" to solve a weight problem instead of focusing on developing an overall diet and exercise plan.

If adhered to, the simple statement made by the Lilly Endowment offers an alternative prescription for action. It suggests the importance of intentional monitoring of all the crucial areas in which development occurs, and the intentional and strategic selection of areas in which to invest key resources.

Monitoring: Outcomes, Inputs, Settings and Systems, and Resources

Funders have driven the outcome accountability message home to direct-service providers. But the results have often been counterproductive, especially when investments in monitoring above the individual program level have been limited or nonexistent. Young people do not grow up in programs; they grow up in families, neighborhoods, and communities that are served or disserved by systems and sectors. The real question is not what a program is providing for youth, but what a neighborhood, community, system, or sector (public education, public health, nonprofit) is providing for youth and their families.

Intentionality and Strategic Selection and Action:
Planning, Prioritizing, and Adjusting

Youth development advocates upped the ante and exponentially increased the options for action by offering a new calculus for youth investment and involvement that broadened the goals, broadened the strategies, and increased the lists of actors, hours, and settings deemed relevant for involvement, if not accountability. Many individuals and organizations took this call to action to heart and brought new levels of intentionality to their youth-focused activities. But, as with monitoring, the challenge is to push the intentionality up several levels. The new mantra: monitoring for action.

Infrastructure:
Funding, Coordinating, and Infusing Knowledge and Purpose

To effectively and consistently undertake the tasks above, we must strengthen the infrastructure. The infrastructure for generating and coordinating nonacademic and nonschool supports for youth is perhaps as fragile and byzantine as the array of direct service providers themselves. Much of the coordinating and grant making is done via committees that represent functionally overlapping initiatives. Progress will not be made until there are permanent institutions in place that have been given the budget and authority to act on behalf of young people and families, not initiatives or systems. These are needed at every level, local to national. Frustration is building fastest at the local levels, however, suggesting this as the place for concentrated experimentation.

Just as we need an infrastructure to monitor and make strategic decisions to promote the youth development movement as a whole, we need community infrastructures to monitor and make strategic selections for and with local youth. So what is needed? Here are specific recommendations for action:

- **Baseline and annual data that track at the individual level** and allow us to develop a picture of what young people need, what they get, how they are doing, and what they are providing to family and community;
- **Baseline and annual data at aggregate levels** that tell us what families, neighborhoods, and systems need, what they get, how they are doing, and what they are providing to young people, families, and communities;
- **Baseline and annual data that estimate, if not monitor, dollars spent** as well as activities delivered by the full array of systems and actors that have youth services as a mandate or interest;
- **Mechanisms for collecting, disseminating, and discussing the data** at the

neighborhood and system levels and for involving young people, families, residents, and frontline workers in the processes;
- **Intermediaries** charged with training, technical assistance, network development, and issue advocacy to use data in ways that strengthen formal and informal support systems;
- **Infrastructure** at the neighborhood and municipal levels to use the data to inform planning prioritizing and reallocation and realignment of resources, accountability, and attention across neighborhoods, organizations, and systems; and
- **Strong and varied local leadership** to keep public and private attention focused on youth, youth outcomes, and community accountability.

The Bottom Line—Pathways to Full Participation

In the previous section we discussed the challenge brought about when the vision is presented to communities in the form of lists. Recognizing the complex challenges that communities face as well as the rich array of resources they bring, one way to provide the focus necessary to monitor and make selections intentionally and strategically is to advance the vision of pathways as our ultimate bottom line (see Figure 6).

To be effective, strategies to engage youth should not be "hit or miss" or isolated opportunities offered in a vacuum. There is a big difference, for example, be-

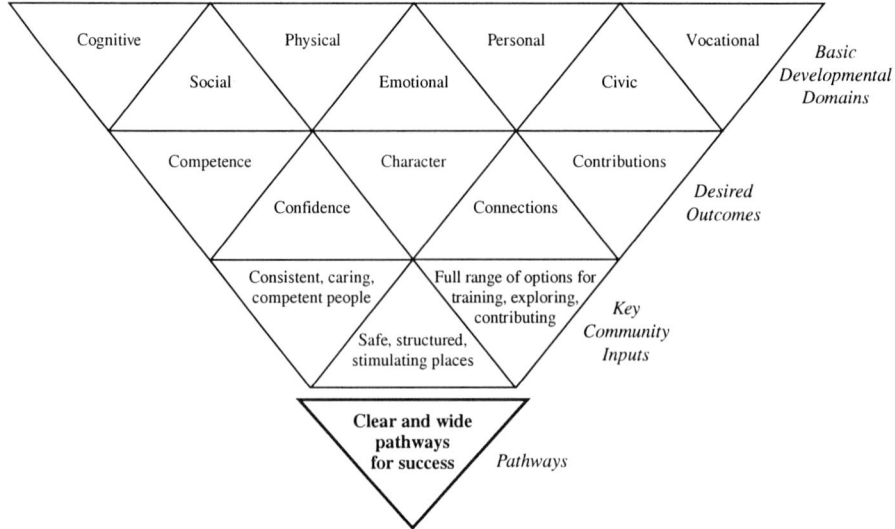

FIGURE 6

Broadened Goals and Increased Options toward Clear and Wide PATHWAYS

tween an isolated community service opportunity and one that attempts to draw youth into related studies and careers. Consider how the "stepping stones" toward increasing skills and responsibilities are clearly and intentionally laid out in Boy and Girl Scout programs and in some faith-based institutions, or how parents attempt to connect their children to the full range of services, opportunities, and supports that they need.

In the end, if created intentionally and strategically, more supports for more youth in more neighborhoods constitute more pathways to success—pathways diverse, wide, and accessible enough for all youth to see, try, and ultimately select from. These pathways offer the basic things young people need: opportunities to learn, work, and contribute in ways that are relevant to them and to others. Pathways should engage young people in roles as full participants in the workplace, the community, and society at large.

The challenge, as we approach the next decade and the next millennium, is to create a robust public idea that inspires sustained public, private, and policy action that focuses on creating more pathways rather than just more programs: pathways that guide youth beyond preparation to full participation and action in their communities.[24]

The Agenda in Action: The Beacons Case Study

Taken together, the recommendations in this chapter appear to present a daunting challenge. First we say that the full list of "beyonds" must be addressed intentionally and monitored. Next we present a list of recurring issues that must be addressed—from building a solid base of sound programming in neighborhoods to building a vocal constituency of youth and adults. Then we say that a broad range of actors, from the general public to organizations to policy makers must be attended to with the same degree of intentionality and monitoring that we advocate for youth. Finally, we say that all this action must be focused on, and result in, more and better pathways to full participation.

Should this picture of what youth need, the range of tasks that need to be tackled, and the range of actors that need to be involved be cause for disillusionment? Is it simply more than we are able to accomplish?

We readily acknowledge the challenges before us. But we also reflect upon the challenges we have already overcome and the successes we have achieved, and conclude that the vision we have laid out is achievable. Further, our hope, and indeed a good measure of our optimism, comes from looking upon one of the successes that emerged in the past decade of promoting youth development: the New York City Beacons.

Initiated in 1991, the Beacons created a web of school-community-family partnerships, coordinated through community centers located in public school buildings. Funded by the New York City Department of Youth and Community Development (DYCD), the Beacons offer a range of activities and services to participants of all ages before and after school, in the evenings and on weekends. With a current funding level of $36 million, the Beacons make up the largest municipally funded youth initiative in the United States (Warren, Brown, and Freudenberg, 1999).

The Beacons, as much as any effort, have embodied and implemented the full range of recommendations we have presented here. As such, they give us cause to believe that what we have called for is an achievable reality.

Beacons and the "Beyonds"

The Beacons were premised upon a sound understanding of the youth development approach, as articulated by the "beyonds":

- **Beyond prevention**—*problem reduction and full preparation for adult roles and responsibilities.* The focus was on positives—people, places, possibilities—but with crime prevention as the hook. Funding was secured as part of a comprehensive antidrug and crime strategy for New York City. Nine centers were proposed instead of an additional prison barge. Notably, a substance abuse prevention curriculum was not proposed, and funding did not hinge on promised reductions in youth crime and drug use. The publicly stated focus was instead on improving community inputs—increasing the number of safe and stimulating places for young people to go, things to do, and people to talk to in neighborhoods where the streets were the only after-school alternatives. Achieving a full range of positive youth and community outcomes, though not touted for accountability purposes, remains the underlying and ultimate goal.
- **Beyond quick fixes**—*deficit remediation, crisis response, problem prevention, and long-term attention to development.* Within the Beacons you may find any number of short-term, targeted activities—summer service programs and six-week prevention courses, for example—but programming for specific issues and age groups is embedded within an ongoing institution committed to building relationships and engaging young people with ample opportunities to contribute and benefit.
- **Beyond basic services**—*human, health, housing and economic services and a full range of supports and opportunities.* Beacons were designed to provide a full array of services, supports, and opportunities, not just for young people but for the full age range. Institutions committed to broad-based development—families, schools, and community-based organizations—were made the key players. Social services, child welfare, law enforcement, and health were brought in later, once the tone had been set. Although activities are most often what bring people through the doors, Beacons staff are prepared to do assessments of the full range of needs and to coordinate services. Over time, as Beacons have been able to demonstrate that they can attract large numbers of youth and families that need critical services, they have been able to bring services or the service dollars on-site.
- **Beyond schools**—*24 hours a day, seven days a week: during the school day and before and after school, including nights, weekends, and summers.* The

driving idea behind the Beacons was to expand the hours, activities, and actors involved in young people's lives beyond what they find in school, and to do this in permanent, accessible places. School buildings were quickly identified as universal, yet underutilized, settings. While community-based organizations are critical for ensuring community ownership and flexible operation, the partnership with schools and government is essential for securing and sustaining resources.

- **Beyond professionals and beyond recipients**—*teachers and youth workers and families, community members, volunteers, young people, and non-youth-focused professionals; young people as recipients and as active agents in their own development and that of their communities and society.* Community engagement and ownership have been instrumental from the beginning. The broad blueprints were filled in by the community as young people, parents, residents, and community associations and councils were engaged in planning their Beacon. Young people and their families were brought in at the beginning to shape the programming and were critical to ensuring a mix of engaging activities and opportunities for participation and leadership both within the Beacon and throughout the community. Parents and young people both teach and take classes (in everything from aerobics to English as a second language) and are key planners of and actors in community initiatives. Young people are engaged as significant, if not primary, change agents in their communities, doing everything from physical revitalization of housing and parks to voter registration and political advocacy.
- **Beyond labeling**—*nonstigmatizing efforts for all youth, including those living in high-risk areas, and those with specific challenges and problems (e.g., dropouts, young parents, court-involved youth).* Initially targeting neighborhoods most in need, the Beacons opened the doors to all members of the community. The neighborhood—not the school—was the focal point. Centers serve, support, and challenge the children, youth, and families of the neighborhood, not the just the student body.
- **Beyond pilots**—*pilot programs and an array of steady services, supports, and opportunities that are affordable, accessible, and attractive enough that at least 80 percent of youth aged 10 to 22 are connected to something for at least 80 percent of their second decade of life.* Beginning with $5 million in municipal "Safe Streets, Safe Cities" funding that helped 10 community-based organizations create community centers inside schools, the initiative continues to stand out in terms of its sustainability and scale. By 1998, the initiative had expanded to 40 Beacons; in 1999 there were 80 Beacons operating—each with a base grant of $450,000 (Warren, Brown, and Freudenberg, 1999).

By implementing these "beyonds," Beacons laid the groundwork for an effective youth development approach. But they did not stop there. What makes the Beacons story especially noteworthy is their simultaneous achievements in terms of sustainability and scale. The Beacons are one of our best examples of beginning with a clear blueprint based on the youth development framework—the full set of "beyonds"—and then strategically selecting elements to highlight, not only to ensure effectiveness but also to ensure scale and sustainability. By the end of 1999, 80 Beacons were in operation. The number alone is impressive, suggesting a level of scale in publicly funded youth programs rarely reached in American cities. But the story is not in the number; it is in the strategy that led to it, a strategy that at every turn opted to promote the goals and principles of youth development while intentionally working to ensure the quality, reach, and longevity of the effort. By using the lenses of effectiveness, scale, and sustainability, we are able to see how they homed in on a highly visible, politically savvy strategy for achieving scale and sustainability while keeping the overall approach of youth development intact.

Any attempt to expand the reach of the youth development philosophy and approach must be balanced with attention to the quality of the efforts and strategic decision making to sustain them over time. Effectiveness, scale, and sustainability—a troika of goals called for by the International Youth Foundation and others—are useful lenses when making strategic decisions about the youth development framework. All of the pieces of the framework are integrally related and important.

This troika was achieved by the combined efforts of the range of actors we discussed as critical to shaping and moving the youth development approach as a public idea. Collectively, they addressed many of the "nagging" issues we presented earlier.

Beacons and the Agenda for Shaping and Moving the Youth Development Approach as a Public Idea

From the beginning, the Beacons effort focused on far more than a single delivery system. Joint accountability was essential—we italicize the number and range of players below to emphasize this point. As discussed above, *youth and families, professionals and volunteers,* and *public and private delivery systems* all worked together to build a solid base of sound programming in *neighborhoods. Schools,* along with established *community-based organizations* and the *Department of Youth Services (DYS),* were key members of an unusually well balanced partnership. No single partner wielded excessive power. *Schools* (selected on the basis of location, not interest) provided space. *Community-based organizations* (competitively selected based on capacity and established *neighborhood* ties) provided the staffing and basic programming. *DYS* provided management and funding.

The *Youth Development Institute at the Fund for the City of New York*—a then-young intermediary organization—acted as the convener of *collaboratives* (e.g., monthly meetings of the *Beacons directors), capacity builder* (e.g., technical assistance and professional development activities for *Beacons directors and staff,* linking to such resources as funding and staff training opportunities, and convening *Networks for Youth Development*—a peer network of *youth organizations* promoting youth development as a field of practice and mastery and committed to accountability and authentic assessment), and as an *advocacy organization* (advocating that public agencies foster collaborative relationships with the Beacons) (Warren, Brown, and Freudenberg, 1999). As such, it assisted actors in the *public and private delivery systems* to develop sustainable infrastructures, strengthen delivery systems, and monitor resources, outputs, and outcomes.

Philanthropic organizations were engaged strategically, with *foundations* coming in as quiet partners supporting training, technical assistance, and evaluation. *Researchers and evaluators* assisted in building an *evidence base* (an evaluation is being conducted by the *Academy for Educational Development,* the *Chapin Hall Center for Children,* and the *Hunter College Center for AIDS, Drugs and Community Health*) (Warren, Brown, and Freudenberg, 1999).

Public opinion and *public policy makers* were attended to equally and strategically. Beginning with the hot topics of drug and crime prevention, politics were never ignored. Positioning and additional *public systems* funding and integration were always goals. The strategies were not all successful, but the diligence never let up—in *city hall,* in the *school buildings,* in the *communities. Parents,* the *public,* and the *press* (movers of public opinion) were key stakeholders, creating a *vocal constituency* that kept the political pressure on. A clear message was articulated, with a simple name (Beacons), simple goal (people, places, possibilities), and simple plan (one per district), which allowed the *media* to monitor resources and outputs, *parents* to label what they knew they wanted for their children and themselves, and vocal public constituencies to rally when the going got hard. Had *DYS* simply given 40 contracts for substance and delinquency prevention to 40 separate community-based organizations with different names, the expansion and even the existence of Beacons schools would be in question. The *vocal constituencies* in the *public* and the *press* saved the Beacons from the chopping block after the change in administration.

Selecting *schools* as the actual settings for this work did more than open up unused facilities in the before- and after-school hours. From the outset, it laid the foundation for a savvy scale and sustainability strategy. Starting with 10 Beacons in 1991, organizers realized that going to scale meant starting big enough to capture attention across *school districts.* The initial placement of these 10 Beacons was also strategic. Putting the Beacons in the worst neighborhoods allowed the political process to work for expansion. *Parents* in less distressed neighborhoods clamored for their own Beacons. The publicly stated goal of at least one in every school district was quickly met—there were 40 Beacons by 1996, doubling again by the end of the decade.

Effectiveness, scale, and sustainability—Beacons schools rate high on all three. On effectiveness, they have not only done a good job of adopting the youth development philosophy; they have done a good job of training to it and evaluating against it as well. But they might not have achieved the Triple Crown had they taken the traditional route—prove effectiveness, slowly increase scale, then (and only then) begin to plan for long-term sustainability. Beacons' master crafters took the best of what is known, pitched it straight, did not overpromise on outcomes, and planned for rapid but sustainable growth from the beginning, building on what already existed. This is the lesson. There is no doubt that the quality of Beacons varies from center to center. But the number of Beacons schools would not have reached 80 if these centers had been established, funded, and evaluated one at a time. We did not build a public school system or a public health system or a public corrections system that way. And we certainly will not link these systems with the existing community-based infrastructure (for youth and community development) that way.

In an increasingly complex society—one in which families are becoming more fragmented, parents' work hours are on the upswing, gun and drug availability is rampant—affluent as well as distressed families are less able to coordinate, much less personally deliver, the supports that they used to provide. Success stories like the Beacons suggest that there are ways to build on and link to services and professionals that exist in neighborhoods while actively engaging parents and young people in securing the supports and opportunities they need. Growing individually and in number, each Beacon school is a dynamic part of the community, responsive to young people, families, and service providers. Much more effective than opening up dozens of cookie-cutter service centers that all provide the same menu of supports, the network of community-based Beacon sites was primed to promote the full youth development framework and engage the full range of actors—families, school and human service officials, community members, teachers, service providers, law enforcement officers, and, most important, young people themselves—in shaping the life and direction of the community. And so, as a result of careful, intentional monitoring and strategic action, the youth development approach flourished in systems and settings beyond its usual purview. This kind of innovative transplanting of the youth development approach will have to be done if we are to see changes at the scale and level needed to change the landscape for young people, especially older adolescents and young adults who are not in college environments.

Conclusion—An Agenda for the Next Decade(s)

In the end, reflecting on the success of the Beacons, we see clearly the value of using a sound youth development framework to broaden the goals and increase the options (the list of beyonds), engaging the full range of actors necessary to build and sustain a public idea, and addressing critical issues.

This analysis comes full circle to embody all of the key points presented in this chapter and, when properly aligned, presents a cohesive picture of an agenda for the next decade(s) (see Figure 7). The top half of the "hourglass" (Figure 6) depicts the youth development idea in terms of broadening the goals and increasing the options. The bottom half (Figure 5) depicts what is needed for a public idea to take hold and have impact. They come together at a critical fulcrum: youth and families in communities and neighborhoods saturated with effective and sustainable services, supports, and opportunities that form clear and wide pathways for preparation and participation. This is the ultimate vision we must pursue. But while we increasingly refine the vision, we must never lose sight of the critical infrastructures required. Pathways are the focal point for a full range of necessary community inputs and a means to a full range of desired outcomes for youth, connected to basic functional areas. All of these areas, outcomes, and inputs must be addressed with intentional monitoring and strategic action. Then and only then

Unfinished Business

FIGURE 7
An Agenda for the Next Decade(s)

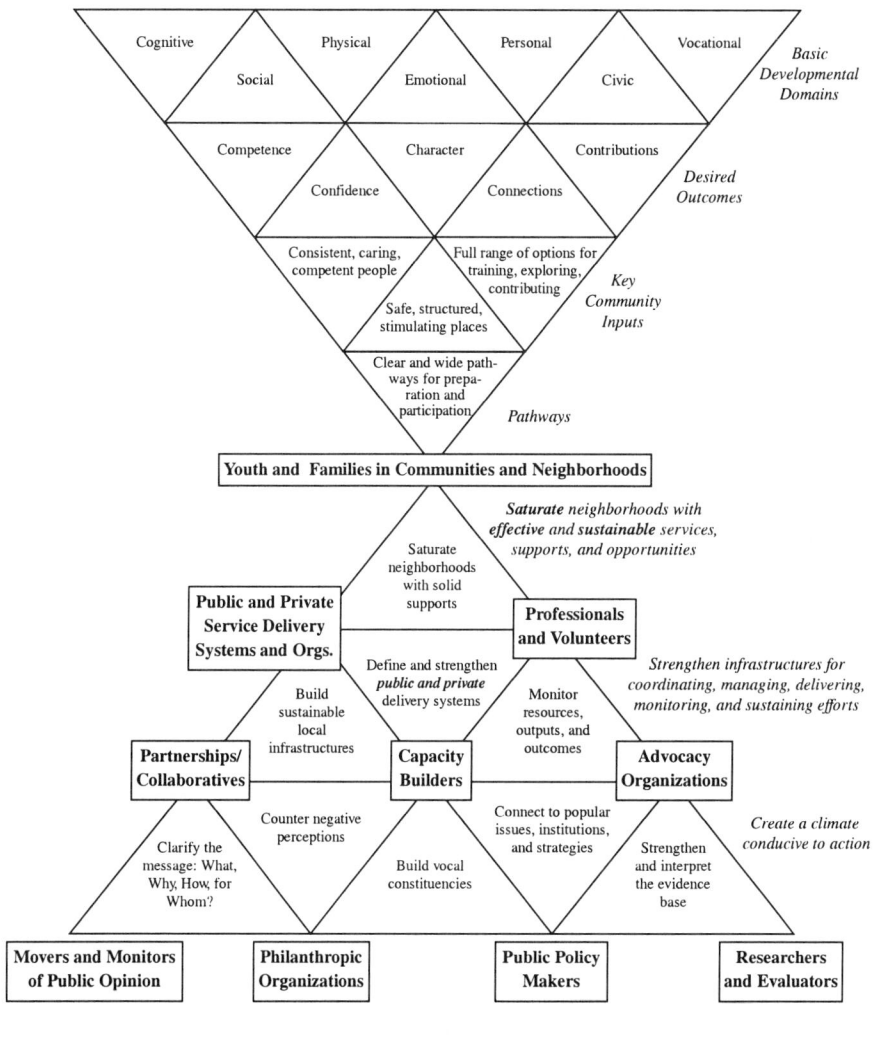

will they come together logically to form clear, coherent, attractive, and wide pathways.

Further, if we are to successfully instill the concept of pathways as a powerful public idea, we must not lose sight of the full range of relevant actors. Public ideas do not become powerful through one sector, actor, or institution. The full power of a public idea is realized only when it takes hold in a number of places, influencing public policy, organizational missions, and private action. Neighborhoods will only become saturated with effective and sustainable pathways when there are strong infrastructures for coordinating, managing, delivering, monitoring, and sustaining efforts, and when there is a climate conducive to action. To ensure that this happens, we must once again stress the importance of intentional monitoring and strategic action—this time referring to the range of actors necessary to shape and sustain a public idea. Then and only then can we hope to achieve effective and sustainable pathways, clear and wide enough for all of our children to traverse.

NOTES

1. This chapter builds directly on "Reflections on a Decade of Promoting Youth Development," a paper commissioned by the American Youth Policy Forum for its volume *The Forgotten Half Revisited*, edited by Samuel Halperin (1998). Our further reflections were prompted by two subsequent events: reading and discussion of *The Power of Public Ideas,* edited by Robert Reich (1988), and discussions with key leaders of the emerging and persistent issues that stand as barriers to investment in the adequate preparation of all young people.
2. Each of the themes obviously needs to be specified within its context, whether in countries around the world or in counties in the United States. But our work suggests that each of these themes has sufficient currency to spark discussion.
3. Competency areas included are originality (creative competency), understanding (personal competency), thinking (cognitive competency), civic competency, our bodies (physical health competency), mental health competency, employability competency, and social competency.
4. See Pittman and Irby (1996); Zeldin (1995); Zeldin, Kimball, and Price (1995); Zeldin and Price (1995).
5. Areas considered include organizational structure that is supportive of youth development; environment factors on which special attention has been focused; a holistic approach to young people; opportunities for contribution; caring and trusting relationships; high expectations; engaging activities; and factors that promote continuity for youth in the program. ("Create safe environment" is one of the subheadings under "environmental factors on which special attention has been focused.")
6. Delbert Elliott (1998), probably one of the best-known and most prolific researchers on youth violence, offers a list of what works and what does not work to prevent or reduce youth violence. The parallels to the youth development arguments on both sides are striking. What works, for example, are individual competency building, multifaceted family-strengthening efforts, and changes in school norms and climate. What does not work includes boot camps and freestanding prevention curricula.
7. In *Adolescents at Risk*, Joy Dryfoos (1990) reports that, beyond the problem-specific information offered, most effective prevention programs focus on the development of social skills, problem-solving skills, and communication skills; engagement or reengagement of youth through participation, leadership, and the building of membership within the group; the establishment of new norms and expectations for behavior sanctioned by the group; and the development of different and deeper relationships with adults (different structures for interaction were established and adults were trained to work differently with youth).
8. Public/Private Ventures selected a different but overlapping list of concrete deliverables to spark community-level capacity building in its Community Change for Youth Development (CCYD) demonstration project. Many initiatives successfully convey the importance of the individual interventions selected (e.g., reducing gun violence, ensuring reading skills). But America's Promise and CCYD are two examples of initiatives that have successfully conveyed the importance and feasibility of providing the interventions as a package. Both convey the idea of thresholds and cumulative im-

pact. The assumption is that young people who get these five things are significantly better off than those who only get two or three.

9 Term coined by the Chapin Hall Center for Children at the University of Chicago.

10 By their own admission, both America's Promise and CCYD have fared less well in reaching all youth than they have in addressing the package of needs. CCYD selected specific high-need neighborhoods, targeting 12- to 20-year-olds within them. Their sites have had much more success attracting the younger youth into programming than the older ones, primarily because they run into the tough issue that older youth want and need jobs. The question is, How much should we push communities to find strategies for engaging older youth, or, short of this, to what extent should we communicate the implications of failing to adequately address the needs of this population?

America's Promise has an even broader mandate to reach disadvantaged youth from birth on. The organization is pushing hard to get communities to accept all five resources, not to pick and choose. But it is vague to silent on the five age groups (0-4, 5-9, 10-14, 15-19, and 20-24, if communities track young people out of high school into careers and college). And it has not explicitly articulated goals for working with marginalized or disconnected youth—those out of school, out of work, involved with the courts, or just uninvolved.

11 Compelling data have recently been released in an edited volume, *America's Disconnected Youth: Toward a Preventive Strategy*, ed. D. Besharov (Washington, D.C.: CWLA Press, 1999). These data strongly suggest that most young people are at least marginally connected to school and the labor force, or both, until the age of 16 or 17, but that disconnection after 17 quickly becomes more common—jumping from 4 to 8 percent among whites, 5 to 13 percent among blacks, and 9 to 15 percent among Hispanics. By age 19, almost 17 percent of both males and females have been disconnected for at least one 26-week period. Disconnection appears to be relatively benign in small quantities, but toxic in multiple doses. Youth disconnected during three or more of the transitional young adult years experienced significant hardship: at ages 25 to 28, their median family income was only about $18,000 for men and $15,000 for women; about 44 percent of the long-term disconnected men and 56 percent of the women were in poverty; 34 percent of the women received Aid to Families with Dependent Children, and 48 percent received food stamps; and men were six times more likely to have spent time in jail or a youth correctional facility.

12 Notable local examples include Philadelphia's Urban Retrievers, a four-pronged leadership training program created by and for youth; Coleman Advocates for Youth's Youth Making a Change (San Francisco); and LISTEN, Inc. (Washington, D.C.).

13 The Safe and Sound Community Promises campaign asks adults to promise to bring positive energy to the lives of children and youth in their neighborhood; learn something about the needs of children and the resources available to them; and make their voice heard on public issues that affect the well-being of children and youth. Youth are asked to promise to respect others' differences; establish integrity through discipline, honesty, responsibility, and morality; be prepared to learn at all times; and maintain a positive attitude, self-confidence, and enthusiasm.

14 Five years ago, the National Network for Youth coined the term "community youth development" to reflect a challenge to its members—calling for them to go beyond their commitments to high-quality programs and services, to make commitments to link themselves and the young people they serve more firmly into the communities in which they live. The Network's formal language reflects a growing recognition that young people, especially adolescents and young adults, cannot and will not grow up in programs (unless forced). Community supports are critical to their development, as is community involvement.

15 Steven Shinke and colleagues' (1992) evaluation of Boys & Girls Clubs of America (BGCA) programming in housing projects led to a major BGCA expansion, fueled in part by a significant HUD investment. Big Brothers/Big Sisters of America has been able to parlay the Public/Private Ventures evaluation of its mentoring programs into a major organizational expansion that has had spillover effects for mentoring in general (Tierney and Grossman, 1995). The Teen Outreach Program, subject of an ongoing control group evaluation spearheaded by Philliber and Associates, did not attract government funding, but it did keep the school based pregnancy and dropout prevention program from dying and allowed it to go slowly to scale (Joseph et al., 1997).

16 The Federal Interagency Forum on Child and Family Statistics recently released the second annual indicators report on children and youth, *America's Children: Key National Indicators of Well-Being*. While there are dozens of factbooks and compendiums of national and state data, this report is the product of an interagency working group that came together to select official indicators for the country. Marketed correctly, the release of these numbers could carry at least a fraction of the weight that the current release of leading economic indicators does. Youth development advocates may write off the exercise because it does not capture enough positives. But it has other equally important weaknesses that limit its utility as a powerful tool for social marketers. First, many indicators beg for

comparisons—at the national or the county level. International comparisons lit a fire under Americans in the 1980s when the international teenage pregnancy and childbearing data were reported by the Alan Guttmacher Institute, and they continue to generate sparks in education (e.g., the TIMMS study). Second, most of the categories (e.g., education, health, family security) beg for a consistent mix of indicators. The current mix of resource, status, and behavior indicators is not even across the categories.

17 Many communities have supplemented the Kids Count data with local survey data. Search Institute's Healthy Communities • Healthy Youth initiative has provided hundreds of communities with local data on the self-reported assets, behaviors, and needs of their middle and high school students. The Center for Youth Development has convened representatives from over 20 different youth-mapping projects and has helped eight communities implement their YouthMapping process; further, the Center is encouraging the use of a common set of indicators in its mobilization cities. And an ever-growing number of communities, often with the backing of local foundations, are investing in customized surveys to map youth needs and community resources, neighborhood by neighborhood. Increasingly, these needs and assets assessments are linked to real change initiatives. For example, extensive, issue-specific surveys of youth, parents, and service providers in Detroit (sports and recreation) and Philadelphia (after-school opportunities) fed directly into large planning and service improvement efforts.

18 Obviously, families are the "steadiest" of the steady hand actors. It is critical that efforts reinforce the centrality of families as the key actors in young people's lives. Families must provide critical supports and opportunities to their children, and they must play a critical brokering function, monitoring their children and their communities and acting as a conduit for connecting youth to critical services, opportunities, and supports.

19 For example, the members of the National Youth Employment Coalition have completely embraced youth development, making adherence to sound youth development principles one of three areas in which programs self-assess. (The other two are organizational effectiveness and youth employment and training practices.) Prevention curricula coordinators in state and local public school systems used the paradigm shift to argue for consolidation of the separate prevention curricula and better integration with the core academic curricula. Communities That Care, a community risk-focused prevention training system developed by Dr. David Hawkins and Dr. Richard Catalano of the University of Washington, has received major funding and promotion from the U.S. Department of Justice.

20 In New York City, the Youth Development Institute at the Fund for the City of New York has emerged as an exemplar of a local intermediary. Similarly, the Indiana Youth Institute, Chicago Youth Agency Partnership, Hampton Coalition for Youth, YouthNet of Greater Kansas City, Community Networks for Youth Development (San Francisco), and the Urban Strategies Council (Oakland, California) have all played key roles in helping develop effective, sustainable, and large-scale local efforts for and with youth.

21 The Community Networks for Youth Development writes: "TA [technical assistance] intermediaries provide the valued services of (1) helping agencies to self-assess their needs, and (2) identifying and obtaining resources to meet those needs, which includes doing the legwork to find resources and sorting through the vast array of what is available to surface useful items and people. Youth workers and program managers want these things to be done but rarely have the time themselves" (Needle, 1994, p. 3).

22 A key finding of the report is that "Americans believe that parents are fundamentally responsible for the disappointing state of today's youth" (Farkas et al., 1997, p. 13).

23 Youth development advocates are understandably biased toward encouraging young people as independent actors and, more important, protecting young people from hazardous or punitive home situations. These elements should not be lost, but rather should be balanced with a recognition of the wisdom of parents and the central role they play in the lives of young people. As with early childhood, a major support for parents could be the teaching of good parenting skills for adolescents based upon lessons learned from parents and backed up by research and practice in youth development.

24 For a more in-depth discussion of pathways, please see "Youth as Effective Citizens on Developing and Deploying Young Leaders" (forthcoming from the Forum for Youth Investment).

REFERENCES

Berlin, G., and A. Sum
1988 "Toward a More Perfect Union: Basic Skills, Poor Families and Our Economic Future." Occasional Paper No. 3, Ford Foundation Project on Social Welfare and the American Future. New York: Ford Foundation.

Catalano, R., M. Berglund, J. Ryan, H. Lonczak, and J. Hawkins
1999 *Positive Youth Development in the United States: Research Findings on Evaluations of Positive Youth Development Programs.* Seattle: University of Washington School of Social Work, Social Development Research Group.

Dryfoos, J.
1990 *Adolescents at Risk.* New York: Oxford University Press.

Elliott, D.
1998 "Prevention Programs That Work for Youth: Violence Prevention." Paper prepared for the Aspen Institute's Congressional Program, "Education and the Development of American Youth," February 13-16, Charleston, South Carolina. Boulder: University of Colorado.

Farkas, S., and J. Johnson, with A. Duffett and A. Bers
1997 *Kids These Days: What Americans Really Think about the Next Generation.* New York: Public Agenda.

Federal Interagency Forum on Child and Family Statistics
1998 *America's Children: Key National Indicators of Well-Being.* Washington, D.C.: Federal Interagency Forum on Child and Family Statistics

Halperin, S. (ed.)
1998 *The Forgotten Half Revisited: American Youth and Young Families, 1988-2008.* Washington, D.C.: American Youth Policy Forum.

Joseph, A., S. Philliber, S. Herrling, and G. Kuperminc
1997 "Preventing Teen Pregnancy and Academic Failure: Experimental Evaluation of a Developmentally Based Approach." *Child Development,* 64(4),729-742.

Moore, M.
1998 "What Sort of Ideas Become Public Ideas?" in R. Reich (ed.). *The Power of Public Ideas.* Cambridge, Mass.: Harvard University Press.

Needle, L.
1994 "Background Paper: Youth Development." San Francisco: Community Networks for Youth Development.

Networks for Youth Development
1998 *A Guided Tour of Youth Development,* Second Edition. New York: Youth Development Institute.

Networks for Youth Development
1998 *The Handbook of Positive Youth Outcomes,* Second Edition. New York: Youth Development Institute.

Pittman, K., and M. Irby
1996 *Preventing Problems or Promoting Development: Competing Priorities or Inseparable Goals?* Baltimore: International Youth Foundation.

Pittman, K., and M. Wright
1991 "Bridging the Gap: A Rationale for Enhancing the Role of Community Organizations in Promoting Youth Development." Commissioned Paper No. 1 for the Task Force on Youth Development and Community Programs at the Carnegie Council on Adolescent Development. Washington, D.C.: Center for Youth Development and Policy Research.

Reich, R.
1988 "Introduction," in R. Reich (ed.). *The Power of Public Ideas.* Cambridge, Mass.: Harvard University Press.

Schinke, S., M. Orlandi, and K. Cole
1992 "Boys & Girls Clubs in Public Housing Developments: Prevention Services for Youth At Risk." *Journal of Community Psychology.* OSAP Special Issue.

Secretary's Commission on Achieving Necessary Skills
1991 *What Work Requires of Schools: A SCANS Report for America 2000.* Washington, D.C.: U.S. Department of Labor.

Sipe, C.
1996 *Mentoring: A Synthesis of P/PV's Research: 1988-1995.* Philadelphia: Public/Private Ventures.

Task Force on Education of Young Adolescents
1989 *Turning Points: Preparing American Youth for the 21st Century.* New York: Carnegie Council on Adolescent Development.

Warren, C., with P. Brown and N. Freudenberg
1999 *Evaluation of the New York City Beacons: Summary of Phase I Findings.* New York: Academy for Educational Development, with the Chapin Hall Center for Children at the University of Chicago and Hunter College Center on AIDS, Drugs and Community Health.

William T. Grant Commission on Work, Family and Citizenship
1988 *The Forgotten Half: Pathways to Success for America's Youth and Young Families.* Washington, D.C.: William T. Grant Commission on Work, Family and Citizenship.

Zeldin, S.
1995 *Opportunities and Supports for Youth Development: Lessons from Research and Implications for Community Leaders and Scholars.* Washington, D.C.: Center for Youth Development.

Zeldin, S., M. Kimball, and L. Price
1995 *What are the Day-to-Day Experiences That Promote Youth Development? An Annotated Bibliography of Research on Adolescents and Their Families.* Washington, D.C.: Center for Youth Development.

Zeldin, S., and L. Price (Guest eds.)
1995 Special Issue: "Creating Supportive Communities for Adolescent Development: Challenges to Scholars." *Journal of Adolescent Research,* 10(1).

Part II. ARENAS OF ACTION THAT DRIVE YOUTH DEVELOPMENT

Public opinion. Policy. Philanthropy. Advocacy. Research. Practice. However you label these arenas (we acknowledge that our term "arenas of action" is far from perfect), it is clear that each plays a critical role in the lives of youth. These six arenas are helpful in that they bring under one umbrella the various ways in which most individuals and organizations that affect the lives of youth tend to identify themselves. There are associations of policy makers (e.g., the National League of Cities' Institute for Youth, Education, and Families). There are affinity groups of philanthropists (e.g., Grantmakers for Children, Youth, and Families). There are networks of advocates (e.g., the National Association of Child Advocates). There are societies for researchers (e.g., the Society for Research on Adolescence). There are networks of practitioners (e.g., the National Network for Youth).

The existence of such networks alone makes the arenas of action a useful framework for reporting progress and directions in the field. But there is another important rationale for using this framework to organize the chapters that follow. In our opinion, some of the most cutting edge work, and some of the most positive outcomes for young people, are achieved in the spaces where two or more of these arenas intersect. While intentional efforts to link and leverage ongoing work across arenas exist, they remain insufficiently understood and undervalued.

We present this framework, then, not as a list of options for readers to pick and choose from, but as a critical set of realms to consistently keep in perspective and bridge.

We acknowledge that our decision to use the six arenas as an organizing tool came *after* the contributions to this volume had been commissioned and collected. We further note that the original process that led to this book was premised on the explicit valuing of expediency over comprehensiveness—to

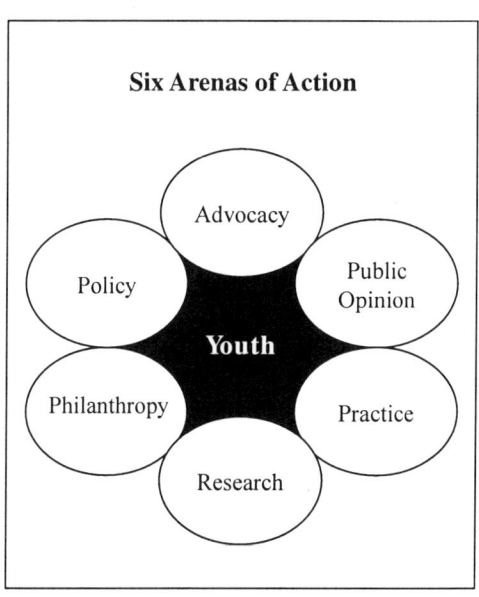

create a quick snapshot to push conversations forward, even if the snapshot turned out to be uneven or incomplete.

Nevertheless, we are able to present a picture of the current reality and future directions of youth development work in most of the arenas. Notably missing, however, is advocacy. While most of the authors consider themselves youth advocates in one fashion or another, and while many chapters were written from this perspective, there is a discrete body of knowledge and action specific to advocacy that is not represented here. Also lacking is a critical practice perspective, such as that offered by Andrew Hahn and Gordon Raley in their 1998 article, "Youth Development: On the Path toward Professionalization."

CONTENTS OF PART II WITH ORGANIZATIONAL SKETCHES OF CONTRIBUTING AUTHORS

2. Perceptual Barriers to Valuing and Supporting Youth

Susan Nall Bales

The FrameWorks Institute continues Susan Nall Bales's long-standing interest in interdisciplinary communications research on social issues. Public opinion research, media effects, and linguistic analysis are the focus of FrameWorks. Advisers include the National Center for Children in Poverty director Larry Aber, communications scholars Frank Gilliam and George Lakoff, and media activists Lori Dorfman and Michael Pertschuk. Susan's portfolio includes work on adolescence and public opinion funded by the W. T. Grant Foundation; on children's issues funded by the David and Lucile Packard Foundation; and on global interdependence funded by the Benton Foundation.

3. The Policy Climate for Early Adolescent Initiatives

Gary Walker

Public/Private Ventures (P/PV) is a national nonprofit organization whose mission is to improve the effectiveness of social policies, programs, and community initiatives, especially as they affect youth and young adults. In carrying out this mission, P/PV works with philanthropies, the public and business sectors, and nonprofit organizations to (1) develop or identify social policies, strategies, and practices that promote individual economic success and citizenship, and stronger families and communities; (2) assess the effectiveness of these promising approaches and distill their critical elements and benchmarks, using rigorous field study and research methods; (3) mine evaluation results and implementation experiences for their policy and practice implications, and communicate the findings to public and private decision makers, as well as to community leaders;

and (4) create and field-test the building blocks—model policies, financing approaches, curricula and training materials, communication strategies, and learning processes—that are necessary to implement effective approaches more broadly.

4. A Matter of Money: The Cost and Financing of Youth Development

Robert P. Newman, Stephanie M. Smith, and Richard Murphy

The Center for Youth Development and Policy Research (CYDPR) is dedicated to contributing to better futures for all youth in the United States. The CYDPR's mission is to be both opportunistic and strategic on a national and local level in shifting the public debate and commitment from youth problems to youth development. One of the Center's primary goals is to support and strengthen public-private partnerships that can ensure community-wide investment and involvement in building an expanded information base and infrastructure for youth development.

5. The Scientific Foundations of Youth Development

Peter L. Benson and Rebecca N. Saito

Search Institute is an independent, nonprofit, nonsectarian organization whose mission is to advance the well-being of adolescents and children by generating knowledge and promoting its application. Search Institute conducts research and evaluation, develops publications and practical tools, and provides training and technical assistance. The Institute collaborates with others to promote long-term organizational and cultural change that supports the healthy development of all children and adolescents.

6. Measuring Deficits and Assets: How We Track Youth Development Now, and How We Should Track It

Gary B. MacDonald and Rafael Valdivieso

Founded in 1961, the Academy for Educational Development (AED) is an independent, nonprofit organization committed to solving critical social problems in the United States and throughout the world through education, social marketing, research, training, policy analysis, and innovative program design and management. Major areas of focus include health, education, youth development, and the environment. Whether the objective is to improve adult literacy in South Africa or early childhood development in the United States, the AED uses its knowledge and experience to connect people with resources and opportunities.

2 PERCEPTUAL BARRIERS TO VALUING AND SUPPORTING YOUTH

Susan Nall Bales

While significant time and research have been aimed at understanding the way Americans think about children's issues, little of this work has directly addressed youth. The question of whether Americans think differently about young children than they do about teenagers has long plagued children's advocates in such mundane ways as choosing between images of children for promotional materials or policy campaigns. While images of little kids might invite sympathy and protectiveness, it has been reasoned, pictures of teens may incite fear and harsh judgments. The simple answer of using categorical monikers—children, kids, and so on—obscures the different needs of adolescents, making it hard to introduce programs that relate to sexuality and work, for example, without their sounding like a non sequitur. Sooner or later, in order to understand the opinion climate that determines how youth issues will be greeted by the public, communications research on youth images had to be undertaken.

This chapter, supported by a grant from the David and Lucile Packard Foundation, is one small step in that direction. It summarizes a series of research endeavors undertaken in 1999 and 2000 to discern what Americans think about youth, why they think what they do, the consequences this has for youth advocates, and how we might best engage Americans in a discussion about positive youth development. This body of research was supported by the W. T. Grant Foundation, as part of a multiyear grant to apply the perspective of strategic frame analysis to youth issues, and supplemented by six focus groups supported by the Packard Foundation.

The research base upon which this chapter relies includes:

1. A summary and analysis of recent survey research related to the public's attitudes concerning adolescents, and six related issue areas: education, sex, substance abuse, violence, the influence of media, and juvenile justice (Bostrom, January 15, 2000);
2. An analysis of the conceptual frames that ordinary people use

to reason about teenagers, based on a series of in-depth interviews (Aubrun and Grady, February 28, 2000);
3. A content analysis of the representation of adolescents in television entertainment programming for the period September 20–November 21, 1999, on the six broadcast networks (Heintz-Knowles, 2000);
4. A catalog of framing options, derived from cognitive-cultural analysis (Aubrun and Grady, April 4, 2000);
5. A summary of six focus groups conducted with parents in three cities in early 2000 (Bostrom, May 2000); and
6. A content analysis of the representation of adolescents in TV news programming for the periods September 29–October 24 and November 28–December 5, 1999, on ABC, CBS, NBC, and CNN evening news and on local evening news on three affiliates in each of five cities (Los Angeles, Chicago, Boston, Seattle, and Columbia, South Carolina), resulting in a sample of 9,678 news stories (Amundson, Lichter, and Lichter, 2000).

These papers were published together in 2000 as *Reframing Youth Issues,* Working Papers of the FrameWorks Institute and the Center for Communications and Community at UCLA. While this chapter draws from this collection of work, the conclusions are solely that of the author, and are meant to invite, not supplant, a closer reading of the original research. Readers should refer to the original manuscripts for primary sources.

ABOUT STRATEGIC FRAME ANALYSIS

Strategic frame analysis is an approach to communications research and practice that pays attention to the public's deeply held worldviews and widely held assumptions. It was created by a multidisciplinary team of scholars and practitioners capable of studying those assumptions and testing them to determine their impact on social policies. Recognizing that there is more than one way to tell a story, strategic frame analysis taps into decades of research on how people think and communicate. The result is an empirically driven communications process that makes academic research understandable, interesting, and usable to help people solve social problems.

The term *frame,* as defined by the political psychologist Shanto Iyengar, "refers to subtle alterations in the statement or presentation of judgment and choice problems, and the term 'framing effects' refers to changes in decision outcomes resulting from these alterations" (1991, p. 21). According to the linguist Deborah Tannen, the frame triggers "an expectation about the world based on prior experience, against which new experiences are measured and interpreted" (p. 17). In short, "frames are conceptual tools which media and individuals rely on to convey, interpret, and evaluate information" (Neuman, Just, and Crigler, 1992,

p. 149). This is significant because how people understand social issues is critical to their support of, or opposition to, particular public policies. Referring to government programs as handouts, for example, brings to bear cultural models of laziness, but not of suffering. Frames tell us how to interpret a message, and even what counts as part of the message and what can be ignored, by evoking particular cognitive models and not others.

This approach is strategic in that it not only deconstructs the dominant frames that drive reasoning on public issues, but it also identifies those models most likely to stimulate public reconsideration and enumerates their elements (reframing). Strategic frame analysis offers policy advocates a way to work systematically through the challenges that confront the introduction of new legislation or social policies, to anticipate attitudinal barriers to support, and to develop research-based strategies to overcome public misunderstanding.

The perspective that informs this chapter is that of strategic frame analysis.

FINDINGS FROM THE RESEARCH

Frame Distortion: Conflicts between Perceptions of Youth and the Reality

There are dramatic differences between the way American adults view teenagers and the descriptive data that should inform our views of what teens think and do. Strategic frame analysis would assert that adults cannot see teens as they are because the frames that control who we think they are get in the way. When the facts don't fit the frames, the facts are rejected, not the frames.

There are a number of critical areas of distortion. First, adults believe that teens today are "different" than they were in the past. At the core of this concern is a feeling that today's teens have rejected traditional American values. Bostrom reports that "only 16% of Americans say that 'young people under the age of 30 share most of their moral and ethical values.' This puts young adults' values only above homosexuals, welfare recipients, and rich people" (Bostrom, January 15, 2000, p. 4). A Gallup poll found that, when asked what word applied to young people in their teens and 20s today, compared to young people in that same group 20 years ago, adults chose "selfish" (81%) and "materialistic" (79%) for youth today, and "patriotic" (65%) and "idealistic" (49%) for the youth of yesteryears (ibid., p. 5).

"While adults have serious reservations about American youth," Bostrom concludes, "the reality is that teens place high value on honesty and hard work, and the vast majority are thinking and planning seriously for the future" (ibid., p. 6). Among those values teens say they rank highest are "being honest" (8.6 on a 10-point scale), "working hard" (8.4), "being a good student" (7.9), and "giving time to helping others" (7.6). And majorities of teens say they volunteer, attend church or synagogue weekly, read the newspaper regularly, and attend cultural events (ibid., p. 7).

And, "while the public tends to blame parents, the reality is that most parents have open, trusting relationships and a solid bond with their teenage children," Bostrom concludes. Indeed, when asked who they most rely on for making important decisions or for facing problems, parents are the top choice, with 63% of teens saying they rely on their parents a "lot." There has been an important shift in responsibility, she notes. "While in 1997, the public was equally likely to blame kids' problems on social/economic pressures as well as irresponsible parents (41% and 44% respectively), in the improved economy, they are more likely to blame parents (37% blame social/economic pressures, 49% parents)" (ibid., p. 10).

In fact, Youniss and Ruth have shown that, on virtually every social indicator, "youth today are at least as healthy or healthier than their parents' generation." Drawing from national databases and trend analysis, they report that "the percentage of youth who work part-time has remained constant or risen a bit 1970 to today" and "SAT scores have remained constant since 1970." The proportions of high school students who volunteer have not changed since 1975, and the proportion of high school seniors who say religion is very or quite important in their lives has remained high and constant from 1975 to the present.

What's going on here? Are adults simply "misinformed" about the lives and attitudes of today's youth? Can a simple recitation of the facts set the record straight? Using data provided by Youniss and Ruth, we tested parents' reaction to a news story that presented positive data about the status of adolescents today.

Over the course of six focus groups with parents, we observed astonishing unanimity in the way adults discounted positive statistics about youth. Confronted with what was presented as a "true news story" about recent trends among teenagers, adults consistently overlooked the positive data (which dominated the story) and focused instead on the few negative trends. When asked to reexamine the story and to explain why they thought it was indeed negative when there were so many positive trends, they first said they thought the numbers were not correct. When informed that they were indeed correct, they often found ways to reinterpret the numbers in order to result in a decline or a "not good enough" conclusion.

MODERATOR: "The title of this story is, 'Some Kids Doing Better, Others Fall Behind.' For the most part it is a very positive article stating that basically school achievement has stayed on a par with what it was in the seventies for the state of Virginia . . . We have a 40 percent of all youth that is now volunteering in programs. Overall, a kind of positive article. We're wondering . . ."

"It's too positive."

MODERATOR: "What particular pieces of it made it seem not true for you?"

"Well, 40 percent of youth involved in community service. That seems awfully high . . ."

MODERATOR: "Okay, if you had made a guess on what percentage of teens volunteer, what percentage would you have guessed?"

"Ten, twenty."

"Twenty."

"Fifteen."

"Way under twenty."

"Did it say volunteer community service because that . . ."

"Can be criminal."

MODERATOR: "What else in there other than the percentage of volunteering seems unrealistic?"

"The chance of being involved in a teenage violent crime is about as high as being hit by a meteor. Either [sic] they are not reporting incidents. That is highly possible. You can get beat up by another kid and not tell anybody because he is embarrassed or whatever, or it is a lie, I think. I don't see how that ratio could be true."

MODERATOR: "If you were reading this in your newspaper at home, what would you do with it?"

"It would lead you to believe that your children are safe and things are good."

MODERATOR: "But the tone of your voice sounds a little cynical. You don't believe that."

"I would think that the state was getting ready to do something legislatively . . ."

"They are going to cut something because we're doing so great or they are going to take something away. I would think that this was not something that was written independently by some reporter who just had this observation. He was either paid, robbed, or given the information."

"The flip side of that, we were talking earlier where it is just not reported as often that good things that teens—that young people are involved in. Maybe that is why the number would shock you so bad because you just don't hear about it. So when you see this really big number that just seems completely impossible, maybe it is true. We just don't hear enough about it because we're hearing more about the violence and the drug use and the drinking and driving, the races on the streets and kids are hitting poles and getting killed. You hear about that . . . Why do they do this? You don't hear about the community volunteers all the time, so when you do get this big outlandish sounding number, it takes you by surprise."

"Well, you don't see it . . . Where do you know outside of church groups where your youth are actually going out in the community and doing something? Where? Where are they?"

"I see kids in hospitals, Candy Stripers."

"I was going to say personally I wouldn't know because I haven't volunteered to do it. I see them at church because I go and I'll see them in the mall because I go. But perhaps if I went and served at a soup kitchen, I might see it jack full of teenagers. Because my butt is at home eating my soup in front of the TV, I don't see them."

"How did they do this poll?"—Mothers of young children, Richmond, Virginia

"It says the school achievement is measured by the national assessment of education progress. Most people don't know what that is. They say national. Does that come out of Washington? Is that an organization run by whatever party is in power to cook the books of the stats to make it look like, Hey, we've done a great job when maybe we haven't."

"Kids today use marijuana less than their parents did. Maybe, maybe not, but it doesn't mention anything about other substances. Alcohol. I know amphetamines . . ."—Fathers of teenagers, Richmond, Virginia

"Where did they get the statistics from?"
"That's what I'd like to know, because it's not my neighborhood."—Mothers of teenagers, Riverside, California

Where, then, are Americans getting the views that fly in the face of reality? What accounts for a distortion so powerful that it "trumps" all incoming data or reconfigures it to fit within the negative stereotypes?

The Pictures in Our Heads: Images of Youth in the Media

"Television is a cultural storyteller," says Katharine Heintz-Knowles, in explaining the importance of entertainment programming in shaping the attitudes and beliefs of viewers. Its dual role, she asserts, is as both a reflection of currently held belief systems and an influence on newly forming belief systems. "Even when viewers recognize that the content they are viewing is fictional, its messages and images gradually shape expectations and beliefs about the real world."

To identify the stories we are being told about teenagers today through entertainment television, Heintz-Knowles examined one episode of each prime-time series that aired during fall 1999 between September 20 and November 21 on six networks (ABC, CBS, NBC, Fox, WB, and UPN). Those with youth characters (defined as between the ages of 13 and 21) were analyzed according to a set of codes that sought to measure youth activity and concern on TV against real-world data. In brief, this study shows that adolescent characters on television are not connected to a wider community, including their own family. TV teens are seen as independent and isolated, living in an adolescent world whose problems are mainly social in nature. They do not require anyone's help beyond their small, immediate peer group, and in fact their parents are often portrayed as ineffective or as causing problems. Heintz-Knowles concludes that TV reinforces the notion of today's teens as self-absorbed and interested only in trivial matters. Her key findings are as follows:

- TV youth are most often shown dealing with problems relating to romantic relationships, friendships/popularity, and family issues. In the sample, there was not a single instance of a youth character involved in a conflict or problem that was societal in nature (homelessness, poverty, environmental concerns).
- In programs with a primarily youth cast, adolescents are often shown as capable of solving their own problems without adult help.
- In programs with a primarily adult cast, youth characters often act as catalysts creating problems adults must fix.
- TV parents are most often shown as absent or ineffective, although some programs feature supportive and effective parent characters. Many youth charac-

ters exist in a world void of parental involvement. In some instances, parents are identified as the root of youth characters' problems. In other cases, while they may not be the cause of their children's problems, they are shown as ineffective or uninvolved in their children's lives.
- The most common activity identified for youth characters is socializing—at school and elsewhere. They were twice as likely to be shown socializing at school than engaging in academic work there. Twelve percent of youth characters were shown to participate in some form of school-oriented extracurricular activities.
- The second most common activity was "hanging out," defined as socializing behavior off school grounds. Just under 10 percent of youth characters were shown doing chores at home or working at low-wage employment.
- When discussing youth, adult characters most often use terminology that sets adolescents apart as young and childlike.

Among Heintz-Knowles's conclusions is the speculation that current television programming "reinforces a common stereotype of teens as self-absorbed." And, "while the portrayal of youth as self-reliant sends an empowering message to youth viewers, it can also convey a sense that youth do not need connections to their families or the larger community." Finally, "youth are talked about in terms that set them apart from adults."

In their parallel analysis of television news, Amundson, Lichter, and Lichter (2000) found, overall, a paucity of news reporting about youth; only one out of every 12 stories on local newscasts, and only one out of every 25 stories on network newscasts dealt with young people. These stories were "overwhelmingly episodic in nature, focusing on particular events and discrete occurrences, without providing any thematic context or otherwise linking them to broader trends or issues" (p. 32). Indeed, only 7 percent of the local coverage was deemed thematic. The three most frequently reported topics of youth news on the local stations were crimes involving youth as victims, accidents involving young people, and violent juvenile crime, accounting for nearly half (46%) of all coverage of youth. Five other frequently reported topics were also negative: property crimes committed by juveniles, domestic violence or sexual abuse, alcohol abuse, individual health problems, and other risky behaviors. This study concludes: "Together, these eight topics, which all emphasize the dangers and negative outcomes associated with youth, accounted for nearly 60 percent of all discussions" of youth (p. 11).

An analysis of the visual backdrop to news reports about youth found that the local news emphasized school settings. The criminal justice system accounted for one out of every four visual backdrops in local news. "When not shown in school, youths were most likely to be seen as part of community activities or in a crime-related or other socially dysfunctional setting. A mere 2 percent of [young people] were portrayed in the home, while just one percent were shown in a work setting" (p. 9).

To chart the implications for policy solutions, we asked Amundson, Lichter, and Lichter to count the instances in which a reporter or source specifically voices some concern about the risks or dangers that are faced by young people. The 242 sound bites that resulted were concentrated in two areas: violence (33%) and other at-risk behaviors (31%), such as drug and alcohol use and dangerous driving. "Only about one in three expressions of concern were accompanied by any discussion of the locus of responsibility for solving whatever problem was indicated." And, of these assignments, parents and youth themselves accounted for 37 percent of the responsible agents, followed by schools (30%) and government (26%) (p. 14).

Our study sample was limited to television, leaving us open to criticism that more influential segments of the public may be more reliant on newspapers for their information and, therefore, exposed to more thematic and policy-oriented coverage of adolescents. The work of other researchers would refute this hypothesis. Recently, the Berkeley Media Studies Group analyzed three California newspapers over the course of a year to determine what kind of attention was being paid to young people with what probable policy consequences. They found that "two topics dominate youth coverage: education and violence," and "no other topic receives even a third as much attention. Education received 26 percent of the coverage. Violence stories comprised 25 percent of all youth coverage. Thus, these print media show violence as a factor in young people's lives as often as schools." As these researchers point out, "only 3 young people in 100 perpetrate or become victims of serious violence in a given year" and "treating violence and education nearly equally exaggerates the frequency of violence." Finally, "in the yearlong sample, about half the youth stories focus on a problem; many fewer describe a solution." The most-often cited solution is greater law enforcement. The study concludes that "the relative absence of solution frames reinforces the notion that violence is inevitable" (Dorfman, 2000).

There are a number of older content analyses that support and extend these conclusions. Content analyses of the depictions of youth by the media have consistently revealed a bias toward negative coverage in which youth are most likely to be featured in the context of crime stories (Kunkel, 1994; Berkeley Media Studies Group, 1995, 1997; Woodruff 1998; Dorfman and Woodruff, 1998; Dorfman, 2000).

During the month of November 1993, Dale Kunkel examined coverage of children's issues in five major newspapers *(Atlanta Constitution, Chicago Tribune, Houston Chronicle, Los Angeles Times, New York Times),* as well as nightly newscasts on three major networks (ABC, CBS, NBC). He found (Kunkel, 1994) that coverage of violence accounted for nearly half (48%) of all TV coverage of children, with only slightly less (40%) in the newspapers. By contrast, the issue of children's health accounted for only 11 percent of the stories in each medium. Only one in three stories addressed any public policy concerns. Kunkel concluded that this imbalance "seems to skew the information the press provides to the public, which in turn diminish the public's perception of the relative importance of other child-related concerns" (www.childrennow.org, online version).

In a study titled "Frames on Children and Youth in US Newspapers" (1995), the Berkeley Media Studies Group (BMSG) studied four major papers during one week and concluded that when children appear in the news, it is most often as

Perceptual Barriers to Valuing and Supporting Youth 63

victims of violence and crime (p. 4). Moreover, "virtually every time youth or teenagers were used as examples . . . it was in a negative context . . . The phrases reflect our stereotypic icons of youth: 'teenage mothers,' 'student athletes on drugs,' 'teenagers too embarrassed to ask about sex,' high school graduates who know 'less than nothing about computers,' and 'troubled teen-agers.' Writers assert that 'much violent crime is impulsive, committed by young people,' and 'liquor is quicker for youthful consumers'" (p. 8).

In a 1997 update to their original content analysis, focused on children's health in three months' coverage from both national and regional newspapers and National Public Radio, the Berkeley Media Studies Group (p. 6) found that "younger children appear to be far more newsworthy than teens." Most coverage of children's health problems presented no solutions at all, and when an approach was discussed, it was most often "in the form of information to parents about what they could do to protect their children." Children or youth themselves were quoted in only 8 percent of the pieces, and only one piece quoted a young person talking about a positive program. In reviewing the frames of presentation, BMSG concluded that "parental responsibility is repeatedly stressed, while the public health approach to children's health and safety appears in a few rare but significant pieces." In other words, the vast majority of the news coverage of youth is "episodic" and tends to attribute responsibility to parents and the youth themselves, rather than to institutions or policies.

In a statewide study of youth and race on local TV news, based on 26 California stations, Dorfman and Woodruff (1998) found that "violence appears to be particularly newsworthy when it involves children or youth" and more than two-thirds of violence stories did involve youth. They also found the reverse to be true: "when youth appeared on the news, it was most often as the victim or perpetrator of violence" (p. 81). Fifty-three percent of all youth stories involved violence. Finally, in order for youth to be portrayed positively, they had to "perform an extraordinary feat," such as flying solo across the country or winning a national beauty contest (p. 81). They conclude: "despite the fact that most young people are not violent, local television news draws a direct link between youth and violence, and this likely contributes to cementing negative views in the minds of viewers . . . [S]tories about productive, nonviolent youth are the exception rather than the rule" (pp. 83-84).

Additionally, Dorfman and Woodruff uncovered important differences in the roles TV accorded youth of color compared to white youth. More white youth were given opportunities to speak in local news stories. In every violence-related role in which youth did speak—either as a victim, a witness of violence, a criminal, or a suspect—youth of color were heard in these roles in higher proportions than their white counterparts. A higher percentage of white youth spoke in the role of victim of unintentional injury. There were also marked differences in the circumstances in which white youth and youth of color were used for "person on the street" interviews, with youth of color being far more likely to be shown in situations related to crime, drug dealing, and gangs (p. 82).

Kill the Camera: Public Perceptions of Media's Role

Participants in the spring 2000 focus groups understand that media influence their perceptions of teens. They understand that news is skewed toward the teens "that shot somebody," and that the "bad teens are the ones that make the headlines." They also understand that the opposite is true: good news does not make it on the news. "They [media] don't do these reports on teens that are in poetry contests and win or working in the soup kitchens—a list of kids that made the honor roll. You don't hear that . . . So when you think of a teenager, you are automatically going to associate with the bad rap that they have gotten just by a few." And, as one mother of a teen put it, "When you expect and assume that kids are doing everything that they are writing about, what chance do they have? You assume they are already doing it" (Bostrom, May 2000, p. 14).

These opinions are stunning in their articulation of the way that media drives reasoning and risk assessment. Yet, while adults know they are "under the influence," they nevertheless continue to reason, to assess risk, and to judge policy options on the basis of this distorted coverage.

The most powerful example of this occurred in focus group participants' reactions to the news story described earlier in this report that put forward positive trend statistics about teens and acknowledged changes in community behavior that accounted for these changes. As the quotations attest, these adults did not believe the statistics, found technical manipulations in the data, or redefined the statistics as negative. Few could explain why positive trends might exist among today's teens. According to Bostrom, "People reacted to the positive statistics with disbelief and skepticism. They were so focused on trying to fit the statistics into their knowledge of the world that they largely ignored the suggested solution of nurturing communities" (Bostrom, May 2000, p. 17).

How does this negative assessment square with adults' own observations of the youth around them? Often uncomfortably. A father of younger children spoke up in one focus group about teens in his neighborhood: "I have some extremely intelligent, articulate, young—12 to 16 year olds. Surprisingly, actually, to speak with such perfect English, respectful. Sometimes it shocks me" (ibid., p. 12).

As Aubrun and Grady assert, most Americans "tend to resolve this contradiction by judging their own experience to be exceptional, rather than by challenging the media frames. This reflects a broader pattern of Americans' response to the contradiction between what they know at first hand and what media and public discourse tells them" (February 2000, p. 2). "The position of the media has the effect of making their own experience and attitudes seem unusual or even aberrant. They tend to discount what does not fit the media frame as exceptional, rather than questioning or challenging the frame" (ibid., p. 3).

In fact, their interviews show that "the same people who are able to articulate this stereotype, and who attribute it to their neighbors, often hold a much more benign view themselves. In fact, they very often feel more sympathy than resentment toward teenagers" (ibid.).

Aubrun and Grady's interviews demonstrate as well that most adults "are aware (at times) that this negative model is a negative stereotype rather than an accurate representation of the teens that they know: 'You know that there've got to be hundreds of thousands of them that are going to college and that have made national honor society or . . . who are trying to do the right things. But you hardly ever hear about them'" (ibid.).

Personal experience does play a strong role in resisting these stereotypes, however, and Aubrun and Grady found that "parents of teenagers or those who interact regularly with teenagers are much less susceptible to the media portrayals of teens. These people either reject media accounts outright or concede that they must be true in some abstract sense (or TV wouldn't be saying so), but not in any practical sense" (ibid., p. 6). "The more people's views are informed by 'face time' and the less by the media, the more likely they are to share . . . the empathic view of teenagers" (ibid., p. 20). In an increasingly age-segregated society, however, the prospects are fewer and fewer for adults to countermand media stereotypes of teen monsters and heroes with abundant firsthand knowledge of normal teens, going about the everyday business of chores and school, athletics, arts, and volunteering.

In sum, the absence of an experiential base for some adults, and the power of media images to trump personal experience for others, leave most adults with few alternatives to the images provided by their daily feed of news and entertainment. And while they may understand this to be the case, and resent the media for it, they nevertheless will find their reasoning directed by these images.

Framed: Deconstructing Elements of the Negative Stereotype

In order to fashion a strategy to "reframe" youth for public support, we need to understand more precisely what aspects of youth culture and behavior are especially important to adults. There are three major problems in adult perceptions of youth that must be addressed:

- Their lack of a relationship to work and the values it is presumed to confer;
- The central and exclusive role accorded parents, often with an emphasis on safeguarding youth as effective and appropriate parenting; and, relatedly,
- The relatively weak role accorded community and government in supporting youth and families.

Bostrom speculates that, at the core of adult anxiety is the contradiction between "having to grow up too fast to the negative realities without having to shoulder the positive, character building responsibilities" (Bostrom, May 2000, p. 2). This combination of fear and concern over the way our world has changed turns teens into the canaries in the mine shafts, first to experience the worst of technology, consumerism, violence, drugs, and a culture out of control. As Aubrun and Grady note, "people's negative attitudes toward teens often seem to reflect anxieties about the direction that American society is taking" (February 2000,

p. 7). Teens become proxies for a whole series of changes—from moms in the workforce to videogames in the bedroom—that Americans do not feel to be improvements in society. In this sense, discussions about "teens today" are as much about whether America is on the right or wrong track morally as they are about specific aspects of teen life.

While many adults say teens today are "growing up too fast," they also believe that they are maturing more slowly. By this, they mean that it takes young people longer "to develop adult competence and self-sufficiency now than it took their parents and grandparents" (ibid., p. 11). Adults believe that teens are coddled and spoiled, and that this experience is detrimental to their development of ideals and acceptance of responsibility:

> "The average teenager has a real easy life . . . They just do what they damn well please, when they want to do it."
>
> "I think most teenagers probably have more things available to them than we ever did as we grew up, because most families are dual income families. I think because of that they have the opportunity to do a lot more than we ever did. And because of that I think they also take things for granted."
>
> "I had a lot of responsibilities. Both my mom and dad worked and so I had to do a lot of things."
>
> "I remember I had responsibilities, too. I was second of eight kids, so I would come home and help mom. Usually she already had dinner started and stuff, but I had to do my things." (Bostrom, May 2000, pp. 7-8)

Given that adults today are rarely exposed to youth performing chores, either at home or work, it is little wonder that the comparison between their own adolescence and that of today's teens finds the latter sorely wanting, with important consequences. The values adults associate with maturity are, for the most part, values associated with the adult world of work: responsibility, discipline, teamwork, commitment, self-restraint, goal-orientation, and so on. "Given the importance of work as a defining American cultural value, teens' perceived distance from the work world also contributes to the view that they are irresponsible" (Aubrun and Grady, February 2000, p. 12). A logical approach to countering this notion that youth today lack these values would be to demonstrate that youth are indeed working, and learning these values in the process. Indeed, data provided by James Youniss show that "the percentage of youth who work part-time has remained constant or risen a bit 1970-today." Yet, when focus group participants were confronted with these statistics, they either denied the data or found a way to convert the motivation for working to selfishness and consumerism:

> "Not the kids I know. Usually they are working to help themselves be able to buy one of those things."
>
> "Car insurance."
>
> "Clothes."

"Video games. But I can't name a kid who works to help his actual family situation."—Mothers of teens, Riverside, California

It is ironic that evidence of workforce participation is unable to break through the media frame of irresponsible youth, and yet this should not deter us from pursuing other ways to get across the fact that kids do learn these essential positive values from their daily experiences. It is no accident that the recent White House Conference on Teenagers was subtitled "Working to Help Families Raise Responsible Teenagers," with both core words—work and responsibility—built into the discussion.

The second major issue that requires addressing is that of the parent's appropriate role in teen development. Aubrun and Grady found "the near-absence of a cultural model that emphasizes teens' need for mentoring from adults outside the nuclear family . . . American models . . . often fail to acknowledge this nearly-universal aspect of human development, in effect reinforcing the widespread idea that the nuclear family bears sole responsibility for guiding the development of youths" (Aubrun and Grady, February 2000, p. 2).

In many of the focus group discussions, adults weighed policy options with specific reference to whether they supplanted parents, leading Bostrom to conclude that many adults are "highly sensitive to what they viewed as any infringement on parent's rights, including actions by schools." Parental involvement is often the panacea for all that troubles teens. Indeed, this sense of ownership is so strong that one mother of a teen actually bemoaned the fact that teens might go to other family members for advice, rather than their parents (Bostrom, May 2000, p. 16). In an exercise that involved discussing the impact of declining numbers of counselors in schools, adults were wary of the notion that counselors might have a role beyond the academic, and would be taking over the role of teaching values that they so firmly believe belongs to them.

In reviewing the photos of teens and commenting on their life prospects, focus group participants often tried to discern the parents behind the teen. Neatness and good grooming demonstrated good parenting—"I think he comes from a good family," or "I think she has a parent or parents very involved in her life" (ibid., p. 11). Similarly, athletic and volunteer participation implied the guiding hand of an involved parent (see below), who was assumed to be present simply because someone had to drive the youth to and from these activities. In sum, as one interviewee expressed this near-universal opinion, "I think everything starts at home" (Aubrun and Grady, February 2000, p. 13).

Bostrom concludes that "adults see no other actor in the equation other than parents and teens, making it particularly difficult to shift people from an assumption of parental responsibility to societal responsibility" (May 2000, p. 2). Despite the many cues in the focus groups to look to social solutions, "the only role for communities that most see is organizing youth activities," says Bostrom (p. 5). "Because of their strong sense of parental responsibility and their cynicism about politics, focus group participants see few social solutions other than teen centers and a vague sense of community support."

This leads to the third important issue for youth advocates: trying to find a role for society that does not threaten the parent-child relationship.

While adults may not see a role for government writ large, they nevertheless do look to communities to "provide role models" and mentors, and they want to see teens included in the community, including civic activities (Bostrom, May 2000, p. 6).

And, as Aubrun and Grady report, adults believe that teens would benefit from being more integrated into the community (February 2000, p. 17). By exposing young people to older adults, people believe that teens will learn more traditional values like respect and responsibility, and be less subject to peers whom they largely see as negative.

It is instructive and thought-provoking to note that focus group participants faced with a specific call to action that invited them to support other parents who were trying to keep their town from being overrun by bars and liquor advertising did feel compelled to respond. Rather than acting together as a political force, they chose more individualist remedies that reinforced their roles as parents, for example, educating their kids about alcohol and advertising.

REFRAMING FOR PUBLIC SUPPORT

There are a number of lessons that emerge from these findings that can be tested by youth advocates. At the same time, the FrameWorks Institute will be continuing its work on reframing youth in a series of subsequent research efforts that include testing the media effects of these very reframing suggestions to determine exactly what impact they have on policy preferences. While the following should be viewed as suggestions, they are the best research-based suggestions we can offer at this point.

1. Don't use the word *teenager*. As Bostrom concluded, "the associations are so powerful that 'teenager' may be an unsalvageable word for advocates hoping to create a positive or sympathetic view of 13–19 year olds."

The terms *youth* or *adolescent* are preferable. Better still is the term *adolescence,* which underscores the fact that kids are in process, passing through a stage, on the way to adulthood. While "adolescence" is a shared experience, and one that can invite empathy from adults, the word *teenager* reinforces assessments of difference. Similarly, the term *young people* reinforces commonality.

Moreover, advocates should be proactive in talking about adolescence as a stage we all go through with its common challenges of learning responsibility, commitment, and teamwork.

Aubrun and Grady suggested reminding adults what it was like to be a teenager; the focus groups found that while this did result in more positive assessments of today's youth (Bostrom, May 2000, p. 8), it had negative consequences as well. Comparisons between the world in which today's adults grew up and the one in which they see teens growing up fuel their fears and make them even more mindful of the need to protect their children. While one might have speculated that it would drive adults to consider more environmental influences on teens, and to push adults into a more societal mind-set, we did not see much evidence of this happening. So powerful is the notion of community as external threat that this comparison incites protection to the exclusion of other considerations. At the same time, this assessment of their own youth compared to that of today's teens only emphasizes to them the perceived responsibilities they shouldered compared to the spoiled, self-absorption of youth now.

Again, we suggest concentrating on adolescence as a shared stage in the transition to adulthood. "Remind people that teenagers are still in a developmental stage, rather than . . . some special, bad category of person," say Aubrun and Grady (April 2000, 10). "What they are today is not what they will be tomorrow."

Experts should address the challenges of adolescence and attempt to explain the need for youth to be accepted in and by the community, to be given roles of responsibility, and to be mentored. This advice should be given not solely as parental advice but as advice to the community in how to guide young people toward healthy development, community leadership, and citizenship. While many people understand the basic tenets of young child development (or think they do), few talk about adolescent development with any confidence. This is an opportunity for experts to shape a vision of healthy youth development that connects to adults' longing for greater responsibility and deeper values among today's youth.

2. Show youth involved in sports, volunteer, and other extracurricular activities like performance arts. Assessments of youth shown involved in these activities were universally positive. "When I see a girl in sports, I immediately think she has a chance to succeed in life," explained a father of a teen (Bostrom, May 2000, p. 13). Reacting to a picture of a young boy volunteering at what appeared to be a soup kitchen, one mother commented, "He is going to be an asset to his community just because he is already at a young age involved in community."

Recognizing that it is going to a take a critical mass of positive images to reverse the negative stereotypes, and that these new images will need to be carefully chosen so as not to directly confront the reigning frame, we urge advocates to be aggressive in spotlighting adolescents involved in these kinds of activities. Showcase them on websites, involve them in news conferences, and put them before civic bodies.

When composing photos meant to illustrate "children's issues," expand the age base to include adolescents by using teens in sports dress or clearly identified in volunteer affiliations.

3. Explain what youth are doing in terms that derive from the values associated with work: responsibility, teamwork, commitment, self-restraint, goal-orientation, learning leadership. One of the most compelling suggestions from Aubrun and Grady is that we emphasize "teens as learners" (April 2000, p. 10). "One aspect of teens that bears constant reinforcing is that they are involved in a learning process. Frames that emphasize this aspect of adolescence strike a positive chord of self-improvement, and suggest that the job of people around teens is to be good 'teachers.'"

What they are learning must be made explicit again and again. Adolescents on the field are learning to strive and to struggle to set goals, to work as a team.

Another suggestion is that "teens are searchers." This allows us to stress that they are looking for ways to contribute to their communities, to find their place, to make their mark, and to shape their world. They are idealistic, and it is important that the community find ways to use their idealism, not to shut them out and reinforce their cynicism. If teens are searchers, then we are all guides.

This is a major translation challenge: to connect the images that have the greatest potential for reframing youth in a positive light with the exact attributes that adults want to see them exhibit. Do not let the picture speak alone; interpret for your audience what is being learned on the playing field and on stage. Otherwise, people are likely to toggle back and forth between thinking this is "play," and not connected to the values of "work."

In advocating for work-specific programs, like summer jobs for youth, stress the values they will acquire and the importance of giving young people responsibility and mentors from whom to learn commitment, goals, and responsibility.

4. Use coaches and volunteer leaders to attest to the values and hard work of today's youth. We need to sanction positive information about youth. One way to do that is to lodge the information in messengers whom the community trusts on these issues. Coaches and volunteer leaders not only fulfill this requirement, but, to the degree that they are not acting in their role as parents (a parent of a teen on the team, for example), "they can help to underscore community responsibility rather than reverting to parental responsibility" (Bostrom, May 2000, p. 2).

Moreover, because coaches and volunteer leaders see hundreds of kids, they can make group pronouncements with some authority, "The kids I see coming through these programs are on track for achievement, focused, responsible, and learning what it means to work as a team, as a member of society." This kind of statement—describing many kids, not merely the exceptional—helps balance the equation for the public.

Special technical assistance and training should be given to coaches and volunteer leaders so that they can comfortably make these assessments, and so that they are press-ready for questions. Without this kind of training, they are likely to revert to individualized, human interest accounts that will only reinforce the notion that it is one good teen in a hundred that is performing well.

5. Use older Americans to attest to the value and values of today's youth. When a book about today's seniors titled *The Greatest Generation* is high on the bestseller list, and older Americans are courted on both sides of the political aisle as pivotal to the presidential election, their pronouncements on just about anything are newsworthy.

But older Americans are important to reframing youth in a very singular sense: they convey values. Their endorsement of youth automatically contests the frame of "valueless youth."

Enlisting older Americans willing to make these pronouncements is often not easy. As was demonstrated in an earlier set of focus groups (see Bales, ed., 1999), the lone senior citizen who asserted that "most kids are OK" was shouted down by her peers. Interestingly, most of these seniors (located outside Phoenix, Arizona) had little direct contact with youth, including their own grandchildren. They were almost solely reliant on the media to tell them how youth were faring in their community and in the country. Direct contact (see below) that leads to positive assessments and a willingness to publicly witness for youth are prerequisites to this strategy.

But it is not enough. Too often, public interest groups enlist seniors and then instruct them to talk about the importance of youth to their social security. The problem with this teens-as-assets model, as Aubrun and Grady point out (April 2000, p. 10), is "that its natural implication is that teens are something to be exploited. This conflicts with the idea that teens are developing and in need of further positive investment from adults, such as mentoring." Moreover, when teens don't "perform," it allows us to liquidate our portfolio.

Using seniors wisely means inviting them to attest to the values that they see youth exhibiting in their places of worship, volunteer activities, and in the community. It means engaging them in sanctioning the good talk about today's youth, and connecting what they see to their own generation's commitment, sacrifice, and teamwork. It means sending a message that today's youth are not "different" from those of previous generations, a very important point to make! Their call to action, as Aubrun and Grady suggest (April 2000, p. 10), can be that elders need to "weigh in" on the side of youth, to see that they are not pulled in the wrong direction. "We have the power to help youth stay on track for achievement," is a great message coming from a senior. Engaged in this way, seniors can become a very powerful force for reframing youth for the general public.

6. Avoid the "hero youth" model, which exceptionalizes the example and casts suspicion on the less accomplished majority. Past content analysis suggests that teens are most likely to appear in news as "monsters or heroes," or as victims or perpetrators. Indeed, it is the "exceptional" teen that makes the news in the first place.

There are two problems with using this "human interest" approach to reframe public attitudes about youth. First, as the research of Shanto Iyengar (1991) suggests, the public cannot connect vivid case studies to broader social solutions. The personalization of social issues results not in greater political salience but in a focus on the individual travails of unfortunate and isolate people. Second, as the research of Franklin D. Gilliam Jr. and colleagues has demonstrated, the presentation of heroic deeds by young people or by African Americans does not effectively reverse people's negative stereotypes associated with these groups. To the contrary, Gilliam shows that people "reframe" the hero to correspond to their stereotype (white) and that they feel worse about the group in general when presented with the triumphant individual. Gilliam concludes that exceptions often serve to reinforce the notion that the group can and should do more to succeed, setting up what has been termed "new racist" reasoning with respect to the African American experiment.

The goal of reframing youth cannot be to exceptionalize them one at a time, to show one or two good kids and to expect the public to make the connection. Nor does the answer lie in presenting people with the facts about teens in America today; as our experiment with the positive news trends strongly suggests, those facts will be rejected. The answer has to be to begin to chip away at the underlying values that lead adults to reason falsely about youth today and to do this by showing groups of kids, by putting forward trusted messengers speaking on behalf of kids, and by connecting youth group activities to those very values that make youth more like adults and less like aliens.

Avoid the irresistible youth who has organized the entire city's park cleanup and, instead, focus on the group activity: ordinary kids getting together to solve a problem, working together, while doing chores and homework. Try to instill the idea that there are thousands of kids like these in every city and state.

7. Show youth in situations in which their work and volunteer support are altruistic and solve a social problem. Earlier focus groups we conducted on children's issues found a public hungry for solutions to help kids (see Bales, ed., 1999). To the extent possible, youth should be shown involved in solving community problems, especially in consort with people of other age groups. At the same time, it is important to be careful in this kind of framing so as not to suggest that the youth should solve their own problems, a common adult frame that merely passes the responsibility on to the victim. By showing youth involved in environmental issues, with elderly people, with younger children, the idea of youth "learning to be adults" will be conveyed, and their "difference" from previous generations undermined. We need to move youth from the problem side of the equation to the problem-solver side.

8. Given the invisibility of normal youth on TV news and entertainment, work with local faith and nonprofit groups to include the voices and profiles of youth in as many ways as possible and to expose as many adults as possible to normal, unnewsworthy adolescents; make the point that they are the norm, not the exception. Invite youth in, and draw explicit attention to the fact that they are not the exception that the media would have us believe. As one focus group participant said, "Include teens. Not just in sports, but in civic activities."

The more direct contact adults have with youth who are not their own, the better. Previous focus groups (Bales, 1999) found the only venue for this kind of outreach to be adults' places of worship or community centers and clubs.

Take this report to religious leaders and invite them to help solve the problem of Americans' distorted image of today's youth by promoting more age-integrated activities—mentoring, group outings, volunteer days. Do the same with business, professional, and civic clubs; invite them into the solution and suggest ways to foster more understanding of today's youth on an ongoing basis.

Do not allow this activity to be portrayed as only involving "good" youth or the "cream of the crop," but rather about educating communities about the everyday lives of ordinary young people in their community. Avoid awards programs and other "exceptional" activities, and substitute the idea of a community assessment of how well we are doing to nurture youth and keep them on track for achievement.

9. Train youth advocates to talk about today's youth as good kids, on track for achievement, learning to be leaders, etc., and to create social accep-

tance for this observation. There are many programs in place that bring youth before adults—essay contests, awards programs, and the like. It is important that speech and debate coaches, teachers, and other mentors enlist young people in becoming advocates for others. They can do this by talking about the kids they know and the overall trends in their schools, and by deemphasizing their specialness. They can do this by talking about how they strived to succeed, how hard the competition was, and how many kids deserve credit for hard work. Media literacy programs that help young people understand how they are being portrayed in the media can raise their awareness and energize their activism.

For parents and other adults, it is important that we make it okay to talk about teens as good people. We need to inform our social networks that they should question the media stereotypes more and their own eyes less. We need to stand up for kids in conversations with other adults, to help them sanction their own positive impressions.

10. Challenge your local news media to do a better job of describing the world of adolescence today—including research from experts in adolescence, interviews with coaches, teachers, volunteer supervisors, employers, and older Americans who come in regular contact with kids, and interviews with normal kids. Aubrun and Grady suggest that we refer to the "silent majority of teens," who are doing their chores, doing well in school, and not doing drugs (April 2000, p. 10). The "news value" is in revealing the stereotype as just that, and this model invites the investigative reporter into the story.

Brainstorm a series of stories that begin to portray the normal lives of everyday kids—the kids "behind the headlines." If you have a local newspaper or station interested in civic journalism, meet with editors and publishers to discuss how local media can take on this problem of reframing youth for public support. Provide lists of local experts on youth, and train these experts in advance to talk about teens in ways that open up the conversation to programs and policies, not merely to parent involvement.

Teens are hot just now, with cover stories in *Newsweek* and *U.S. News & World Report.* The trick for advocates is to come up with ideas for series that get context into the news coverage—group stories, trend reports, examples of kids doing civic and teamwork.

Remember, as Richard Rodriguez has said, "The stories invent us." Make sure the story you are telling about youth today is one the public can hear, and one that promotes a discussion of how communities can help kids weather the transition from adolescence to adulthood.

REFERENCES

Amundson, Daniel R., Linda S. Lichter, and S. Robert Lichter
2000 "What's the Matter with Kids Today? Television Coverage of Adolescents in America." Washington, D.C.: FrameWorks Institute and the Center for Communications and Community.

Aubrun, Axel, and Joseph Grady
April 4, 2000 "Reframing Youth: Models, Metaphors, Messages," in S. Bales (ed.), *Reframing Youth Issues.* Washington, D.C.: Working Papers, FrameWorks Institute and Center for Communications and Community, UCLA.

Aubrun, Axel, and Joseph Grady
February 28, 2000 "How Americans Understand Teens: Findings from the Cognitive Interviews," in S Bales (ed.), *Reframing Youth Issues.* Washington, D.C.: Working Papers, FrameWorks Institute and Center for Communications and Community, UCLA.

Bales, S.N. (ed.)
1999 *Effective Language for Communicating Children's Issues.* Washington, D.C.: Coalition for America's Children with the Benton Foundation.

Bales, S. N.
1999 "Communicating Early Childhood Education: Using Strategic Frame Analysis to Shape the Dialogue." *Bulletin of Zero to Three,* 19, no. 6.

Ball-Rokeach, S., M. Rokeach, and J. Grube
1984 *The Great American Values Test: Influencing Behavior and Belief through Television.* New York: Free Press.

Berkeley Media Studies Group
1997 *Children's Health in the News.* Washington, D.C.: Benton Foundation.

Berkeley Media Studies Group
1995 *Media Advocacy Workshop Workbook.* Berkeley: Berkeley Media Studies Group.

Bostrom, Meg
May 2000 "Teenhood: Understanding Attitudes toward Those Transitioning from Childhood to Adulthood," in S. Bales (ed.), *Reframing Youth Issues.* Washington, D.C.: Working Papers, FrameWorks Institute and Center for Communications and Community, UCLA.

Bostrom, Meg
January 15, 2000 "The 21st Century Teen: Public Perception and Teen Reality," in S. Bales (ed.), *Reframing Youth Issues.* Washington, D.C.: Working Papers, FrameWorks Institute and Center for Communications and Community, UCLA.

Dorfman, L. (ed.)
2000 *Youth and Violence in California Newspapers.* Berkeley Media Studies Group, issue 9.

Dorfman, L., and K. Woodruff
1998 "The Roles of Speakers in Local Television News Stories on Youth and Violence." *Journal of Popular Film and Television,* 26(2): 80-85.

Dorfman, L., K. Woodruff, V. Chavez, and L. Wallack
1997 "Youth and Violence on Local California Television News." *American Journal of Public Health,* 87, 311-316.

Gilliam, F.D., Jr.
Forthcoming "The Welfare Queen Experiment." *Nieman Reports.*

Gilliam, F. D., Jr.
1998 "Race and Crime in California," in Michael B. Preston, Bruce A. Cain, and Sandra Bass (eds.), *Racial and Ethnic Politics in California.* Berkeley: Institute for Governmental Studies Press, University of California.

Gilliam, F.D., Jr., and S. Iyengar
1998 "The Superpredator Script." *Nieman Reports,* 45.

Gilliam, F.D., Jr., and S. Iyengar
1997 "Prime Suspects: The Effects of Local News on the Viewing Public." Paper presented at the annual meeting of the Western Political Science Association, Portland, Oregon.

Gilliam, F.D. Jr., S. Iyengar, A. Simon, and O. Wright
1996 "Crime in Black and White: The Violent, Scary World of Local News." *Harvard International Journal of Press/Politics,* 1: 6-23.

Heintz-Knowles, Katharine E.
April 9, 2000 "Images of Youth: A Content Analysis of Adolescents in Prime Time Entertainment Programming," in S. Bales (ed.), *Reframing Youth Issues.* Washington, D.C.: Working Papers, FrameWorks Institute and Center for Communications and Community, UCLA.

Iyengar, S.
1991 *Is Anyone Responsible? How Television Frames Political Issues.* Chicago: University of Chicago Press.

Kunkel, D.
1994 *The News Media's Picture of Children.* Oakland: Children Now.

Neuman, W., M. Just, and A. Crigler
1992 *Common Knowledge: News and the Construction of Political Meaning.* Chicago: University of Chicago Press.

Tannen, Deborah
1993 *Framing in Discourse.* Oxford and New York: Oxford University Press.

Woodruff, K.
1998. "Youth and Race on Local TV News." *Nieman Reports.*
Youniss, J., and A. Ruth
2000 *Interim Report: Positive Indicators of Youth Development.* Unpublished manuscript. Washington, D.C.: Catholic University of America.

3 THE POLICY CLIMATE FOR EARLY ADOLESCENT INITIATIVES

Gary Walker

While considering what I would write for this essay on the "policy climate" for improving the lives and prospects of young teens, I asked random contacts—cab drivers, people sitting next to me on trains and planes, bored conference colleagues, a woman on a particularly slow and long elevator ride—what struck them when they thought about young teens in today's world. Their responses without exception expressed worry and concern; so I asked what they thought should be done and who should do it.

Over six months I talked in some depth to 26 different people from all walks of life. An unscientific survey, I admit, but the conversations were always fascinating, always went on longer than I expected (elevator interview excepted), and were remarkably consistent on five themes.

First, once they had gotten past some early griping and statements of "not understanding them," it was not hard for most to sympathize with the dilemmas of being a young teen. No matter their age, they could remember their own lives during those years as full of confusion and uncertainty. Some shook their heads in disbelief and appreciation that they had made it through adolescence at all.

Second, most thought that today's youth had it harder than they had. *None wanted to be young now.* They cited the availability of weapons and drugs, the media's demoralizing impact, the need for more education to "make it," the fast pace of change in today's world and how difficult that made it to maintain "traditional values" (no matter the age, race, ethnicity, apparent income or social class, they all felt the erosion of values). One woman cab driver said it succinctly: "Oh, we were poorer, but these are the days of *mental* hardship for kids."

Third, they mostly blamed parents, the public schools and the media for those teens who could not meet current challenges. No matter how difficult the challenge, they felt these basic institutions had the responsibility to support and guide youth.

Fourth, they had few specific positive ideas on what to do. They were stumped by how to make parents do better; mostly stumped by how to improve the schools (with a few saying the schools needed more competition); and mostly stumped by how to control the media (with a few advocating strong censorship).

But, when pressed, they usually turned back to parents—and beyond that, to fatalism. As one said, "You're talking about teens. This is the period they make the right choices or don't, and there's no way to guarantee they'll make the right ones." A few said maybe more Boys & Girls Clubs would help. Several thought churches should get more involved.

Fifth, they had very little to no confidence that public policy had any solutions. Most just shook their heads and said they could not imagine what the public sector might do, except improve the schools—and their confidence in that was not high. A few said the law needed to be clearer about the consequences of wrong decisions.

You might think that this uncertainty over what to do arises because the people I talked to do not specialize in the issue of what to do; they are not "youth experts." And, no doubt, most issues benefit from reflection and evidence. On the other hand, this is not an arcane problem. Most of these people are parents; all had been youth. Many had lived through, or had close acquaintance with, difficult young teen lives.

The lengthy discussions I had with several people in my random sample led me to conclude that the reason for the confusion is deeper and more diverse than a lack of specialization. It has to do, I think, with the complex, transitional, and inconclusive nature of the early teen years themselves; with a conviction that the basic institutions that are responsible for or influence youth are failing; with a belief that there are no good alternatives; and with an American political and social culture that is instinctively distrustful of public solutions to problems of individual and family behavior.

In short, the underlying reasons for the lack of solutions are grounded in some hard realities that even the most specialized knowledge does not resolve and at best can only confront.

Since the "policy climate" for an issue as fundamental as improving the lives and prospects of young teens is, in a democracy, rooted largely in the opinions and common sense of ordinary citizens, I take the concerns and opinions expressed by this random group of strangers seriously. They were without exception a thoughtful group of people, none of whom expressed hostility to or seemed uncaring about teens. If this sample was skewed, it was toward tolerance to young teens. But other than that, they left an impression similar to the one I get when looking at polls and newspaper articles: concerned and baffled about what to do.

This essay examines and builds on the gleanings from my informal survey and tries to sketch out the opportunities and limits—the "policy climate"—that seem to characterize America in the late 1990s. Although the common concern of citizens for young teens can be seen as suggesting a receptive climate for improved policies, their sense of frustration at the performance of such basic institutions as families and schools, their frustration at not being able to intuit or articulate what might be done to counter that frustration, and their lack of confidence in public policy as being capable of finding solutions do not make for a truly receptive climate. And even the most perfect solution, if there were such a creature, needs to be recognized and believed in, in order to be adopted as durable policy.

AMERICA'S VIEW OF PUBLIC SOCIAL POLICY

No one would claim that American political culture embraces public social policy as a tool of first resort for improving social conditions or solving social problems. Quite the contrary: we generally view it as a tool of last resort, when private solutions clearly do not work and when the condition or problem is serious and highly visible. The major public social policy initiatives of the 1930s required a national depression to gain support; those of the 1960s and 1970s required riots.

This reluctance to use social policy is our historical political culture, and rarely has it been more evident than in the 1990s. In that broad sense, it is incontrovertible that the "policy climate" is not favorable to wide-scale public efforts to improve the lives and conditions of adolescents.

Further, even when we do resort to public social policy, we are not patient with it: we want to see progress; we want to see problems solved quickly. If we suspect social policy is not solving problems—or is perhaps creating other problems—we ultimately abandon our public initiatives. The major initiatives of the War on Poverty, and the Aid to Families with Dependent Children (AFDC) welfare entitlement, are recent examples.

The general reluctance to use public policy to confront social concerns has hardened over the past 20 years. The most vocal advocates for public social policy claim this abandonment is a national moral failure, rooted in our country's extreme individualism and social Darwinism. There is an undeniable but only partial truth to that claim. For many people, including most of those I spoke with, the bigger and more practical reason for this hardening is the perception that social policies are ineffective—that they fail. This perception is not confined to one party or political stripe. An enthusiastic supporter of public social policy, Democrat and former secretary of labor Robert Reich did not advocate for continuation of the relatively large several billion dollars youth title of the Job Training Partnership Act because, he said, the evidence was clear: employment training programs for youth do not work.

Secretary Reich's view is perfectly reflected in an "ordinary citizen's" letter to the editor in the Sunday *Philadelphia Inquirer* of May 3, 1999:

> Personally I don't think that the average taxpaying, law-abiding citizen is numbed to the atrocities that occur daily. I just think we don't know what to do about them. What's the answer? I have no idea.

Changing that perception is not solely a matter of improved communication and more ethical politics, difficult as those are to achieve. A substantial body of evidence supports that discouraging conclusion. It is not entirely the work of morality and communication that two major social programs with strong survival records—Head Start and the Job Corps—both have evidence that they work and a positive image among political leaders and the public alike.

Critics maintain that the evidence is selective because better programs were not evaluated; the evaluation methods were too rigid; the implementation periods were not long enough; and there are more promising approaches to try. I think each of those arguments has merit, but they are too fine-tuned to overcome the widespread perception that is now in place. It will take counterevidence, and a significant body of it, to dent the evidentiary crust that has formed over our country's general reluctance to use public social policy in matters of social behavior.

The "outcomes movement" that has developed among many policy-influential individuals and institutions is a major effort to confront the perception of failure. Most public social legislation now requires strong evaluation components; many philanthropic initiatives do as well. This is, of course, an opportunity to create counterevidence, but it is also a risk: unless these new initiatives are a substantive improvement over those previously evaluated, these future evaluations are likely to produce more skepticism (Walker and Grossman, 1999).

The strong performance of the American economy these past nine years, the relative decline of the Pacific Rim economies, and the collapse of Soviet communism all strengthen the notion that the public sector is not the way to solve problems: let the private sector do it. The privatization of many social functions and the heightened emphasis on "civil society" to address critical issues à la 1997's President's Summit on youth issues are the outgrowths of all these converging forces. They simply reflect the public's low opinion, shown in poll after poll, of the public sector as a solution to problems of social behavior.

I have painted a negative picture of the overall view of public social policy, historically and currently, not because I think it is always fair or always works out well, but because it just *is*—a deep current in American life, part of its character, with strengths and weaknesses, not necessarily or always mean-spirited and, more important, not simply a short-term trend. It is an independent force to be reckoned with as we consider the prospects for improved public social policy with regard to early adolescents, one deeply intertwined with America's great successes as well as its shortcomings.

THE NATURE OF THE ISSUE

The *general* social policy climate in the United States is, thus, difficult and resistant. But the climate for a *particular* social policy initiative can be less resistant depending on a number of factors.

My reading of the past 30 years is that three factors are especially important:

- The immediate moral power of the issue, that is, its capacity to push the "fairness" button in American leaders and the broader electorate, based on recent events;
- The resolve, resources, and political-communications strategies of its key advocates; and
- The clarity and urgency of the solution.

I do not mean by this to reduce American politics to a rational and predictable framework of rules and conditions; that would ignore both the ambiguities and downright contradictions inherent in any complex array of human relationships and behavior and would underrate what a powerful individual on a mission can accomplish. Nonetheless, our political behavior does have its general characteristics and patterns—a framework you can most often count on to hold. I think the above three factors are generally useful and reliable components of a strategy to put a major piece of social policy in place.

The first two factors have to do with getting an audience for the issue, to have it considered as an exception to the country's general resistance to social policy. The various civil rights campaigns of the 1950s and 1960s are the most obvious examples.

The third factor has to do with the formulation and implementation of the solution: is it comprehensible, compelling, and intuitively doable? It is difficult to get sustained and widespread support for a policy initiative that does not have those features. The solution does not have to be *easy* to do—desegregating the schools and enforcing fairness in public accommodations and in employment have been anything but easy. It just needs to be understandable.

The group of people I talked with are all concerned about young teens—they all had sympathy for the challenges teens face in growing up. Compared with the respondents to surveys like that done in 1997 by Public Agenda, my interviewees are more sympathetic to teens than is the voting public at large. But along with their sympathy, I did not sense either moral outrage or the sense that the public at large *has* to do something. Nor did they convey much sense that unfairness is at the root of the problem. Rather they see the problems of young teens as being in part intrinsic to being a young teen and in part caused by social forces well beyond the reach of social policies and programs. They are sorry that the world has become so challenging and sorry that early adolescence is such a difficult time in human life. They do not see a way to change either.

Part of the reason for their attitude has to do with the fact that there is no long-standing, sustained, and powerful national advocacy movement for young teens; the voters are not roused, but rather sorry and puzzled. And certainly there have been, over the past few years, an increasing number of articles and editorials saying that Americans have lost their capacity to be morally outraged. To whatever degree that is true, it would combine with the lack of a powerful advocacy movement to produce a potent lassitude.

But part of the reason that there is no powerful and sustained advocacy movement is the very nature of the early teen years as perceived by most adults and as reflected in my interviews. Adults see adolescence as a confusing and trying time, full of new thinking, experimentation and hormonal change, ups and downs in mood—hard to characterize easily, hard to predict, hard to explain in terms of cause and effect. The people I talked to were not hostile to the state of adolescence; they just did not think that much could be done about it, unless it is by parents or schools. In the end, to them, adolescence is something to "get through"—so internally driven as to be impervious to outside influence.

Another reason it is difficult to mount and sustain a campaign for adolescents is that the information available about early teens supports divergent views. On the one hand, we hear that young teens are very dangerous to themselves and others, are having babies irresponsibly, are using drugs, and are performing poorly in school—are, in short, a disaster. The media coverage of births at proms and the recent string of school shootings by so-called ordinary kids adds to the impression that all teens are at risk of such behavior. And, indeed, some very respected youth advocates and experts say precisely that: that all youth are at risk. This would seem to be the basis for a movement to increase the public's receptiveness to policy aimed at adolescents (though what its content would be is a separate issue).

But there is an opposing point of view, which stresses that in fact most teens are not so different now than they were decades ago and that things are better in some respects. The *New York Times* recently carried two major stories in a three-day period about teenagers, one headlined "Birth Rates for Teenagers Declined Sharply in the 90s," which reported that from 1991 to 1996, for the first time "in decades and decades," birth rates dropped, as did sexual activity, while use of contraceptives increased. Both liberals and conservatives took credit.

The other story outlined a number of adult myths about teenagers:

- **Myth No. 1: Youth are becoming more violent and criminally dangerous.** "Wrong," says the article, and presents compelling evidence that adults are the real threat and that youth violence is neither on the rise nor happens very often.
- **Myth No. 4: Drugs remain a threat to young people.** "Wrong," says the article . . . the evidence is that adults are the problem. Youth drug use dropped in the 1970s and has remained low ever since.
- **Myth No. 5: Teenagers are naturally rebellious and impulsive risk-takers.** Wrong again. The article says they largely reflect their parents.

These differing views do not coalesce into a powerful image on which to build public policy. You can take a middle course and say that we should not be reassured by recently encouraging trends, that the early teens are fragile years, that these are indeed times of "mental hardship" for teenagers, and demand a public response. But that brings us to the third factor: clarity of solution. What is it we are proposing to do and to what end? And that is hard to say without some rough consensus on what the problem is.

The more problem oriented the goal is, the easier it is to be clear about what to do. And that is in fact what we have been doing for the past 25 years: defining a problem (teen pregnancy, drug abuse, poor school performance) and then proposing a concrete program to solve it. This approach can meet the three conditions laid out above and often has.

But it is precisely this approach that continues to produce such weak results. Evaluation after evaluation has concluded that the program it examined did not have much enduring effect on teens' lives. In the summer of 1997, a conference was held in Chicago solely to discuss three recent evaluations of major public programs designed to address one or more of the above-mentioned adolescent problems—and the fact that none showed any significant effectiveness.

This has led to the widely held view among youth professionals and experts that deficiency-oriented programming is the culprit and that a more positive, youth development approach must be devised. This approach promotes a broader view of youth than the problem-oriented approach might imply and focuses on youth's assets and potentials. It is about successful development as opposed to problem solution.

The difficulty with youth development vis-à-vis the three conditions laid out above is that it is not clear what it means in policy or in operation—it is hard to visualize—and is thus hard to rally around. It also does not strike a "fairness" chord, especially when it is accompanied by the claim (as it often is) that *all* youth are at risk. That claim strikes many people, and influential ones at that (remember the *New York Times* articles above), as excessive. It also brings disagreement: large numbers of people think youth need more and firmer discipline, which is not what the phrase "positive youth development" brings to mind.

However, there is some evidence that recognizable pieces of the youth development approach work. For example, everyone would agree that a caring adult is a critical element of youth development, and Public/Private Ventures' 1995 impact evaluation of Big Brothers Big Sisters offers clear evidence that a caring adult can be provided in a social intervention and can have substantial impacts on first drug use and school performance and behavior—not by focusing on problems, but by promoting friendship and trust between an adult and youth who were previously strangers.

Evaluations of Boys & Girls Clubs have also produced compelling evidence about their effects on negative behaviors, and Girls Incorporated and YMCAs have generated operational evidence about their usefulness to youth development. This evidence has been fairly widely disseminated and has helped sustain interest in two particular aspects of youth development that have been the focus of strong national advocacy and media attention: mentoring and after-school programming.

Mentoring has in fact been a subject of favorable attention for almost a decade now. The 1997 President's Summit made it the first of its five-part agenda and is being promoted by retired general Colin Powell and his America's Promise organization. It has the support of a number of foundations; of the brand-name Big Brothers Big Sisters; and of an increasing number of influential leaders in politics, business, and public agencies.

The after-school issue (what do children do with that time?) has begun to receive more and more attention. It is also one of Powell's agenda items and has been well promoted as a social policy topic by both the Carnegie Corporation and the strong advocacy of Hugh Price, president of the National Urban League. In mid-April of 1998, *Newsweek* carried the issue on its cover and detailed it in a strong article.

So there are two specific initiatives for younger teens that are alive and well in the policy world. They both have the potential to meet all three of the conditions for policy advance that I noted above. The Clinton administration has already set out a proposal for a major after-school initiative in which the Mott Foundation is participating. Two other influential foundations—the DeWitt Wallace-Reader's Digest Fund and George Soros's Open Society Institute—are investing millions in after-school programming. Congress just gave $20 million to Boys & Girls Clubs of America. The Department of Justice has a multimillion dollar mentoring initiative. A number of cities and a number of philanthropies are mounting large initiatives to provide these and other supports and opportunities for young teens.

This is good news for policy advocates for adolescents, particularly those who espouse a youth development approach. It means that in spite of the generally cautious climate for social policy in America, and in spite of the ambiguous nature of adolescence and the evidence about its current condition, there are some policy actions with enough clarity and urgency to have made it to the arena of real policy discussion. So there is a receptive climate—but how receptive? Our judgment on that is important, for it will shape our future actions and strategies.

OPPORTUNITIES AND LIMITS

To better understand the specific opportunities and limits likely to make up the social policy climate for early adolescent initiatives, it is helpful to examine mentoring and after-school programming in more depth. Besides meeting the three conditions laid out earlier, they have several other instructive commonalities.

The Commonalities of Mentoring and After-School Programming

First, the two concepts are very basic. There is nothing more basic than a young person's need for a caring adult, and that, I think, is the most powerful reason for mentoring's continued popularity. After-school activities are also basic; like mentoring, they are easy to visualize and are doable. Most adults remember doing them in their youth—much as they remember having caring adults—and it does strike their sense of fairness that today's youth do not have these basic supports.

Second, they are identified with "brand names" in which people have confidence: Big Brothers Big Sisters *is* mentoring in the public's eye, and Boys & Girls Clubs and Little Leagues are well known and highly regarded for their after-school activities.

Does this mean that brand names are the only way social policy can accomplish mentoring and after-school activities? Not necessarily. The brand name simply casts a favorable light on the effectiveness of a generic activity. But it does seem obvious that the closer the identification the proposed policies have with these brand names, the stronger their chances of being adopted. The problem with the claim "we know what to do for youth, it's only lack of political will that prevents us from doing it" is that clearly we too often do not know *how* to do it. It is one thing to say that it is obvious youth need caring adults; it is quite another to say we know how to create deliberately through policy those caring adults. Brand names are the "Good Housekeeping Seal of Doability."

Third, neither model is primarily or dominantly associated with national public policy or with public institutions. Mentoring has almost no association with public policy, and though many after-school activities are indeed school-operated, many are not. The very words "after school" free the phrase from institutional capture; most of us think as much of volunteer adults coaching athletic leagues, or of Boys and Girls Clubs, YMCAs, or 4-H. In an age of particularly low confidence in public policy, this private association is particularly useful.

Fourth, the strength of mentoring and after-school programming is associated to a considerable degree with their capacity to reduce negative behavior. That is, as much as mentoring and positive after-school activities are seen as elementary and basic to growing up, their power to shape public policy is still tied not to their potential for *promoting* positive youth development but to their potential for *reducing* negative behavior. The largest amounts of public funds at the federal level going specifically to mentoring are located in the Department of Justice's Office of Juvenile Justice Delinquency Prevention. The interest in after-school programming for early adolescents as a public policy initiative is firmly tied to the widespread perception, based on strong advocacy and communication efforts, that those are the hours when a high proportion of teenage sex and crime occurs.

The Implications for Policy

So what do these four commonalities mean for the policy climate when added to the three conditions noted earlier (fairness button, strong advocacy, and clear solution)? The most obvious overall implication is one of tight limits. Barring the sort of unusual occurrence and extraordinary leadership that can upset all ordinary rules, I think that the opportunities in the foreseeable future for new and major public policy initiatives aimed at early adolescents are very limited, especially at the national level.

I also suspect that at the national level such unusual occurrences as the string of shootings in early 1998 and 1999 are less likely to lead to major "developmental" initiatives than to a mix of measures that are mostly punitive (harsher sentences, treatment as adults) and restrictive (restricted access to guns, driving licenses and adult media). The latter will be harder to implement, since adult financial interests are involved.

Tight as the restrictions are, they do not deny any opportunity for action at the national level; they simply define a narrow avenue for successful strategy. That avenue requires that we view public interest in activities like mentoring and after-school programming not as narrow, modest items that are too limited and oriented to negative behavior to warrant an all-out effort, but as good-as-they-come opportunities to gain public support for the very basic developmental supports that all youth need. The nonprofit and philanthropic organizations that believe American society is shortchanging its youth could have great impact if they organized around these opportunities to ensure that they develop roots in policy and implementation, and that they in fact, backed by credible evidence, reduce the negative behaviors Americans want their social policy to affect.

There are alternatives to getting behind these modest and narrow opportunities and pushing them. One is to put efforts and resources behind leaders and strategies aimed at changing our country's attitudes toward adolescents *and* toward the use of public policy.

My read, much as I dislike it, is that either one of those changes is a long shot, and both together come close to impossibility. There may be small victories in both regards accomplished by exceptional individuals, but I do not believe they will form the basis for large-scale changes in attitudes toward teens and public policy, mostly because American attitudes toward those two topics have as much truth and merit as they do misperception and dysfunction. They are neither mostly wrong nor mostly immoral.

Another alternative is to forget national policy and concentrate on states, localities, and the private sector. This is the age of devolution—exploit it. This alternative is persuasive not only because of devolution but because the local level is where many of the adults, resources, and decisions that influence youth are located—and where all these influences manifest themselves concretely. In addition, given the previous difficulty in convincing the public that social interventions for early adolescents are effective, issues of local design, implementation, and evaluation require increased attention. The voting public will most likely need some form of concrete proof that an approach works before it will even consider it nationally.

The local-state option has so much merit that its greatest downside is that it will win too much of the available energy and resources. Pride in idiosyncrasy, accompanied by the fact-insensitive local boosterism that so marks American history, might make for bursts of local activity and communication, some of which might be very successful. But if they do not satisfy the three conditions noted earlier, they are probably not good candidates for national policy embrace.

"So what?" you might ask. Let us focus on spreading things that work through state and local channels, avoiding the national level to the maximum extent possible. This strategy is appealing in two ways: first, there is a substantive need for greater work in the area of local-to-local and state-to-state policy communication and adaptation; and second, it is a wonderfully resourceful reaction to constrictive national opportunities.

However, we would be shortsighted to ignore the national level. That level is, in the end, where significant and equity-producing resources reside. It is important to remember that devolution itself requires the distribution of federal resources and that their continued distribution as well as their growth will ultimately depend on a national sense that these resources are used effectively. The history of devolution funding over the past three decades does not offer any confidence that such funding will persist solely on the grounds of its philosophy; it will be examined, and if found lacking, it will be reduced or discontinued. It may not be replaced by a significant national initiative without convincing evidence that some local initiatives are effective.

The federal government is also the only possible guarantor of any real equity in the application of effective policies. A solely local-state strategy, no matter how successful, will finally meet the wall of unequal resource capacity.

So what does all this amount to? Is there any optimal strategy that would be most likely to take advantage of the "policy climate" I have described—a climate that is narrow at the national level, more wide open at the state and local levels, and yet connected by the need for federal resources?

The Elements of a Strategy

It would be foolhardy to assert any one optimal strategy that can promise the greatest policy benefit to young adolescents. But as I think back on the people I interviewed, the outlines of a broad strategy do emerge. It contains five basic elements.

1. Ensure that new local and state initiatives promote national opportunities. At first blush, this might sound unnecessarily limiting; what is the point of local experimentation if it must conform to national constraints? The point here is that local experimentation should aggressively tie itself to national opportunities—for it is the perceived success or failure of those opportunities that will have a great deal to do with national attitudes about the usefulness of public social policy. It will do little good over the long run to act as if the public will is a blank slate that can be created anew "when the time is right."

In fact, the public will is constantly being created; the time is always now. The current openness to mentoring and after-school programming may be limited opportunities, but they are opportunities nonetheless. Their success or failure in the new round of state and local initiatives will play a significant role in our country's willingness to consider other policies that may be useful to early adolescents.

This is easier said than done. The desire for innovation in local and state government, and in the world of philanthropy, almost amounts to a cult. That desire, combined with the call by many youth advocates for policies that are more "comprehensive, integrated, holistic, and sequential," conspires to discount or ignore these apparently limited opportunities.

I think this is a serious mistake. These opportunities are not only politically important; they are substantively capable of creative adaptation to more complex ideas. They are the building blocks for improved policies, and an improved policy climate.

2. Use simple and clear language to explain initiatives. This seems obvious as a matter of all communication, and especially so in a policy climate that is narrow and distrustful. I think of the letter to the editor quoted earlier, in which the writer said she did not believe most people were numb to the problems of the world—they just did not know what to do about them. She will need to be convinced that there are things that can be done, in language she can understand.

The youth field has on the whole taken a different tack. It emphasizes the complexity of the problems youth face and how correspondingly complex the solutions must be. The language of "comprehensive, integrated, holistic, and sequential" may serve as broad guideposts for those designing initiatives, but it will never serve to improve the policy climate. Unlike science and medicine, youth policy is not an area of human activity where jargon creates respect and trust. The jargon barrier only creates distance from the possibility of durable policy and substantial resources.

We have to be able to say in ordinary language what it is we are proposing to do. This will conflict with the youth field's desire for professionalism, but clarity must take precedence over that desire if the goal is an improved policy climate.

I think it will also improve local implementation, which bears on the next point.

3. Produce evidence that initiatives make a difference in relation to priority issues. The distinctions between *preventive* and *reclamation,* between *deficiency* and *developmental,* are not without meaning, but they are mostly debates internal to the small world of aficionados who spend their lives thinking about youth policy and programs. They are largely irrelevant to the forces and considerations that make up the public policy climate, which are primarily concerned with the solutions to priority issues.

Those priority issues are not hard to name; they have to do with adolescent crime, drugs, pregnancy, school performance, and preparation for employment. I think it is very unlikely that we can create a durable and improved policy climate for early adolescent initiatives unless we can show that our initiatives effectively address those issues.

From that perspective, the debates noted above are in a sense diverting us from larger truths: we need more and improved preventive policies *and* reclamation policies, for there will always be youth who need each. And we need to address deficiencies in ways that are effective—that are developmentally appropriate and yet sensitive to considerations of community safety and order—which means that punishment and discipline, as well as supports and opportunities, must be possible in our policy initiatives. All these options are necessary for a policy climate that is responsive to the variety of actual human needs; each one must have evidence that it makes a difference relative to these priority issues if it is to generate and maintain significant public support.

That evidence does not, especially for younger adolescents, need to show that the issue is totally resolved. Our social quest is for resolution; our immediate policy climate quest is for progress. Thus, Public/Private Ventures' impact evaluation of Big Brothers Big Sisters does not show that a mentor in the early adolescent years forecloses future problems in the youth's life. It does show that it, at a minimum, forestalls them for 18 months. This sort of "forestalling evidence" is not only important for policy purposes, it will also assist us in our implementation of "comprehensive, holistic, integrated, and sequential" programming. The latter, of course, will still be composed of discontinuous and discrete parts. That is the nature of external interventions in any human life. Credible knowledge of their distinct contribution to achieving progress on the priority issues is critical to policy and practice.

4. Use and develop brand-name institutions. The marketability of policies and ideas is greatly enhanced if known and respected organizations are living examples of those policies and ideas. There are a number of such institutions in the early adolescent area: Boys & Girls Clubs and Big Brothers Big Sisters are obvious examples. We should ensure their soundness, their spread in fact and in influence, and their use as standards for all like activities.

This is a hard message to disseminate in a social policy world with a general culture of innovation, funding sources that pursue innovation separately, the natural forces of local idiosyncrasy and a historical moment that rhetorically favors the particular over the national. Nonetheless, I think its value to creating a more open social policy climate is critical: they are the only trusted brand names we have to work with. They need not be the owners of all policy initiatives or their operation; they should be involved, used, and strengthened to the maximum extent possible.

5. Articulate roles for each sector (public, private, and nonprofit) and for each primary institution that most people judge should be responsible for a youth's development (family, school, and church). Collaboration is a popular word, and thus the involvement of multiple sectors would appear to need little emphasis. So I will not repeat the substantive arguments that support it. But there are several aspects to the word *collaboration;* in my judgment the one that is most talked about is overemphasized, while the most critical aspects receive much less attention than they deserve.

The aspect that receives the most attention is the process and goal of working together. That aspect of collaboration sounds (and is) both high-minded and difficult. It implies ongoing process and consensus. Issues of class, belief, culture, negotiating, style, and so on, are all important.

To focus on the "working together" aspect of collaboration, however, overemphasizes its most difficult aspect, and sometimes exacerbates it. As a rallying cry, it is substantively empty, and it tends to draw skepticism from those with practical operational experience in any sector.

The aspect of collaboration that counters "working together's" orientation toward complexity and process is "role definition." The concreteness of defining sectoral roles and responsibilities not only helps ensure that the initiative has beef, it also helps ensure that the comparative advantages of each sector are used and not ignored or blurred by the goal or process of working together. Working collaboratively can thus mean mostly working apart, each sector doing what it does best. That is generally the best way for people from different sectors to accomplish common goals.

The second aspect of collaboration that deserves more attention is political—the sense most people have (including my interviewees) that family, school, and religion are primarily responsible for the behavior of youth. Other forces *influence* youth, but those three institutions are *responsible.*

The accuracy of this judgment can be debated endlessly. The important point is that to develop policy initiatives without addressing the role of those primary institutions is to invite criticism from any number of seemingly incompatible political forces. It is also to ignore what are in fact elements critical to substantive effectiveness.

Addressing the role of these primary institutions does not always mean defining a role; sometimes an actual role for each primary institution will just not be viable or sensible. But it is important to communicate that their importance has been acknowledged and considered, and if no role is envisioned, the reasoning behind that decision. This will not satisfy all critics, but it will convince some who otherwise would have a knee-jerk reaction to any less-than-dominant role for primary institutions.

CLOSING THOUGHTS

There is no question that our political culture does not tend toward excess when it comes to devising social policies and spending taxpayer money on adolescents—especially on adolescents in poor communities. A more generous attitude, one that tolerates the errors of excess, would no doubt provide stability, direction, and opportunity to many more young people than currently have them.

Some will argue that changing that political culture is the first order of business and that it must be done directly, through advocacy and communication. I too believe that advocacy and communication are vital, but I am skeptical that moral argument alone will change our culture. The lack of confidence in public social policy as an effective means to solve critical issues is too powerful for moral arguments to overcome, except for occasional small victories. Guilt over inaction is significantly blunted by a reasonable disbelief in the effectiveness of action.

The critical complements to advocacy and communication are seizing the modest and concrete opportunities that do exist at the national level and building on them at all levels. To do so requires an understanding and acceptance of limits on the social policy climate that are not always uplifting but that do form the pathway to building a more positive social policy climate. Clarity, evidence, brand names, sectoral roles, primary institutions—using these factors to exploit national opportunities is in my judgment the most effective way to transcend the rather chilly climate that exists for early adolescent initiatives.

REFERENCES

Males, M.
1998 "Five Myths, and Why Adults Believe They are True." *New York Times,* April 29, p. D9.
Males, M.
1998 "The Children of the Glum." *New York Times,* May 2, p. A22.
Walker, Gary, and Jean Grossman
1999 *Philanthropy and Outcomes: Dilemmas in the Quest for Accountability.* Philadelphia: Public/Private Ventures.

4 A MATTER OF MONEY: THE COST AND FINANCING OF YOUTH DEVELOPMENT

Robert P. Newman, Stephanie M. Smith, and Richard Murphy

> Slowly, (General Colin) Powell is coming around to the view that government, too, must do more, not in—God forbid—running programs but in helping to fund the nonprofits we already know work. While avoiding the usual Washington scramble for money, he admits that the pending $200 billion-plus transportation bill got him thinking. Youth development programs are "as good a place to invest as highways in Kansas," he says. So why not more public investment?[1] ("Long after the Trumpets," *Newsweek,* May 11, 1998)

During the final days of putting together this chapter, two images kept running through our minds at the Center for Youth Development and Policy Research (the Center). The first was of a meeting two years ago with a group of foundations in one city interested in after-school programming and, in particular, the Center staff's role in the development of Beacon Schools. As the meeting progressed, it became clear that these funders were primarily interested in expanding funding support to after-school programs. They were very interested in tying their additional funding support to demonstrable youth and program outcomes. This discussion was positive and productive until the funders announced the amount of money they envisioned granting to each program . . . $25,000—$25,000 to expand the number of young people served by each program, to expand program hours to all current and newly enrolled youth, and to show such outcomes as improved school attendance and reading scores. That meeting was the first time the Center used the following three questions to add a dose of reality to situations in which serious groups of people state their interest in doing "something" for children and youth after school:

1. At what age would you leave a young person home alone after school from 3 P.M. to 7 P.M.?
2. How much would you spend to take care of one young person for one day for four hours from 3 P.M. to 7 P.M.?
3. How many hours of structured activities would you want for a young person for one week during the school year (not counting time in school)?

People inevitably ask a follow-up question when they hear question 2: "Do you mean what I'd spend for my kid or . . . ?" Their voice trails off, realizing that they have already developed their own personal cost system and standard level. For example, the group of funders described above eventually realized that their $25,000 add-on grants would barely pay for a dozen youth to participate in year-round, quality programs. It would also be next to impossible to prove that (per youth, per program, per activity) their dollars had an appreciable impact on the outcomes they wanted to measure.

The second image is a more haunting one; it was on the front page of the *New York Times* on October 14, 1998. In the picture, Wendy Williams, age 13, leans against a tree in front of her trailer park home in Dixon, Illinois. The reporter describes what it means to be Wendy among the working poor in a time of raging prosperity, receiving taunts about her clothes, her living space, and even what lunch she brings to school. The article goes on to say:

> Unlike young people a generation ago, those today must typically pay fees to play for the school sports teams or band. It costs $45 to play in the youth summer soccer league. It takes money to go skating on weekends at the White Pines roller rink, to play laser tag or rock-climb at the Plum Hollow Recreation Center, to mount a steed at the Horseback Riding Club, to gaze at Leonardo DiCaprio and Kate Winslet at the Plaza Cinemas, to go shopping for clothes at Cherryvale Mall. To be without money, in so many ways is to be left out. (Johnson, 1998, p. 1)

In many discussions on youth development, the need for infrastructure and outcomes is discussed at length, but we do not spend equal time on the dollars needed to help achieve the desired outcomes. The Center hopes "A Matter of Money" will advance the dialogue concerning the real dollars required to get the desired outcomes for all of America's youth.

INTRODUCTION

The accelerated trend over the past decade toward empowering our nation's young people to succeed has fostered a new awareness and commitment to this most valuable resource. Unfortunately, the money required to support this commitment and realize change has not kept up the pace. Our youth cannot truly be a priority until we back up our good intentions with the funding needed to demonstrate this priority.

Securing the financial resources necessary to provide the supports and opportunities our youth need to become healthy, productive members of society requires answers to some fundamental questions:

- How much do we currently spend?
- How much should we spend?
- What are the best mechanisms to harness and equitably distribute the necessary funds?

The Center is by no means the first to venture these questions. In preparing its 1992 landmark youth development document, *A Matter of Time: Risk and Opportunity in the Nonschool Hours,* the Carnegie Council on Adolescent Development undertook an exploratory study into the funding patterns of nonprofit organizations that provide youth development services. The Council examined the finances of several national youth-serving organizations and looked at both foundation and government spending on youth development programs. Since 1994, the Finance Project has produced a large number of studies examining issues and methods central to improving "the effectiveness, efficiency, and equity of public financing for education and other children's services." In her 1998 *Safe Passage: Making It through Adolescence in a Risky Society,* Joy Dryfoos, an independent researcher, provided an overview of existing government financial commitment to youth development.

Some progress has been made through new initiatives in education finance reform and services integration, providing more effective delivery of social, health, and education services for children and youth from the school up to the government level. However, the issue of increasing financial commitment to youth development continues to be addressed in targeted and fragmented ways. Many would contend that this is the "nature of the beast" and that the meager available resources should support the development of those youth in most desperate and immediate need. This being understandable in light of current limited funds, we must not lose sight of the ideal:

Adequate and secure funding for the developmental supports and opportunities that *all* youth need on the road to a productive, healthy, and economically viable adulthood.

This chapter is an initial attempt to establish a framework and formula for assessing the financial resources and mechanisms necessary to move American society closer to this ideal. The Center, like all of the others who have investigated issues around these questions, has come to understand just how daunting a task it is. We do not pretend to have all of the answers. Rather, we hope the information and ideas presented here will lead to increased efforts at all levels to determine the resources we must be prepared to invest in our youth.

WHAT IS YOUTH DEVELOPMENT?

> One can define *youth development* as the ongoing growth process in which all youth are engaged in attempting to (1) meet their basic personal and social needs to be safe, feel cared for, be valued, be useful, and be spiritually grounded, and (2) to build skills and competencies that allow them to function and contribute in their daily lives. (Pittman, O'Brien, and Kimball 1993, p. 8)

This definition accurately describes youth development as a process that all young people go through on the way to adulthood. As the definition implies, it is a process or journey that automatically involves all of the people around a youth—family and community. Young people will not be able to build essential skills and competencies and feel safe, cared for, valued, useful, and spiritually grounded unless their families and communities provide them with the supports and opportunities they need along the way. Thus, youth development is also a process in which family and community must actively participate. As Hugh Price, president of the National Urban League, put it so succinctly in 1998, youth development is "what parents do for their children . . . on a good day."

Youth development then is a combination of all of the people, places, supports, opportunities, and services that most of us inherently understand that young people need to be happy, healthy, and successful. Youth development currently exists in a variety of different places and forms, and under all sorts of different names.

People, programs, and institutions involved in youth development are working toward positive results in the lives of youth. Some have clearly defined these desired positive results—or outcomes—in an attempt to more effectively work toward them. There are many efforts to define the outcomes of youth development, and while language may differ from place to place, most express the results that most people want for their own children. These outcomes include but move above and beyond the academic skills and competencies that are the focus of most schools. The Center has identified these outcomes as the following:

Aspects of Identity
- A sense of safety and structure
- High self-worth and self-esteem
- Feeling of mastery and future
- Belonging and membership
- Perception of responsibility and autonomy
- A sense of self-awareness and spirituality

Areas of Ability
- Physical health
- Mental health
- Intellectual health
- Employability
- Civic and social involvement

There are a number of well-known factors in youth's lives that contribute to reaching these positive developmental outcomes. Search Institute has identified 40 assets, internal and external, that form a foundation for healthy development of young people. The 40-asset framework covers eight categories (support, empowerment, boundaries and expectations, constructive use of time, commitment to learning, positive values, social competencies, and positive identity) and provides communities a tool with which to measure these assets in their youth's lives.

People, programs, and institutions that work with youth are engaged in youth development if there is strong evidence of the following practices:

Supports: motivational, emotional, and strategic supports to succeed in life. The supports can take many different forms, but they must be affirming, respectful, and ongoing. The supports are most powerful when they are offered by a variety of people, such as parents and close relatives, community social networks, teachers, youth workers, employers, health providers, and peers who are involved in the lives of young people.

Opportunities: chances for young people to learn how to act in the world around them, to explore, express, earn, belong, and influence. Opportunities give young people the chance to test ideas and behaviors and to experiment with different roles. It is important to stress that young people, just like adults, learn best through active participation and that learning occurs in all types of settings and situations.

Quality services: services in such areas as education, health, employment, and juvenile justice that exhibit (1) relevant instruction and information; (2) challenging opportunities to express oneself, to contribute, to take on new roles and be part of a group; and (3) supportive adults and peers who provide respect, high standards and expectations, guidance, and affirmation to young people.

Youth development is not a highly sophisticated and complicated prescription for "fixing those troubled kids." Youth development is about people, programs, institutions, and systems that provide all youth—"troubled" or not—with the supports and opportunities they need to empower themselves. For a nation with such a rich diversity of youth, this requires youth development in all shapes and sizes:

- An adult who volunteers time to mentor or tutor a young person;
- A school that partners with community-based organizations to keep its doors open until 10 P.M. and provide all youth a safe, supervised place to be with homework support, activities, and physical and mental health services;
- A leadership development program that offers rival gang members neutral territory where they can relate to one another as individuals and build skills;
- A city government that engages youth in the policy-making process through youth councils and youth positions in government departments;
- A religious institution that provides youth access to computers and the necessary training; and
- A local business that employs youth in meaningful and relevant work.

These, in addition to the important national youth-serving organizations like Boys & Girls Clubs, 4-H, and Boy and Girl Scouts, are a sampling of the myriad types of youth development supports and opportunities that all too few youth are able to take advantage of. The challenge is to make such supports and opportunities the rule rather than the exception for all youth.

THE IDEAL: YOUTH DEVELOPMENT FOR ALL YOUTH

The ideal, as we stated before, is adequate and secure funding to provide youth development supports, opportunities, and services for all youth. Many youth, but by no means all of them, will reach adulthood whether or not they enjoy those supports, opportunities, and services along the way. Yet merely reaching adulthood is not a successful outcome of the youth development process. We need adults who are mentally and physically healthy, socially and civically engaged, and economically viable. In order to become this type of adult, youth need the active involvement of their families and communities.

Families, Communities, and Schools

Families are the primary venue for youth development. However, the ability of families to support the positive development of their youth varies greatly, based on a host of factors, including financial resources, available time, number of parents and youth in a family, physical and health circumstances, and special needs of a youth. The list goes on and on. Families contribute to youth development in ways that may never be calculated but are easily recognizable, extremely valuable, and vital to support.

Likewise, the number and quality of supports and opportunities that communities offer their youth vary greatly based on the level of resources and structured collaboration that community members (governments, schools, community-based organizations, businesses, and individuals) bring together.

At this point, some might argue defensively that most communities already spend a large portion of their resources to support their youth. After all, according to the National Center for Education Statistics, in 1996-1997 this country spent $274.1 billion on public school education for 51.4 million students.[2] And public education often receives the largest portion of most state budgets. Does this money support youth development? It does for the youth who are lucky enough to attend schools that provide the developmental supports, opportunities, and services described earlier. All of the principles, practices, and outcomes of youth development must be integrally and intentionally incorporated into the classroom and throughout the school. However, in too many schools, a focus on youth development does not begin until after-school programming begins. Of course, this assumes after-school programming exists—either in the school building or in the community.

We know then that we are far from the ideal: not all families can provide the necessary youth development supports, and communities are failing to do so even with the large amounts of money they spend on education and noneducation youth services. *What could the ideal look like?*

1. Children and youth are safe and have loving and supportive families, a sense of community and belonging, a spiritual connection, meaningful and developmentally appropriate activities, involvement, and partnerships, and they receive an education that prepares them to lead healthy, self-supporting, meaningful, productive, and responsible lives;
2. Youth development is considered a public responsibility;
3. Youth development infrastructures are in place from the community to the federal government level;
4. Adequate and protected government funding is available for youth development systems and providers;
5. Standards of performance are established for youth development activities provided outside of the family; and
6. Information about youth development is collected in ways that will enable us to make informed and responsible decisions.

Our picture of the ideal, as you can see, is not just a picture of more money and more programs. It is a picture of a system of publicly and privately funded supports and opportunities to which all youth have access. It is a picture of an ideal that involves making a financial commitment to provide youth with the tools we know they need to build a successful life. It is an ideal that is within our grasp, but it will not come cheaply.

THE COST OF YOUTH DEVELOPMENT

How much will it cost us? This is a question that gets asked when planning any integral component of public infrastructure: roads and highways, sewage systems, housing developments, filtration systems, health facilities, shopping districts, police departments, and even schools. Answering this question helps to determine what investments the public is willing to make. Youth development, as General Colin Powell has argued, must be considered one of these public investments.

Since the continued health of the entire nation and its economy relies on the successful outcomes of youth, the cost of youth development, which involves billions of dollars just like other major public investments, should not be borne by only one segment of the population. Families, neighborhoods, businesses, community-based organizations, health care, schools, government, foundations, and individuals are all responsible for providing youth development opportunities and supports. If youth development is to become a support system for youth rather than just a fragmented collection of targeted programs, we must all consider ourselves responsible for its cost.

Time Is Money

In attempting to quantify the cost of youth development, we have chosen to focus on the period in which a vacuum exists in the support system for youth: the hours of a typical youth's day, week, and year when families and schools, in particular, are often unable to address youth needs. The significance of these vacuum hours was brought to public attention in 1992 by the Carnegie Council in their seminal document *A Matter of Time*. It examined how young people spend their time and emphasized the link between unstructured time and youth engagement in risky behaviors. Moreover, *A Matter of Time* showed us how, given youth development supports and opportunities like the ones we have discussed above, youth will often make positive decisions about how to fill this vacant time.

FIGURE 1

How Young Adolescents (Ages 9-14) Spend Their Waking Hours

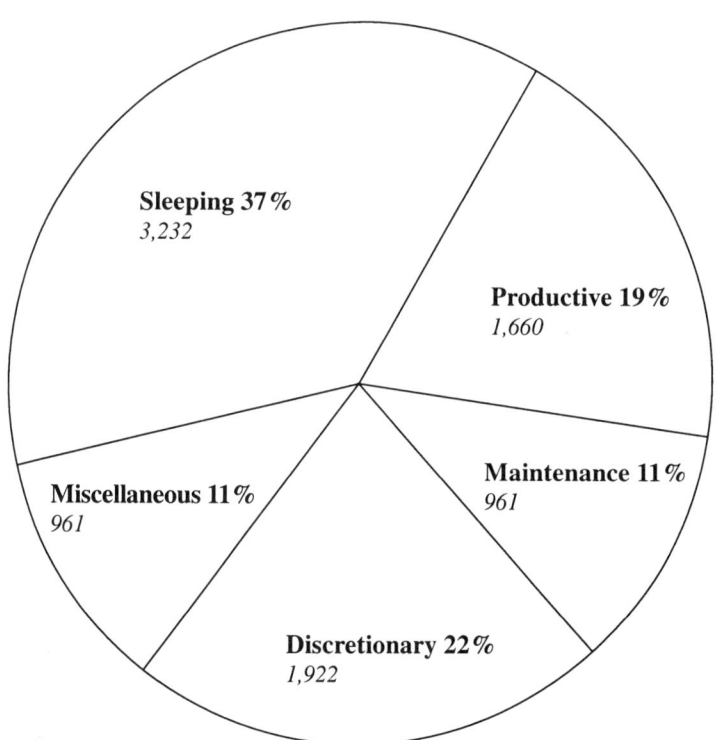

A Matter of Time, 1992

A Matter of Money

This chapter tries to complete what *A Matter of Time* began. We have developed one possible framework and formula for assigning a cost to the supports and opportunities we all know youth need.

How Much Time?

Two graphs help us answer this question by breaking down a year in the life of a youth into hours. Figure 1 is from the *A Matter of Time* report; Figure 2 is from the New York City Department of Youth Services (DYS).[3] Five categories are shown in Figure 1: *sleeping, productive* (school, studying, and jobs), *maintenance* (household chores, work and errands, personal care, and eating), *discretionary* (reading, visiting, church, television, playing, hobbies, art and activities, and sports and outdoor activities), and *miscellaneous*. Although Figure 2 uses different categories, the two charts yield similar results.

The hours in the *sleeping* and *productive* categories of Figure 1 are similar to those in the categories *asleep* and *in school* shown in Figure 2. For the sake of

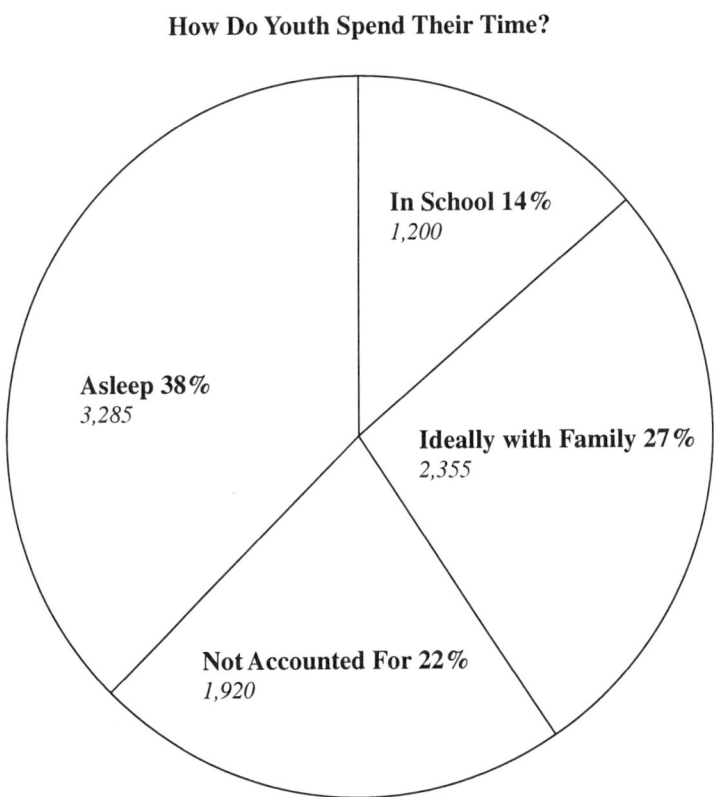

FIGURE 2
How Do Youth Spend Their Time?

In School 14%
1,200

Asleep 38%
3,285

Ideally with Family 27%
2,355

Not Accounted For 22%
1,920

New York City Department of Youth Services, 1991

comparison, let us try to balance the remaining categories. If we assume that youth in Figure 1 spend 50 percent of their *maintenance, discretionary,* and *miscellaneous* time with family, that equals 1,922 hours per year, making it comparable to the 1,920 hours *not accounted for* in Figure 2.[4]

These efforts by the DYS and Carnegie indicate that outside of time spent with family, in school and asleep, there are about 1,920 hours per year currently not accounted for, hours in which youth are looking for something to do. These hours are the focus of these calculations. How much would it cost to provide 1,920 hours of youth development opportunities and supports to the 47 million school-age youth (youth ages 6 to 17 years old) in this country? We do not have the definitive answers, but we hope to provide a logical model to get some answers.

Since there is no "system" like education for youth during the time that is unaccounted for, we cannot easily calculate the associated costs. Instead, we will look at the costs of some programs that can fill the unaccounted-for hours with positive supports and opportunities. These programs are either based on youth development principles in purpose and design, or are preventive but operate with youth development principles and practices. These programs include Big Brothers Big Sisters, Teen Outreach Program, the After-School Corporation in New York, Boys & Girls Clubs of America, and Girl Scouts of America. Programs like these and others, both national and local in nature, can and do help to fill the time not accounted for (see Table 1).

Table 1. *Cost of Youth Development Programs*

Organization	Annual Cost/Youth	Hours/Youth	Unit Cost (Cost/Hour) per Youth
Big Brothers Big Sisters[5] (mentoring)	$1,000	260	$3.85
Teen Outreach Program[6] (prevention)	$572	60	$9.53
The After-School Corporation[7] (after-school)	$1,000	540	$1.85
Boys & Girls Clubs[8] (recreation)	$139	NA	NA
Girl Scouts of America[9] (recreation and service)	$135	NA	NA

Assumption—1,200 hours

It is not likely that every hour of a youth's life can be or should be accounted for with programs. Therefore, we assume that on average 14 hours per week (728 hours per year) may always be not accounted for, especially with older youth. Based on this assumption, there are 1,194 hours per year (1,922 minus 728) that youth need developmental supports and opportunities. For the sake of simplicity, however, our calculations are based on the rounded figure of 1,200 hours.

How Much Money?

Table 1 provides some insight into the costs of some recognizable programs and can help to estimate the cost of youth development during times that are unaccounted for. As incredible as this figure may seem, there are at least three important reasons why it is so low.

Table 2. *Cost of Youth Development per Youth for 1,200 Unsupervised/ Unstructured Hours*

Allocation of Time	Hours per Year	Cost per Hour	Cost per Year
After-school (3 P.M.-7 P.M.)	720	$1.85	$1,332
Mentoring	260	$3.85	$1,001
Prevention	60	$9.53	$572
Recreation, Scouts, service, etc.	160	Annual	$155
Total	1,200	$2.55 avg.	$3,060

Table 3. *Potential National Cost of Youth Development*

Number of U.S. School-Age Youth (6 to 17 years old)	Total Cost of Youth Development for 1,200 Hours per Year
47,107,102	$144,147,732,120

Using the following information, we are able to calculate in Table 2 and Table 3 that the estimated cost of ensuring that developmental opportunities and supports are available to all school-age youth in the United States for 1,200 hours per year would be $2.55 per hour, per youth ($3,060 per youth annually): $144 billion per year.

1. We take a very optimistic look at the hours spent by a youth with family during a year. For example, Figure 2 suggests that, of their waking hours, youth spend three hours per day Monday through Friday with family and 30 hours on the weekends. In many cases, however, this is an unrealistically large amount of time to spend with family. Consider that just a 5 percent increase in the need for opportunities and supports (based on 1,200 hours per year) would result in an additional 60 hours annually or just over one hour per week per youth. Such a small increase could result in an increase of $7.2 billion per year.
2. Each of the programs listed would state that the reported costs do not represent the actual costs of providing their services and opportunities. They do not include staff payments for a variety of miscellaneous expenses that are not or cannot be reimbursed. They do not calculate the time spent beyond 40 hours, by many staff members, to put together proposals for

funding or to attend evening events or visit schools and families on behalf of one of their participants.
3. Most providers of youth development will admit that to ensure consistent, high-quality services, supports and opportunities would cost more than what is currently funded. Many of these programs cannot train and develop their staff like other sectors of the economy. They cannot offer benefit and retirement plans, they cannot afford to hire highly trained staff and meet ideal staff-to-youth ratios, nor can they provide all the resources and equipment that would make their program ideal.

Making a Public Investment

Who pays? Even if there was support to fund youth development fully with a dedicated or protected funding stream, where would the $144 billion necessary come from? Youth development is an investment that must be made by each sector of the wider community—public and private. Until we more accurately assess the current nature and level of youth development funding, it will be difficult to tell what part of this $144 billion will require new revenues from the various sectors. It is nonetheless necessary to contemplate the role of each sector of society that has a responsibility and stake in making this crucial public investment.

Families and Neighborhoods

As has been acknowledged, families and neighborhoods are the primary venue for youth development, yet the financial capacity of families and neighborhoods to support such development varies greatly. While the goal is for society as a whole to ensure that all youth have equal access to the necessary supports and opportunities, some families are able to make a greater contribution than others. Citizens and policy makers need to engage in a dialogue that examines the responsibility that all families and neighborhoods have to their children.

Federal, State, and Local Governments

Given the greater capacity of government funds to address the developmental needs of all youth, the roles at each level of government must be critically examined. To facilitate this, the Center has applied the same formula used to calculate the potential national cost of youth development to each state and to the 50 most populous cities. This yielded an estimated cost of youth development for each state and locality (see Appendix A).

When considering federal government influence on state policy, the case of the minimum drinking age is instructive. All states now have the same minimum drinking age of 21 because the federal government made it a prerequisite to obtain certain funding from the Department of Transportation. Some states balked at first, but they all needed the funding.

A similar scenario can be developed for youth development. Using some of the aforementioned revenue, the federal government can allocate funds to the states with the stipulation that there be a 100 percent match. Such matching efforts, however, are often difficult for smaller or poorer states. The reality is that some states do not have the economic base to raise enough revenue to meet the matching stipulation and would have to rely on multiple funding efforts.

At the local level there is a need for examining and supporting the effectiveness of models using dedicated taxes and other secure revenues for youth development, such as those in Pinellas County, Florida; San Francisco; and Oakland. These will likely become valuable models for emerging initiatives in other cities and counties across the country, such as the Priority One: Put Kids First initiative now under way in Bartholomew County, Indiana. Priority One's coalition of concerned community citizens from business, education, and social services arenas has recognized the need for a countywide structure for "providing children and youth (ages 0 to 20) with the resources necessary to develop into healthy, contributing adults" and so has formed the Bartholomew County Youth Development Commission in collaboration with United Way.

Dedicated taxes, however, are no panacea. The fixed nature of dedicated funding can act as a safety measure for ensuring a minimum level of adequate funding, but it might also eventually act as a barrier to increased or new funding. Dedicated taxes are a start, a bridge to getting protected and secure funding for youth development. Communities must give youth development the same funding priority as other such essentials as police and sanitation departments.

Governments can also require these communities to provide new types of information about how resources are allocated to serve young people in a community. We discuss this new type of information in a section titled "YouthBudget."

Business and Philanthropic Sectors

Recent economic prosperity indicates a greater potential capacity for the business and philanthropic sectors to contribute significantly to the public investment in youth development. *Enabling them to do so will entail clarifying their level of responsibility to youth and devising effective mechanisms for their investments in youth.* Analogous to the federal-state match, government at all levels can provide incentives to the business and philanthropic communities to provide funding and support for youth development programs. Similar to tax abatement and tax credits given for commercial development, the government can offer financial incentives to these communities when they provide developmental supports and opportunities to youth. In fact, in fall 1998, Maryland Advocates for Children and Youth made just such a recommendation to their state legislature.

Calculating the Return on Investment

But is it worth it? Is it worth $144 billion to ensure that all youth have access to developmental supports and opportunities in their vacant hours?

Return on investment is a key indicator of the worthiness of any public investment. Prompted by a 1996 report by the Pacific Research Institute for Public Policy that compares the costs of incarceration to the savings in the social costs of crime, the Center has attempted a similar calculation for the return on investment for every dollar spent on youth development.

In constructing a framework for our calculation, we must make some assumptions.

Assumption #1: The best we can expect from a young person receiving youth development in principle and practice is a high school diploma, and for this person to live a healthy, productive, responsible, and civically engaged life (a very conservative expectation). According to the U.S. Census Bureau, the high school graduate can expect to make an annual salary of $22,895 (versus $40,478 with a bachelor's degree or $63,229 with an advanced degree).

Assumption #2: Assuming that this person receives an annual 3 percent cost-of-living increase for the next 40 years of employed life, he or she will have earned a salary of $1,726,312 over their employed lifetime. (This figure does not account for demotions or job changes at lower salaries, but shall serve as a working number for this example.) Based on our current tax structure this individual will pay approximately $293,473 in taxes (17% of total income).

Assumption #3: Let's assume that this person spends $1,035,787 (60%) and manages to save $397,052 (23%). That would result in a total of $1,329,260 going back to society before retirement either through taxation or consumer spending.

Our current estimates for the cost of youth development suggest that for twelve years a young person should be the beneficiary of a $36,720 total investment in developmental opportunities and supports ($3,060/year x 12 years). This would be in addition to the $78,768 average cost of a public education ($6,564 x 12 years). This is not to suggest that there is or should be a difference between youth development and schools. In fact, at "better" schools, youth development is a seamlessly integrated part of the educational experience.

A Positive Return

Based on this rudimentary (and conservative) example, Table 4 indicates that the return on investment (with no consideration of future value) for providing youth development opportunities and supports to a youth would be $1,213,772 ($1,329,260 − $115,488). **An investment of $2.55/hour for 1,200 hours per year to develop youth into economically and socially viable adults plus a developmental education can result in a gain of $10.51 for every dollar invested.**

One final and important note on this rudimentary example is that it calculates only the tangible benefits of an economically and socially viable adult. It is more

A Matter of Money

difficult to calculate other benefits society gains from adults who contribute time and service to nurturing healthy families and communities.

Table 4. *Potential Return on Public Investment in a Youth*

Investment	
$3,060/yr for 12 years of 1,200 hours of supports and opportunities (6-17 yrs. old)	$36,720
$6,564/yr for 12 years of public education (grades 1-12)	$78,768
Total basic investment (12 years)	$115,488
Minimum Expectation	
Average annual salary (with just a high school diploma)	$22,895
Annual cost of living allowance	3%
Years of continuous employment	40
Total income (lifetime)	$1,726,312
Taxes (17% of total income)	$293,473
Consumption (60%)	$1,035,787
Personal savings w/o accrued interest (23%)	$397,052
Total contributions to society (taxes + consumption)	$1,329,260
Return on Investment	
Return on investment (contributions to society – investment)	$1,213,772
For every dollar invested, society gains	**$10.51**

HOW DO WE MEASURE UP TO THE IDEAL?

Ideally, we as a society will see the value of making the sounder public investment: adequate and secure funds to help all youth achieve positive outcomes. Yet before committing $144 billion to youth development, the public should demand to know how the current funding situation for youth development measures up to the ideal. This entails investigating the other two questions fundamental to providing our youth the supports and opportunities they need to become healthy, productive members of society:

- How much do we currently spend?
- What are the best mechanisms to harness and equitably distribute the necessary funds?

Answering these questions requires examining the sources as well as financing and distribution mechanisms of youth development funds and the organizational structure around these—no small task. While the barriers we encountered in this undertaking were lessened by an increasing number of such investigations, our efforts verified the findings of the Carnegie Council (Stern, 1992, p. 100) that "the difficulty in obtaining consistent and reliable data frustrates efforts to determine clearly the amount of funds from different sources available for youth development purposes." Dryfoos (1998, p. 222) reiterated similar sentiments in her chapter "Tracking Resources through the State and Federal Maze," in which she emphasized the "complexity of the U.S. system (or nonsystem) for supporting youth programs."

Money for youth development work comes from four general sources: private (families and individuals); philanthropy; local, state, and federal governments; and the business community. Having examined private philanthropic funds for youth development, the Carnegie Council found that while national youth-serving organizations get most foundation dollars targeted to adolescents, foundation grants for youth are less than the average size of grants for all other purposes. Moreover, the Council did not find corporate support to be a significant source of revenue for youth development (Stern, 1992, p. 106).

Still, because of the greater capacity of government funds to address the developmental needs of all youth, the Center's primary concern tends toward public financial commitment to youth development. Federal funding, in particular, plays a central role: excluding education, the federal government apparently spends more for children's programs than do state and local governments (Gold and Ellwood, 1994, p. 7). Moreover, the Carnegie Council (Stern, 1992, p. 124) observed that "without appropriate federal financial support, it is likely that community-based youth development programs will not be adequately funded." Yet the federal government does not live up to its potential in this regard: major national youth development organizations receive a smaller percentage of their funding from government than do other charitable organizations (Stern, 1992, p. 95); important youth development programs such as school-to-work, summer jobs for youth, and after-school centers often come up for cuts and do not have enough consistent funding.

Federal Spending

Unfortunately, there is no one definitive source to consult in measuring U.S. federal government expenditures for youth. There is still no such thing as a federal youth or children's budget. Researchers on this topic have made use of different combinations of documents as well as direct information from federal agencies to compile their own lists of federal programs and spending for children and youth. Findings in terms of specific numbers and programs vary among the lists, depending on the definition of youth and children and programs that serve them. Variable inclusion of Medicaid and education programs seems to account for some of the greatest discrepancies in the lists we examined. Notably, appearing on only two of the lists is 4-H (a program of the U.S. Department of Agriculture's Extension Service), which the Carnegie Council (Stern, 1992, p. 95) identified as probably "one of the largest youth development programs operating in voluntary settings under the direct supervision of the federal government." Also of importance, 4-H appears to be one of the few federal programs outside the Department of Education that targets all youth.

In 1992 the Carnegie Council identified, for fiscal years 1989-1991, 13 "federal programs targeted at adolescents" and 23 "federal programs which may include services for adolescents" for a total of $6.7 billion (Stern, 1992, pp. 92-94).

A Matter of Money

In 1994 the Finance Project compared two sources (the 1995 *Green Book* and Jule M. Sugarman's *Expenditures for Children: Existing Data and Perspectives on Budgeting*) that estimate "federal spending on children's programs," with the *Green Book* total estimate at $119.6 billion for 27 programs and the Sugarman estimate at $177.1 billion for about 40 programs (Gold and Ellwood, 1994, pp. 18-19).

Dryfoos compiled a list of "selected federal funds for youth-related programs, FY 1997," which identified 60 federal programs spending a total of about $245.3 billion. For the same fiscal year, the Pacific Research Institute identified more than 150 federal programs "targeted specifically at children" for a total of $54.4 billion (Dryfoos, 1998, pp. 245-247).

For fiscal year 1998, the Children's Defense Fund identified 57 "key children's programs" for a total of just under $40 billion.[10] Also for fiscal year 1998, the *Children and Youth Funding Report* identified 82 programs within the Departments of Labor, Health and Human Services, and Education, for a total of just over $144 billion.

The Pacific Research Institute for Public Policy identified more than 150 federal programs in five categories (nutrition; social and juvenile services; education, training and compensatory; education; health programs) targeted specifically at children, with a total of $54.4 billion in 1997 (Lopez, 1998, p. 13).

The wide variation among the above figures certainly supports the Pacific Research Institute's claim that "the current magnitude of government efforts is not readily apparent" (Lopez, 1998, p. 1). Even putting aside the differences in numbers and programs, the various lists bear out several observations regarding federal spending on youth and youth development.

Federal monies for children and youth are fragmented (Dryfoos, 1998, p. 232, and Stern, 1992, p. 125).

One estimate puts the number of federal entities with responsibility for federal programs serving children and families at 82, including 19 congressional committees, 26 subcommittees, 12 departments, and 25 agencies within departments (Dryfoos, 1998, p. 10). Monies in many of these federal entities support similar yet isolated programs for youth, and often such programs are merely small segments of much larger initiatives with a different focus.

Federal monies for youth often support crisis intervention-oriented programs and categorical problems (Stern, 1992, pp. 97 and 125).

Most federal dollars for youth go to after-the-fact intervention programs and strategies designed to respond to and change specific problem behaviors rather than to developmental programs that foster healthy behavior.

Most federal monies for youth do not support programs that make positive development of all youth a priority.

In 1992 the Carnegie Council observed that "relatively few federal dollars are targeted specifically at adolescents, fewer yet could be seen as youth development programs" (Stern, 1992, p. 95). Add to this the fact that among programs for youth of any age almost all federal dollars outside of education seem to go to programs targeted for youth designated as at risk.

While the question of measuring how much the federal government is spending on youth development seems to continue without a satisfactory answer, we still must agree on how best to go about determining this answer. To do this, a consensus must be reached on which of the myriad federal "programs for children and youth" can actually be counted as youth development and, within this, which of these programs address the positive development of all youth versus targeted populations. Youth-serving organizations as well as funding and intermediary organizations (especially those that have helped to develop the research on this question) will need to be involved in achieving this important consensus.

Federal Funding Mechanisms

Once we have answered "how much," we must then move on to "how." That is, how are the monies for youth development organized and distributed and what works best? At the federal government level, we have already observed how monies for youth are widely dispersed among a fragmented array of departments, agencies, and committees. No centralized agency is responsible for youth or even for overseeing or coordinating money for all federal government youth-related initiatives. There remains no federal government entity to oversee programs and funding, which would help to ensure the ideals set forth in the Young Americans Act as called for by the Carnegie Council in 1992 and again by Dryfoos in 1998.

The Family and Youth Services Bureau of the Administration for Children and Families within the U.S. Department of Health and Human Services (HHS) would be the federal government entity one might naturally look to for such coordination and leadership, especially given its important role in educating others about the principles and practices of youth development. Yet its funding level at over $3 billion (1997) also seems restricted to a crisis intervention–oriented focus. In late 1998, HHS awarded grants totaling just over $1 million to nine states ($120,000 each) to "help the states identify, develop, and strengthen effective youth development strategies." While such a small sum could never hope to adequately address the positive developmental needs of all youth, these funds have been targeted for efforts that "focus on at-risk youth, such as homeless, runaway, abused and neglected, those served in the child welfare and juvenile justice systems."

At the federal level, there appear to be no financing mechanisms that protect or dedicate funds for youth—any youth—outside of the normal appropriation system. Even the "Youth Development Block Grant" remains elusive, though attempts to initiate such a measure in some form occurred in 1992 and 1995. With the federal government devolving more and more power over funds and decisions for youth, this course does not seem to be changing.

State Spending and Funding Mechanisms

It is just this process of devolution of power to states that makes examination of youth development structures and funding at the state level so crucial. This was observed by the Carnegie Council in 1992, when it called for more investigation

A Matter of Money

of this matter. The Carnegie Council, the Finance Project, the National Association of Child Advocates (NACA), and Joy Dryfoos have all provided important pieces of this picture: overviews and perspectives on state outlays for children and youth, as well as analysis of innovative programs and practices such as comprehensive community schools, and integration and collaboration at the governmental level for youth education, health, and welfare services. "Children's budgets," produced both by state governments and state child advocacy organizations, have also contributed greatly to the knowledge base on this issue.

Nonetheless, the most readily available information at the state level tends to be on education and entitlement service funds. Determining what youth development structures and programs, never mind funds, exist at the state level is usually difficult. The Carnegie Council in 1992 observed that "it is not possible to obtain nationwide data on funds spent on youth issues by state and local governments" (Stern, 1992, p. 101). More recently, the director of NACA's Multi-State Budget Watch Project remarked that attempts to assess youth development expenditures and services at the state level were mostly unsuccessful.[11]

The importance of the task, however, remains. Once again recognizing the greater capacity of government funds to address the developmental needs of all youth, the Center believes the states' increasingly central and still-evolving role in this process must be given serious consideration and analysis. The Center has attempted some of the basic groundwork, which could lead to the necessary analysis at the state level. In an informal telephone survey that canvassed state governments, we tried to gauge awareness of youth development as well as the possibility of determining states' financial and programmatic commitment to it. In doing so, three broad questions were posed:

1. What state monies go to youth development strategies and programs? Inherent in this question is another: what, if anything, does youth development mean to a particular state government?
2. Do those youth development dollars, strategies, and programs target all youth or a specific group?
3. Under what sort of organizational structure and by what means and mechanisms are those youth development dollars acquired and distributed? Specifically, are the youth development funds in fragmented areas of state government or is there an identifiable structure around them? In what sort of funding streams do those monies have their source? Are any of those funding streams protected outside the normal appropriation systems?

Calls to 10 states resulted in substantive findings for only six: Kansas, Ohio, Iowa, Missouri, Minnesota, and New York. For the most part we did not, nor did we expect to, get complete answers to any of the questions in any one state. We were curious to see what kind of information this sort of inquiry would produce. Not surprisingly, the information we were given largely mirrors the three main findings at the federal level: fragmentation; a crisis-intervention orientation; and lack of support for all youth in funding, programs, and structures for youth. The extent to which this is true for each state varies greatly. In fact, findings from states in our limited canvassing represent a veritable spectrum of the different levels of financial and programmatic commitment to youth development. They fall anywhere from nonexistent and highly fragmented youth development structures and funding to well-defined and dedicated structures and funding streams.

The following are four important general observations from the canvassing:

1. There are very different awareness levels and definitions of youth development in each state.

    Figures for state spending on youth development are really only comparable if the operating definitions, goals, and target groups for youth development are similar. There might be some worth, for example, in comparing levels of expenditure for the Special Delinquency Prevention Program in New York and the Youth Development/Youth Service in Minnesota.

2. In most states, it is very difficult to find youth development initiatives that target all youth.

    In some states our investigation led to the Extension Service (4-H). In others it led to initiatives with titles and missions that give the impression of being "for all youth," yet in which the funding usually targets youth at risk and problem behaviors. There is a need for examining and determining the effectiveness of more all-youth approaches of the type found in Minnesota and New York (see Appendix B).

3. There is a need for examining and determining the effectiveness of the different organizational structures around youth development funds.

    This, of course, is difficult when in many cases there is either no defined structure or the structure is frequently changing, as we observed in our canvassing. Nonetheless, the different types of structures found in such states as Iowa, Missouri, Minnesota, and New York offer good chances for such evaluation.

4. Finally, the understanding of "dedicated" and "protected" funds varies from state to state, as do the methods for achieving this.

    When examining the amount of spending for youth development in a state, it is also crucial to examine closely the financing mechanisms and the extent to which funds are dedicated and protected. The New York and Minnesota youth development legislation and the Iowa increased allowable growth legislation are just some of the mechanisms that merit examination. Also notable is the expanded role of the Children's Trust Fund in Ohio. Most states have such a trust fund with similar revenues dedicated to child abuse and neglect prevention, yet it is unclear to what extent they currently do, and potentially could, support more development-oriented initiatives.

Local Spending

Answering the fundamental questions on youth development spending and mechanisms for counties, cities, and towns is a task not yet undertaken by many. As an intermediary working with localities to build comprehensive youth development infrastructures, these are questions the Center frequently confronts. In an attempt to adequately address the question of spending in our work with localities, the Center developed a "YouthBudget" analysis to examine and document how resources are allocated to serve young people in a community.

YouthBudget

YouthBudget analysis is a critical step toward identifying a community's priorities and equity of investments for young people. Through this process, sometimes referred to as children's budgets, communities can begin to assess their current levels and areas of investment and devise plans for future spending. YouthBudget entails a three-step process for gathering and analyzing data on a community's spending for youth:

1. Identify the target population served by a funding stream or budget allocation;
2. Identify the type of funded programs and services: development, prevention, treatment, rehabilitation, or incarceration; and
3. Integrate the above information to provide a picture of which youth are getting which services, and of financial investments in a community at large.

In reality, communities undertake and employ YouthBudget in different ways suited to their immediate needs. In collaboration with the Center, the United Way of Central Indiana and D. Bonnet Associates carried out a YouthBudget analysis for public and philanthropic spending on children and youth in central Indiana. In this analysis, spending for youth was examined according to type of funding source, purpose, and age group (see Appendix C). Findings reflected some of the same trends we have already observed in federal and state spending for youth:

- Philanthropic and government spending on children and youth in the nine-county area totaled $1.68 billion per year; an average of $4,416 per person ages 0 to 18;
- Education accounts for three-quarters of the total;
- Public money—federal, state, and local—goes mainly toward health, education, and welfare, in that order; and
- Foundation and United Way funds go mainly toward child and youth development ($11.4 million) and education ($5.94 million).

The data produced by such a YouthBudget analysis can be invaluable in planning comprehensive infrastructures of services and programs for youth development for all youth. Imagine if we had access to such data in all localities and at all levels of government!

Local Funding Mechanisms

At the local level, there have been notable innovations in both the organizational structures and financing mechanisms around youth development. The Children and Families Program of the National League of Cities (NLC), in particular, has paid close attention to these issues, with substantial research in youth master planning, child care systems, city and school partnerships, and financing of municipal policies and programs for children and youth.

The following are three important findings from research conducted by the NLC:

1. Cities are spending more on services for children and families;
2. City officials expect funds for services for children and families to decrease while the demand for services increases as the result of changes in federal policy; and
3. Cities seem to rely most on general revenues and fees for service in financing children's services. Far fewer rely on dedicated taxes, bond issues and impact fees (National League of Cities, 1997, pp. 1-4).

In 1997, the NLC identified 20 cities of different sizes that used some sort of dedicated tax for services to children and youth. Taxes ranging from income, sales, and property to food and beverage, cigarette, and bedroom may support one specific service, such as libraries, recreation facilities, and child-care centers, or they may be used to fund citywide comprehensive youth development strategies and initiatives (see Appendix D).

Dedicated taxes and other protected funds that fall into this latter category have the most potential for ensuring the supports and opportunities all youth need to become healthy and productive members of society. The Juvenile Welfare Board of Pinellas County, Florida, is perhaps the longest-existing such entity at

A Matter of Money 113

the local level. The Florida legislature in 1949 created an independent special taxing district in the county that was dedicated to children's services. This taxing authority led to the creation of the Juvenile Welfare Board, which, over the years, has moved away from "smaller, categorical efforts and toward more comprehensive approaches" (Carnegie Corporation, 1992, p. 106).

Recent examples of dedicated structures and funding mechanisms at the local level include:

San Francisco's "Proposition J," established in 1991—The 10-year San Francisco Children's Fund amended the city charter to mandate that 2.5 percent of the property tax be set aside each year to expand services to children and youth under 18. As a result, San Francisco will spend $160,000,000 between 1991 and 2003 on the following types of programs: child care, job readiness, training, placement programs, health and social services (including prenatal services), educational programs, recreation programs, delinquency prevention programs, and library services. The funds may not be used for law enforcement services, purchase of property or services benefiting children only incidentally or as members of a larger population that includes adults. The fund is administered through the Mayor's Office of Children, Youth and Their Families, which, in 1997-1998, oversaw the approximately $13 million raised through Proposition J.

Oakland's "Measure K," established in 1996—The 12-year Oakland Children's Fund designated 2.5 percent of the city's budget to direct services to children and youth. In fiscal year 1997-1998, the amount available for grants was $5,264,709, with up to 80 percent allocated for grants to qualified organizations and up to 20 percent allocated for youth-initiated projects.

WHY DO WE FALL SHORT OF THE IDEAL?

Through examination of the current public investment in youth development, we, and others, have consistently identified the shortcomings that impede our ability to provide positive developmental supports and opportunities to all youth.

Devaluation of Adolescents

Raising healthy youth from ages 0 to 21 requires a comprehensive and balanced approach to supporting healthy development at each stage. Unfortunately, adolescents are often the forgotten and undervalued segment of America's youth population. Policy makers and society as a whole focus a great deal less positive attention—and as a result fewer supports and opportunities—on adolescents than on younger children. Adolescents who are from poor and disenfranchised backgrounds face even greater obstacles to healthy development. Providing the supports our adolescents need will require a critical examination of and change in society's attitude toward them. Consider the following editorial from *Life* magazine in July 1998:

Teenager. The word itself is uttered as an insult. Friends commiserate, as though having teenage children were an affliction. Or they warn, "just wait until she or he is a teenager." It turns other innocuous words into pejorative terms like teenage mother, teenage driver. We treat this group, these citizens, as we would dare treat no other: what if the malls imposed curfews on, say, people over 60? Or refused to let people in their forties shop without chaperones? You would think, if all people did was read the paper and watch the evening news, that children upon turning 13 automatically enter a state of psychosis that lasts for seven years, and sometimes longer. But look at the teens around you. In my community, teenagers attend church, raise funds for charity, read to the elderly, clean up the rivers, baby-sit, wash cars, shovel snow, stack books in the library. They also get pregnant, drop out of school, play lousy music and hang out in the park drinking beer. But mostly, the good outweighs the bad, just as it does in every other age group. Yet bad teenagers are the only portion of an age group that becomes the norm for the entire group. (*Life,* July 1998, p. 10)

Lack of Consensus on Youth Development

Now, more than 10 years into the youth development movement, there still seems to be a lack of consensus about both the meaning and the concept of youth development—inside and outside of the field. A random Internet search for "youth development" will bring up sites as distinct as the "Minnesota Youth Development Page," which highlights that state's comprehensive positive youth development initiatives for all of its youth, and the "York County Youth Development Center" page, which outlines specific services for adjudicated delinquent juveniles at this Pennsylvania county detention center. In Georgia, our telephone query was immediately referred to the Youth Service Department, which oversees a number of youth development centers that again are detention centers for adjudicated youth.

While it is very possible that important youth development work is going on in such detention centers, this once again points to the issue of identifying youth development as either services and opportunities that aim to change negative behaviors for a targeted group of youth or as supports and opportunities that promote healthy development in all youth. This distinction becomes very important when the term and concept travel outside the field. Do the public officials, the policy makers and budget makers, and the public at large identify youth development as work with troubled kids or with their own kids? These perceptions matter very much, as they will ultimately guide the direction of public dollars and support.

Lack of Integrated Structure around Services and Funds for Youth

The fragmentation of monies and services for youth has now been identified frequently at both the federal and state government levels. As previously mentioned, several innovative reforms to change this are under way in some states and localities, yet integrated strategies and structures are still lacking on the whole. Moreover, these innovative strategies and structures, such as comprehensive community schools and other integrated health-social services-education delivery systems, need to be designed from a perspective of positive youth development for all youth.

Lack of Adequate and Protected Funding

We have seen some large numbers next to youth services, some (but not many) of them related to youth development. The reality, however, is that even the meager youth development–related funds are not protected and dedicated in a way that will sustain the long-term, comprehensive process that *is* youth development. Increased funds for youth development will be most effective only if they are adequate and secure. Innovative legislation at the state level and such financing mechanisms as dedicated taxes at the local level, need to be further examined for their effectiveness and potential to be brought to scale. Until there is protected and dedicated funding for all youth, we will never be able to provide all of our youth with the supports and opportunities necessary to become healthy, productive members of society.

MOVING TOWARD THE IDEAL

We have so far looked at what the ideal situation is for creating an environment of positive youth development for all youth and how our current situation falls short of that ideal. Others who have gone through this process have then moved ahead to try to gain support for plans and measures reflecting the ideal:

1. In *A Matter of Time,* the Carnegie Council (1992) called on local, state, and federal governments to take several steps to increase their commitment to adolescents. In particular, at the federal level, the Council called for funding and infrastructure to back up the 1989 Young Americans Act and create a comprehensive national youth policy.
2. In 1991, the Association of New York State Youth Bureaus sought support for legislation authorizing $100 per year per youth in federal aid (total $7 billion) for local government to

contract with community organizations for services addressing developmental needs of the general youth population and youth with special needs.
3. Numerous failed legislative attempts in the last decade include the 1992 Comprehensive Services for Youth Act, which authorized $250 million for youth development services to be provided at the local level with coordination at the state and federal levels, and the 1995 Youth Development Community Block Grant, which reallocated existing federal funding for preventive youth programs into a more cohesive approach.
4. More recently, Joy Dryfoos (1998) has called for a "Safe Passages Movement" of integrated school and community services, which would establish infrastructure at the federal, state, and local levels and require $710 million in the first two years for start-up and grants to states and communities.

While none of these "ideals" has yet to become a reality, the Center is working alongside others in the youth development field to continue to support initiatives that move the public sector toward shouldering its responsibility for youth by creating both an integrated government infrastructure and dedicated funding for all youth. This is the ideal we must all continue to support. Given the comprehensive nature and long-term goals of the youth development movement, we believe the ideal will most likely be achieved through a series of key incremental steps that must include the following factors.

New Types of Information

There is a saying in the human services field that "you collect information about what you fund and you fund what you know." The most readily accessible information on youth is about what is wrong with them or what they have done wrong. Is it any wonder that we fund so many crisis-intervention programs and strategies designed to respond to and change specific problem behaviors rather than developmental programs that foster healthy behavior?

It is very easy to find out how many teenagers are parents, how many do drugs, how many dropped out of school, and how many have committed a crime. On the other hand, how would you find out how many youth are abstaining from sex or practicing safe sex, how many youth have positive and caring relationships, how many youth are doing community service and are leaders in their community? How would you find out how many and where the youth development–oriented after-school and out-of-school time programs are in a community, city, county, or state? How much of your tax dollars or charity donations goes toward the positive development of young people? We must seek new types of information that enable us to support ongoing healthy development of all youth and do not restrict us to fixing specific problem behaviors.

A Matter of Money 117

Developmental Indicators

Along with identifying the positive outcomes we want our youth to achieve, it is important to identify ways to determine whether youth are successfully achieving those outcomes. What evidence indicates that a young person is mentally healthy? What indicates her or his potential to be successfully employed in today's economy? Over the past several years, work has been done to identify positive developmental indicators on the program level. The Center is currently in the process of working with localities to define, collect, and analyze an initial set of youth development and community indicators. These well-defined indicators and outcomes can be used to inform us about supporting the wellness of our youth. For this work to go to scale and have national implications, the federal and state governments need to embrace the collection of positive and developmental indicators about youth. These data, complemented by the Annie E. Casey Foundation's *Kids Count* data, would begin to give us a true picture of the status of all our youth.

Cost Projections

The public needs to know how much it should be investing in the future—their youth. The federal, state, and local governments have a responsibility to determine exactly how much youth development costs for the population they serve. Precedents for this type of calculation are abundant, albeit for prevention and intervention programs. In fact, most of our entitlement programs are based on such calculations. The Center's formula for devising a youth development cost projection at the national, state, and local levels is one example of how this could be done (see pp. 102-103 and Appendix A). Policy makers, funders, and advocates at all levels must join the effort to determine the cost of youth development so that funding for positive developmental supports and opportunities can become a priority rather than an "extra."

Data on Existing Funding and Supports

There are many programs that provide opportunities and supports to young people, but who knows what they are, where they are, and how many there are? In order to improve the provision of services, supports, and opportunities to all youth, communities need to know what currently exists. The Center has introduced YouthMapping in over 30 communities where youth have used their eyes and their feet to answer these questions by identifying community resources useful to their families, friends, or themselves. This process provides communities with baseline information about supports and opportunities for youth in a community. This identification process needs to continue at the local level, but with intentional and committed support from the federal and state levels. Such information should also be updated regularly and used in community decisions about resources for youth.

Likewise, in order for the public to make a wise investment of its youth development dollars, a community needs information on the nature and level of current funding. YouthBudget analyses examine and document how resources are allocated to serve young people in a community. This includes the type of program or service funded and the specific youth population targeted. It can also go a level deeper, generating information about who provides the funding and how many young people are served. Such inquiries into expenditures related to young people are a critical step in identifying a community's *priorities* and its *equity of investments*. Through this process, communities can begin to assess their current levels and areas of investment and devise plans for future spending. Such analysis ought to be done from the city and county to the state and federal levels.

Building on the After-School Momentum

Increased public attention to and investment in quality after-school opportunities for school-age youth are encouraging signs that the public is recognizing the value of youth development. There has recently been an outpouring of support and funds for after-school programs at all levels: federal, state, local, and philanthropic. This positive momentum could provide the necessary vehicle for increasing public understanding of and commitment to youth development on a national scale. Beyond the traditional "after-school" hours, youth need developmental supports and opportunities during evenings, weekends, summers and other school vacations. Some of the recent after-school initiatives that could have positive implications for a wide-scale youth development movement include the following.

Federal

In January 1998, the U.S. Department of Education and the Charles Stewart Mott Foundation announced the development of a public-private partnership to ensure that young people have opportunities for growth and learning during nonschool hours. The Mott Foundation has pledged a minimum of $55 million over five years to support the federal proposal to expand before- and after-school programs for youth through the 21st Century Community Learning Centers Program.

The purpose of the centers is to provide quality extended learning opportunities for children in safe and disciplined school-based programs through building collaborations with schools, community-based organizations, universities, and employers. The federal budget for fiscal year 2000 doubled the previous year's allocation to $453 million for the 21st Century Schools, with congressional members of both parties considering increasing after-school funding as a "win-win" deal.

State

In 1998, the California legislature passed the After-School Learning and Safe Neighborhoods Partnership Programs. This initiative provides elementary and

A Matter of Money

middle schools and their community partners expanded opportunities to promote the educational and social development of children and youth. Fifty million dollars in grant funds will be available to provide learning supports and safe and stimulating environments in the hours immediately following school.

The $50 million will be available annually for three-year grants. A 50 percent local match (cash or in-kind) from the school districts, government agencies, community organizations, or the private sector is required. The grants will be based on an allocation of $5 per day per student, with the maximum grant for one school year totaling $75,000 for elementary schools and $100,000 for middle schools.

These funded programs must operate on school sites a minimum of three hours per day and until at least 6 P.M. on every regular school day. These programs will maintain a student-to-staff ratio of 20 to 1.

Finally, this bill would also require that up to $550,000 of the funding be allocated to local education agencies for technical assistance and training. In addition, the bill would appropriate $500,000 from the General Fund to the State Department of Education for state operations for implementation.

Local

According to *Evaluation of the New York City Beacons—Summary of Phase I Findings* (Warren et al., 1999):

> The New York City Beacons provide an excellent example of the "scaling up" of a targeted after-school/out-of-school initiative to a comprehensive neighborhood improvement program. Crucial to this scaling up was the ongoing leadership and support, financial and otherwise provided by New York City government under two administrations (of differing political parties). This support not only provided funds to allow the initiative to quadruple in size; it also sent an important message to local-level practitioners about the importance of the initiative and the city's substantial commitment to developing the capacity of community-based organizations to provide opportunities for youth development and to address local community needs. What began as an ambitious and comprehensive initiative in 10 sites became institutionalized in city policy, with its own assistant commissioner, as one of the major ways that the city helps youth, families, and neighborhoods thrive. (p. 9)

In Baltimore, the Safe and Sound Campaign has proposed an initial investment of $57.1 million for three years to make possible permanent systemic change to ensure that all of Baltimore's children and youth have access to cultural, recreational, and intellectual after- and out-of-school experiences. Further, in developing its plan for use of the initial investment, Baltimore has also proposed a budget for its after-school program called YouthPlaces. Using information from experts in the field of youth development, Safe and Sound has determined that a quality YouthPlace in Baltimore will cost approximately $854,000 to serve 500 youth for 740 hours per year.[12]

Philanthropy

The sole purpose of the After-School Corporation (TASC) in New York City, established and entirely funded by the Open Society Institute, is to advance the quality and availability of in-school and after-school programs. This intermediary serves as a resource and infrastructure to help disparate after-school initiatives evolve into viable, sustainable programs. TASC will encourage the creation of after-school environments that meet basic needs of youth and stimulate their social and academic development in lively and productive settings. TASC planned to help fund 20 or more programs starting in the 1998-1999 academic year, establishing new programs and augmenting existing ones.

In order for the after-school momentum to successfully contribute to a large-scale youth development movement, several criteria must be met:

1. The efforts need to focus on all youth;
2. After-school programs should intentionally contribute to positive youth development outcomes;
3. The funding for after-school programming must be done realistically so as not only to provide services for youth but also to allow for staff and organizational development, adequate salaries, appropriate and quality equipment and supplies, technical assistance, and evaluation of best practices;
4. Community-based organizations should be equal players in the provision of after-school programming; and
5. Finally, the funding ought to be protected by whatever means necessary. If the political winds change, youth should not be the victims.

Sustainability

Youth development is an investment that must be made by each sector of the wider community—public and private. In determining each sector's level of responsibility, we must give precedence to mechanisms that account for interrelated roles as well as the need for sustainability, which requires long-term secure and adequate funding. We need to institute mechanisms that will provide adequate funds for youth development for at least 15 to 20 years before we can expect to see widespread positive results. Leaders in each of the sectors—families and neighborhoods; federal, state, and local governments; business and philanthropy—must be prepared to make a commitment to sustainability.

One possible scenario for both starting up and sustaining a youth development funding stream could have involved making use of the fiscal year 1998 federal budget surplus and continued deficit reduction. If the federal government had allocated the surplus of $80 billion to the states with a dollar-for-dollar match, it could have resulted in a start-up amount of $160 billion for a youth development funding stream. As for sustainability, consider that in 1997 the federal government paid $241 billion in interest on the deficit, practically equal to what it paid for national defense ($266 billion). As the deficit is reduced, can funds that are no longer paying interest pay for youth development?

Leadership

Good things are happening for youth due in large measure to the work of many people who have spent their entire careers attempting to create a developmental infrastructure for youth. We will not attempt to list them all, but suffice it to say they are in federal, state, and local governments; in communities; in national and local nonprofits; and in foundations and businesses.

In preparing this chapter, many of the documents reviewed, conversations conducted, and experiences gained suggested that there has not been enough of the "right" type of leadership supporting youth development for all youth. If there is to be a national youth development infrastructure with adequate and secure funds, the federal government must provide leadership: an individual with power and the will to provide a vision and set an example for the country. This individual could be the president, the vice president, a cabinet member, the Speaker of the House or the Senate majority leader.

This leadership can manifest itself at the federal level through policy and legislation by ensuring that revenue is generated and allocated for youth development; that the philanthropic and corporate communities have incentives to fund youth development; and that information is collected and gathered about youth development spending, utilization, and outcomes. Beyond these duties, the federal government can also take the lead in ensuring "real" coordination at all levels of government.

This leadership is needed to complement the leadership efforts in local communities like Baltimore; Milwaukee; Indianapolis; Albuquerque; and Hampton, Virginia, where foundations, elected leaders, academics, community organizations, and families are making strides in creating the ideal for their youth. Federal leadership could support state-level efforts in Hawaii, California, Maryland, and New York, where they are looking at new ways of collecting positive information about youth and finding creative mechanisms for funding youth development opportunities and supports for youth. And finally, federal leadership is needed to complement the efforts of a retired general who has come to realize that in order to give all youth a first chance we must build an infrastructure of supports and opportunities. Strong and effective public infrastructure requires significant public investment.

CONCLUSION

As the Center has investigated these issues concerning the cost and financing of youth development, we may have produced more questions than answers about how to increase public investment in our nation's youth. Nonetheless, we believe that these questions must be asked in order to provide developmental supports and opportunities for *all* youth.

To better educate youth advocates in both the public and private sectors as to the financial resources required to help all youth achieve positive outcomes, we explored the dollars and financing mechanisms that do and should exist for youth. Keeping our ideal of *youth development for all youth* in mind, the Center set out to investigate how current efforts measure up to the ideal and how we could move more confidently in the direction of that ideal.

Findings

Of the limited data and general information available on youth development services and spending, we were able to reaffirm the following observations:

- Spending is fragmented among a vast array of disparate government entities and is undertaken in the absence of a comprehensive strategy for youth;
- Spending is primarily for programs providing crisis intervention rather than development; and
- Spending primarily targets at-risk youth as opposed to all youth.

Moreover, we found the following to be potential root causes of these trends in spending:

- **Devaluation of adolescents.** A comprehensive strategy for all youth eludes us in part because policy makers and society as a whole focus a great deal less positive attention—and as a result fewer supports and opportunities—on adolescents than on younger children. Adolescents who are from poor and disenfranchised backgrounds face even greater obstacles to healthy development. Providing the supports our adolescents need will require a critical examination of and change in society's attitude toward them.
- **Lack of consensus on youth development.** Both the terminology and concept of youth development have yet to take widespread root in the policy and funding arenas. The use of the term itself is often inconsistent or unclear, which, among the other problems this causes, makes it difficult to translate the concept into more dollars for all youth.
- **Lack of integrated structure around services and funds for youth.** Fragmented programs and funding for youth must become more responsive to and accountable for all youth. This will only come about with a comprehensive and integrated strategy and structure grounded in developmental principles and practices.

- **Lack of adequate and protected funding.** Funds are not protected and dedicated in the manner necessary to sustain the long-term, comprehensive process that is youth development. Increased funds for youth development will be most effective only if they are adequate and secure.

In moving away from these circumstances and toward the ideal of adequate and secure funding for developmental supports and opportunities for all youth, we must seek ways to apply tangible and "fundable" numbers to our ideal. Through examination of the time and costs associated with youth in nonfamily, out-of-school circumstances, our estimate points to a cost of $3,060 per youth per year (1,200 hours) for providing youth development supports and opportunities to all school-age children and youth in the United States. This calculation provides a baseline sum of $144 billion. This figure may best be understood when it is broken into categories of time (see Table 5).

Table 5. *Category of Time (Annually)*

	Hours	Cost/Youth	Total Cost
After-school (3 P.M.-6 P.M. for 180 days)	720	$1,836	$86,488,639,272
Summer (6 hours per weekday for 8 weeks)	240	$612	$28,829,546,424
Other out-of-school time (school breaks, holidays, and weekends)	240	$612	$28,829,546,424
Total	**1,200**	**$3,060**	**$144,147,732,120**

Recommendations

The Center's method for devising such a baseline number is just one way this could be done. There needs to be further investigation and collaboration on applying more concrete costs and financing mechanisms to youth development.

At the same time, we must move toward the ideal by:

- **Seeking new types of information.** Information we need to move ahead includes data on youth development services and opportunities now in existence at local, state, and federal levels, and the costs associated with them; developmental indicators; and formulas and methods for calculating youth development costs.
- **Building on the after-school momentum.** Public attention to, and investment in, quality after-school opportunities for school-age youth could provide the necessary vehicle for increasing public understanding of, and commitment to, youth development on a larger scale.
- **Making a sustainable public investment.** Youth development is an investment that must be made by each sector of the wider community—public and private. Examination of federal-state matching, local dedicated taxes, and incentives for business and philanthropy could lead to models for providing adequate and sustainable funding for youth development.

Finally, we will be unable to reach our ideal of adequate and secure funding for developmental supports and opportunities for all youth without strong leadership. National intermediaries must work to cultivate this leadership at all levels of government, and at the grass roots, by creating constituencies. Ultimately, these leaders and constituents are the only ones who can bring about increased public investment and commitment to youth development.

NOTES

1. P.L. 105-178, passed June 9, 1996.
2. National Center for Education Statistics at http://nces.ed.gov/fastfacts.
3. A more current time analysis was recently presented in Public/Private Ventures' *Support for Youth*. Although a bit different from these two graphs, it is consistent with the figures presented.
4. It could be argued that 50 percent is questionable. Surely some families spend more time with their youth than do others, but for the sake of these calculations, we will use this figure.
5. Although Big Brothers Big Sisters uses volunteers, P/PV determined that it cost approximately $1,000 to train, develop a match, and supervise a volunteer, disproving the myth that volunteers are free. Cited from Tierney et al., p. 52.
6. Cited from "The Cost of Doing the Teen Outreach Program, Cornerstone Consulting, p. 1.
7. Cited from The After-School Corporation organization overview, p. 10.
8. Cited from Stern, p. 21.
9. Cited from Stern, p. 29.
10. www.childrensdefense.org.
11. Personal communication with Nancy Sconyers, director of NACA's Multi-State Budget Watch Project.
12. These Baltimore figures are lower than those used earlier. The earlier figures are based on the costs of the programs highlighted. In reality, all levels of government will have to make their own determination of the real costs of youth development.

REFERENCES

Alter, Jonathan
1998 "Long After the Trumpets." *Newsweek,* May 11, p. 41.
The Annie E. Casey Foundation
1998 *Kids Count Data Book.* Baltimore: The Annie E. Casey Foundation.
Carnegie Corporation of New York
1992 *A Matter of Time: Risk and Opportunity in the Nonschool Hours.* New York: Carnegie Council on Adolescent Development.
Cornerstone Consulting
1997 *The Cost of Doing the Teen Outreach Program—Sample Case Study from the Field: Roanoke, Virginia.* Houston: Cornerstone Consulting.
Dryfoos, Joy G.
1998 *Safe Passage: Making It through Adolescence in a Risky Society.* New York: Oxford University Press.
Feister, L., E.R. Reisner, C. Marzke, and A.M. Castle
1999 *Executive Summary of the Preliminary Report of Beating the Odds from 3-6pm: Evaluation Results from the TASC After-School Program's First Year.* Washington, D.C.: Policy Studies Associates.
Gold, Steven, and Deborah Ellwood
1994 *Spending and Revenue For Children's Programs.* Washington, D.C.: The Finance Project.
Johnson, Dirk
1998 "When Money Is Everything, Except Hers." *New York Times,* October 14, p. A1.
Lopez, Naomi
1998 *The State of Children: What Parents Should Know about Government's Efforts to Assist Children.* San Francisco: Pacific Research Institute for Public Policy.
Motley, Isolde
1998 *Life,* July, Vol. 21, Issue 8, p. 10.

National League of Cities
1997 *New Directions for Cities, Families, and Children: Financing Municipal Policies and Programs for Children and Youth.* Washington, D.C.: National League of Cities.

Pittman, Karen J., Ray O'Brien, and Mary Kimball
1993 *Youth Development and Resiliency Research: Making Connections to Substance Abuse Prevention.* New York: Center for Youth Development and Policy Research/Academy for Educational Development.

Pittman, Karen J., and Shepherd Zeldin
1994 *From Deterrence to Development: Putting Programs for Young African-American Males in Perspective.* Washington, D.C.: The Urban Institute.

Stern, Leonard W.
1992 *Funding Patterns of Nonprofit Organizations That Provide Youth Development Services: An Exploratory Study.* A report prepared for the Task Force on Youth Development and Community Programs of the Carnegie Council on Adolescent Development.

Tierney, Joseph P., and Jean Baldwin Grossman, with Nancy L. Resch
1995 *Making a Difference: An Impact Study of Big Brothers/Big Sisters.* Philadelphia: Public/Private Ventures.

Warren, Constancia, with Prudence Brown, and Nicolas Freudenberg
1999 *Evaluation of the New York City Beacons—Summary of Phase I Findings.* New York: Academy for Educational Development, Inc., with Chapin Hall Center for Children at the University of Chicago and Hunter College Center on AIDS, Drugs and Community Health.

APPENDIX A. THE COST OF YOUTH DEVELOPMENT IN THE FIFTY STATES

(1,200 hours per year at $2.55 per hour = $3,060 per year per youth)

States	School-Age Population (6-17 yrs. old)	Annual Cost of Youth Development (,000,000)	States	School-Age Population (6-17 yrs. old)	Annual Cost of Youth Development (,000,000)
Alabama	796,211	$2,436	Montana	174,664	$534
Alaska	123,947	$379	Nebraska	313,876	$960
Arizona	826,085	$2,528	Nevada	278,130	$851
Arkansas	471,143	$1,442	New Hampshire	198,306	$607
California	5,594,626	$17,120	New Jersey	1,267,781	$3,879
Colorado	700,477	$2,143	New Mexico	353,295	$1,081
Connecticut	496,985	$1,521	New York	2,911,622	$8,910
Delaware	121,176	$371	North Carolina	1,248,673	$3,821
District of Columbia	66,842	$205	North Dakota	123,711	$379
Florida	2,206,101	$6,751	Ohio	2,008,464	$6,146
Georgia	1,383,379	$4,233	Oklahoma	621,966	$1,903
Hawaii	203,243	$622	Oregon	578,590	$1,770
Idaho	264,079	$808	Pennsylvania	1,951,549	$5,972
Illinois	2,106,369	$6,445	Rhode Island	149,760	$458
Indiana	1,084,840	$3,320	South Carolina	690,247	$2,112
Iowa	518,548	$1,587	South Dakota	146,075	$447
Kansas	474,251	$1,451	Tennessee	946,741	$2,897
Kentucky	724,997	$2,218	Texas	3,836,373	$11,739
Louisiana	888,304	$2,718	Utah	531,475	$1,626
Maine	215,897	$661	Vermont	102,222	$313
Maryland	822,447	$2,517	Virginia	1,121,226	$3,431
Massachusetts	913,843	$2,796	Washington	995,430	$3,046
Michigan	1,784,539	$5,461	West Virginia	329,498	$1,008
Minnesota	863,972	$2,644	Wisconsin	947,285	$2,899
Mississippi	564,514	$1,727	Wyoming	101,546	$311
Missouri	961,782	$2,943			

Source for Population and Households: The Right Site—Easy Analytic Software, Inc. (EASI).

A Matter of Money

APPENDIX A (cont.). THE COST OF YOUTH DEVELOPMENT IN THE FIFTY MOST POPULOUS CITIES

(1,200 hours per year at $2.55 per hour = $3,060 per year per youth)

States	School-Age Population (6-17 yrs. old)	Annual Cost of Youth Development (,000,000)	States	School-Age Population (6-17 yrs. old)	Annual Cost of Youth Development (,000,000)
Albuquerque, NM	$79,765	$244	Milwaukee, WI	100,887	$309
Atlanta, GA	65,535	$201	Minneapolis, MN	47,206	$144
Austin, TX	93,826	$287	Nashville-Davidson, TN	85,066	$260
Baltimore, MD	105,915	$324	New Orleans, LA	87,682	$268
Boston, MA	67,670	$207	New York, NY	1,149,524	$3,518
Buffalo, NY	47,630	$146	Oakland, CA	57,291	$175
Charlotte, NC	75,249	$230	Oklahoma City, OK	85,290	$261
Chicago, IL	461,572	$1,412	Omaha, NE	64,485	$197
Cincinnati, OH	61,292	$188	Philadelphia, PA	237,157	$726
Cleveland, OH	80,315	$246	Phoenix, AZ	212,937	$652
Columbus, OH	111,808	$342	Pittsburgh, PA	47,323	$145
Dallas, TX	181,462	$555	Portland, OR	75,957	$232
Denver, CO	79,132	$242	Sacramento, CA	67,893	$208
Detroit, MI	194,457	$595	San Antonio, TX	213,113	$652
El Paso, TX	139,413	$427	San Diego, CA	192,854	$590
Fort Worth, TX	87,667	$268	San Francisco, CA	80,884	$248
Fresno, CA	80,882	$247	San Jose, CA	138,717	$424
Honolulu, HI	52,085	$159	Seattle, WA	66,248	$203
Houston, TX	345,841	$1,058	St. Louis, MO	58,813	$180
Indianapolis, IN	129,754	$397	Toledo, OH	57,306	$175
Jacksonville, FL	120,420	$368	Tucson, AZ	80,871	$247
Kansas City, MO	74,066	$227	Tulsa, OK	64,865	$198
Long Beach, CA	72,508	$222	Virginia Beach, VA	79,363	$243
Los Angeles, CA	582,414	$1,782	Washington, DC	66,842	$205
Memphis, TN	117,335	$359			
Miami, FL	62,771	$192			

APPENDIX B. MINNESOTA: PARTICIPATION AND AGES IN YOUTH DEVELOPMENT AND SERVICE (IN %)

Program	Offered By			Participant Ages			
	Community Groups	Schools	Community Education	5-8	9-12	13-15	16-18
Youth Service and Service-Learning							
Peer Tutoring	11	82	35	43	61	73	76
Peer Helpers	9	73	27	24	43	67	71
Work w/Children	31	48	59	30	40	55	58
Work w/Elderly	37	54	46	30	46	53	53
Hunger Relief	41	51	30	33	43	56	52
Environmental	42	65	39	47	59	65	61
Peer Mediations	16	70	20	30	51	60	52
Other	4	6	6	5	5	7	1
Youth Involvement and Leadership							
Civic Groups	31	45	20	5	15	38	49
Serv/Ldrsp Prog	41	70	49	16	41	67	71
Ldrsp Dev For Gr	33	57	37	14	36	59	61
Youth Clubs	74	36	33	65	75	76	71
Other	3	6	5	1	2	6	8
Youth Enrichment Activities							
Sport	62	81	79	80	83	81	79
Wellness/Fitness	44	70	73	61	67	73	72
Visual Arts	35	70	67	61	68	69	64
Performing Arts	55	77	74	73	83	84	78
Education Clubs	13	68	32	28	42	59	59
Other	0	4	6	5	6	5	5
Youth Community Career Connections							
Career Awareness	25	84	33	16	34	70	79
Career Counseling	10	79	11	5	12	52	75
Internships	11	37	9	0	1	11	35
Career Mentors	15	47	12	0	3	22	45
Voc Ed Clubs	5	47	2	0	2	24	44
Work Experience	16	74	19	1	3	29	73
Apprenticeships	8	22	6	0	0	5	2
Other	1	2	2	0	0	2	3
Youth Support Network or Services							
Parent Involvement	44	75	69	67	67	69	67
Adult Mentors	26	34	25	23	31	36	33
Chem Abuse Prev	51	83	47	58	75	81	82
Dropout Prev	20	63	18	13	25	54	59
Teen Preg Support	42	57	26	5	17	59	64
Family Crisis Couns	52	48	13	48	53	58	59
Indiv Crisis Couns	40	35	9	32	39	47	47
Other	3	4	2	2	3	3	2

Cited from *Community Education Youth Development/Youth Service 1997 Report* (Minnesota Department of Children, Families and Learning Community Education and Minnesota Commission on National and Community Service).

A Matter of Money

APPENDIX C. YOUTHBUDGET: SPENDING ON YOUTH IN CENTRAL INDIANA

Spending by Purpose and Source: All Counties

Purpose	0-4 Preschool	5-9 Elementary School	10-15 Middle School	16-18 High School	Total
Alcohol & Other Drug Abuse	187,775	273,412	150,999	92,971	705,157
Basic Skills & Workforce Development	37,412	122,062	2,386,999	2,265,682	4,812,155
Child Care	16,261,621	16,396,696	1,604,556	112,052	34,374,925
Child & Youth Development	923,926	4,395,683	5,694,569	3,290,032	14,304,211
Education	8,124,251	476,011,035	529,973,236	256,575,680	1,270,684,202
Family Abuse & Violence	1,122,811	1,083,057	1,227,228	601,688	4,034,784
Health & Well-Being	45,662,335	63,912,148	39,059,772	19,375,183	168,009,439
Individual & Family Support	24,735,032	24,049,559	24,410,188	12,286,312	85,481,091
Juvenile Justice & Child Welfare	16,124,306	16,695,864	26,461,081	15,533,554	74,814,805
Support for People with Disabilities	16,413,078	2,855,549	2,408,971	1,160,553	22,838,151
Teen Parenting	27,644	0	142,645	296,866	467,154
Total	129,620,192	605,795,065	633,520,243	311,590,573	1,680,526,073

Spending by Purpose and Source: All Counties

Purpose	Federal	State	Local	Foundation and UW	Total
Alcohol & Other Drug Abuse	313,993	362,474	0	28,690	705,157
Basic Skills & Workforce Development	4,582,130	0	0	230,025	4,812,155
Child Care	32,665,155	593,169	0	1,116,601	34,374,925
Child & Youth Development	581,574	179,154	2,403,149	11,140,333	14,304,210
Education	35,188,211	1,229,560,197	0	5,935,794	1,270,684,202
Family Abuse & Violence	1,728,627	218,236	1,416,878	671,043	4,034,784
Health & Well-Being	167,192,311	149,832	429,590	237,706	168,009,439
Individual & Family Support	83,821,556	106,019	0	1,553,516	85,481,091
Juvenile Justice & Child Welfare	56,271,262	8,196,414	9,717,354	629,775	74,814,805
Support for People with Disabilities	16,258,030	5,719,639	0	860,482	22,838,151
Teen Parenting	44,603	0	0	422,551	467,154
Total	398,647,452	1,245,085,134	13,966,971	22,826,516	1,680,526,073

Cited from *Public and Philanthropic Spending on Children and Youth in Central Indiana* (November 1997, D. Bonnet Associates).

APPENDIX D. EXAMPLES OF CITIES THAT USE A DEDICATED TAX FOR CHILDREN

City	Type of Dedicated Tax	Contact
Albany, California	A library tax is levied as a special property tax to extend library hours and services to offset cuts in library services by the County. (Library Services Act of 1994 Ordinance No. 94-06.) Fund generates about $250,000.	Assistant to the City Administrator, 510/528-5710
Albuquerque, New Mexico	A portion of a dedicated municipal Quality of Life Tax was used to fund Child Development Centers. The tax has been sunsetted, but there has been an increase in the amount allocated by the city since then.	Director, Dept. of Family and Community Services, 505/768-3000
Ames, Iowa	A Local Option Tax supports a subsidy to child care centers for low- and middle-income families.	Mayor, 515/239-5106
Chandler, Arizona	By 1993 Executive Order, $400,000 per year from the city's sales tax (.5%) is used to fund the Youth Enhancement Program. The money is derived from increased funds projected to be received as a result of a city sales tax increase. The Fund is administered by the United Way.	Recreation Superintendent, 602/786-2485

Cited from National League of Cities, *New Directions for Cities, Families, and Children* (1997, pp. 6-7).

A Matter of Money

APPENDIX D (cont.). EXAMPLES OF CITIES THAT USE A DEDICATED TAX FOR CHILDREN

City	Type of Dedicated Tax	Contact
Freeport, Illinois	A portion of the food and beverage tax established in 1993 is used for children and family programs (Chapter 882-Food and Beverage Privilege Tax). Taxes are levied on alcoholic beverages at retail stores and on beverages or prepared food in any retail food facility. $.02 of every $1 taxed is used to fund a food pantry, a community clinic, early childhood centers, a drug and alcohol commission, and a coalition for a safe community.	Mayor, 815/235-8200
Greensboro, North Carolina	A dedicated municipal tax for the Greensboro Housing Partnership Fund passed in 1988. One cent of every $100 levied in property tax is allocated for the exclusive use of housing. It generates about $1.3 million per fiscal year.	Director of Housing and Community Development, 910/373-2349
Kent, Washington	In 1989, a mandatory funding base for human services was established. The City Council adopted Resolution No. 1205, which mandates that 1% of the city's General Fund be designated as a Human Services Fund through which dollars are distributed to nonprofit agencies that serve families and children.	Human Services Planner, 206/850-4789
Madison, Alabama	A .5-mill property tax for a library fund for construction of the Madison Public Library was created in 1989 by referendum. It generates $65,000-$70,000 per year. (Resolution No. 89-23-R.)	Finance Department, 205/772-5600

APPENDIX D (cont.). EXAMPLES OF CITIES THAT USE A DEDICATED TAX FOR CHILDREN

City	Type of Dedicated Tax	Contact
Manhattan, Kansas	Use of 1.5 mill of property tax for social services was begun in 1988. This year's funding is about $130,000. A Social Service Advisory Board oversees the use of the funds and the development of programs to meet social service needs of the community.	Assistant City Manager, 913/537-0056
Modesto, California	A Park and Recreation Facilities Fund is generated from a bedroom tax on each dwelling unit constructed. Started in 1965 to improve and expand parks, playground and recreation facilities, each unit is taxed $15 for the first bedroom and $5 for each additional bedroom not to exceed $30. It generates $20,000 per year.	Recreation Superintendent, 209/491-5902
Muskegon, Michigan	A city income tax was created in 1993. The City Commission promised that part of the levied tax would be put toward the services the citizens wanted, one of which was a city recreation program.	Director of Leisure Services, 616/724-6704
Oakland, California	Recently passed Measure "K," which amends the city charter to establish the Oakland Children's Fund. It designates 2.5% of the city's budget to children and families' programs, and establishes a 19-member Planning and Oversight Committee for planning, oversight, and evaluation of the use of the funds.	Mayor, 510/238-3611

APPENDIX D (cont.). EXAMPLES OF CITIES THAT USE A DEDICATED TAX FOR CHILDREN

City	Type of Dedicated Tax	Contact
Pasadena, California	Residents have approved a property tax to support library services beginning in 1993. It first passed with 79% support. More recently it garnered 86.5% of the vote.	Library Director, 818/405-3867
Portland, Texas	A half-cent sales tax for a community center was passed by ballot in 1993. Revenues aid in paying the debt service on the bond issue the city granted.	Park and Recreation Director, 512/777-3301
Roanoke, Virginia	A dedicated municipal tax on cigarettes was used to finance construction and renovation of a juvenile justice system facility.	Director of Human Development, 540/981-2302
Roswell, New Mexico	The city levies a cigarette tax specifically for youth programming. It usually generates $45,000-$50,000 a year.	Recreation Director, 505/624-6720
Scottsboro, Alabama	A one-cent sales tax dedicated to building and renovating high schools was created by an ordinance of the City Council in 1995 (Ordinance No. 394). It raised $2 million in its first year.	Mayor, 205/574-4510
Seattle, Washington	The city voters passed a Families and Education Levy, raising $8.5 million a year for seven years for children and family support services.	Family and Youth Director, 206/386-1010
South Holland, Illinois	In addition to all other village taxes, special taxes from property millage are dedicated to an array of funds that include a recreation fund, a library fund, and a drug education fund.	Assistant to the Mayor, 708/210-2900

APPENDIX D (cont.). EXAMPLES OF CITIES THAT USE A DEDICATED TAX FOR CHILDREN

City	Type of Dedicated Tax	Contact
Springfield, Missouri	A one-mill property tax earmarks $.11 of every $100 for public health centers that provide child health and immunization clinics. This year it has brought in $1.2 million.	Director of Public Health and Welfare, 417/864-1657

5 THE SCIENTIFIC FOUNDATIONS OF YOUTH DEVELOPMENT

Peter L. Benson and Rebecca N. Saito

In this chapter, we examine the status of youth development research and propose the kind of scientific work needed to responsibly advance the field. At the most general level, the term *youth development* connotes a focus on supporting or promoting, during the second decade of life, the positive developmental processes that are known or assumed to advance health and well-being. These processes include such multidimensional domains as competence, mastery, positive identity, resilience, caring, connection, and belonging.

Youth development is sometimes characterized as "the other side of the coin," that is, complementary to a risk-reduction or deficit-reduction paradigm that accents naming and reducing obstacles to positive human development (e.g., poverty, family violence, victimization, abuse, neglect, negative peer or adult influence). Youth development as an approach moves in the direction of naming and promoting core positive developmental processes, opportunities, and experiences.

The opportunities and resources that promote positive youth development have been categorized in many different ways: primary and secondary supports and services (Wynn et al., 1994); formal, informal, and nonformal programs, places, and opportunities (Saito et al., 1995); structured and unstructured time use (Carnegie Council on Adolescent Development, 1992); and asset-building communities (Benson et al., 1998), to name but a few. Each of these frameworks has played a role in building the theoretical foundations for understanding the many ways to promote the healthy development of children and youth.

Youth development occurs in a wide range of settings. This review suggests that there are four primary settings in which youth development principles are applied and in which youth development can and does occur. These four move from the specific to the general and are not necessarily discrete categories. They are:

- **Programs.** These are semistructured processes, most often led by adults and designed to address specific goals and youth outcomes. A program can be considered a youth development program when it *intentionally* incorporates experiences and learnings to address and advance the positive development of children and youth. This category incorporates a range of programs from those that are highly structured, often in the form of curriculum with step-by-step guidelines, to those that may have a looser structure but incorporate a clear focus on one or more youth development activities (e.g., service learning). Schools, national voluntary youth organizations, and community-based organizations are primary, but not exclusive, delivery systems.

- **Organizations.** This category includes "place-based" youth development opportunities, i.e., settings in which a wide variety of activities and relationships occur that are designed to improve the well-being of children and youth. Using the definition offered by Costello, Toles, Spielberger, and Wynn, these are "structures in which people and resources are coordinated for a definite purpose" (1998, p. 2). Examples include school-based after-school recreation and cocurricular activities, Parks and Recreation centers and leagues, community centers, amateur sports leagues, faith-based youth development opportunities, and the myriad places and opportunities developed by community-based and national youth organizations (e.g., YMCA, YWCA, Girl Scouts, Boy Scouts). These kinds of settings can mobilize a wide range of formal and informal youth development inputs.
- **Socializing systems.** Youth are embedded in an important array of complex and omnipresent systems intended to enhance processes and outcomes consonant with youth development principles. These include schools, families, neighborhoods, religious institutions, museums, and libraries.
- **Community.** This is the most general of the four categories, the most difficult to define, and perhaps the most potentially powerful source of youth development. For now, we use the concept of community to include not only the geographic place within which programs, organizations, and systems intersect, but also the social norms, resources, relationships, and informal settings that can dramatically inform human development, both directly and indirectly.

In defining a science of youth development, we need to know which of these four settings we are addressing. Although there are some scientific issues that inform all of them (e.g., the conceptualization of developmental targets, the conceptualization and measurement of outcomes), each setting presents unique theoretical and evaluation demands.

OVERVIEW OF CURRENT RESEARCH

This section presents an overview of illustrative research, seeking less to catalog all current research and more to set the stage for enumerating the scientific issues each raises.

Programs

Most scientific work on youth development programs has concerned the evaluation of impact; indeed, it is the youth development setting that is most amenable to evaluations using a classic experimental design.

Recently, the Social Development Research Group at the University of Washington completed an important meta-analysis of 25 program evaluations that met specific criteria related to program content and standards (Catalano et al., 1998). The program criteria include a focus on promoting competencies and social, emotional, or cognitive development; the target population is youth aged 6 to 20. Program evaluations were required to show significant effects using a strong research design with comparison groups and to measure behavioral outcomes.

Some of the outcomes these programs improved were self-control, assertiveness, problem solving, interpersonal skills, social acceptance, school achievement, completion of school work, graduation rates, parental trust, self-efficacy, and self-esteem. At the same time, in some studies, data showed a decrease in such negative outcomes as alcohol, tobacco, and other drug use; hitting, carrying weapons, and vehicle theft; school failure, skipping classes, and school suspensions; negative family events; and teen pregnancy.

Among the early researchers who studied the impact of positive youth development were Conrad and Hedin (1981), who studied youth participants in a variety of experiential education programs. Their sample consisted of 4,000 adolescents in 30 programs, surveyed pre- and post-program. Six programs had comparison groups composed of students in nonexperiential programs. Students in the treatment group demonstrated improvement in personal and social development, moral reasoning, self-esteem, and attitudes toward community service and involvement.

A few other quasi-experimental studies of service-learning programs, which include treatment and comparison groups with pre- and post-tests, show improvement in ego and moral development (Cognetta and Sprinthall, 1978), and sense of social responsibility and competence (Newman and Rutter, 1983).

Organizations

Research on organizations with a youth development accent tends to address both the evaluation of impact *and* the question of access. Wynn et al. (1987) describe 22 studies on the impact of community supports on adolescents, including a summary of the sample, the measures used, whether control or comparison groups were used, analytic methods, and significant findings. The Carnegie Council on Adolescent Development (1992) issued a report titled *A Matter of Time* in which four evaluations of community youth organizations are reviewed. Quinn (1995) reviewed several studies in which participation in extracurricular community service and national voluntary organizations appears to promote prosocial behavior and reduce high-risk behaviors. Leffert et al. (1996) review studies related to seven organization types (sports and recreation, camps, service, mentoring, drop-in centers, school-to-work, and support for teen parents).

In one of the more comprehensive syntheses of the scientific literature on adolescent development, Scales and Leffert (1999) include a section on studies related to constructive use of time, including participation in youth organizations. Some of the outcomes they describe are associated with involvement in youth development settings. They include:

- Increased self-esteem, increased popularity, increased sense of personal control, and enhanced identity development;
- Better development of such life skills as leadership and speaking in public, decision making, and increased dependability and job responsibility;
- Greater communication in the family;
- Fewer psychosocial problems, such as loneliness, shyness, and hopelessness;
- Decreased involvement in risky behaviors, such as drug use, and decreased juvenile delinquency;
- Increased academic achievement; and
- Increased safety.

Most of the studies and evaluations conducted to date and cited in these reviews do not use experimental or quasi-experimental research designs, but instead marshal an important array of correlational and anecdotal evidence.

Many of the evaluations of youth development organizations focus on a particular program of curriculum, such as the evaluation of Boys & Girls Clubs of America's alcohol and other drug abuse prevention program called SMART Moves (Boys & Girls Clubs of America, 1991). This evaluation included five public housing sites, each with two control groups: one public housing site without a Boys & Girls Club and one public housing site with a Boys & Girls Club that did not use SMART Moves. Of particular interest to us as we explore the evidence of impact by youth development organizations, this study found that Boys & Girls Clubs appeared to have a positive impact on youth (and adults) in public housing sites, regardless of whether they used the SMART Moves initiative. These outcomes include a reduction in alcohol and drug use, drug-related crimes, and drug trafficking.

Ladewig and Thomas (1987) conducted telephone interviews with a stratified random sample of U.S. adults who were grouped into three categories: former 4-H members (N = 709), former members of other voluntary youth organizations (N = 743), and nonparticipants (N = 309). Adults who had participated in voluntary youth organizations, including 4-H, attained higher education levels and were more likely to be involved in civic and community service, be employed, and report higher incomes than were nonparticipants.

An important line of inquiry seeks to document how much access American youth have to organizations and programs that—at least theoretically—have a youth development intent or legacy.

Estimates of participation in formal youth development organizations range from about half to nearly three-quarters of youth. Quinn (1995) reviews data from the 1988 National Education Longitudinal Study in which 71 percent of the 25,000 eighth graders in their national sample participated in some form of structured youth program outside of school. Participation in national voluntary youth organizations (e.g., Boys & Girls Clubs, 4-H, Scouts, "Ys" or other youth groups) makes up the largest category (50%), followed by nonschool team sports (37%), religious youth groups (34%), summer programs (19%), and hobby clubs (15%). Data from a sample of 99,462 youth in grades 6 through 12 in 213 U.S. cities and towns indicate participation in structured youth organizations by 59 percent of youth (Benson et al., 1998). Participation appears to peak at about eighth grade, and remains relatively high until eleventh grade, when participation decreases.

Youth in urban areas, particularly those whose families have lower incomes, have less access to (National Commission on Children, 1991) and lower participation in (National Center for Education Statistics, 1990) formal youth development organizations. Youth of color also have lower participation rates than do their Caucasian cohorts (National Center for Education Statistics, 1990; Saito et al., 1995).

In Minneapolis, in an effort to strategically advance access to youth development organizations, youth ages 7 to 14 were asked through surveys and focus groups to identify activities and dynamics they would most like to access (Saito et al., 1995). The following are among the key findings:

- Seventy-seven percent voiced interest in increasing access to gyms and recreation centers where the environment provides a safe place to gather with friends, with an accent on informal rather than formal dynamics. The theme, as stated by one interviewee:

    I want a place where you feel comfortable, a place that's familiar, a place where you know the people there, a place where you can come and go, and not have to stay the whole time and do only what the staff tells you to do.

- Sixty-five percent of youth said they would like more contact with an adult they can trust and who respects them;
- Fifty-nine percent said they would like to spend more time with their parents or guardians; and
- Forty-seven percent said they would like to have an older teenage or adult mentor.

There has been little documentation or evaluation of these kinds of more informal youth opportunities. These settings, which fall somewhere in the program-to-organization continuum, are often called "safe places" in the research and policy literature. These are semistructured and loosely supervised places (e.g., open gyms, drop-in centers, parks) where young people can go and spontaneously choose from a variety of activities. Halpern (1992) underscores the importance of safe places for young people to gather, where some modicum of supervision and structure is available, particularly for inner-city youth.

These places, opportunities, and relationships hold great but untapped potential as sources of positive youth development. They are most likely to occur in neighborhoods or smaller communities of place or association. Relatively little is known about levels or impact of participation in these informal resources because systems of monitoring and evaluating their impact do not exist.

Socializing Systems

It can be argued that most of the scientific work on youth development occurs around the program and organizational dimensions. Most of the policy work, too, is devoted to strengthening and expanding youth development through program and organizational vehicles.

When we expand to socializing systems and community, we move from specific settings and places constructed to deliver on youth development targets to complex entities where youth development becomes an approach or philosophy designed to inform, reform, or transform existing systems. Included here are schools, religious congregations, public safety and courts, neighborhoods, employers, and families. There are, we will argue, a growing number of social scientists and practitioners who seek to draw youth development perspectives into these important spheres of developmental influence. For example, a number of middle school reform initiatives are premised wholly or in part on mobilizing the climate, norms, and relationships of schools to better meet developmental needs (Connell, 1996; Scales, 1996). Uniting Congregations for Youth Development, a multiyear, multisite pilot project supported by the DeWitt Wallace-Reader's Digest Fund, sought to equip congregational leaders to both transform congregational environments around core youth development principles (e.g., empowerment, intergenerational relationships, skill and competence building) and unite congregations of all faith traditions within a city to trigger and support community-wide youth development initiatives (Roehlkepartain, 1998). Other efforts are emerging to draw youth development principles and strategies into a wide range of other systems, including neighborhoods, park and recreation departments, city and county government, and employers.

Our intent here is not to synthesize what is being learned from these system transformation efforts but to enumerate how such work informs the scientific agenda for youth development. More will be said about this after a brief discussion of community-based youth development initiatives. For now, however, let us note that system-changing approaches to youth development demand scientific attention to conceptualizing inputs (e.g., norms, climate, relationships, informal and formal curricula, symbols, ritual), defining change indicators, and expanding evaluation methods.

Community Initiatives

Youth development as an approach or philosophy now informs a rapidly increasing number of community initiatives as well as state-based and regional mobilizations designed to orchestrate multiple local efforts. These initiatives are literally everywhere.

Applications of the varied concepts of community are now common in a number of applied areas, including alcohol and other drug use prevention (Hawkins and Catalano, 1992), student learning and achievement (Comer, 1997; Epstein, 1996), and health promotion (Walberg et al., 1997). The theme running through these community-based theoretical and action formulations is the assumption that both child and adolescent well-being require the engagement and participation of multiple community forces and sectors. Recent studies have helped to define several of the dimensions of this engagement. The initial publication of the National Longitudinal Study of Adolescent Health (Resnick et al., 1997) concludes that youth's connectedness to such multiple support networks as family, school, and community serves as an important protective factor across multiple domains, including emotional health, violence, substance use, and sexuality.

In an analysis of the variability of violent crime in 343 Chicago neighborhoods, Sampson, Raudenbush, and Earls (1997) suggest that the level of social cohesion within neighborhoods, combined with the level of shared commitment to take action when what is understood as the common good is threatened, is strongly linked to rates of violence, beyond what is accounted for by demographic factors like income and residential stability. What is particularly germane is that the definition of the common good—the glue that unites neighbors in shared purpose and action—has to do with the welfare of neighborhood children.

Community as an analytical and applied construct holds high promise. However, efforts to mobilize and sustain the engagement of multiple community systems and energy face considerable obstacles (Center for the Study of Social Policy, 1995). Community is, of course, a complex construct that occasionally is touted as a panacea for most social and human problems. Some of this potential extension of the concept may be caused by relatively recent efforts to conceptualize the dimensions and dynamics of community that inform human development. Some of the current interest in community may reflect a growing despair about the efficacy of more historical approaches to changing problematic trends in child and adolescent health outcomes, which typically viewed the individual child or adolescent as the appropriate target of change (Dryfoos, 1990). For a variety of reasons, then, there appears to be a kind of cultural readiness to explore community-based approaches to human development and a demand to deepen the inquiry into how knowledge of the influence of the community can be translated into effective community change efforts.

One of the driving forces behind community-based youth development initiatives is the relatively new thinking about the cumulative effect of exposure to multiple youth development resources and inputs. Consonant with the well-demonstrated "pileup" effect of risk factors related to negative health indicators is an emerging body of work on the "pileup" of protective factors. Benson and his colleagues (1998) show that as the number of developmental assets increase, risk behavior patterns decrease and thriving behaviors (e.g., school success, affirmation of diversity, prosocial behavior) increase. Similarly, Jessor et al. (1995) document that increases in the number of protective factors cause several problem behaviors to decrease. This evidence of the predictive power of redundancy (i.e., engagement in multiple systems and places attentive to developmental inputs and resources) encourages the pursuit of initiatives designed to mobilize multiple settings and actors. More often than not, "community" becomes the conceptual tool for such multisector mobilization.

Setting the Stage

In proposing the key scientific issues for advancing the practice and effectiveness of youth development, we recognize that the terrain includes, at an elementary level, all four of the settings we have just described (i.e., programs, organizations, systems, community). Each is an important sphere of youth development influence. This expansive view of youth development has important scientific and practical implications. The following chart shows a set of dimensions defined by the sphere of influence under discussion.

	Spheres of Youth Development Influence			
Dimension	Program	Organization	System	Community
Theoretical complexity	Less		→	More
Complexity of implementation strategies	Less		→	More
Time needed to implement change	Less		→	More
Evaluation complexity	Less		→	More
Length of time needed to observe real change	Less		→	More

Practical and scientific complexity increase as we move along the continuum of spheres from program to community. This presents a major problem for youth development and the evolution of its scientific foundations. There is considerable political, policy, and funding pressure in the United States when it comes to initiatives focused on children and adolescents to (a) demonstrate effect and (b) do so in a short time frame. Such pressure tends, as a practical matter, to favor action at the less complex program and organizational levels and the utilization of classic experimental methods that can show experimental and control group differences. These two pressures feed each other: programs are amenable to the scientific method; the scientific method is best applied to programs and much less so to the system or community spheres.

As we move to an exploration of what a science of youth development should look like, we firmly stand on the expansive side. We advocate that the pursuit of knowledge about the more complex arenas of system and community change is as important, if not more so, than is the pursuit of knowledge about programs. Efforts that work to broaden the purpose of youth programs and organizations to include community change and development certainly move us in the right direction. Some now argue that in the long run *understanding and effecting system and community change will do more developmental good for more youth than will a focus on the proliferation of programs.* Underneath this assumption lies the ultimate scientific question: If we are to move the developmental needle forward for American youth, where should we focus our resources and energy?

RATIONALE FOR BUILDING THE SCIENTIFIC FOUNDATIONS OF YOUTH DEVELOPMENT

Youth development as an approach to action and practice has high face validity among practitioners working in such settings as schools, agencies, and youth-serving organizations. Practice, we would argue, is considerably ahead of the scientific foundations of this work. As we review the research literature, we find kernels of encouragement for establishing youth development as a viable approach. But we see little evidence of the kind of systematic inquiry necessary to guide, shape, refine, and fuel the approach.

One could argue that youth development is now at the crossroads faced earlier by the prevention field. In about 1970, prevention became an approach that generated programs, professions, and professionals. Issues of accountability emerged, and now that field is undergirding its work with what is becoming known as prevention science (Morrissey et al., 1997). The fact that prevention science exists as a unifying area of inquiry, and because this work claims a deeper research base than does youth development, prevention—and the allied concepts of deficit and risk reduction—takes the scientific and moral high road in policy discussions of what works. And that translates into funding.

Hence, it is in youth development's best interest to advance a science of youth development. Science matters in American policy circles, and although this may be a cultural bias, it is the way it is. But there are other compelling reasons to advance scientific foundations. Among these are the importance of learning how to increase the effectiveness of what we often call the "people, places, and opportunities" of youth development; of discerning how to take effective practice to scale; of advancing the sustainability of good and effective work; and in informing the training of youth development practitioners.

One issue we want to highlight here is the relative lack of people and places doing research on issues germane to youth development. The potential power of the youth development paradigm is not matched by a like commitment to and investment in research. What we seem to have here is an example of the classic split between theory and application. If the field is about practice, it is too soft, too "second class" to warrant academic attention, just as sociology divorces itself from social work and "pure" psychology pushes clinical psychology to the other side of the campus. We do not know how to fix this. But academic fields like child and adolescent development tend not to help us much in understanding the people, places, and opportunities that shape lives. What, after all, do we really know about the impact or possibility of Little Leagues, parks and recreation, bands, orchestras, dance, drama, ceremony, family rituals, middle school athletic teams, libraries, museums, natural intergenerational community, congregational programs, working at a Burger King, shopping malls, people on the street, conversations across the backyard fence, service learning, national and community-based youth organizations, or summer camps? What do we know about these individually—and perhaps more important—in combination?

The answer, of course, is "not enough." University-based departments and scholars underplay the real-world settings we seek to mobilize. This translates into a missed opportunity, an underutilized resource for strengthening the underpinnings of the youth development field. In any review of where we are as a field, with few exceptions, the following two facts dominate:

1. Most academics will not "play" in the field of youth development; and
2. A disproportionate ratio of the scientific work (research and evaluation) is conducted by intermediary nonprofits (e.g., Search Institute, P/PV, Academy for Educational Development [AED]) or university-affiliated centers of applied research (e.g., Chapin Hall Center for Children).

It would be advantageous to the future of youth development to alter this profile so that our work becomes more respectable within the academy. By so doing, we increase the intellectual capital for our work and at the same time legitimate ourselves among key gatekeepers instrumental to the shaping of policy and the allocation of public resources.

The key point is this: *if we are to close the gap between theory and application, we need first to articulate models to guide the science of youth development and then buttress these arenas of scholarship with the necessary professional resources (e.g., refereed, multidisciplinary youth development journals, research conferences, funding).*

CONCEPTUALIZING THE SCIENTIFIC ISSUES

If one commissioned 10 writers to compose reviews of what we know about youth development, 10 very different papers would emerge. Perhaps a few studies and a few names would be constant. Ultimately, the overlap in references cited would be minimal. (The exercise of commissioning 10 reviews may be an intriguing method for unleashing needed debate and dialogue about what is inside the youth development box and what is outside.)

Our point is that the conceptual terrain for youth development is murky. There is no readily known and accessible literature. The work by definition is multidisciplinary, multilanguage, and multisector. We therefore suggest the following conceptual framework for the field of youth development and a scientific agenda needed to guide and inform its evolution.

In mapping out the scientific terrain, we begin with this working definition: *youth development mobilizes programs, organizations, systems and communities to build developmental strengths in order to promote health and well-being.* In this definition, each of the elements brings conceptual challenge. Figure 1 presents a conceptual framework for defining each of the elements.

In this model (Figure 1), the elements within the inputs (I) cell are not intended to be exhaustive. The inputs are organized into programs, organizations, systems, and community, each of which holds myriad formal and informal possibilities for

FIGURE 1
Conceptual Framework for Youth Development Theory and Research

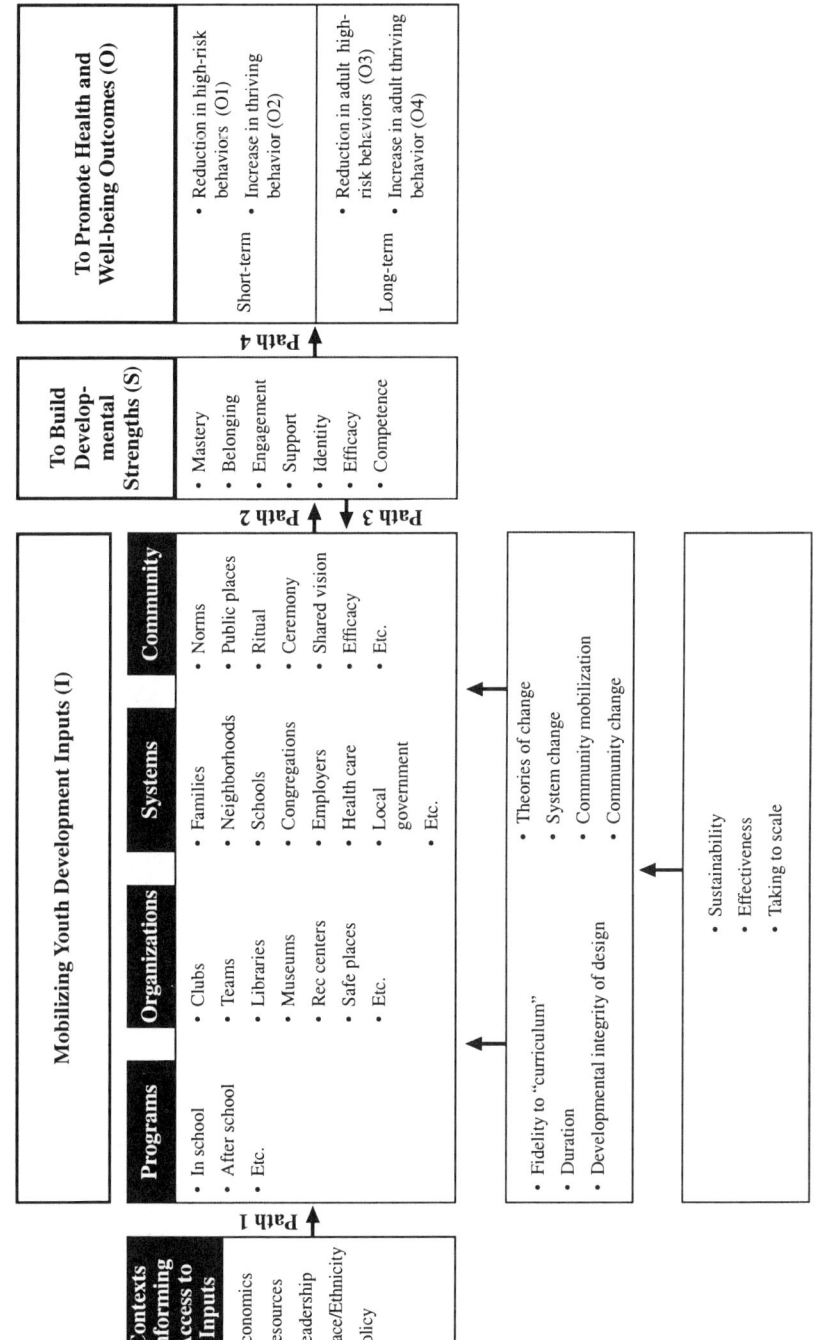

building developmental strengths. Similarly, the cell that names the developmental strengths (S) represents a rather quick way to name the territory of developmental processes. This list, from mastery to competence, should be seen as illustrative.

We use Figure 1 as a visual map for articulating what we see to be eight theoretical, definitional, and research issues germane to a science of youth development.

Core Issue #1

Conceptualize the arena of inputs (I). Currently, lists of inputs dominate the field. But little deep work has been done to name dimensions and categories of inputs (though an attempt is made earlier in this chapter to begin differentiating elements of a typology); establish the developmental resources within each input (e.g., relationships, norms, climate, opportunity for active engagement); integrate and evaluate current models; or establish criteria by which to evaluate the efficacy and accessibility of inputs. Work on conceptualizing the service infrastructure of cities is a helpful beginning (Whalen and Wynn, 1995).

Scientific literatures not often incorporated into input deliberations add value to this conceptual task. Among these are the areas of socialization theory, school climate, school reform, social movements, chaos theory, and the anthropological literature on ceremony and ritual. It is also suggested that a scientific approach to conceptualizing youth development inputs should include not only institutions, programs, and services (the more formal or organized face of inputs), but also the informal, natural, and nonprogrammatic capacity of community (Benson, 1997). The encouragement here is to think expansively—within a well-reasoned theoretical model of inputs.

Core Issue #2

Conceptualize the arena of developmental strengths and assets (S). We know there are many lists floating through the youth development field, but we have done little critical reflection on them. They need to be examined in light of developmental theory and differences in age- and gender-related developmental processes. Consensus on the model is less important than are good scientific rationales for proposed elements. However, the ways in which the strengths are conceptualized and communicated may have significant, practical import when community mobilization is a youth development strategy.

Core Issue #3

Establish the links between I and S. This is represented in Figure 1 as path 2. The field assumes that inputs (I) generate developmental strengths (S). The research on path 2 is quite weak. We know far too little about which inputs promote which

The Scientific Foundations of Youth Development 147

strengths or how much developmental energy emanating from I establishes a particular developmental strength (S). Some scholars (e.g., Bronfrenbrenner and Lerner) who advance the theoretical underpinnings of ecological approaches to human development open the door to the intriguing notion that adolescents—in their search for and attainment of belonging, identity, and connection—shape people and places included in I (path 3). Establishing the links between I and S should be an area of work in which we more directly invite the participation of basic research scholars in the field of human development.

Core Issue #4

Investigate the "pileup" effect of I. In the risk-reduction and deficit-reduction paradigms, important work has been done in examining the additive nature of risks (in essence, risks are cumulative in influence and there is evidence of their interaction). In youth development, our assumptions about the power of developmental inputs (I) are rather unsophisticated. The lack of a research tradition here unintentionally fuels what could be a naive assumption that *a* program, *a* relationship, *a* developmental resource produces the strengths and outcomes we seek. A reasonable hypothesis is that multiple inputs are needed to grow developmental strengths. We need to build a knowledge base about input "pileup" effects. A driving hypothesis could be that "youth development requires multiple inputs from multiple sources over a sustained period of time" (Pittman and Irby, 1998).

Core Issue #5

Clarify youth development outcomes. Ultimately, youth development's case for itself hinges on establishing the link between S and O (see path 4). The field's work here is in its infancy. Is youth development only about promoting positive developmental outcomes? Or is it equally interested in the connection of I and S to the reduction of health-compromising behaviors? We suggest that the field would gain from a deliberate search for effect in these four outcome domains.

Short-Term Outcomes	**Long-Term Outcomes**
Reduction of youth health-compromising behaviors (O1)	**Reduction of adult health-compromising behaviors (O3)**
Alcohol use	Alcohol dependence
Tobacco use	Drug dependence
Teen pregnancy	Crime
Violence	
Promotion of youth thriving (O2)	**Promotion of adult thriving (O4)**
School success	Work effectiveness
Affirmation of diversity	Parenting effectiveness
Positive nutrition	Civic engagement

Note that the connection of I and S to O1 (reduction of health-compromising behaviors) lies in the territory now commonly referred to as protective factors. And note that I and S connected to O1 and O2 lies in the territory of resiliency research, particularly when the focus is on youth known to experience risk factors. A science of youth development, then, claims both of these (i.e., resiliency and protective factors) as allied fields of inquiry.

We also make the distinction between short- and long-term outcomes. There is a theoretical rationale, grounded in lifespan developmental psychology, to suggest that developmental strengths (S) during the second decade of life are predictive of adult outcomes. Parenting competence, work competence, and morbidity and mortality rates could well be so informed. If such connections could be documented, via longitudinal and retrospective research, the case for youth development as an approach gains additional credibility. Extant longitudinal data sets (e.g., Werner and Smith, 1992) should be examined to determine what can currently be claimed about these connections.

Core Issue #6

Establish baseline data for I and S. National studies of children and adolescents tend to be designed to name and count deficits, risks, and obstacles. We need good baseline descriptive documentation of access to I and attainment of S for three reasons: (1) to guide our investment in change making; (2) to have clearer benchmarks against which to judge progress; and (3) to make visible and known an alternative set of social indicators so that a language of youth development can more readily emerge among policy makers, scholars, practitioners, and the general public.

Core Issue #7

Understand the contexts that shape the accessibility to inputs (path 1). Among these contexts are family and community-level economics; the strength and challenges of culture, including race-ethnicity; the norms, resources, volunteer base, and leadership within community; and public policy—local, state, and federal.

Core Issue #8

All of the core issues named to this point have to do with the interconnections among inputs, strengths, and outcomes. These are all issues of human development. More precisely, they tend to be applied developmental science issues. Below the cell marked (I) in Figure 1 are two remaining cells that together begin to frame a different set of issues. These are about the strategies of *change making*, of effectively mobilizing inputs. In the case of programs (and to a lesser extent, organizations), the issues include fidelity to curriculum, the duration of exposure (e.g., 6 sessions, 12 sessions), and qualities of the youth-youth worker relationship. These issues are well known and much discussed in the evaluation literature on prevention programs.

When we move to mobilizing inputs at the system and community levels, however, we are faced with complex and perhaps enigmatic change, reform, and transformation issues. To understand these, we need to move into such areas as theories of change, the evolution of social norms, the mobilization of public will, and social movements. New theoretical frameworks (e.g., systems theory and chaos theory) need to be explored. And new evaluation methods must be developed and refined (Connell et al., 1995; Fulbright-Anderson, Kubisch, and Connell, 1998).

Pittman and Irby, in an important reflection on the status of the youth development paradigm, suggest that effectiveness, scale, and sustainability are three useful lenses for "strategic decision-making about the youth development framework" (1998, p. 13). These three are, of course, particularly crucial for directing practice and action. Our view here is that the critical questions are the following:

- What features of each input increase its capacity to build developmental strengths?
- What resources (people energy, policy, financial resources, system change, leadership, etc.) are needed to expand accessibility to inputs within a geographic space and across many communities?
- What sustains professional, citizen, volunteer, system, and program attention and commitment to maximizing and growing access to I?

Youth development shares with adolescent psychology an interest in inputs (I) and strengths (S). Unlike adolescent psychology, it seeks practical knowledge in service of advancing the links between I and S. Hence, youth development easily expands to include outcomes, "what works," best practices, and policy. We suggest here that a science of youth development must expand beyond these applied issues to include the rigorous exploration of change making.

In our view, these eight core issues should become central to laying the scientific foundations of the field. We offer these three hypotheses:

- The state of the science on these eight issues is in its infancy;
- The resources needed to build scientific foundations (dedicated researchers, funding, professional encouragement) are fragile; and
- Building the scientific foundations of youth development is necessary to advance its practice.

NAMING THE SCIENTIFIC AGENDA

In this section, we try our hand at articulating a knowledge-generating agenda in more common social science categories. We restate concerns named in the eight core issues and extend beyond them to several additional issues.

The Conceptual Agenda

- Theoretically define the territory of youth development inputs (I).
- Theoretically define the territory of developmental strengths (S) and how these might vary by social-demographic variables.
- Conceptualize the territory of outcomes.
- Build theoretical models to posit how inputs (I) inform the development of strengths (S).
- Create theories of change to inform change making at the system and community levels.

The Measurement Agenda

- Develop psychometrically sound measures of developmental strengths (S).
- Develop measurement tools for short-term thriving indicators (O2).
- Develop instrumentation to explore the quality and effectiveness of inputs (I).

The Predictive Agenda

- Explore linkages of inputs (I) to strengths (S).
- Explore linkages of strengths (S) to outcomes (O).
- Explore variability in I to S and S to O linkages, by gender, race-ethnicity, socioeconomic status, and related social-demographic categories.
- Explore the additive nature of inputs (I) in predicting strengths (S).
- Explore the additive nature of strengths (S) in predicting outcomes.
- Launch retrospective and longitudinal inquiries to discern long-term consequences of youth development strengths.

The Baseline Agenda

- Develop indicators and measures to establish community-level and national benchmarks for inputs and strengths.
- Conduct baseline studies.

The Evaluation Agenda

- Conceive and conduct additional experimental studies in the tradition of P/PV's pioneering mentoring study (Tierney, Grossman, and Resch, 1995), expanded to look at the impact of multiple inputs.
- Develop indicators of change for organizations, systems, and community.
- Develop comprehensive evaluation strategies for system and community initiatives.

The Contextual Agenda

- Study the role of context (economics, culture, etc.) in access to and utilization of inputs and the attainment of strengths.

The System Agenda

- Conceptualize the input potential of schools, congregations, youth organizations, family, and neighborhood.
- Design and evaluate interventions to mobilize and transform systems.

The Community Change Agenda

- Create models to define and describe the dynamics of a community that broadly promotes developmental strengths.
- Conceptualize how communities can be mobilized to maximize input accessibility.
- Design and evaluate initiatives to mobilize communities.
- Define the indicators and manifestations of *sustainable*, strength-building community.

THE BIGGER PICTURE

We recognize that this chapter offers an expansive and comprehensive view of youth development and the science needed to undergird it. The science is necessarily multidisciplinary, basic and applied, theoretical and empirical, and multi-method. It overlaps with other ongoing fields of inquiry in such areas as prevention, resiliency, and protective factors. We suggest that this comprehensive view is necessary both to position youth development as a dominant paradigm of thinking, action, and policy and to guide the formation of effective change making at the local level.

There are also a number of high-level questions that require greater discernment. These questions tend to be philosophical or strategic in nature. Although no one study can answer them directly, we propose that building a more comprehensive body of knowledge and a deeper research community is necessary to inform them. The following are examples of some higher-order questions:

- Would we gain by expanding our thinking to include how developmental strengths are built across ages 0-20 or 0-24? If so, to what extent could we influence development in years 0-10 to better inform development in the second decade of life?
- Are there indigenous or cross-cultural sources of wisdom about building developmental strengths that should be incorporated into our work?

- Can community be altered?
- Do we gain more by focusing on adults (e.g., teaching, training) or by focusing on youth (e.g., empowering, engaging, mobilizing)?
- Do we gain more by focusing on some youth (e.g., high-risk, urban) or on all youth?
- How does the paradigm of youth development intersect with other paradigms (e.g., risk reduction, economic development)? Is there a "pileup" effect here (i.e., do developmental strengths advance when all these paradigms coexist in a community)?
- What is the ideal ratio of energy and resource allocation for changing programs, organizations, systems and communities?

REFERENCES

Benson, P. L.
1997 *All Kids Are Our Kids: What Communities Must Do To Raise Caring and Responsible Children and Adolescents.* San Francisco: Jossey-Bass.

Benson, P.L., N. Leffert, P.C. Scales, and D.A. Blyth
1998 Beyond the "Village" Rhetoric: Creating Healthy Communities for Children and Adolescents. *Applied Developmental Science,* 2(3), 138-159.

Boys & Girls Clubs of America
1991 *The Effects of Boys & Girls Clubs on Alcohol and Other Drug Use and Related Problems in Public Housing Projects.* New York: Boys & Girls Clubs of America.

Carnegie Council on Adolescent Development
1992 *A Matter of Time: Risk and Opportunity in the Nonschool Hours.* Washington, D.C.: Carnegie Council on Adolescent Development.

Catalano, R.F., M.L. Berglund, J.A.M. Ryan, H.C. Lonczak, and J.D. Hawkins
1998 "Positive Youth Development in the United States: Research Findings on Evaluations of Positive Youth Development Programs." Paper submitted to U.S. Department of Health and Human Services, Office of the Assistant Secretary for Planning and Evaluation and National Institute for Child Health and Human Development.

Center for the Study of Social Policy
1995 *Building New Futures for At-Risk Youth. Findings from a Five-Year, Multisite Evaluation.* Washington, D.C.: Center for the Study of Social Policy.

Cognetta, P.V., and N.A. Sprinthall
1978 "Students as Teachers: Role Taking as a Means of Promoting Psychological Development During Adolescence," in N.A. Sprinthall and R.L. Mosher (eds.). *Value Development as the Aim of Education.* Schenectady, N.Y.: Character Research Press.

Comer, J.
1997 *Waiting for a Miracle: Why Schools Can't Solve Our Problems—And How We Can.* New York: Dutton.

Connell, J.P.
1996 *First Thing First: A Framework for Successful School-Site Reform.* White paper prepared for the Ewing Marion Kauffman Foundation, Kansas City, Mo.

Connell, J.P., A.C. Kubisch, L.B. Schorr, and C.H. Weiss (eds.)
1995 *New Approaches to Evaluating Community Initiatives: Concepts, Methods and Contexts.* Washington, D.C.: The Aspen Institute.

Conrad, D., and D. Hedin
1981 *National Assessment of Experiential Education: A Final Report.* St. Paul, Minn.: University of Minnesota.

Costello, J., M. Toles, and J. Wynn
1998 *Promoting Youth Development in Organizations That Serve Adolescents: The Implications of Organizational Factors.* Commissioned paper for the Youth Development Directions Project. Philadelphia: Public/Private Ventures.

Dryfoos, J.G.
1990 *Adolescents at Risk: Prevalence and Prevention.* New York: Oxford University Press.
Epstein, J.L.
1996 "Perspectives and Previews on Research and Policy for School, Family, and Community Partnerships," in A. Booth and J.F. Dunn (eds.). *Family-School Links: How Do They Affect Educational Outcomes?* Mahwah, N.J.: Lawrence Erlbaum Associates, Inc.
Fulbright-Anderson, K., A.C. Kubisch, and J.P. Connell (eds.)
1998 *New Approaches to Evaluating Community Initiatives: Theory, Measurement, and Analysis.* Washington, D.C.: The Aspen Institute.
Halpern, R.
1992 *Rebuilding the Inner City: A History of Neighborhood-Based Initiatives to Address Poverty.* New York: Columbia University Press.
Hawkins, J.D., and R.F. Catalano
1992 *Communities That Care: Action for Drug Abuse Prevention.* San Francisco: Jossey-Bass.
Jessor, R., J. Van Den Bos, J. Vanderryn, F.M. Costa, and M.S. Turbin
1995 "Protective Factors in Adolescent Problem Behavior: Moderator Effects and Developmental Change." *Developmental Psychology,* 31, 923-933.
Ladewig, H., and J.K. Thomas
1987 *Assessing the Impact of 4-H on Former Members.* College Station: Texas A&M University.
Leffert, N., R.N. Saito, D.A. Blyth, and C.H. Kroenke
1996 *Making the Case: Measuring the Impact of Youth Development Programs.* Minneapolis: Search Institute.
Morrissey, E., A. Wandersman, D. Seybolt, M. Nation, C. Crusto, and K. Davino
1997 "Toward a Framework for Bridging the Gap Between Science and Practice in Prevention: A Focus on Evaluator and Practitioner Perspectives." *Evaluation and Program Planning,* 20(3), 367-377.
National Center for Education Statistics
1990 *National Education Longitudinal Study of 1988: The Profile of the American Eighth Grader.* Washington, D.C.: U.S. Government Printing Office.
National Commission on Children
1991 *Speaking of Kids: A National Survey of Children and Parents.* Washington, D.C.: U.S. Department of Education.
Newman, F.M., and R.A. Rutter
1983 *The Effects of High School Community Service Programs on Students' Social Development.* Madison: University of Wisconsin.
Pittman, K., and M. Irby
1998 "Unfinished Business: Reflections on a Decade of Promoting Youth Development." Unpublished paper.
Quinn, J.
1995 "Positive Effects of Participation in Youth Organizations," in M. Rutter (ed.). *Psychosocial Disturbances in Young People: Challenges for Prevention.* New York: Cambridge University Press.
Resnick, M.D., P.S. Bearman, R.W. Blum, K.E. Bauman, K.M. Harris, J. Jones., J. Tabor, T. Beuhring, R.E. Sieving, M. Shew, M. Ireland, L.H. Bearinger, and J.R. Udry
1997 "Protecting Adolescents from Harm: Findings from the National Longitudinal Study of Adolescent Health." *Journal of the American Medical Association,* 278, 823-832.
Roehlkepartain, E.C.
1998 *Building Assets in Congregations: A Practical Guide for Helping Youth Grow Up Healthy.* Minneapolis: Search Institute.
Saito, R.N., P.L. Benson, D.A. Blyth, and A.R. Sharma
1995 *Places to Grow: Perspectives on Youth Development Opportunities for Seven- to Fourteen-year-old Minneapolis Youth.* Minneapolis: Search Institute.
Sampson, R.J., S.W. Raudenbush, and F.C. Earls
1997 "Neighborhoods and Violent Crime: A Multilevel Study of Collective Efficacy." *Science,* 277, 918-924.
Scales, P.C.
1996 *Boxed In and Bored: How Middle Schools Continue to Fail Young Adolescents and What Good Middle Schools Do Right.* Minneapolis: Search Institute.
Scales, P., and N. Leffert
1999 *Developmental Assets: A Synthesis of the Scientific Research on Adolescent Development.* Minneapolis: Search Institute.

Tierney, J.P., J.B. Grossman, and N.L. Resch
1995 *Making a Difference: An Impact Study of Big Brothers/Big Sisters.* Philadelphia: Public/Private Ventures.

Walberg, H.J., O. Reyes, R.P. Weissberg, and C.B. Kuster
1997 "Afterword: Strengthening the Families, Education, and Health of Urban Children and Youth," in H.J. Walberg, O. Reyes, and R.P. Weissberg (eds.). *Children and Youth: Interdisciplinary Perspectives* (pp. 363-368). Thousand Oaks, Calif.: Sage.

Werner, E.E., and R.S. Smith
1992 *Overcoming the Odds: High Risk Children from Birth to Adulthood.* Ithaca, N.Y.: Cornell University Press.

Whalen, S.P., and J.R. Wynn
1995 "Enhancing Primary Services for Youth through an Infrastructure of Social Services." *Journal of Adolescent Research,* 10(1), 88-110.

Wynn, J., J. Costello, R. Halpern, and H. Richman
1994 *Children, Families, and Communities: A New Approach to Social Services.* Chicago: Chapin Hall Center for Children, University of Chicago.

Wynn J., H. Richman, R.A. Rubinstein, and J. Littell
1987 *Communities and Adolescents: An Exploration of Reciprocal Supports.* Washington, D.C.: William T. Grant Foundation Commission on Youth and America's Future.

6 MEASURING DEFICITS AND ASSETS: HOW WE TRACK YOUTH DEVELOPMENT NOW, AND HOW WE SHOULD TRACK IT

Gary B. MacDonald and Rafael Valdivieso

HOW WE MEASURE YOUTH DEVELOPMENT NOW

The United States is perhaps the most data-driven society on the planet. Virtually everything Americans think and do is affected by data in some way: the way we live, the purchases we make, the attitudes we hold and the decisions we make about how we are educated, how and in what we invest, who does or does not benefit from resources—indeed, the values we share.

It is not hyperbole, therefore, to say that data rule in our society. One subject on which data particularly rule is that of our young people. Perhaps no other population is more thoroughly poked, prodded, and scrutinized than citizens who are between birth and the age of 21. Adults have an apparently fathomless need to know everything they can about young people: how they behave, what they like and do not like, what they buy and why, how they spend time, how they perform (or do not) in school, how they get into trouble, what they think about adults and each other, and so on and so on.

Over the past 20 years, literally thousands of studies have been conducted about young people (so many, in fact, that parents in many school jurisdictions nationwide have rebelled by refusing to allow their children to be surveyed). Many of these studies are one-time-only, small in scale, or focused on very specific issues. On the other hand, some studies—the studies that this chapter discusses—are national in scope and regularly administered, thus representative of the youth populations they target and useful for purposes of comparison. These are the studies whose findings are routinely reported in national and local media; routinely provide background for significant policy, legal, and resource-allocation decisions affecting young people; and routinely form the basis for what might be called our "national dialogue" on young people. In a very real sense, these studies have defined many of the ways we perceive young people, particularly adolescents, today.

The influential studies or reports on studies that form the basis of our discussion include:

- *Youth Risk Behavior Surveillance,* administered by the U.S. Centers for Disease Control and Prevention (1998) (hereafter *YRBS*);
- *Kids Count Data Book* (1998), compiled from several sources and published annually by the Annie E. Casey Foundation (hereafter *Kids Count*);
- *America's Children: Key National Indicators of Well-Being,* compiled from several federal data sources by the Federal Interagency Forum on Child and Family Statistics (1998) (hereafter *KNIWB*);
- *Trends in the Well-Being of America's Children and Youth,* compiled from federal and other data sources by Child Trends, Inc., a national research organization, for the Department of Health and Human Services' Office of the Assistant Secretary for Planning and Evaluation (1997) (hereafter *Trends*);
- *Juvenile Offenders and Victims: A National Report,* compiled from several federal data sources and published by the U.S. Department of Justice's Office of Juvenile Justice and Delinquency Prevention (hereafter *JOV*) (Snyder and Sickmund, 1995); and
- *Report in Brief: National Assessment of Educational Progress: 1996 Trends in Academic Progress,* compiled from numerous federal, state, and local sources and published by the U.S. Department of Education's National Center for Education Statistics (hereafter *NAEP*) (Campbell et al., 1998).

Among them, these studies or reports on studies contain data on many aspects of a young person's life. They are by no means the only data we could have considered, but, in our judgment, the data we discuss have the advantage of being perceived by policy makers and media alike as being authoritative in their particular fields. We discuss each of the studies or reports on studies individually in the following pages.

Before we do so, however, it is important to note *what* we are looking for and *why* in each source. Our working assumption is that most national data about young people currently measure *deficit* outcomes, by which we mean negative or undesirable outcomes, such as substance use and abuse, violence, criminal activity, failure to complete school, and so on, or negative or undesirable conditions in the lives of young people, such as poverty. As we work our way through each of our data sources, our intention is to investigate whether this working assumption is accurate. We also focus where possible on the criteria used to select the outcomes or conditions being measured. In addition, we are concerned about the *impact on perceptions* of the data contained in each of our sources. What kind of picture of young people does each source, and the sources collectively, create? We attempt to characterize these pictures in each case for subsequent discussion.

Youth Risk Behavior Surveillance

The *YRBS* national survey has been administered five times since 1990 by the U.S. Centers for Disease Control and Prevention (CDC); surveys in selected states (never more than 40), territories (never more than four), and large cities (never more than 17) have also been administered four times since 1990. Survey samples are limited to 9th to 12th graders in all locations and are considered representative in most but not all locations in which the survey is administered. The data reported in our source are from the period of February through May 1997.

The *YRBS* is the most comprehensive ongoing survey of health-risk behaviors among young people in the United States (as distinguished from the occasional national poll that may ask similar types of questions of young people). Because of its federal imprimatur, *YRBS* findings are closely watched by policy makers at all levels. Survey-to-survey fluctuations in such key indicators as sexual behavior and substance use draw pointed attention in the media, the Congress, and state and local governments. Indeed, this is CDC's intent:

> These *YRBS* data are already being used by health and education officials to improve national, state and local policies and programs to reduce risks associated with the leading causes of morbidity and mortality. *YRBS* data also are being used to measure progress toward achieving 21 national health objectives and 1 of the 8 National Education Goals. (*YRBS*, 1998, p. 2)

YRBS monitors six categories of priority health-risk behaviors in its sample population: behaviors that contribute to unintentional and intentional injuries; tobacco use; alcohol and other drug use; sexual behaviors that contribute to unintended pregnancy and sexually transmitted diseases (STDs, including HIV infection); unhealthy dietary behaviors; and physical inactivity.

The report on the 1997 *YRBS* summarizes its findings as follows:

> In the United States, 73% of all deaths among youth and young adults 10-24 years of age result from only four causes: motor vehicle crashes, other unintentional injuries, homicide, and suicide. Results from the national 1997 *YRBS* demonstrate that many high school students engage in behaviors that increase their likelihood of death from these four cases—19.3% had rarely or never worn a seat belt; during the 30 days preceding the survey, 36% had ridden with a driver who had been drinking alcohol; 18.3% had carried a weapon during the 30 days preceding the survey; 50.8% had drunk alcohol during the 30 days preceding the survey; 26.2% had used marijuana during the 30 days preceding the survey; and 7.7% had attempted suicide during the 12 months preceding the survey. Substantial morbidity among school-age youth, young adults and their children also result from unintended pregnancies and STDs,

including HIV infection. *YRBS* results indicate that in 1997, 48.4% of high school students had ever had sexual intercourse; 43.2% of sexually active students had not used a condom at last intercourse; and 2.1% had ever injected an illegal drug. Of all deaths and substantial morbidity among adults ≥25 years of age, 67% result from two causes—cardiovascular disease and cancer. Most of the risk behaviors associated with these causes of death are initiated during adolescence. In 1997, 36.4% of high school students had smoked cigarettes during the 30 days preceding the survey; 70.7% had not eaten five or more servings of fruits and vegetables during the day preceding the survey; and 72.6% had not attended physical education class daily. (*YRBS*, 1998, pp. 1-2)

The *YRBS* is, of course, unabashedly focused on negative behaviors and minces no words in describing their incidence among young people. Aggregating so many negative facts about youth health behaviors in one place, however, gives the simplistic impression that young people are mildly to seriously out of control. This is particularly true when studies like the *YRBS* fail to report or discuss the reverse of their negative findings. What about the often substantial percentages of young people who do *not* report negative behaviors? In the 1997 *YRBS,* for example, *96 percent of young people did not* miss one or more days of school during the 30 days preceding the survey because "they had felt unsafe at school or when traveling to or from school" (*YRBS*, p. 8)—and this at a time of increased national anxiety about school safety. Another unhighlighted bright spot is the *nearly 98 percent of young people who do not* inject illegal drugs.

Kids Count Data Book

Kids Count is a data collection and dissemination project of the Annie E. Casey Foundation, which annually updates national and state-specific data on 10 indicators of child well-being: percentage of low-birth-weight babies; infant mortality rate; child death rate; rate of teen deaths by accident, homicide, and suicide; teen birth rate; juvenile violent crime arrest rate; percentage of teens not attending school and not working; percentage of children in poverty; and percentage of families with children headed by a single parent. Data on each of these indicators are collected and reported at both the national and state levels. The annual *Kids Count Data Book* reports data collected in previous years (the *Kids Count Data Book* we discuss here reports 1995 data) and compares it to a baseline year (in this case, 1985).

Although it is not billed as such, *Kids Count* functions as a kind of report card for the nation as well as for specific states on how well or poorly each of the indicators is faring. Indeed, *Kids Count* annually ranks states as to how well or poorly they are doing. Thus we learn, for example, that in 1995 New Hampshire led states in the 10 reported indicators and the District of Columbia took up the rear. Because *Kids Count* is the only national report of its kind that actually ranks states

Measuring Deficits and Assets

in order of accomplishment, policy makers at all levels and the media pay close attention to it.

One could ask why *Kids Count* selected the 10 indicators that it analyzes. The selection criteria are interesting:

1. **Data must be from a reliable source.** All the indicator data used in this book come from U.S. government agencies. Most of the data have been published or released to the public in some other form before [*Kids Count* uses] it.
2. **The statistical indicator must be available and consistent over time.** Changes in methodologies, practices, or policies may affect year-to-year comparability. Program and administrative data are particularly vulnerable to changes in policies or program administration, resulting in data that are not comparable across states or over time.
3. **The statistical indicator must be available and consistent across states.** In practical terms this means data collected by the federal government or some other national organization. Much of the data collected by states may be accurate and reliable, but unless all the states follow the same data collection procedures, the statistics are not likely to be comparable.
4. **The data item should reflect a salient outcome or measure of well-being.** [*Kids Count* focuses] on outcome measures rather than programmatic or service data (such as dollars spent on education or welfare costs), which are not always related to the actual well-being of children.
5. **The data item must be easily understandable to the public.** [*Kids Count* is] trying to reach an educated lay public, not academic scholars or researchers. Measures that are too complex will not be effective.
6. **The data item must have a relatively unambiguous interpretation.** If the value of an indicator changes, [*Kids Count* wants] to be sure there is widespread agreement that this is a good thing (or a bad thing) for kids.
7. **There should be a high probability that the measure will continue to be produced in the near future.** [*Kids Count* wants] to establish a series of indicators that can be produced year after year in order to track changes in the well-being of children (*Kids Count,* 1998, p. 175).

What is interesting about these criteria are the types of indicators that satisfied them. Apparently only data on the negative outcomes *Kids Count* watches can currently be considered reliable, consistent over time and across states, salient, easily understood, unambiguous, and likely to continue being produced in the near future. We will return to the *Kids Count* criteria later.

What does the 1998 *Kids Count Data Book* tell us? The following list consists of national data compiled between 1985 and 1995:

- Percentage of low-birth-weight babies: 7 percent worse.
- Infant mortality rate: 28 percent better.
- Child death rate: 18 percent better.
- Rate of teen deaths by accident, homicide, and suicide: 3 percent worse.
- Teen birth rate: 16 percent worse.
- Juvenile violent crime arrest rate: 66 percent worse.
- Percentage of teens who are high school dropouts: 9 percent better.
- Percentage of teens not attending school and not working: 18 percent better.
- Percentage of children in poverty: steady at 21 percent.
- Percentage of families with children headed by a single parent: 18 percent worse (*Kids Count,* 1998, p. 27).

A mixed national picture of young people emerges from the *Kids Count* data, and it is not altogether a bad one. Percentages of infant mortality, child death, high school dropouts, and teens not in school and not working are all decreasing. On the "hot button" indicators that tend to preoccupy the attention of policy makers, however, things are not getting better: more teens are dying by accident, homicide, or suicide; more teens are giving birth; juvenile violent crime arrest rates are way up; the same percentage of children remain in poverty; and families with children headed by a single parent are increasing significantly. The impression that lingers is that young people are still in trouble, in some cases badly so, despite some modest improvements in their lives.

America's Children: Key National Indicators of Well-Being

The *KNIWB,* like the entity that created it, represents a promising evolution in the packaging and dissemination of U.S. government data. In 1997, an executive order created the Federal Interagency Forum on Child and Family Statistics. The forum includes representatives of eight U.S. government departments (Agriculture, Commerce, Defense, Education, Health and Human Services, Housing and Urban Development, Justice, and Labor), the National Science Foundation, and the Office of Management and Budget. The forum's job is to produce the *KNIWB* on an annual basis; two editions have so far been published, the latest in 1998.

KNIWB brings together in a single document federal data on 23 key indicators of important aspects of children's lives, including their economic security, health, behavior, social environment, and education. Several of these indicators are identical or similar to those used by *Kids Count,* which, in our view, corroborates the salience of such indicators in the current policy-making environment (low-birth-weight babies, child mortality, teen mortality, teen birth rate, serious violent crime offending rate, high school completion, teens not attending school and not working, children in poverty). In addition, *KNIWB* analyzes the following data:

Measuring Deficits and Assets

- Percentage of children under 18 living with parents with at least one parent employed full-time;
- Percentage of households with children under age 18 that report any of three housing problems;
- Percentage of children under age 18 in households experiencing food insecurity with moderate hunger;
- Percentage of children under age 18 in households experiencing food insecurity with severe hunger;
- Percentage of children under age 18 covered by health insurance;
- Percentage of children under age 18 with no usual source of health care;
- Percentage of children under age 18 in very good or excellent health;
- Percentage of children ages 5 to 17 with any limitation in activity resulting from chronic conditions;
- Percentage of children ages 19 to 35 months who received combined series immunization coverage;
- Percentage of 8th-, 10th-, and 12th-grade students who reported smoking daily in the previous 30 days;
- Percentage of 8th-, 10th-, and 12th-grade students who reported having five or more alcoholic beverages in a row in the last two weeks;
- Percentage of 8th-, 10th-, and 12th-grade students who have used illicit drugs in the previous 30 days;
- Rate of serious violent crime victimizations per 1,000 youths ages 12 to 17;
- Percentage of children ages 3 to 5 who are read to every day by a family member;
- Percentage of children ages 3 to 4 who are enrolled in preschool;
- Average mathematics scale scores of 9-, 13-, and 17-year-olds;
- Average reading scale scores of 9-, 13-, and 17-year-olds; and
- Percentage of high school graduates ages 25 to 29 who have completed a bachelor's degree or higher.

"Special Features":

- Percentage of children ages 1 to 5 with 10 or more micrograms of lead per deciliter of blood; and
- Percentage of children under age 6 participating in child care and early childhood education programs on a regular basis. (*KNIWB,* 1998, pp. v-vi).

There are four points of interest to highlight about *KNIWB*'s indicators. First, the forum's criteria for selecting these particular indicators are quite similar to the criteria *Kids Count* uses. *KNIWB*'s indicators were chosen because they are:

- **Easy to understand** by broad audiences;
- **Objectively** based on substantial research connecting them to child well-being and based on reliable data;
- **Balanced** so that no single area of children's lives dominates the report;

- **Measured regularly** so that they can be updated and show trends over time; and
- **Representative** of large segments of the population, rather than one particular group (*KNIWB*, 1998, p. viii).

We will question later just how connected to child well-being, how balanced, and how representative most of these indicators really are, but for the moment it is interesting to note that the concurrence between *Kids Count* and *KNIWB* criteria for selection of indicators may reflect a kind of consensus, at least within the research community, about what is worth reporting to Americans about their children.

The second item of interest about *KNIWB*'s indicators is that they have not remained static from year to year. The 1998 *KNIWB* contains data on most but not all indicators reported in the 1997 *KNIWB*. The specific changes in indicators are less important here than the reasons these changes were implemented:

> Some of the changes reflect improvements in the availability of data for certain key indicators. Some changes better clarify the concept being measured or reflect the expanded nature of the indicator. Many of the changes are the result of an evaluation done by the National Center for Health Statistics Questionnaire Design Research Laboratory to help make the report clear and user-friendly to a non-technical audience. All the changes reflect the many helpful comments and suggestions for improvements that were received from readers and users of the 1997 report. (*KNIWB*, 1998, p. viii)

The willingness of so influential a source of national data to make changes in response to evaluations and user input gives us hope that the kinds of changes in national data collection that we recommend in the section titled "How We Should Measure Youth Development" have at least a chance of becoming reality.

The third item of interest about *KNIWB*'s indicators is that they are not all about negative outcomes. In fact, some of the indicators are directly pertinent to the positive youth development components of a child's life that we would like to see much more widely measured. These indicators include percentage of children under age 18 in very good or excellent health (81%); percentage of children under age 18 covered by health insurance (85%); percentage of children ages 3 to 5 who are read to every day by a family member (57%); percentage of children ages 3 and 4 who are enrolled in preschool (45%); percentage of children under age 6 participating in child care and early childhood education programs on a regular basis (60%); and percentage of high school graduates ages 25 to 29 who have completed a bachelor's degree or higher (32%, up from 26% in 1980).

Fourth, the *KNIWB* provides encouraging evidence of what we hope will become a trend: at the conclusion of each of its sections on indicators, the report highlights other types of data that are not being collected or reported now but

Measuring Deficits and Assets

should be. For example, in the section on behavior and social environment, the report recommends new research on indicators of positive behavior:

> Indicators of positive behaviors with proven relationships to enhancing child well-being need to be developed. Examples might include participation in extra-curricular activities such as school clubs and sports, scouting, attendance in churches and synagogues, or volunteering at community organizations. (*KNIWB*, 1998, p. 40)

We could not agree more. This is the kernel of our recommendations later in this chapter. It is gratifying to observe that the idea appears to be gaining currency in some quarters.

Having said all that, what did the *KNIWB* data show? Unfortunately, too much to be discussed in any detail here. However, a short summary is possible. Like the findings of *Kids Count, KNIWB*'s data are mixed. On the one hand, most kids are healthy; most kids are immunized properly; most kids (but not yet enough) are being read to daily by a family member; math scale scores are rising; the high school completion rate is increasing, as is the college completion rate.

On the other hand, more kids are smoking, drinking, and using drugs; reading scale scores have not improved among 13- and 17-year-olds and are declining among 9-year-olds; children under 18 continue to represent a very large segment of the poor population (40%) even though they are only about one-fourth of the total population; and children living in poverty consistently rank lower in all categories of indicators.

Here we must stop on the horns of a common dilemma: many of the *KNIWB* findings appear to be directly contradicted by the *Kids Count* findings discussed earlier. For example, *KNIWB* reports that birth rates among adolescent females *declined* between 1991 and 1996, whereas *Kids Count* says the teen birth rate has grown 16 percent *worse* between 1985 and 1995. Similarly, *KNIWB* reports that "in recent years, there has been a decline in the rates for which youth ages 12 to 17 . . . were the perpetrators of serious violent crime" (*KNIWB*, 1998, p. iv), whereas *Kids Count* says that the juvenile violent crime arrest rate grew 66 percent *worse* between 1985 and 1995. There are other disparities between the two reports. Who is telling the "truth"?

A researcher might explain that such apparent contradictions are related to differences in what or who is being counted; the periods of time being measured; the way in which survey questions are worded; and other, more technical aspects of manipulating data. But the vagaries of research are lost on the nontechnical public and, too often, the media. While Americans depend on data, they are also skeptical of data, and this is why. In the minds of many people, whatever impression is left today by the findings of a particular study is likely if not certainly to be contradicted, and thereby confused, by the findings of another study tomorrow. This is a problem not so much of *what* we measure but of how we *report* what we measure. Both require much more care.

Trends in the Well-Being of America's Children and Youth

It would not be an overstatement to call *Trends* the mother of all data compendiums about America's young people. It is to the *KNIWB* what the *Titanic* is to a rowboat. Published in 1997 for the second time by the U.S. Department of Health and Human Services, *Trends* contains comprehensive analysis of multiyear data on 90 indicators of child well-being divided into five sections and 17 subsections. To give the reader a flavor of the contents of *Trends,* the 17 subsections include child population characteristics; family structure; neighborhoods; poverty and income; financial support; parental and youth employment; housing; mortality; health conditions; health care; social development; behavioral health: physical health and safety; behavioral health: smoking, alcohol, and substance abuse; behavioral health: sexual activity and fertility; education: enrollment and attendance; education: achievement and proficiency; and education-related behaviors and characteristics. If nothing else, *Trends* makes clear that "the data available for tracking the well-being of children and youth at the national level are fairly extensive" (*Trends,* 1997, p. 7).

Trends begins with a clarion call for better data on children and youth:

> There remain major gaps in the federal statistical system that must be filled if we are to have a complete picture of the quality of our children's lives.
>
> We have few measures of social development and health-related behaviors for very young and pre-teenage children which are measured on a regular basis. For example, we lack good indicators of school readiness for young children. Measures of mental health for any age child are rare, though one such measure was recently added to the National Health Interview Survey. Positive measures of social development and related behaviors are also sparse, *with the result that the current set of indicators may present a gloomier picture of our children's overall well-being than is in fact the case. New indicators which reflect the positive developments we desire for our children and youth clearly need to be developed and incorporated into the federal statistical system.* [Emphasis added.]
>
> We have very few indicators available that reflect important social processes affecting child well-being that go on inside the family and within the neighborhood. Measures of parent-child interactions, critical to the social and intellectual development of children, are only now beginning to work their way into regularly repeated national surveys ...
>
> Finally, data which can be used to track the well-being of children at the state and local levels are much less plentiful than at the national level. As state and local governments take on increasing levels of responsibility for the design and implementation of government programs of all sorts affecting children, youth and their

Measuring Deficits and Assets

> families, the need for such information is increasing. *The federal statistical system is positioned to play a significant role in increasing the availability of such data for use at the state and local level.* [Emphasis added.] (*Trends,* 1997, pp. 7-8)

These remarks are heartening not only because of their source but also because they suggest that managers of influential national data resources have come to see the importance of positive developmental outcome indicators in forming a more accurate and complete understanding of our children's lives.

The overwhelming amount of data in *Trends* make them impossible to summarize in this brief discussion. However, a random sampling of *Trends* data is not particularly encouraging. One reason that this may be true is because the report goes far back in time (as far as 1960 in many cases) to compare data to 1995. This sometimes produces startling visual contrasts, as in the graph (*Trends,* 1997, p. 29) that shows a 60 percent increase between 1960 and 1995 in births to unmarried mothers aged 15 to 19. Or an equally disturbing chart (*Trends,* p. 115) that shows the skyrocketing rate of homicides since 1970 among black males aged 15 to 19.

All of the data reported by the *YRBS, Kids Count,* and *KNIWB* are repeated or expanded in *Trends* and tell the same story. It does, however, introduce an innovation by reporting data on various "social development" factors in children's lives. These indicators include:

- Percentage of high school seniors who rate selected personal goals as being "extremely important."
- Percentage of 12th-grade students reporting that good grades have great or very great importance to peers.
- Percentage of 12th-grade students reporting peer disapproval of intentionally angering a teacher in school.
- Percentage attendance and religiosity among high school seniors.
- Percentage of persons aged 18-20 who registered to vote and percentage who voted.
- Percentage of students who watch six or more hours of television per day, by age (*Trends,* 1997, pp. 176-195).

In this section of the report we learn, for example, that between 1976 and 1995, high school students have most often rated as extremely important the following goals, in order of priority: being successful in my line of work (78%); having a good marriage and family life (62%); having lots of money (20%); making a contribution to society (20%); being a leader in my community (12%); and working to correct social and economic inequalities (10%). Only about 50 percent of 12th graders report that good grades have great or very great importance to their peers. About one-third of 12th graders (32%) report regular weekly religious attendance, and slightly fewer (30%) report that religion plays a "very important" role in their lives. From 1972 to 1992, more young people aged 18 to 20 registered to vote than voted in each of six presidential elections (48% vs. 39%, respectively, in 1992).

And 9-year-olds are twice as likely as 17-year-olds to watch six or more hours of television per day (19% vs. 8%, respectively, in 1994) (*Trends,* 1997, pp. 176-195).

Trends also reports data in two other areas that are developmental in nature. One has to do with the participation of 3- to 5-year-olds in "literacy activities," such as being told a story three or more times a week (58% nonpoor vs. 49% poor), or visiting a library in the past month (41% nonpoor vs. 28% poor). In addition, *Trends* tracks the percentage of students in 4th, 8th, and 12th grade who read for fun (in 1994, 45%, 22%, and 24%, respectively) (*Trends,* 1997, pp. 308-313). The significance of these developmental indicators is not that those selected by *Trends* are the only or even the "right" indicators, but rather that information about them opens a different and refreshing perspective on young people that we rarely get in the other data to which we have become accustomed. It turns out that data really can tell us more about young people than, so to speak, sex, drugs, and rock and roll.

Juvenile Offenders and Victims: A National Report

Of all our data sources, this one is the house of horrors. *JOV* is filled with so much disturbing information that it induces a kind of protective numbness in the reader and even, perhaps, in the authors, who let the data speak for themselves rather than trying to summarize "highlights" across sections. Still, *JOV* fulfills a vital purpose because, for the first time, it brings together in one document the answers to questions about juvenile crime and the juvenile justice system that our crime-sensitive society wants to know. The 1995 report was so popular that it was reprinted in 1996, though much of the crime data it contains are no more recent than 1991 or 1992. The authors address this issue by noting that "although some newer data are now available, the patterns displayed in this report remain accurate" (*JOV,* 1995, p. iii).

Some of the random facts that emerge from *JOV* include:

- Any juvenile between ages 12 and 17 is more likely to be the victim of violent crime than are persons past their mid-20s (pp. 20-21).
- Recent large increases in the homicide rates of black and older juveniles are the result of increases in firearm homicides (pp. 24-25).
- Suicide rates increased between 1979 and 1991 for both white and nonwhite youth ages 15-19 (p. 27).
- Young children are at most risk of violent victimization at dinner time—older juveniles, at the end of the school day (p. 30).
- Victims attributed about one in four personal crimes to juvenile offenders in 1991 (p. 47).
- Juveniles were responsible for about one in five violent crimes in 1991 (p. 47).
- Five percent of juveniles were arrested in 1992; of those, less than one-half of 1% were arrested a violent offense (p. 51).

- Growth in homicides involving juvenile offenders has surpassed that among adults (p. 56).
- Nearly half (47%) of juvenile homicide offenders are white. However, when population differences are taken into account, black juveniles kill at a rate six times that of white juveniles (p. 57).
- In 1992, juveniles were responsible for 9% of murders, 12% of aggravated assaults, 14% of forcible rapes, 16% of robberies, 20% of burglaries, 23% of larceny-thefts, 24% of vehicle thefts, and 42% of arsons (p. 101).
- If trends continue as they have over the past 10 years, juvenile arrests for violent crime will double by the year 2010 (p. 111).

And so on. In the midst of so much damning evidence, evidence that has convinced most Americans that adolescents are hooligans, it is easy to forget a defining fact about this information: *only a handful of adolescents ever get into trouble with the law.* Ninety-five percent of our teenagers do not. This fact might be more prominent, indeed comforting, if we spent as much time and money investigating what the vast majority of teenagers are doing who do not commit crimes as we do tracking the few who do.

Some of *JOV*'s data do, however, debunk some widely held beliefs about adolescent behavior. For example:

> *The initiation of delinquency and the initiation of substance abuse appear to be independent events.* [A review of the] findings of the National Youth Survey to investigate the links between delinquency and substance abuse [revealed] . . . that the onset of minor delinquency in a child's life generally occurs prior to the onset of alcohol use. Thus alcohol use cannot be a cause for the onset of delinquency. Similarly, since serious offending generally begins prior to the use of marijuana and hard drugs, their use cannot be viewed as a cause for the initiation of more serious delinquency. The sequencing of minor delinquency to alcohol use, to more serious offending, to marijuana and hard drug use most likely reflects overlapping, independent and developmentally determined delinquency and substance abuse patterns. Drug use does not cause the initiation of delinquent behavior, nor delinquent behavior the initiation of drug use. However, they may have the same root causes, such as family background, family structure, peer associations, peer influences, school history, psychosocial attributes, interpersonal traits, unemployment and social class. (*JOV*, 1995, p. 63)

Many of these "root causes" are the same developmental components of a child's life that we believe need much more scrutiny from research.

REPORT IN BRIEF. NATIONAL ASSESSMENT OF EDUCATIONAL PROGRESS: 1996 TRENDS IN ACADEMIC PROGRESS (UPDATED 1998)

This report provides the major results of the 1996 *NAEP* science, mathematics, reading, and writing long-term trend assessments. These results chart trends going back to the first year in which each *NAEP* assessment was given: 1969/1970 in science, 1973 in mathematics, 1971 in reading and 1984 in writing. Trends in average performance over these periods are discussed for students at ages 9, 13, and 17 for the science, mathematics and reading assessments, and for students in grades 4, 8 and 11 for the writing assessment.

NAEP makes clear that, from the early 1970s through 1996, the performance of America's schoolchildren has been relatively consistent:

- **Science.** The overall pattern of performance in science for 9-, 13- and 17-year-olds is one of early declines followed by a period of improvements. Among 17-year-old students, declines in performance that were observed from 1969 to 1982 were reversed, and the trend has been toward higher average science scores since that time. Despite these recent gains, the overall trend was negative, and the 1996 average score remained lower than the 1969 average. After a period of declining performance from 1970 to 1977, the trend for 13-year-olds has been one of increasing scores. Although the overall linear trend was positive, there was no significant difference between the 1996 and 1970 average scores for these students. Except for the decline from 1970 to 1973 in average science scores for 9-year-olds, the overall trend shows improved performance, and the 1996 average score for these students was higher than that in 1970.
- **Mathematics.** At all three ages, trend results indicate overall improvement in mathematics across the assessment years. Among 17-year-olds, declining performance during the 1970s and early 1980s was followed by a period of moderate gains. Although the overall pattern is one of increased performance, the average score in 1996 was not significantly different from that in 1973. The performance of 13-year-olds across the trend assessments shows overall improvement, resulting in a 1996 average score that was higher than the 1973 average. After a period of relative stability during the 1970s and early 1980s, the average score for 9-year-olds increased. The overall trend for this age group was one of improved performance, and the average score in 1996 was higher than in 1973.
- **Reading.** At age 17, the pattern of increases in average reading scores from 1971 to 1988 was not sustained into the 1990s. Although the overall pattern is one of improved performance across the assessment years, the average score of 17-year-olds in 1996 was not significantly different from that of their counterparts in 1971. Thirteen-year-olds have shown moderate gains across the trend assessments, and in 1996 attained an average score that was higher than that in 1971. The performance of 9-year-olds improved from 1971 to 1980, but declined slightly since that time. However, in 1996 the av-

erage score for these students remained higher than that of their counterparts in 1971.
- **Writing.** Among eleventh graders, an overall pattern of declining performance is evident in the average writing scores across the assessment years. In 1996, the average score attained by these students was lower than that in 1984. The average writing score of eighth graders has fluctuated, reaching a low point in 1990 and rebounding in 1992. However, no consistent pattern of increases or decreases across the assessments was evident, and the 1996 average score for these students did not differ significantly from that of their counterparts in 1984. At grade 4, no significant changes were observed in students' average writing scores from 1984 to 1996. (*NAEP,* 1998, p. 4)

In short, children's overall learning gains have been modest at best over the past 25 years and in some areas—writing in particular—performance is declining. What are we to conclude from this information? That American public school students are slackers incapable of learning more? That the schools and educators themselves are underachievers who fail to provide our children a first-rate education? That we expect too much and demand too little of our kids in the classroom? All of these conclusions and many more, mostly negative, have been reached by others when confronted with such data as *NAEP*'s. The plain fact is that our children are not performing as well academically as we want them to.

We believe that these six sources of data tell us a great deal, not only about America's kids but also, and more important for our purposes, about the ways we study young people today and the things we want to know about them. It is clear that we are fixated on negative outcomes; most of the information just discussed was obtained because someone somewhere wanted to know what is not working or what has gone wrong in the lives of children. Undoubtedly, the data on negative outcomes will continue to be collected because, like the mountain to be climbed, they are there for the taking. And whole industries have grown up to collect, manage, package, and use negative data. But there is also evidence that, at the federal level anyway, managers of data are beginning to rethink the developmental indicators that are commonly monitored and conclude correctly that negative indicators alone do not tell the full, or even the right, story about America's kids. We want to encourage that trend.

And what about the power of so much negative data to shape our views of young people, particularly adolescents? Even in our small sample of studies, the big picture the data project about the status of children in America is pretty grim. Untrained to make the fine (and defining) distinctions that researchers can, and bombarded daily with an unceasing flow of negative (and often conflicting) factoids, the public aggregates what it should not and concludes from the evidence received that America's kids—*usually, everyone else's kids*—are in big-time trouble. Most data simply make kids look bad in one way or another.

No one set out deliberately to make kids look bad, and making them look that way did not happen overnight. There is a history behind our fixation on negative outcome indicators.

HOW WE BECAME ENAMORED OF THE NEGATIVE

The research indicators we are discussing were, like most social indicators, developed to be used for at least one of the two following purposes: (1) for measuring, analyzing, and understanding, as well as monitoring and reporting on, social changes not necessarily tied to specific governmental policies or programs; and (2) for decision making and evaluating and assessing governmental social programs and policies (Zill, 1995).

The idea of using government statistics to monitor social changes is an old one; it goes back to antiquity in some cases. The earliest statistics were simply outputs of government record keeping. Indeed, the term *statistics* refers to "matters of state" in modern history. Most statistics used in this tradition have been demographic or based on the characteristics of populations. The U.S. population census was required by the Constitution to provide the basis for determining congressional districts, although the gathering of social statistics did not begin in earnest until the 1850 census (De Neufville, 1975).

Indicators developed for decision-making purposes, which include a good number of the indicators discussed so far, are tied to such specific social problems as unmarried young women giving birth or students dropping out of high school. The same indicators are also used to measure the success of specific policies and programs designed to address these problems.

Using a limited set of indicators to make decisions about and assess government social policies and programs dates back to the 1960s, particularly to the advent of the program innovations of Lyndon Johnson's "Great Society." Initially, indicators were used by social analysts to assist policy makers who wanted to shape new program initiatives (e.g., eradication of poverty and racial integration) during a period when resources were abundant and underused and when there was far more confidence in the efficacy of government action than exists today (Schick, 1971).

Also during the 1960s, people who in earlier decades would have been considered social deviants in need of punishment and control came to be seen as people who needed help, program intervention, and treatment. As a result, all sorts of rehabilitation programs were developed for abusers of drugs and alcohol, youth who had committed delinquencies, members of gangs, students who were truants and dropouts from school, unemployed youth and young adults, and so on. The continuation of such programs depended, of course, on data to monitor their effectiveness.

By the early 1970s, however, government resources, confidence, and the will to innovate began to decline. Thus was ushered in a new era of policy research, program evaluation, and accountability to the public that has lasted to this day. What have also lasted are the social research indicators developed to support a now discredited past.

How those indicators have come to be used over the past 30 years has evolved considerably. Beginning in the 1970s, *prevention* of social problems became more important to policy makers than *treatment.* As the cost of rehabilitation programs mounted and the public grew more skeptical of their value, the notion of "nipping problems in the bud" gained currency. Doing so would, of course, save money later on. By the end of the decade, government was firmly in the prevention business—primarily at the secondary school–age level—and has remained so ever since.

Prevention raises a tricky question, however: who should be in these programs? For the most part, policy makers have concluded that young people deemed to be "at risk" of developing social problems are the likeliest candidates for prevention efforts. But who is at risk? At first, the term *at risk* was applied to young people who lived in proximity to older youth and adults who had already demonstrated social problems. The logic here was that if you were in the presence of trouble, you were more likely to create it. Actually causing trouble also qualified you as at risk. Eventually, however, *at risk* also came to encompass a broader set of indicators—indicators that are not based on your behavior or relationship to others but rather on your membership in a demographic category with which trouble has been associated.

For example, if you are a poor youth, then you are more likely to be a criminal because criminals are more likely to come from the ranks of the poor. Or if you are a poor, unmarried, African American, adolescent female, then you are more likely to become pregnant because of the higher prevalence of pregnancy in this group. Or all males up to the age of 25 pay higher car insurance rates because as a group they have a higher incidence of accidents. When considering these proxy indicators of at-risk status, it has not mattered historically to policy makers that the indicators make up false deductive reasoning, i.e., that one's mere membership in a particular group does not automatically denote a particular condition or behavior. But it does matter to groups negatively tarred by these broad brushes, who, by the 1980s, made their voices heard and caused policy makers to back off. By the 1990s, more analysts and researchers were using indicators of at-risk behavior based on direct measures of specific precursor behaviors in individuals. For example, if in the past a student has been retained or held back in a grade, then that student would be more likely to drop out at a later grade based on research among other students who have been retained (Bradby, Kauffman, and Owings, 1992).

But even these more direct indicators of at-risk status have not inspired universal confidence. With regard to school dropouts, for example, Gleason and Dynarski (1998) studied a large national sample and concluded:

> The key finding . . . is that commonly used risk factors are weak predictors of dropping out. The analysis showed that many students with numerous risk factors stayed in school and many with no evident risk factors dropped out. The risk factor that was best able to predict whether middle school students were dropouts—high absenteeism—correctly identified dropouts only 16 percent of the time. Using risk factors was better than using no information at all, but it was not as good as their widespread use might indicate. (p. 9)

It would be interesting to replicate this study in other "at-risk" areas to determine whether risk factors do, in fact, predict anything worthy of policy and resource attention.

PREVENTION VERSUS DEVELOPMENT?

The evolution in thinking just discussed has produced what amounts to a self-justifying and very powerful incentive for activities that seek to prevent bad things from happening to our young people. Data are obviously a key component of this incentive. We tell ourselves that we must find an effective way to prevent a given problem from happening to or among young people; then we use research to chart how effective our efforts have been by tracking the presence or absence of the problems we target. The assumption underlying this approach is that the absence of problems means that young people are developing appropriately.

From a developmental perspective, there are at least three flaws in this rationale. First, while there is plenty of evidence that negative behaviors or conditions impede the positive development of young people, there is no evidence of which we are aware that the absence of such behaviors or conditions in and of itself equates with positive development. That is, the absence of measurable problems in a child's life does not necessarily mean that the child is developing in positive ways—or, as leading youth development advocate Karen Pittman has often said, "Problem-free is not fully prepared." In addition, it is difficult if not impossible to measure behaviors that *could have happened but did not* as the result of a prevention input.

Second is the thorny issue of causality: can we draw credibly causal lines between a prevention "input," say, programs to prevent unwanted teenage pregnancies, and a desired outcome, in this case decreases in such pregnancies? Not really. For many years now, trends in births to teenaged mothers have risen and fallen without apparent connection to widespread and increasing prevention efforts. The same holds true for trends in adolescent drug use and smoking behaviors. Third, and most important, our focus on prevention efforts and the negative outcomes they seek to avoid is a focus on only a fraction of our young people, not all of them, and only a fraction of each young person we target, not the whole kid.

The development perspective offers a different approach that begins with three commonsense questions: What kind of human beings do we want *all* of our children to be? What skills do we want them to possess? What do we want them to be able to do to succeed in adolescence as well as adulthood? The answers to these questions are the same as those any responsible parent would give and go well beyond those that narrowly focused prevention programs seek to provide. We will discuss the development perspective in more detail in the next section. Suffice it to say here that what we want our children to acquire is a rich array of social and intellectual knowledge, attitudes, and competencies that will enable them to be caring people and productive citizens.

Are the prevention and development approaches related? Compatible? Partners? Adversaries? Just what is the relationship between the two? This is a reasonable question at a time when youth development is a fast-growing new field, and prevention, a longtime toiler in the vineyards of youth work, is increasingly being scrutinized for effectiveness.

In our view, prevention and youth development are two faces of the same coin. There are considerable data to prove that prevention of negative behaviors is more likely to be achieved when young people benefit from developmental supports and opportunities on a consistent, day-to-day basis over the course of childhood and adolescence (Zeldin, Kimball, and Price, 1995). Youth development inputs may thus be said to be, in effect, naturally preventive. By the same token, the most effective prevention inputs are almost always developmental in nature. That is, prevention that works is fundamentally based on the principles and best practices of youth development. Indeed, the literature of youth development—drawn from over 30 years of rigorous social science research—is significantly based on studies of effective prevention programs. As we noted previously, the principal way in which prevention and youth development diverge is that development is comprehensive while prevention is specific. In addition, prevention inputs usually target a particular period of time in a young person's life, whereas youth development inputs must occur every day throughout childhood and adolescence.

In some sense, the distinctions between prevention and development that some attempt to draw are distinctions of language. We do not yet possess a shared vocabulary of youth development—a vocabulary that would, for example, permit prevention practitioners to recognize that some if not most of what they do well is actually developmental in nature.

There is also fear among many in the prevention field that the ascendancy of youth development will somehow supplant prevention. This is particularly true among those who work with at-risk populations of young people who are more likely to be poorer, inner-city persons of color. The fear here is that to abandon prevention efforts among these populations is to abandon them altogether. But we do not advocate the supplanting or abandonment of prevention programs. On the contrary, we advocate that prevention efforts be reorganized and redefined in ways that would render them fully and explicitly developmental in principle as well as practice.

DEFINING YOUTH DEVELOPMENT

In order to determine what we should be measuring in the development of young people, we must first have an understanding of what we define as youth development. There are a number of theoretical constructs in the fast-growing field of youth development that seek to provide this definition. For purposes of simplicity, and because we believe it to be the most comprehensive definition, we have selected the Center for Youth Development and Policy Research's Opportunities and Supports model as the basis for our discussion in this section of the chapter.

The center's model identifies a number of outcomes that denote healthy development in young people as well as the opportunities and supports that are essential to the achievement of these outcomes. The following paragraphs provide detail.

Desirable Youth Outcomes

Aspects of Identity: Young people have a positive identity when they express perceptions of self-confidence and well-being, and when they feel connection and commitment to others. Programs often try to enhance the following aspects of identity:

- **Safety and structure:** the perception that one is safe in this world on a day-to-day basis and that some events are predictable;
- **Self-worth:** the perception that one is a good person who can and does make meaningful contributions;
- **Mastery and future:** the perception that one can and does "make it" and has hope for success in the future;
- **Belonging and membership:** the perception that one values, and is valued, by others in the family and surrounding community;
- **Responsibility:** the perception that one has control over one's own actions, and is accountable for those actions and for their consequences on others;
- **Spirituality and self-awareness:** the perception that one is unique and is ultimately attached to families, cultural groups, communities, higher deities or principles.

Areas of Ability: Young people demonstrate ability when they gain knowledge, skills, and attitudes that result in the following kinds of competencies:

- **Physical health:** the ability and motivation to act in ways that best protect and ensure current and future health for oneself and others;
- **Mental health:** the ability and motivation to respond affirmatively and to cope with positive and adverse situations, to reflect on one's emotions and surroundings, and to engage in leisure and fun;
- **Intellectual:** the ability and motivation to learn in school and in other settings; to gain the basic knowledge needed to graduate from high school; to use critical thinking and creative problem solving and expressive skills; and to conduct independent study;
- **Employment:** the ability and motivation to gain the functional and organizational skills necessary for employment, including an understanding of careers and options and the steps necessary to reach goals;
- **Civic and social:** the ability and motivation to work collaboratively with others for the common good and to build and sustain caring relationships with others;
- **Cultural:** the ability and motivation to respect and respond affirmatively to differences among groups and individuals of diverse backgrounds, interests, and traditions.

Measuring Deficits and Assets

Developmental Opportunities

Opportunities: An opportunity exists when young people have ongoing, challenging and relevant chances for:

Formal and Informal Instruction and Training

- **Exploration:** the chance to learn and build skills through guided exploration and instruction, and to test, explore, and discuss ideas and choices critically;
- **Expression and creativity:** the chance to express oneself through different mediums and in different settings, and to engage in both learning and play;

"Adult" Roles and Responsibilities

- **Group membership:** the chance to be an integral group member (groups include families, schools, clubs and youth organizations) by fully taking on the responsibilities of membership;
- **Contribution and service:** the chance to have positive influences on others through active participation in formal or informal community- and family-based activities;
- **Part-time paid employment:** the chance to earn income and to be a part of the workforce, when such work is done within a safe and reasonably comfortable setting.

Developmental Supports

Supports: Support exists when young people are involved in ongoing relationships with others that are characterized by:

Emotional Support

- **Nurturance and friendship:** to receive love, friendship, and affirmation from others, and to be involved in caring relationships.

Motivational Support

- **High expectations:** to know that one is the object of high expectations from others, and to be given the opportunities, encouragement, and rewards necessary to meet high expectations;

- **Standards and boundaries:** to receive clear messages regarding rules, norms, and discipline, and to be involved in discussing and modifying the boundaries as appropriate.

Strategic Support

- **Options assessment and planning:** to receive assistance in assessing and planning one's life options, and to be involved in relationships characterized by coaching, feedback, and discussion;
- **Access to resources:** to receive assistance in gaining access to current and future resources through involvement with and connections to people and information.

The outcomes, opportunities, and supports listed above were not selected arbitrarily or at random. They derive from an exhaustive secondary review of more than two decades of social science research. This review showed clearly that young people are more likely to develop in positive ways (and to avoid problem behaviors) if they possess the aspects of identity and areas of ability the model defines, and if they benefit on an ongoing, consistent, day-to-day basis from the model's developmental opportunities and supports.

Taken together, the various components of the center's model paint a comprehensive and rich picture of an individual child's life—a much more comprehensive picture than any we currently paint with the data we collect. It is instructive, in fact, to note how few of the youth development model's components are being measured in any consistent or meaningful way today. As a consequence, we know far less about our young people and the true state of their development than we may think we do or than we need to know to make the decisions that would truly serve developmental goals.

HOW WE *SHOULD* MEASURE YOUTH DEVELOPMENT

Several basic conditions need to change before widespread changes in the content of data collection can reasonably be implemented. First, government and the media must understand that what we need to know about the development of our young people goes well beyond the narrow information requirements of the prevention industry. As a society interested in its own perpetuation, what would we really rather know about our kids: that more and more of them (yet still a small number) smoke, or that more and more of them (a really significant number) volunteer for community service? That kids get pregnant, or that kids have mastered the Internet? That kids are arrested for violent crimes, or that kids feel loved and protected at home?

Second, there needs to be much wider acknowledgment among adults that *young people are the experts in their own development.* That is, young people intuitively know that they need to develop in positive ways and will do so if helped along the way. The focus we want to highlight here is one of action: of young people acting upon themselves and their environment rather than being acted upon; of young people being agents of change in their own lives rather than passive bystanders in the developmental process. Young people do not have all the answers, and they may not always know what to do, but they are rarely given credit for the many competencies they do possess and the contributions they are willing and able to make.

Third, we need to get over our collective skepticism about measuring the "warm and fuzzy" side of youth development. It is not only possible but also essential to learn how young people feel about themselves, their families, their peers, and their lives. Similarly, adult perceptions of young people are important to understand. Attitudes and beliefs are powerful motivators for or against positive development. Yet, as a society, we have somehow decided that, for example, learning a child's views about the quality of her or his home life is "soft" (i.e., unimportant) data, while counting the number of employed adults in that household is "hard" data. Data about feelings and perceptions are routinely considered soft because they are self-reported. However, if we were more systematic in our collection of soft data and more intentional in our use of it to drive policies and programs, we might develop greater respect for this underused resource.

Fourth, and perhaps most important, research methods need to be made more practical and user-friendly at the community, neighborhood, and organizational levels. Currently, the data that galvanize our attention are collected or compiled mainly by national agencies in costly, large-scale studies. But there is nothing inherently expensive or complicated about research if individuals and organizations understand how to do it correctly and then make effective use of the data they collect. Our ideal would be an environment in which, in addition to national studies, communities throughout the country are routinely defining and tracking the indicators of youth development most meaningful to them. If that were to happen, the result would be a community-based pool of data that tell a much richer story about the ways in which our young people are (or are not) developing than any we can write today.

What, then, besides negative outcomes, should we be measuring consistently in the development of our young people? In some sense, the answer to this question is a matter of practicalities. For example, what would it be reasonable for national agencies to track in annual or periodic surveys? What would it be reasonable for communities or organizations within communities to track in ad hoc local studies? And because we will never have sufficient resources to measure every developmental aspect of every child's life nationwide, or even locally, what "basket" of selected developmental indicators would open a meaningful window into the developmental lives of our kids? Our purpose in this chapter is not to provide definitive answers to these questions but rather to pose the questions and suggest options and examples that can serve as a basis for discussion.

At the national level, we would like to return for a moment to the criteria that Kids Count uses to select the 10 indicators that it analyzes (see page 158). We believe that the same criteria could and should be applied to the collection of youth development data by national agencies. This would entail the addition of developmental indicators in certain national surveys. Rather than do this piecemeal, we recommend that some entity, such as the Federal Interagency Forum on Child and Family Statistics, convene a panel of national experts in youth development who could define the developmental indicators that need to be tracked. The forum could then work with its member departments to add the specified indicators to appropriate survey instruments. Because some or all of the developmental indicators may not "fit" easily into surveys that have been designed for other purposes, there may be some incentive at the federal level to create a new survey process that focuses solely on developmental factors. That eventuality would, of course, be dependent on the importance attached by policy makers to developmental data.

Data Collection in Four Domains

We believe that there are four domains in which it is important to gather data about youth development: among young people themselves; among adults (both parents and nonparents); among organizations that serve or interact in some way with young people; and at the community level in terms of the policy, resource and service environment. The domains of young people and adults lend themselves easily to national data collection; the domains of organizations and communities are probably better addressed at the community level.

Young People

In the domain of young people, some of the indicators that we believe would be interesting to track nationally include percentages of adolescents who:

- Report daily intergenerational contacts with caring adults within and outside the home;
- Volunteer in community service projects three or more hours per week;
- Believe that they are the object of high expectations at home and in school;
- Believe that their environment is safe;
- Believe that they have the ability to "make it" in life;
- Report participating in a school or community decision-making process on issues that have a direct impact on their lives;
- Report respecting differences among groups and individuals of diverse backgrounds, interests, and traditions;
- Report working with computers five or more hours per week;
- Report reading for pleasure at least once per week;
- Report visiting a library twice or more per month; and
- Report mentoring or tutoring younger children at least once per week.

The list could go on, but we believe that these indicators illustrate the direction we would like national surveys to take when asking questions of young people.

Measuring Deficits and Assets

One heartening aspect of changing national data-collection efforts to include developmental indicators is that these indicators do not need to be created from scratch. There are an increasing number of surveys that can serve as examples and provide guidance to national researchers. One such example of a survey currently in use, albeit at the community level only, asks a variety of development-based questions of young people. The survey was developed by Search Institute (1995), which is interested in determining how many external and internal developmental "assets" are possessed or experienced by the middle and high school students it surveys for private clients in cities throughout the United States. These assets fall into general developmental categories, including family and community support, empowerment, boundaries and expectations, constructive use of time, commitment to learning, positive values, social competencies, and positive identity. The more assets a young person possesses or experiences, the more likely it is that he or she will thrive and succeed and the less likely it is that he or she will engage in problem behaviors. Among survey instruments in widespread use, the Search Institute instrument is somewhat unusual in that it combines questions about indicators related to development with questions about risk-taking and problem behaviors.

Another survey of young people that contains a number of development-based questions is one designed for use by the W. K. Kellogg Foundation's Kellogg Youth Initiative Partnerships (KYIP Youth Survey, 1998c). The survey was administered for the first time in 1998 among all eighth and eleventh graders in the three Michigan sites in which KYIP operates: Calhoun County; a portion of north Detroit; and Marquette and Alger Counties in the Upper Peninsula. It will be repeated periodically in future years. The indicators the survey investigates are tied directly to a set of long-term developmental outcomes for youth that KYIP is working to promote in the three sites. These outcomes include the following:

1. **Young people intentionally participate in their own development.** "Intentionally participate in their own development" is defined as young people thoughtfully and deliberately seeking opportunities to learn, grow, and serve; setting goals for themselves; and participating in decision making about issues that affect their lives.
2. **Young people have multiple opportunities in their daily lives to learn, grow, and develop.** "Learning" is defined as the acquisition and application of knowledge and skills; "growth" is defined as emotional maturation; "development" is defined as the achievement of positive developmental outcomes.
3. **Young people have consistent, ongoing relationships with caring adults.** A "caring adult" is defined as someone 21 years of age or older who has frequent contact with, or is consistently available to, a young person; and who offers a young person attention, respect, high expectations, discipline (when necessary), and affection over time.

4. **Young people develop measurable areas of ability and skills and higher levels of thriving behaviors.** These include high academic motivation and attainment, and the development of civic and social competencies.
5. **Young people lower their participation levels in negative risk-taking behaviors.** This includes less or no use of alcohol, tobacco, and other drugs, and less involvement in delinquent behavior.
6. **Young people experience key aspects of a positive identity, such as a sense of belonging, responsibility, self-efficacy, self-worth, and a positive view of the future** (Academy for Educational Development, 1998, pp. 24-25).

We have quoted at some length from these outcomes because KYIP is that still-rare project in which community-based outcome objectives are all based on principles of youth development and in which research to measure progress is substantially linked to developmental outcomes.

Another interesting data set was developed in the 1996 Public Agenda survey—released as *Kids These Days: What Americans Really Think about the Next Generation (KTD)* (Farkas et al., 1997)—a survey of 2,000 adults and 600 young people nationwide that deserves to be repeated on a regular basis. Among the developmental indicators this survey investigated was the percentage of young people 12 to 17 years old who said they would feel "very comfortable":

- Running an errand for a neighbor who needed help (67%);
- Watching a younger child for a neighbor as a favor, without getting paid (59%);
- Doing volunteer work once a week at a place like a hospital or church (55%);
- Helping to feed poor or homeless people at a place like a soup kitchen (51%);
- Volunteering to tutor kids at school (47%);
- Spending time once a week with very old people who need company (44%) (p. 47).

In addition, Public Agenda studied the percentage of young people ages 12 to 17 who said the following statements came "very close" to their point of view:

- I can always trust my parents to be there for me when I need them (81%);
- If I ever need to talk to an adult, there is someone other than my parents I can go to (70%);
- Faith in God is an important part of my life (66%);
- I can always trust my friends to be there for me when I need them (62%);
- I am usually happy (61%);
- I am good at helping other kids with their problems (48%);
- Many of the adults in my neighborhood know me by name (46%) (p. 45).

Adults

Because they are so important in the development of young people, adults are a natural target for study. Again, the 1996 Public Agenda survey provides illustrative guidance. It is a treasure trove of data on adult attitudes and beliefs about teenagers, children, parents, problems facing today's kids, ways to help young people, general views of helping and helping behaviors, and volunteerism.

The Kellogg project, KYIP, has also developed a survey of adults (W. K. Kellogg Foundation, 1997) in its three sites that was first administered in 1997 and will be repeated in future years. As with KYIP's youth survey discussed earlier, the adult survey is tied directly to the early and intermediate outcome objectives that KYIP works with its communities to promote among adults. These outcomes, and their associated measurement indicators, include the following:

- **Adults commit their resources to foster strong systems that promote positive youth development opportunities and supports.** Indicators: adults volunteer in youth-related activities; give money and materials to youth-related activities; believe that youth are a top priority in the community; believe they are making a contribution to young people in the community; and have contact with young people.
- **Adults have consistent, ongoing caring relationships with young people.** Indicators: adults can identify young people with whom they have consistent, ongoing caring relationships; can specify extent of contacts with young people (i.e., frequency, length); and express interest in, and respect and concern for young people.
- **Adults enable young people to be active participants in decision making about issues that affect their lives.** Indicators: young people can name examples of adults seeking and incorporating their views in decision-making processes; and adults create and sustain decision-making opportunities for young people (Academy for Educational Development, 1998, p. 26).

Organizations

There are fewer precedents for studying the domain of organizations in youth development, although there is increasing conviction among service providers that this needs to be done. A pioneering advocate for "best practices" in organizations and programs that serve youth is Networks for Youth Development, an entity based in the Fund for the City of New York's Youth Development Institute. Networks published *A Guided Tour of Youth Development* (Networks for Youth Development, n.d.) in the mid-1990s, which has been influential in the field of youth work in identifying specific things that youth-serving organizations can do to promote youth development. The chapter headings include Organizational Structure That Is Supportive of Youth Development; Environmental Factors on Which Special Attention Has Been Focused; A Holistic Approach to Young People;

Opportunities for Contributions; Caring and Trusting Relationships; High Expectations; Engaging Activities; and Factors That Promote Continuity for Youth in the Program. Each chapter lists specific objectives that could also be used as indicators. Under Engaging Activities, for example, *A Guided Tour* recommends that organizations:

1. **Balance individual and group activities.**
   - Workshop training or group sessions are supplemented with individual counseling sessions on participant needs or opportunities for individual study, activity, etc.
   - Large group, small group, and one-to-one activities are available.

2. **Instill curiosity to learn from a broad range of experiences.**
   - Activities involve questioning, experimentation, and exploration (e.g., field trips, guest speakers, etc.).
   - Activities are interactive and "hands-on" and based upon experiential learning.

3. **Incorporate fun.**
   - Nontargeted laughter occurring during activities.
   - Active participation, including team-building activities, opening up meetings with some type of game, the use of games and role plays in presentation, etc.
   - New activities are constantly added to programs.
   - Staff exhibits sense of humor.

4. **Provide developmentally appropriate activities.**
   - Similar activities and topics are structured differently for different developmental/age groups.
   - Staff/participant ratios and group sizes vary with age of group.

5. **Foster creativity/flexibility.**
   - Activities/workshops/classes involving arts, music, theater, dance, etc.
   - "Choice" activities where youth can make decisions on parts of programs that they would enjoy within the larger youth program.
   - Assessment of creative outlets upon entry to agency (Networks for Youth Development, pp. 28-29).

Networks has pilot-tested and is now refining a peer assessment process based on *A Guided Tour* that involves Network member agencies assessing best practices in youth development among themselves and in other youth-serving agencies.

Measuring Deficits and Assets 183

The Center for Youth Development and Policy Research has also reviewed various approaches to organizational best practice in youth development, including the Network's approaches, which were summarized in the Center's *Best Practice in Youth Development: People, Programs, Organizations and Communities* (1996). It contains not only specific practices that promote youth development but also illustrative measurement indicators for each practice designed to help organizations understand how they can track progress.

The first practical survey application of the work of the Network for Youth Development and the Center occurred coincidentally in KYIP. The Center for Youth Development and Policy Research is a member of KYIP's external evaluation team, which assisted the Kellogg Foundation in developing two organizational surveys for KYIP: one for community organizations that do not serve young people directly but have some interaction with them (W. K. Kellogg Foundation, 1998a) and one for organizations that serve young people directly (W. K. Kellogg Foundation, 1998b). The two surveys were fielded for the first time in late 1998 among a convenience sample of organizations in each of KYIP's three sites and will be repeated in future years.

Like the other KYIP surveys discussed in this chapter, the organizational surveys are tied to its outcome objectives for organizations. These outcomes, and their associated measurement indicators, include the following:

1. **Youth-serving organizations are structured and function in ways that promote positive youth development.** "Structure" is defined as an organization's mission and internal organization and capacity. "Function" is defined as operations—for example, programs and activities.

    Structure Indicators:
    - Boards of directors understand and support positive youth development.
    - Staff are trained in positive youth development principles and practices.
    - Organizational mission statement is supportive of positive youth development.

    Function Indicators:
    - Programs are intentionally planned, implemented, and evaluated to achieve specific developmental goals.
    - Young people participate in decision making about programs.
    - Young people play a pivotal role in implementing programs.
    - Young people evaluate programs regularly, and their evaluations are used in planning.

2. **Organizations collaborate and coordinate with other organizations to promote positive youth development.** "Collaboration" is defined as formal and informal, ongoing working relationships. Within or outside collaborations, "coordination" is defined as consistent consultation with relevant parties regarding specific issues and activities.

   Indicators:
   - Organizations are collaborating to promote positive youth development (e.g., organizations have agreements to work together).
   - Organizations assume specific responsibilities within comprehensive collaborative actions.
   - Organizations can name examples of coordination to achieve various aspects of positive youth development.

3. **Organizations create and sustain strong systems of developmental opportunities and supports for young people.** [Please refer to the center's Opportunities and Supports model earlier in this section for definitions.]

   Indicators:
   - Organizations can name multiple opportunities and supports they provide for young people.
   - Organizations regularly create new opportunities and supports.
   - Organizations sustain opportunities and supports over time (Academy for Educational Development, 1998, p. 27).

Communities

Finally, we come to communities and how we might better understand whether a particular community is supportive of youth development as this chapter defines it. We believe that assessments of conditions within communities that indicate positive youth development is happening would flow cumulatively from the types of data we recommend be collected among young people, adults, and organizations. But we would like to posit an illustrative selection of indicators about which data could tell communities how well they are doing:

- Young people from appropriate age groups are regularly and meaningfully involved—at both the public and private levels—in making decisions about the issues and events that affect them.
- Young people's ideas are regularly solicited, accepted, and acted upon by community institutions of all kinds (e.g., government, schools, police, churches, service providers, media, businesses).

- Public policies address the developmental needs of young people and explicitly support the ability of community institutions in general and parents and other caretakers in particular to meet those needs.
- Employers acknowledge the developmental needs of young people and enable as well as encourage all employees—not just caretakers—to help meet those needs.
- An adequate mix of public and private funding is available to address the developmental needs of young people; or, if not, the public is willing to make up the difference through increased taxation or charitable contributions.
- Community-wide resources available to young people—services, safe places to go, positive things to do, and caring adults—are regularly assessed for adequacy and effectiveness, preferably by young people themselves; effective mechanisms exist to fill gaps and make changes as necessary.
- Every community institution offers young people opportunities to volunteer and contribute.
- Every community institution and business employs young people or offers them opportunities for employment mentoring and job shadowing.
- A majority of adults—whether or not they are caretakers—have positive daily contact with young people and perceive them positively as citizens with valuable contributions to make to the community.
- A majority of stories about youth are positive in all media.

In conclusion, we have attempted in this chapter to present a persuasive case for a new approach to the kinds of information we need in order to understand more fully and in much greater depth the real developmental lives of young people. We have also tried to provide practical examples of the types of data we could collect as well as examples in current use that are available to readers for further investigation.

Our kids deserve a better deal when it comes to the data we collect about them. For decades now, young people have been portrayed inadequately, incompletely, and much too harshly by our most authoritative data resources. Worse, the data we now collect tell us little or nothing about what we really need to know to help our young people grow up more positively. That fact has increasingly serious consequences for American society. Redefining how we know youth development is happening will not solve every problem, nor will it be easy. But it is the right thing to do.

REFERENCES

Academy for Educational Development
1998 *KYIP Revised Evaluation Plan.* Unpublished internal document.
Annie E. Casey Foundation
1998 *Kids Count Data Book: State Profiles of Child Well-Being: 1998.* Baltimore: The Annie E. Casey Foundation.
Bradby, Denise, Phillip Kauffman, and Jeffrey Owings
1992 *Characteristics of At-Risk Students in NELS: 88.* Washington, D.C.: National Center for Education Statistics.

Campbell, J.R., K.E. Voelkl, and P.L. Donahue
1998 *Report in Brief, NAEP 1996 Trends in Academic Progress.* (Publication No. 98-530). Washington, D.C.: U.S. Department of Education, National Center for Education Statistics.

Center for Youth Development and Policy Research
1996 *Best Practice in Youth Development: People, Programs, Organizations and Communities.* Washington, D.C.: Academy for Educational Development, Center for Youth Development and Policy Research. Unpublished monograph.

Centers for Disease Control and Prevention
1998 "Youth Risk Behavior Surveillance—United States, 1997." *CDC Surveillance Summaries* (August 14), and *MMWR* 47(No. SS-3).

De Neufville, Judith Innes
1975 *Social Indicators and Public Policy: Interactive Processes of Design and Application.* New York: Elsevier.

Farkas, S., J. Johnson, A. Duffett, and A. Bers
1997 *Kids These Days: What Americans Really Think about the Next Generation.* Washington, D.C.: Public Agenda.

Federal Interagency Forum on Child and Family Statistics
1998 *America's Children: Key National Indicators of Well-Being, 1998.* Washington, D.C.: U.S. Government Printing Office.

Federal Interagency Forum on Child and Family Statistics
1997 *America's Children: Key National Indicators of Well-Being, 1997.* Federal Interagency Forum on Child and Family Statistics, Washington, D.C.: U.S. Government Printing Office.

Gleason, Philip, and Mark Dynarski
1998 *Do We Know Whom We Serve? Issues in Using Risk Factors to Identify Dropouts.* Princeton: Mathematica Policy Research, Inc. See also Dynarski, Mark, and Philip Gleason (1998). *How Can We Help? What We Have Learned from Evaluations of Federal Dropout-Prevention Programs.* Princeton: Mathematica Policy Research, Inc.

Networks for Youth Development
n.d. *A Guided Tour of Youth Development.* New York: Fund for the City of New York, Youth Development Institute.

Schick, Allen
1971 "From Analysis to Evaluation." *Annals,* 394, p. 57.

Search Institute
1995 *Search Institute Profiles of Student Life: Attitudes and Behaviors.* Minneapolis: Search Institute.

Snyder, Howard N., and Melissa Sickmund
1995 *Juvenile Offenders and Victims: A National Report.* Washington, D.C.: U.S. Department of Justice, Office of Juvenile Justice and Delinquency Prevention.

U.S. Department of Health and Human Services, Office of the Assistant Secretary for Planning and Evaluation
1997 *Trends in the Well-Being of America's Children and Youth, 1997.* Washington, D.C.: U.S. Government Printing Office.

W. K. Kellogg Foundation
1998a *Kellogg Youth Initiative Partnerships (KYIP): A Survey of Community Organizations.* Battle Creek, Mich.: W. K. Kellogg Foundation.

W. K. Kellogg Foundation
1998b *Kellogg Youth Initiative Partnerships (KYIP): A Survey of Youth-Serving Organizations.* Battle Creek, Mich.: W. K. Kellogg Foundation.

W. K. Kellogg Foundation
1998c *Kellogg Youth Initiative Partnerships (KYIP) Youth Survey.* Battle Creek, Mich.: W. K. Kellogg Foundation.

W. K. Kellogg Foundation
1997 *Kellogg Youth Initiative Partnerships (KYIP) Adult Survey.* Battle Creek, Mich.: W. K. Kellogg Foundation.

Zeldin, S., M. Kimball, and L. Price
1995 *What Are the Day-to-Day Experiences That Promote Youth Development? An Annotated Bibliography of Research on Adolescents and Their Families.* Washington, D.C.: Academy for Educational Development, Center for Youth Development and Policy Research.

Zill, Nicholas
1995 "Back to the Future: Improving Child Indicators by Remembering Their Origins." *Focus,* 16(3).

Part III. LOCATING YOUTH DEVELOPMENT ON THE GROUND: SYSTEMS AND SETTINGS

While the complex array of work associated with supporting positive youth development takes place in the policy, research, practice, philanthropy, advocacy, and public opinion "arenas," young people's daily lives unfold in the context of settings—families, neighborhoods, communities, cultures—which are influenced by discrete systems (e.g., education, social services, health care, recreation, juvenile justice). While each of these systems and settings has the potential to contribute in significant ways to positive development, as a group they constitute a fragmented lot, and their collective power is thus weakened and difficult to measure.

The challenge facing researchers, policy makers, funders, and advocates is to support the systems and settings that directly influence young people's lives. Any book attempting to capture and create momentum behind the "big picture" of youth development must therefore reflect the reality of those systems and settings. As the field evolves, it is critical to proceed strategically, considering the full range of settings and sectors that affect young people.

Clearly this section explores only a small subset of what could be a long list of relevant systems and settings. For example, the most critical setting in which young people develop—the family—is not covered here; similarly, critical systems such as education, health care, higher education, and the community-based youth-serving organizations (CBOs) closely associated with the youth development approach are not fully represented. However, this section does mark an important beginning to these explorations by providing in-depth analyses of two of the most important systems that affect young

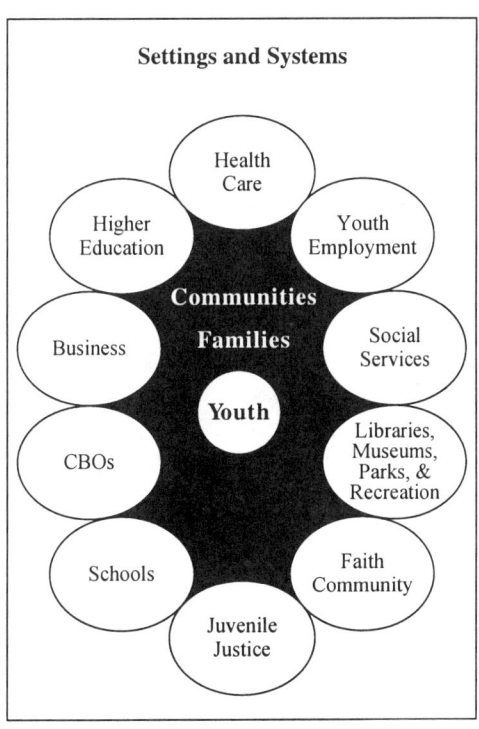

people: juvenile justice and youth employment. In addition, Costello, Toles, Spielberger, and Wynn's chapter provides a broad scan across several sectors (education, community-based youth-serving organizations, and child welfare), identifying common organizational factors that promote or inhibit development.

CONTENTS OF PART III WITH ORGANIZATIONAL SKETCHES OF CONTRIBUTING AUTHORS:

7. How History, Ideology, and Structure Shape the Organizations That Shape Youth

Joan Costello, Mark Toles, Julie Spielberger, and Joan Wynn

The Chapin Hall Center for Children at the University of Chicago was established in 1985 as a research and development center dedicated to bringing sound information, rigorous analyses, innovative ideas, and an independent perspective to the ongoing public debate about the needs of children and the ways in which those needs can best be met. Chapin Hall's primary work is research that addresses two questions: (1) What does our society now do for children? (2) What other approaches might we as a society take to meet our responsibility to children? The Center focuses its work on all children while devoting particular attention to children facing special risks or challenges, such as poverty, abuse and neglect, and mental and physical illness. The contexts in which children are supported—primarily their families and communities—are of particular interest.

8. Juvenile Justice and Positive Youth Development

Robert G. Schwartz

Founded in 1975 as a nonprofit legal service, the Juvenile Law Center (JLC) is one of the oldest children's rights organizations in the United States. The JLC works on behalf of children who have come within the purview of public agencies—abused or neglected children placed in foster homes, delinquent youth sent to residential treatment facilities or adult prisons, or children in placement with specialized services needs. Although the JLC primarily serves the children of Pennsylvania, it also lends expertise to national child advocacy efforts. The JLC's staff attorneys concentrate their efforts on protecting children while reforming the systems meant to serve them by engaging in litigation of key cases, writing, training, public education, advising state and federal government, and serving as an information resource.

9. The More Things Change, the More They Stay the Same: The Evolution and Devolution of Youth Employment Programs

Alan Zuckerman

The National Youth Employment Coalition (NYEC) is a network of 150 youth employment and youth development organizations dedicated to promoting policies and programs that help youth succeed in becoming lifelong learners, productive workers, and self-sufficient citizens. The NYEC shares information about youth policies and programs among practitioners, policy makers, researchers, and advocates.

10. Youth Development in Community Settings: Challenges to Our Field and Our Approach

James P. Connell, Michelle Alberti Gambone, and Thomas J. Smith

In 1999, Gambone & Associates and the Institute for Research and Reform in Education began a cooperative project called the Community Action for Youth Project (CAYP). The mission of CAYP is threefold. First, it aims to disseminate through publication, presentation, and consultation a community action framework for youth development. CAYP is also developing tools to support the use of this framework by funders, managers, planners, evaluators, and technical assistance providers working with community-based youth initiatives and programs. Finally, CAYP provides direct technical assistance to community-based youth initiatives that are using this framework to guide their work.

7 HOW HISTORY, IDEOLOGY, AND STRUCTURE SHAPE THE ORGANIZATIONS THAT SHAPE YOUTH

Joan Costello, Mark Toles, Julie Spielberger, and Joan Wynn

> Almost everything that is great has been done by youth.
> Benjamin Disraeli (1844)

During the second decade of their lives, adolescents may spend as much time in organized settings as they do at home or in other informal settings with friends or family members (Medrich et al., 1992).[1] However, organizations that serve youth are seldom structured to promote youth development. In fact, some of these organizations have mandates, goals, or organizational structures that exist in direct conflict with adolescent needs. Compromises made to accommodate historical and current contexts and missions profoundly affect the way adolescents are viewed and treated.

Young people's lives are touched by multiple organizations, including schools, after-school clubs, sports leagues, cultural programs, church youth groups, courts, child welfare or mental health centers, and places of work.[2] The ubiquity of youth-serving organizations and the amount of time young people spend in them suggest that these organizations have great potential to influence the development of youth, especially those who grow up without supportive families or neighborhoods and who are therefore especially vulnerable.

In this country, government and private funders with an interest in the welfare of youth have focused their funding on preventive or ameliorative programs to reduce such negative behaviors as drug use, unwanted pregnancy, and delinquency, or to alter behavior in young people who have already fallen into these negative patterns. But even if programs like these fulfilled their missions completely, their success could only be measured by the absence of negative characteristics. A nonpregnant, nondropout, non-gang-affiliated, non-drug-abusing youth is not necessarily one who is prepared to live a satisfying, healthy, productive adult life.

For policy makers and practitioners, understanding how the embedded attitudes and mandates of organizations help or hinder youth development has important practical implications.

Focusing questions on structural constraints helps to identify those aspects of organizational practice that have the greatest implications for youth development. This is not to suggest that external influences on organizations are unimportant. Youth-serving organizations persevere under harsh conditions and overcome many obstacles just to maintain organizational coherence and effectively provide services of high quality. But it is clear that money and other resources, which are often quite limited, are not sufficient to generate the changes needed for organizations to promote youth development. Sometimes the organizations themselves are part of the problem.

Although the mission and annual goals of any organization can claim to promote youth development, many factors may limit an organization's ability to achieve that goal. History, administrative structures, funding sources, and accountability requirements may alter the organization's ability to create an environment conducive to the full development of youth. Historical conceptions of adolescence and histories of human service sector organizations have influenced their missions and practices in ways that affect youth development; and social trends have prolonged the period between physical maturity and economic independence, thereby increasing adolescent dependence on formal organizations.

The three human service sectors this chapter considers are education (public schools, in which most children fulfill their legal mandate to attend school), primary supports (activities in which young people participate on a voluntary basis), and problem-focused specialized services (to correct or ameliorate problems). There are, of course, many examples of organizations in each of these sectors that are very good at promoting youth development. We focus here on general factors that potentially promote or inhibit this development, especially in organizations whose services are targeted toward adolescents in urban settings.

For several years, a number of innovative organizations, whose contributions are included in this book, have articulated philosophical and strategic approaches to help organizations—sometimes whole towns—foster youth development. These have distinctive but mutually compatible vocabularies to characterize youth needs and assets, developmental goals, and organizational practices that meet needs and promote development. Most observers tend to agree that organizations are eager to improve the range and quality of their *services to youth.* There is much greater hesitancy, however, to go all the way—to *involve youth* in decisions that affect them and to include their voices (if not their votes) in organizational matters.[3]

We focus here on practices that engage adolescent needs and capacities to exercise control over their lives, including participation in decisions that affect them (Pittman and Wright, 1991; Connell, Gambone, and Smith, 1998; Heath and Roach, 1998). From this perspective, one measure of an organization's orientation toward youth development is its ability or willingness to allow adolescents some degree of autonomy—to take active roles in the organization; to influence matters that are important to them; and to interact in an atmosphere where relationships with adults are characterized by mutual respect, responsiveness, and responsibility. Although organizations can and should attend to providing services that address the other needs of young people, we believe that involving youth in a *joint* effort to promote their development is fundamental to the adoption of a youth development approach that is youth involving as well as youth serving.

We conclude that youth development may need not only a *focus* but a *locus* that links a community development perspective to a youth development perspective. Youth working in collaboration with organizational staff could potentially renew the social fabric of neighborhoods and wider communities and, in so doing, contribute to building their social capital.

HISTORICAL CONTEXT: YOUTH AS A CONCEPT AND A REALITY

Although the concept of adolescence is largely an invention of the twentieth century, evidence of ambiguity about how adolescents are different from children appeared even in the literature of the eighteenth century (Ariès, 1962). The late nineteenth and early twentieth centuries witnessed the development of a new conception of adolescence that profoundly influenced the ways in which institutions viewed and treated young people. Generational distinctions, propelled by social changes associated with industrialization and modernization, implied not the smooth passage of land, skills, and other traditions to the next generation, but a separation of life courses, a break with traditions (Berger, Berger, and Kellner, 1973; Levy, 1966). Young adults who went to work in factories and moved into cities were likely to know as much as if not more than their elders about the changes in economic, social, and civic life. The young posed a threat to the established social order, but they also offered the promise of re-creation and renewal. They did then, and they do now. Ambivalence about youth underlies much of what organizations say and do about them and for them.

In this atmosphere of ambivalence—if not outright fear—G. Stanley Hall's theory of adolescence became popular. He defined adolescence as a biologically driven, stormy period and diminished it by concluding that young people could not be taken seriously, however much they might be amazing, endearing or annoying in turn. Life for the adolescent was marked by "storm and stress," and this period of turmoil was seen as universal to all cultures (Hall, 1904). It is not. Hall's view of youth did not so much reflect reality for adolescents as it created it, laying the groundwork for solutions to the "problems" of youth that treated them as unstable, incapacitated by biological condition, and unable to be rational or responsible. If they were unstable and incompetent, it made sense that organizations and institutions would not take adolescents' opinions seriously or allow adolescents to contribute to decisions.

The Biosocial Gap

In the United States and other industrialized countries, the onset of puberty has been occurring earlier and earlier. Because of improvements in public health—

preventive health care, medicine, and possibly nutrition—the mean age of menarche[4] for girls in industrialized countries decreased by three to four months each decade between 1850 and 1950 before leveling off. Thus, menarche occurs two and a half to three and a half years earlier than it did 150 years ago when, as we discuss later, changes in society's organized responses to youth began to take shape (Brunstetter and Silver, 1985; Petersen, Richmond, and Leffert, 1993; Sprinthall and Collins, 1984). Young people's cognitive capacities to use formal logic, to think hypothetically, and to use abstract reasoning reach adult levels by middle adolescence and facilitate processing complex information to which they currently have unprecedented access (Keating and Clark, 1980; Weithorn and Campbell, 1982). A widening gap between the age at which muscles, reproductive capacity, and cognitive powers mature (biological maturity) and the age at which adolescents are prepared to take on adult economic roles and social responsibilities (social and economic maturity) is a new phenomenon in human history that has been described as the *biosocial gap* (Senderowitz, 1992).

One consequence of the biosocial gap is that young people spend greater amounts of time financially dependent on families or their surrogates because they cannot support themselves and prepare for rewarding employment at the same time, something they could have done a generation or two ago. They are also dependent on teachers and preparatory institutions organized in most respects to teach physically immature children.

Confronted by this disparity between what they are able to do physically and mentally and what they are allowed to do socially and economically, adolescents must find their own ways to make meaningful choices. Because another characteristic of contemporary adolescent life is age segregation and lack of adult presence, often they proceed without adult support and guidance. Csikszentmihalyi and Larson (1984) found that adolescents spend most of their time with peers and relatively little time in formal or informal socialization or interaction with adults. Until recent decades, workplaces supplemented adult family and church contacts by providing opportunities for adolescents to work alongside adults and to infer—if not to hear directly—how adults approached life situations. But those opportunities are fewer in increasingly age segregated workplaces.

Many of the contacts youth have or could have with adults occur in the settings of youth-serving organizations, especially in schools, after-school programs, athletic, and cultural clubs close to home, and for some, in the child welfare, mental health, or juvenile justice systems. If relationships with adults are as important for adolescent development as most writers believe, and if adolescents interact with adults largely in settings organized to serve youth, then the ways in which organizations engage, limit, or promote those relationships are crucial.

The Youth Development Movement

Over the last 30 years, increasing attention has been paid in the human development and practice literatures to adolescent capabilities and the conditions that must be satisfied for adolescents to grow into successful, responsible adults.

Although many common themes surface in this literature, it offers neither a common language nor a perspective on how the findings might guide a practice framework. In the late 1980s, Karen Pittman and others (Marlene Wright, Michele Cahill, and James Connell) began to shape a youth development perspective that focused on the needs and competencies of adolescents—a coherent, holistic framework that would help orient thinking about youth and inform policies to address youth needs. One of the goals of the *youth development perspective* was to shift policy away from a programmatic focus on youth problems to a more comprehensive approach that views youth as assets, as individuals with resources and capabilities that deserve full support and development.

Among the critical components of the *youth development perspective* is the development of youth voice, initiative, and decision making as key aspects of growth toward maturity. Pittman and Wright (1991) distilled from their literature reviews six basic adolescent needs, three of which apply to younger as well as older adolescents—safety and structure, belonging and group membership, closeness and relationships—and three of which become, in our opinion, increasingly critical by middle adolescence—self-worth and social contribution, independence and control over one's life, competence and mastery. If adult life functions require self-worth, independence, and competence, it makes sense that the development of initiative and sound decision-making ability is vital during adolescence. According to Connell et al. (1998):

> [Adolescents] need ample opportunities to try on the adult roles they are preparing for. This means they need to participate in making age-appropriate decisions for themselves and others, ranging from deciding what activities to participate in to choosing responsible alternatives to negative behaviors and taking part in setting group rules for classrooms, teams, organizations, and the like. They also need to practice taking on leadership roles, such as peer leader, team captain, council member or organizational representative . . . Specifically, they need to participate in groups of interconnected members, families, clubs, teams, churches, theater groups and other organizations that afford opportunities for youth to take on responsibilities. They also need to experience themselves as individuals who have something of value to contribute to their different communities. (p. 8)

Young people need to make their mark one way or another. This idea was first articulated in a 1959 paper that reviewed the then-expanding literature on motivation and concluded that achieving personal efficacy and a sense of competence were central elements in human motivation (White, 1959). The need for experience in positions of autonomy, action, and responsibility is so acute in adolescents that in the absence of healthy opportunities to belong, young people will seek or create less healthy versions (Connell et al., 1998). A recent review of the literature on family influences (Galambos and Ehrenberg, 1997) confirms the conclusions of an earlier review of parental influences (Baumrind, 1987), namely, that optimal development occurs when families promote age-appropriate autonomy while maintaining strong family relationships. Organizations with a serious commitment to youth development must recognize that *care and service* to youth are not enough. Attention must also be given to fostering the development of self-worth, independence, and competence through their involvement in organizational life.

A growing body of research on human development emphasizes the importance of the social context of learning and has given rise to renewed interest in Vygotsky's theory that children's development progresses when they undertake tasks beyond their current independent problem-solving ability under adult guidance or in collaboration with more capable peers. He called the range within which their development can be fostered the "zone of proximal development" (Vygotsky, 1978). The adult or more capable peer assists performance through interactions that begin with the learner's current level of understanding and allows the learner a meaningful role in setting the pace and sequence of the instructional task. Relationships between adults and youth that engender learning are characterized by goals shared by the teacher and learner (Rogoff, 1990) and tend to have the characteristics of relationships that young people find satisfying. Such relationships respect the voices of youth. If initiative and good decision making are important capabilities for adolescents to acquire, youth need to be heard, to take on "adult" responsibilities and to make important choices, scaffolded by relationships with adults and more capable peers who share the same goals.

These ideas hold several implications for organizations that serve youth. If the goal in promoting youth development is to prepare youth for the future, to provide for their growth into responsible, contributing adults, then at least three conditions must be met. First, young people's ideas must be heard and respected. Second, youth must be able to take on near-adult roles, that is, to have the opportunity to take responsibility within the organization and to make decisions that have consequences for themselves and for others. Adolescents need to begin to make decisions that determine the course of their own lives—decisions about the paths they take within the organization or about the course of the organization itself. Third, these near-adult roles must be woven into a context of supportive relationships with adults and more capable peers to allow for adolescent choice in an environment that promotes relationships with adults that go well beyond the roles of participant and supervisor.

Staff are unlikely to engage youth in their zone of proximal development unless the organization itself provides opportunities for staff to contribute to the decisions of the organization. As hard as it may be to enable youth to share decision making, it is often just as difficult to allow staff a role in developing the organization and its services (Tharp, 1993).

Do Organizational Structures Support Youth Development Goals?

The foundations of youth-serving organizations in the human services sectors of interest to us—schools, primary supports, and problem-focused services—date to the last decades of the nineteenth century. They were part of a period of massive social reorganization and institution building in the United States and Europe that responded to social dislocations following industrialization and urban population growth. From the mid-1960s to the 1980s, many social reformers, including government and private funders, judged the historic features of older youth-serving organizations to be so cumbersome and resistant to change that they advocated the creation of alternative schools and youth agencies. Now, in the late 1990s, most of those organizations are plagued by the same problems found in the old organizations to which they were the alternative.

In assessing how organizations contribute to youth development, it is important to consider the relationship the organization establishes with the adolescent. This relationship is crucial to the delivery of effective services. In fact, in all human service organizations, the content and quality of the relations between organizations and their clients influence the effectiveness of the service (Hasenfeld and English, 1974): the greater the degree of equality in organization-client relations, the more motivated and committed the clients are likely to be, and the more they will benefit from the services offered (Parsons, 1970). Even the most responsive organizations struggle to balance competing goals—treating participants with respect and allowing for their autonomy while at the same time trying to enhance or change the participants' competencies or behaviors.

In dealing with adult clients, human service organizations must balance their own responsibilities and mandates against the degree to which their services are shaped by client voice and direction. Youth-serving organizations face two additional challenges. They must strike a balance between the perception and treatment of the adolescent as a child or as an adult; an organizational belief in the capacity of youth for responsible initiative and decision making helps determine the autonomy and respect that are afforded youth. Organizations must also consider the mandates under which they work, such as government regulations, board policies, and liability considerations, in the context of federal and state legislative environments that have no coherent view of what age has to do with attaining adult status.

Vulnerable or Responsible: Child-Care Subsidies

Child-care regulations struggle to define the age at which a young person is mature enough to take care of her- or himself. Federal and most state policies do not provide subsidies for child care or other supervised arrangements for children of working parents once they reach 12 years of age, although most parents and youth workers believe that 13-, 14- and 15-year-olds need some supervision and direction. The case for denying child-care subsidies asserts that by the age of 12 young people of working parents can regularly protect and supervise themselves and engage in constructive activities. This policy is not rooted in a sound theoretical framework about young adolescents' needs and capabilities but responds instead to a host of competing and often conflicting pressures on the public welfare system and the agendas of agents inside and outside of the systems of public welfare and child care.

ORGANIZATIONS THAT SERVE YOUTH

In the sections that follow, we examine selected characteristics of organizations within the three human service sectors that interact with youth: public schools—the universal organization for youth because it compels attendance; primary support organizations that offer activities on a voluntary basis during out-of-school time; and problem-focused organizations that become involved when young people need protection or rehabilitation. Although individual organizations within these sectors vary widely with respect to practices and effectiveness, the three sectors share significant history, public support, mandates, and organizational structures that contribute to the ways adolescents are viewed and treated. In each sector, exemplary programs exist in which adolescents flourish; but to endure and multiply over time, exemplary programs must also take root in the organizations themselves. Core beliefs about the way adolescents should be treated often interact with organizational mandates, responsibilities, and histories to create environments that help or hinder these programs in taking a comprehensive approach to adolescent development. In what follows, we attempt to take some common lineages and characteristics of organizations in order to pose questions about the prospects of each to help prepare adolescents for rich and productive lives.

In our examination of the three human service sectors, we consider a variety of factors, including their evolution and history, their mission, the nature of participation, organizational size, autonomy, practice strategies, capacity for relationship building, and opportunities for youth involvement. In this way, we try to identify the organizational constraints that may undermine the capacity of organizations within these sectors to promote youth development. We focus primarily on those aspects of a youth development perspective that allow youth participation—voice, initiative, and decision making—and specifically on those that offer opportunities for young people to make choices about their activities; assume adult or near-adult roles and responsibilities that they share with adults; engage in critical feedback; contribute ideas to institutional decisions; and develop strong, supportive relationships with adults and more capable peers.

In considering some of the influences that compete with a youth development perspective in organizations, it should be noted that, like individuals and families, organizations are creatures with a social inheritance.

Schools

Schools touch the lives of more adolescents than any other institution. The school system is the primary normative institution for children and youth in the United States and holds vast potential for supporting young people in becoming productive, healthy adults. Despite the publicity given to dropout rates, each decennial census reports a greater percentage of this country's young people becoming high school graduates. Although schools have an ostensible mandate to prepare young people for successful adult lives, there are inherent conflicts between what youth need and what schools are able to provide, a circumstance that has been shaped largely by the history of American education. We address only public schools in this chapter; however, many of the influences on public schooling also apply to private schools. The mission and form of schooling express a society's hopes and a defense against its fears. These currents often narrow an individual school's leeway to be responsive to its students.

History

In the early 1900s, in response to the industrial revolution and massive migration to cities, urban elites, "largely business and professional men, university presidents and professors, and some 'progressive' superintendents" joined forces and brought about the consolidation of rural community schools into larger, more centralized, urban institutions (Tyack, 1974). As schools enlarged their catchment areas; added staff, rooms, and rows of desks; and increased the number of grades within each school, schooling became a much larger presence in the lives of young people. Decisions that shaped modern schooling were not made solely for the welfare of children. Changes in the economy created pressure for more children to attend school and to stay in school for more years. As work in factories became more specialized, employers began to demand certificates and credentials for employment, and education became the mandatory route to certification.

Pressure to attend school also came from legislation designed both to protect youth and to ensure that they did not disrupt economic and civic order. Child labor laws were passed to keep children safe from harsh conditions in factories, but also to limit competition with adult workers for jobs. Mandatory school attendance for all children developed, in part, as a response from lawmakers to quell what were feared to be the riotous excesses of what was viewed as a rowdy, unrestrained immigrant population. The logic followed that if children were in school, they were not out on the streets causing mischief and social disorder. By 1903, compulsory schooling was enforced in 31 states (Tyack, 1974). Soon the schools were flooded with a great number and diversity of students.

Large public schools evolved with a dual mandate: to prevent social disorder and to prepare children to become efficient, productive employees in a manufacturing economy dominated by large factories where labor was organized into assembly lines. Discipline, conformity and obedience became the operative social goals of schooling, superseding curriculum.

With this purpose in mind, superintendents like Harris advocated for public schools that were to be governed bureaucratically and dominated by rules, regulations, and clear hierarchies of control. The school replicated the organization of the factory. The model of rational administration found in most factories dictated that workers perform actions but make as few decisions as possible and that rigid hierarchies exist for decision making at the higher levels of the organization. Students, divided into discrete grades, worked through standardized lessons, ruled by a precise series of bells and periods. Teachers, who themselves operated within carefully prescribed roles, guided their practices with standard texts provided by the administration. Principals presided over schools but made all decisions in accordance with district mandates, and superintendents oversaw all operations and made decisions for the entire district. This centralized control of schools stood in stark contrast to the small, community-controlled rural schools that often comprised a handful of students, a single teacher, and no administrators and were marked by nongraded primary education, flexible scheduling and instruction of younger children by older peers (Tyack, 1974).

As schools have increased in size and curricula have increased in specialization, the hierarchical factory model of school structure has persisted. High schools, in particular, have developed rigid and pyramidal authority structures, having been divided into departments each with its own rules and regulations. Schools themselves are accountable to various interests, including local and state school boards, parents, national government standards, and professional accreditation organizations. They are least accountable to the students. These structural characteristics create an environment that has many implications for adolescent development.

If the development of adolescents is fostered in environments in which their voices are respected, where they can take the initiative, and where they can participate in decisions that affect their own fate, then public high schools, in particular, tend not to promote the full development of adolescents. The history of schools as institutions that instill order within the young and prepare them for specialized manual labor has left a structural legacy that presents obstacles to the development of adolescents as near-adults preparing for a different world than the one in which compulsory education began (Newmann and Wehlage, 1995).

Organizational Structures and Dynamics

School size. One characteristic of public high schools that affects their capacity to promote adolescent development is size. The consolidation of public schools into large central campuses occurred at a time when economies of scale were being promoted in business and industry. It was assumed that large schools would be economically efficient because they would require fewer administrative and support staff and could obtain materials and supplies in greater quantity at lower costs. It was also assumed that larger schools would provide a greater variety of resources than would smaller ones (Lee, Bryk, and Smith, 1993). These premises have not been borne out in practice, and larger school size seems to have other, more damaging effects. Research has shown that larger schools actually require more support and administrative staff than do smaller schools (Chambers, 1981). Other studies suggest that the availability of resources for schools is determined less by school size than by the socioeconomic status of the community served by the school (Friedkin and Necochea, 1988).

School size has had an impact on the way schools function as communities. According to some researchers, increasing the size of the school results in a more formal division of labor and a static set of rules, often fostering organizational alienation (Lee et al., 1993). The rigid bureaucratic structures that emerge produce an environment in which there is little room for adolescents to make decisions that actually affect the course of their lives in school or the course of the school itself. Large school size also tends to foster alienation, isolation, and a lack of engagement of both teachers and students—conditions that do not encourage the strong relationships between adolescents and adults that are so necessary to support and guide adolescent decision-making at an adult level.

> **Community Ethos on a Large Scale:**
> **John F. Kennedy High School**
> Sara Lawrence Lightfoot (1983), in her portrait of six good high schools, wrote about the John F. Kennedy High School, a public school in an affluent neighborhood in the Bronx attended by 5,300 students, many of them from lower-income families of diverse cultural backgrounds.
>
> The principal, Bob Mastruzzi, expended a tremendous amount of effort to build and maintain the school as a place where adolescent needs can be met; and students and teachers treated as assets and contributors rather than subjects.
>
> Despite the size of the school, Lightfoot observed a sense of community and belonging among many of the students and faculty. She attributed this quality to the nature of interpersonal relationships inside the classroom and to the administration's acceptance and solicitation of student input and feedback about broader school issues. (pp. 72, 66-67, 69)

Even in small schools, however, there are few roles in which adolescents can take the initiative or assume responsibility and authority. The number of positions in which students can make important plans or choices that have consequences for themselves as students or the school as a whole is few. Students who take these positions of responsibility are largely self-selected, and often the same small group of students can be seen participating in multiple activities. Students are often chosen to participate because they already have confidence and experience in making realistic choices. Faculty often choose participants and are responsible for extracurricular activities rather than serving as advisers to them. In many schools, extracurricular activities become entries on college applications rather than opportunities to explore and organize common interests with a group of peers or to influence school climate. Previous generations may have had access to fewer extracurricular opportunities, but they had more autonomy and were more likely to complain that faculty and administration were *uninterested* rather than too involved or too controlling.

Autonomy. Public school administrators balance an array of conflicting interests from outside the school—parents; local school boards; municipal, county, state, and federal governments; and professional organizations—all of which claim a legitimate role in shaping schools. The degree to which school administrators are prompted to respond to outside influences and are rewarded for avoiding controversy and conflict affects their inclination to allow for administrator and teacher discretion. An administration that aims to be free of mistakes is not likely to generate development in students, faculty, or the organization. School autonomy not only affects the ability of the school to prepare its students cognitively, but also to allow for adolescent responsibility, creativity, and initiative. Private schools have greater autonomy than do public schools, but they are not without their constraints.

One of the major approaches to restructuring schools is school-based management, which features a change in the governance system of a school district by decentralizing decision making from the district's central administration to local schools. School-based governance aims to give school constituents—administrators, teachers, parents, and sometimes students—a greater say in school decisions that affect them. In a study of a group of schools undergoing this type of change in Chicago, researchers found that organizing schools more democratically had strong connections to real, systemic restructuring, which often included greater teacher involvement in an emerging professional community and stronger school-community ties (Bryk, Kerbow, and Rollow, 1997). It can be argued that these changes promote a better environment for students not only academically but also developmentally, and that inclusion of students in the process is beneficial for all involved. According to one researcher, "Schools that were most successful were those where staff, parents and even sometimes students were involved in making decisions" (Wohlstetter, Mohrman, and Robertson, 1997).

Sharing the Power: Brookline High School

Brookline High School, just outside Boston, underwent an administrative and organizational transformation with the arrival of Bob McCarthy. Believing that "the more power you give people, the more responsibility they take" (Lightfoot, p. 173), McCarthy dismantled the top-down, hierarchical arrangement of roles and relationships in the school. His commitment to increasing the sense of community and including more constituencies extended to inclusion of students in school decision-making processes. One of his first acts as principal was to establish a "Fairness Committee" composed of students and teachers to deal with disciplinary problems and, he hoped, to expand its scope to create policy.

McCarthy instituted a "town meeting" in which teachers and students were asked to take responsible roles in the school. Some of the first issues handled by the group regarded absentee policies, hiring decisions, litter and vandalism, and a discipline policy for drugs and alcohol. According to one observer, "Adolescents are offered a piece of the power in exchange for responsible action. It is an uphill battle. Many students prefer a more passive, reactive role, while others are suspicious of bargaining with any adult and do not trust McCarthy's rhetoric" (ibid., p. 318). Though the school's efforts were conscious and deliberate, they were in opposition to the cultural and ideological sweeps of contemporary society and demanded a shift for both staff and students out of the deep grooves of habit, hierarchy and convention. The transition required a great deal of security and leadership on the part of the principal and a lot of work from all the stakeholders.

Teachers whose actions are determined more by rules and regulations than by their own creativity and judgment as professionals have limited latitude in allowing adolescents to make judgments about the course of their studies or the ways in which they will participate in or contribute to the school and the community. Even when school rules accommodate student needs, teachers' judgments about what is in the interest of youth may conflict with the social norms that govern professional identity. Fostering the autonomy of youth may jeopardize continued acceptance by professional colleagues.

Researchers concerned with isolating characteristics of effective schools have often looked at parochial schools, which seem to engender favorable outcomes for the students and families who choose them. Catholic schools are generally more communally organized than are public schools, and students in those schools achieve well academically across the board; in fact, in Catholic schools, differences in social class and ability level do not create the same academic disparities they do in other schools. Among the factors used to explain the success of Catholic schools are a communal school organization, decentralized governance, and a unifying ideology (Lee, 1997). Organized communally, Catholic schools offer frequent opportunities for adults and adolescents to have face-to-face interactions and shared experiences outside the classroom. Teachers in Catholic schools have more diffuse roles and see their duties as extending to all encounters with students inside and outside the school. Teachers see themselves as shapers of character as well as developers of skills, and they experience a strong sense of collegiality. Most Catholic schools operate with remarkable autonomy, linked only loosely to other schools or the diocese. They are able to operate freely and without the rigid bureaucracy of public schools unless they become financially dependent on the diocese. Finally, these schools are organized around an inspirational ideology that insists that both students and teachers be considered from the standpoint of human dignity and asks that people act beyond their own individual interests for the common good. Catholic schools seem to be able to provide for the academic and intellectual growth of their charges and tend to their emotional, social, and moral growth, and are organized and informed by ideas that promote the full development of youth as human beings (Lee, 1997).

Segregation by age level and ability. According to the Vygotskian perspective, children master new skills while in the presence of more advanced peers as well as adults. High schools—most schools, in fact—divide students by grade and by ability level, grouping them homogeneously and thereby limiting their opportunity to develop skills in the company of peers who are already proficient. Peer tutoring or mentoring programs have been developed to mitigate the situation, but such peripheral efforts do not alter the effect of separating students from their older and more advanced peers, whether they are more advanced chronologically or in terms of ability level.

Professionalism. In rural schools before the industrial revolution, teaching was perceived as an employment alternative for unmarried women and required no special training or experience. Driven by the centralization of schools in the early 1900s and the increasing emphasis on certification as a requirement for employment, teaching emerged as a profession. The burgeoning hierarchy and bureaucracy in education brought with them new regulations and standards for teaching and the beginning of teacher training programs designed originally to standardize teaching practices and reduce variation from classroom to classroom. Now teachers must undergo more training than ever, and workshops and professional development opportunities abound. The increasing professionalization of teaching—reinforced by unionization—has several implications for adolescent development that turn on competing notions of what it means to be a professional.

Freidson (1970), in his studies of the health-care system, argues that professionalism contributes to alienation and disenfranchisement of clients as well as to bureaucracy. He contends that embedded in historical notions of professionalism (embodied in documents like the Hippocratic Corpus, which laid out professional standards for physicians) is the notion that professionals attain status through access to specialized knowledge and that clients, lacking professional training, are too ignorant to understand information related to their situations. It follows that the client "should not be treated like an adult, but rather like a child, given reassurance but not information." Historically, the relationship between the client and the professional relies on the client's faith in the professional's superior knowledge and judgment; if patients do ask questions, they threaten the status of the professional.

Applying this line of reasoning to secondary schools, it can be seen that to the degree that the notion of the teacher as professional is based on historical notions of professionalism, and teaching is seen as the process by which an expert (the teacher) imparts technical knowledge, the clients—students—will be treated as children, that is to say, treated as if their judgment is not adequate. In some schools and among some teachers, this reinforces the view that the teacher possesses special knowledge, that adolescents are ignorant, and that their questions are impertinent and threatening to the status of the teacher as a professional. This perspective not only inhibits adolescent questioning, and therefore adolescent cognitive growth, it also increases alienation, causing a rift between adults and students. To the extent that this viewpoint permeates teacher interactions with adolescents, adolescents will be treated as if they are children, and such healthy signs of adolescent growth as spontaneity, questioning, and initiative will be seen as threats to institutional and professional authority and as symptoms of adolescent insubordination and disorder.

In some schools—and in some classrooms in many schools—teacher professionalism defines teachers as both learners and experts. Another perspective on professionalism comes from research on *professional communities* within effective schools. From this perspective, a professional community is one that is distinguished by a mission strong enough to guide instruction but flexible enough to encourage reflection, debate, discussion, and experimentation. In the most effective schools, students and staff cooperate, collaborate, and work for the mission—in what Vygotskians would call the "zone of proximal development." In their review of research, Newmann and Wehlage (1995) found that in the presence of a professional community students had higher cognitive gains and were surrounded by greater social support for learning. This notion of professionalism nourishes relationships between students and adults and provides a place for student voice and initiative in collaboration with adults. It fosters the vision of adolescents working alongside adults to build something of importance to both of them—the enterprise of successful schooling.

There are certain structural characteristics that promote a professional learning community: small school size; an interdependent work structure in which staff have time and responsibility to collaborate on school operations; authority to act, unconstrained by outside regulations (Newmann and Wehlage, 1995). These conditions are rarely found in modern public high schools, where student populations often swell into the thousands; teachers, segregated into departments, are pressed for time to collaborate; and administrators, bound by their mandate to serve the public, must negotiate and often capitulate to the demands of varied constituents—school boards, parents, government agencies, unions, and professional organizations. These characteristics, endemic to most large public schools, present serious obstacles to the formation of an atmosphere of professional community in which adolescents can be seen as valuable contributors to a larger effort and in which they can develop relationships with adults that prepare them for maturity.

Critical Feedback and Debate: Milton Academy

Some schools not only encourage feedback and criticism from students but also foster debate and discussion about the organization itself and the shape it should take. Sara Lawrence Lightfoot (1983), in her book *The Good High School,* noted the importance of criticism at Milton Academy, a New England preparatory school. Everyone is aware and accepting of Milton's institutional imperfections. The school's philosophical grounding in humanism and the administration's acceptance of criticism and conflict encourage students and staff to air their opinions about how the school functions. "Criticism was legitimized, even encouraged," Lightfoot writes. "The stark visibility of the institutional vulnerabilities was related, I think, to a deeply rooted tolerance for conflict, idealism, and to feelings of security" (p. 309). While some students and staff welcomed the atmosphere, others "grew impatient with the conflicts and confusion" (p. 310). Affording opportunities to exercise power, autonomy, and initiative is not without its drawbacks and challenges. However, it is clear that despite structural or historical tendencies of schools to have limited tolerance for student criticism, some schools are able to cultivate and integrate greater participation and criticism from young people.

It is of interest that alternative schools for young people who are ejected from or who drop out of large public schools often embody many of the characteristics of effective schools. Many draw upon experiential education models (Conrad and Hedin, 1981). Although we do not know how common it is, we are aware that many alternative schools involve youth in making decisions, solving problems in the school community, and giving critical feedback to the school about its operations.

Capacity for relationship building. Although size often interferes with relationship building, time is an asset. Students spend a great deal of time in schools over several years and have repeated opportunities to interact with adults and peers and to hear other students' views of those people. Regular doses of contact and the extended duration of the social context allow for the development of close relationships with age peers, older peers, faculty, coaches, and administrative personnel. However, school size and the fragmentation of class schedules and activities can limit opportunities as well as the inclination to invest in nurturing relationships.

Schools offer the most extensive opportunities for youth development because of the time and resources invested both by society and by young people themselves. The best-organized, brightest, and most motivated students typically develop their competencies very well by taking advantage of existing opportunities to lead, to excel, to negotiate, to organize, and perhaps to challenge some aspect of the organization's life. For many students, one good, affirming, caring teacher can make an enormous difference. Despite popular cynicism about teachers, many if not all make connections with young people but cannot devote personal attention to the hundreds of students they meet every day. Even in small schools, specialization has led to the fragmentation of relationships. For the average student, school size is an overwhelming obstacle, but for some students who embrace low-incidence lifestyles, big schools may be their only hope of finding friends and soul mates. It is difficult for schools to step back and consider how they promote all aspects of youth development because the administrative structures represent an effort to balance competing and often conflicting "masters." This delicate balance is often allergic to changes that might set chaos in motion.

Primary Supports

A second human service sector includes organizations that provide a primary source of support by extending what schools and families offer. Primary supports[5] offer a wide variety of cultural, athletic, social, and recreational opportunities. Attendance is voluntary. When they are well organized, primary support activities offer young people, and sometimes parents, opportunities to engage in constructive activities, to explore new interests, to master skills in safe surroundings, and to enjoy the company of respectful and caring peers and adults. Primary supports include a remarkably broad range of organizations from large, national nonprofit organizations with long histories to small, community-based programs operated by part-time staff and volunteers. Park districts and libraries represent widely available government-funded primary supports.

The primary supports enjoyed by most young people are in or near their neighborhoods, although older children and youth may participate in primary support activities located near their schools or in the wider community. Despite the scope and reach of primary supports and differences in their funding levels, origins, and degree of formality, these organizations generally encounter fewer constraints than those encountered by more formal organizations, such as schools or problem-focused services. It is not surprising that the movement to promote a youth development perspective was incubated in the voluntary primary supports sector, where it has been widely embraced.

History

Although the history and life span of primary support organizations vary greatly, some of the oldest of these organizations—the Young Men's Christian Association (YMCA), the Young Women's Christian Association (YWCA), Boy Scouts, and 4-H Clubs—were founded during the late nineteenth and early twentieth centuries, at approximately the same time as the public school system. In the social climate of that time, adolescents were beginning to be viewed as potential problems. From their very beginnings, primary support organizations considered it their mission to nurture youth participants and to provide opportunities for young people to be heard and supported in a changing social world. A brief look at the origins of three organizations—the YMCA/YWCA, the Boy Scouts, and 4-H Clubs[6]—will help to explain why youth development needs and competencies were so central to these as well as many other youth-serving organizations in the voluntary sector.

The YMCA, the oldest of the three, was founded in 1844 in England. It came to North America in 1851 and grew to prominence in the second half of the nineteenth century. The intent of its founder, George Williams, was to create a club for young working men (Young Men's Christian Association, 1998). Currently, YMCA programs serve millions each year. Their organizational structures are flexible; each organization has a national framework and membership, but each individual branch is completely autonomous. The YWCA, a completely independent organization, was formed in 1877 to provide for young working women (Young Women's Christian Association, 1998). Both the YMCA and the YWCA came into being to help youth who were already supporting themselves and handling adult responsibilities.

The Boy Scouts was founded in 1908 by Robert S. Baden-Powell, a cavalry officer who found that boys in England were avidly reading the book he had written in South Africa to train cavalry scouts in stalking and survival. He rewrote the book in a nonmilitary form and named it *Scouting for Boys*. Powell organized scouts into "patrols"—groups of six or seven boys under a boy leader and with adult guidance. The scouts would learn tracking and reconnaissance, mapping, signaling, knotting, first aid, and all the skills used in camping and similar outdoor activities. They also adopted and learned a simple code of chivalry and service that revolved around the completion of at least one good deed per day. Training of Boy Scouts was intended to produce self-sufficient youth who could provide for themselves and survive on their own and who would be able to be contributing members of society (Boy Scouts of America, 1998). The underlying assumption is that youth, assisted by adults, are ready to take on adult responsibility, not that they are dependents with no personal resources or stamina.

The 4-H movement began at the turn of the century, when progressive educators introduced nature study as a basis for a better agricultural education (National 4-H Council, 1998). Boys' and girls' 4-H clubs were formed in schools and churches. Schools and farmers' institutes cooperated to promote production contests, soil tests, and plant identification. Farmers soon saw the practical benefits—a cadre of youth better equipped to pursue agriculture—and national support grew. By 1904, several clubs had exhibited projects, and, by 1914, 4-H clubs had congressional support and federal funding.

4-H clubs pursue a variety of activities and projects. They have an average of 24 members of varying ages who elect their own officers. Each club plans and carries out its projects with the guidance of one or more adult leaders assisted by junior leaders. The structure provides for a great deal of autonomy and member decision making, consistent with the overall objective of 4-H: to develop youth as individuals and as responsible and productive citizens (National 4-H Council, 1998). Guided by adults and by older members, young people initiate and carry out independent projects that afford them great opportunities for control and judgment.

Organizational Structure and Dynamics

Primary support organizations have structures that offer flexibility for empowering youth. However, the education, training, and experience of many staff in this sector are limited; they often lack the skills to create opportunities that fully involve youth. A frequent criticism of the primary support sector is that it is underorganized or too "loose" in structure (Halpern, 1991; Halpern, Barker, and Mollard, 1998). The good news is that it may be easier to build the necessary structure in these organizations than to restructure schools or specialized service organizations to be more responsive. It may be important to preserve some of the looseness and creative chaos that weave through primary support organizations because creating the same structures in primary supports that one finds in the other sectors could duplicate their least helpful features, which would not serve young people very well (Sarason, 1971).

Primary support organizations share a commitment to meeting the normal developmental needs of young people rather than focusing on their problems. A review of the mission statements of 83 programs in the voluntary sector that were nominated as among the best of their kind revealed that over 80 percent include clear, positive, youth-focused developmental language about helping young people explore their own talents and possibilities, such language as to involve, motivate, engage, empower, challenge, enhance, nurture, inspire (Merry, 1998). Many primary support programs are organized around broad goals that encompass not only academic or vocational aspects of young people's lives, but physical, social, and emotional aspects as well. Pittman and Wright (1991) found that the mission statements of major national youth-serving organizations address four of the following five competencies that define a youth development perspective: health and physical competence, personal and social competence, cognitive creative competence, vocational competence, and citizenship competence. According to Pittman and Wright, smaller, community-based programs also strive to build personal and social skills, leadership skills, and an orientation to service. A comprehensive approach, if not contained in the language of a mission statement, can sometimes be seen in the actions of primary support staff and their willingness to provide diverse supports for young people in response to their needs.

> **The Youth Initiative Project**
> The Youth Initiative Project (YIP) was established by five black men who grew up in housing projects in Brunswick, Georgia. They were concerned about the lack of positive opportunities for African American youth in their community, as well as the need for a support system for many young people to "overcome the adversity of living in the projects." YIP provides opportunities for African American youth to be in charge and to see themselves as competent people capable of changing the world around them. The project has three primary activities. First, YIP offers a weekly youth club, organized and run by the youth themselves, at which they plan activities, speakers, and service projects. The project also offers a teen college scholarship program in the form of a pageant where contestants are judged on poise, talent, and creativity. And, finally, each summer the project offers the "Business Adventure" program in which participants are taught basic business and entrepreneurial skills by peer tutors using computer simulations and competency tests.

Voluntary participation. One of the defining characteristics of primary supports is voluntary participation. Even when youth attend programs in order to comply with court orders or parole conditions, the primary support organizations give young people a choice to participate or not. Wynn (1997) suggests that voluntary participation is a distinguishing trait of primary support programs:

> The voluntary nature of participation in primary supports is a defining characteristic both of the sector overall and of participation in individual programs. Primary supports depend to an extraordinary degree on the energy, commitment, and self direction of the participants, both adults and youth. Because neither initial nor continued participation is mandated, participants have to repeatedly choose to affiliate with the group, its standards, and practices. (p. 6)

Because of the voluntary nature of membership, the activities and supports that these organizations provide must be of interest and value to the youth they serve. This selection pressure ensures that organizations will continue to offer programs that attract and engage adolescents. Activities that seem to do this best are those that offer opportunities for the exercise of choice and increase the participant's sense of efficacy and control (Whalen and Wynn, 1995).

Autonomy and flexibility. Organizations in the primary support sector act with considerable autonomy. Because funding comes in so many pieces from so many sources, controls and accountability are often limited. The Boy Scouts, for example, are funded by a wide range of sources: membership fees, sales of *Boy's Life* and *Scouting Life* magazines, local fund-raising efforts, local United Ways, sustaining members, foundations, special events, project sales, investment income, trust funds, bequests, and gifts of real and personal property (Boy Scouts of America, 1998). In fact, the participants themselves can be seen to be funders and fund-raisers. These large national organizations, and the small ones as well, are accountable above all to the young people who are their members and to the vast group of volunteer scout leaders who are on a mission to pass a tradition from one generation to the next.

Even the largest of primary support organizations often stress the autonomy of local units. YMCA literature asserts the subservience of the national system to the mission and the local branches (Young Men's Christian Association, 1998). Individual branches are governed by volunteer boards that make all decisions about programming and services and elect representatives to national boards. Park districts and local nonprofit primary support organizations are often community based and are similarly able to govern themselves without interference from other sources.

At a local level, primary supports offer differing degrees of autonomy for youth to make decisions about their own activities and to influence decisions that help to determine the course of the organization itself. Some of the youth-serving organizations in the voluntary sector depend upon youth leaders. Boy Scout troops are led by boy leaders; 4-H clubs have student officers that facilitate meetings and officiate at club events. Other primary supports organized around youth production and performance depend upon youth to make editorial decisions for youth-oriented newspapers, to make casting and directorial calls for theatrical productions, or to lead food drives and voter registration drives (Wynn, 1997).

A characteristic related to the autonomy of most primary support organizations is their flexibility. They are generally smaller and more loosely structured than schools. They also often operate with limited resources. Pittman and Wright (1991) report on an independent sector analysis that revealed that 79 percent of the more than 17,000 nonprofit organizations that classify themselves as youth development organizations have operating budgets of less than $25,000. In part because of their relatively small budgets, many primary supports depend on volunteers to carry out much of their work. Dependence on volunteer efforts means that these organizations must be flexible in their practices. In the absence of material compensation, volunteer staff need to feel that their work is enjoyable and worthwhile. If organizations want to keep volunteer staff, they must be responsive to them and willing to adapt programs and policies. As a consequence, small organizations often meet the Vygotskian conditions for challenging staff, volunteers, and young people within their "zone of proximal development."

Community Responsibility: El Puente
El Puente is a multiservice, community-based youth program in one of New York City's poorest neighborhoods. Key to the philosophy of El Puente is the notion that young people must be responsible to themselves and their communities. Therefore, young people are actively involved in all aspects of the operations of El Puente—from program planning to implementation. Young people serve on all committees and are expected be active advocates in their communities. They are trained as peer counselors and group discussion leaders. Youth also teach classes in music, aerobics, and dance and are employed in all areas of the center.

Primary support organizations often remain flexible in order to provide services when and where youth can access them (Sherraden, 1992). Some adopt strategies found in adult education—flexibility in scheduling, dress, location, staffing, and instructional approach. The implication is that these organizations adapt to the schedules, locations, and needs of the youth they serve. Put another way, primary supports are more responsive to the demands of their voluntary young consumers than are organizations that mandate youth presence.

Involving Youth Fully: Youth Communications
At Youth Communications in Chicago, young people are charged with all aspects of the task of publishing a monthly newspaper, *New Expressions.* Participants decide what stories to cover and how to cover them; they write the copy, edit each others' work, and manage layout, photography, design, and production. They even sell the ads that help to make the paper possible. While adult staff are available to answer questions and provide some support and direction, the organization operates under the assumption that young people are capable and competent to meet the substantial challenge that producing a newspaper involves. As one *New Expressions* reporter commented, "They take us seriously, very seriously, around here."

This flexibility does not imply an absence of structure. In many primary support organizations, large and small, youth participation is guided by fairly rigid rules, rituals, and codes of conduct. However, the structures developed in these cases are presented as means to an end rather than ends in themselves. Structural components, including symbolic rituals of membership (e.g., uniforms, T-shirts, handshakes, and oaths) create a sense of belonging and safety for youth. The clear structures present in many primary supports create a manageable world and a safe environment in which youth can take responsibility, develop judgment, govern themselves, and, ultimately, contribute to a society beyond the boundaries of the club or group itself.

Professionalism. In primary support programs, unlike in schools, professional status is not the primary requisite for working with youth. Although paid staff and volunteers may have professional certification or affiliation in fields related to their work with youth, adults in these programs often have no identified professional roles. This lack of an acknowledged professional youth work identity, according to Heath and Roach (1998), may have disadvantages as well as advantages. No alliance of interest groups currently represents youth organizations whose staff have no professional recognition beyond the doors of their organization.

Although the absence of professional affiliation may weaken youth workers' effectiveness in political advocacy, it may have a beneficial effect for the youth with whom they work. If Freidson's 1970 analysis of the impact of professionalism on client-staff relationships is correct, then youth workers in primary supports who lack professional status would be more likely to treat youth as equals and be less threatened by their ideas, initiative, and desire to influence organizational decisions. On the other hand, knowledge of human development and the practice skills that promote youth development represent such important tools that their absence can weaken the potential impact of programs (Costello and Ogletree, 1993; Costello, Barden, and Howard, 1995; Brown et al., 1995).

Although the programs offered by different primary support organizations vary widely, the organizations all use similar strategies that can be thought of as a professional foundation for youth work. Pittman and Wright's 1991 review of organizations in the voluntary sector showed the almost universal use of small groups, flexible grouping practices, symbols of membership (e.g., uniforms, T-shirts), and clear structures (e.g., regular meetings, codes of conduct). Other strategies used by primary support programs include an emphasis on group endeavors and group problem solving; a focus on activities and issues of importance; high expectations; tangible products and performances; prospects for advancement and expanded opportunities; and adults who act as caregivers, catalysts, and coaches and provide continuity, sustained support, and flexible responses to youth needs (Wynn, 1997).

Relationships with adults. Another common attribute of primary support organizations is that they offer opportunities for adolescents to develop strong relationships with adults and with peers who may vary in age. Adults often have multiple roles, acting as caregivers, mentors, coaches, counselors, and teachers. At times, they just "hang out" with participants, offering comfortable opportunities for talking and for what one writer refers to as "social integration" (Larson, 1994). Adult relationships with youth in the best of these organizations are characterized by availability, continuity, respect, and reciprocity. Adults who "go the extra mile" in support of youth are also important. At the very least, primary supports offer proximity and time for adolescents to interact with and work alongside adults.

> **Building Competence Together: Outward Bound**
> At Voyageur Outward Bound in Minnesota, students and instructors undertake long, often arduous expeditions by foot or canoe into the Boundary Waters Wilderness area, traveling in groups of nine or fewer across the region of lakes between the United States and Canada. Outward Bound uses physical and mental challenges to build self-reliance, craftsmanship, and compassion in young

people. Courses prepare each student "brigade" to function independently and to assume more and more responsibility. During the final days of the course, students choose their own route through the hundreds of lakes and portages, navigate independently, travel with minimal supervision, and sometimes camp separately from instructors. Student leaders evaluate the day's travel during student-cooked suppers and are given feedback about their own leadership by members of the group. Participants address problems during nightly meetings or call for "problem circles" in order to bring the combined wisdom and thought of the whole group to bear on a particular challenge or conflict. The degree to which feedback is structured or informal varies from course to course, but all courses encourage participant feedback as a tool to refine and improve the group effort and to prepare the brigade to function successfully without instructor input. The course's goal is independence in the context of wilderness travel, including ability to weigh alternatives, consider risks, solve problems, and achieve collective aims in cooperation with peers.

Youth leadership and decision making are sometimes built into the structures of primary supports. Youth may be expected to exercise leadership in planning activities, facilitating discussions, and assisting younger peers formally or informally. Youth may help to chart the course in wilderness and other camping programs, plan activities in scouting and in community service, mentor and coach younger children in athletic programs, and lead tours in museums, to cite a few examples.

These practices are not as commonplace as one might expect, given the relative lack of structural constraints in primary supports. A great deal of knowledge and skill are involved in effective facilitation of youth participation in significant roles. Furthermore, potential threats to adult status may keep organizations from realizing the potential of these practices for promoting youth development.

Expecting staff and administrators in any organization to accept critical feedback from youth is expecting a lot. In a 10-year study of developmental programs for youth, Heath and Roach (1998) found particularly striking benefits to young people who participated in arts programs. Critical feedback, a characteristic of arts education programs and the art world itself, seemed to be a key ingredient. Mutual criticism improved skills and products and signified being taken seriously. Students' cognitive and linguistic development were stimulated because others cared enough to listen to their thoughts and opinions. Organizations that lead camping programs and wilderness trips often encourage debriefing sessions to help the participants not only to reflect on and reinforce what they have learned about themselves, but to hear their own words and others' words "code" the experience in common language.

The primary support sector offers many opportunities to build youth development goals and practices into everyday activities. It is not difficult to foster high expectations and sustain supportive relationships in these programs, particularly if staff are given appropriate opportunities to learn. It is somewhat more difficult to institutionalize higher-level youth development strategies, such as fostering youth initiative, decision making, critical feedback, and shared responsibility. Involved in these critical youth development strategies are public and private values that come together in a particular organization's history as interpreted by its current leaders and staff.

Problem-Focused Services

The third human service sector of interest is the problem-focused services sector. We discuss the child welfare and juvenile justice systems here because these systems have extensive contacts with children and families and much power over them.

History

Child welfare. During the last half of the nineteenth century, charitable organizations were developed to take responsibility for children when the care and protection provided by families or religious congregations were inadequate in quality or quantity. The dislocation of families in a changed economic and social order and the sheer size of the population overwhelmed informal arrangements and prompted the creation of organizations to supplement or substitute for parental care. Residential facilities for children were the largest of these organizations and were intended in part as correctives to the exploitation of child labor in boarding homes and to the exposure of children to the problems of adults in institutions for the destitute (Cmiel, 1995).

Founded around the same time, settlement houses were intended to protect and promote the development of children and the well-being of families. They were hybrid organizations that offered a range of what we would now call primary supports as well as problem-focused services. Settlement houses also offered practical information, skill development, a sense of empowerment for immigrant families, and opportunities for socialization with neighbors in safe, free surroundings (Brown, 1995).

By the turn of the century, government was pressed to take a more active role in the lives of troubled children. Proposals to establish a national Children's Bureau circulated for a decade before it was established to examine and to quantify the state of children's needs, particularly those of the most vulnerable, who were a focus of the first White House Conference on Children in 1909. Since the signing of the Social Security Act in 1935, there has been a gradual shift from private charity to public responsibility for child welfare. For the next four decades, the physical protection and education of neglected children were the primary responsibility of the child welfare system.

In the 1970s, when attention to the rights of children was growing, the prevention of physical abuse of children became a priority expressed in mandated reporting requirements and investigative procedures. Emphases on the interests of children and their entitlement to social inclusiveness were patterned on civil rights legislation of the 1960s. These laws expanded children's rights in education, child welfare, and juvenile justice; and along with their amendments, they have had a continuing influence. The great hope, however—that child welfare caseloads would be reduced—has not been realized (Schuerman, Rzepnicki, and Littell, 1994).

Juvenile justice. The first juvenile court was established at the end of the nineteenth century, and the idea of the court as a just but kind parent spread across the country. Because of their age, young people could become subject to court supervision and incarceration for such behaviors as truancy and running away that would not be crimes if committed by adults. In 1974, the Juvenile Justice and Delinquency Prevention Act ended incarceration of juveniles for these "status offenses" and removed a powerful means of social control from the courts. Since that time, the paths of the child welfare and juvenile justice systems have intersected frequently.

Peer courts. Many juvenile courts throughout the nation are exploring the potential role of peer courts in influencing juvenile delinquency among first-time offenders. Through these courts, young people who are willing to plead guilty to a charge in juvenile court agree to be sentenced and abide by the decision of a peer jury. This jury, or young people trained to act as prosecutor and defense attorney, asks the family and youth directly about the offense and surrounding circumstances. They decide together on an appropriate sentence commensurate with the crime committed. All sentences rendered by the peer court include a requirement that the offender serve on at least one peer jury sentencing another young person.

In the area of juvenile justice, the current emphasis seems to be moving decisively away from promoting positive youth development and rehabilitation toward an emphasis on punishment and promoting public safety. According to a recent report by the Office of Juvenile Justice and Delinquency Prevention (Sickmund, Snyder, and Poe-Yamagata, 1997), juvenile court dispositions in the past tended to be based on the offending youth's individual characteristics and situation, with the primary goal being rehabilitation. Today, they see a renewed interest in punishment. Similarly, a study of trends in the Juvenile Court of Cook County, Illinois, indicates that it is increasingly common for juvenile cases to be transferred to the adult court system. In the early 1980s, a new system of "automatic transfers" was established by Illinois and other states that identified four specific offenses that qualified for this type of transfer. Over the years, the number of offenses deemed serious enough for such a transfer has grown to more than twenty (Reed, Perlmutter, and Gill, 1997).

Common threads. Although there is a good deal of overlap among problem-focused services and their clients, they also tend to be viewed as quite different from each other and from educational and primary services. For example, at least half of all runaways in the United States have fled from state-supported foster homes or correctional institutions (Courter, 1995). As a society, we view children involved in the child welfare system as innocent victims and those in the juvenile justice system as perpetrators. Yet, despite these quite different perspectives and sympathies, the net result for young people in problem-focused services is often remarkably similar. That is, an unknown adult takes control of their lives. For perpetrators, control is justified to protect society; for victims, control is justified to protect them from further victimization.

Although the missions of child welfare and juvenile justice services are narrower than those of schools or primary supports, they are not as narrow as one might think. The child welfare codes of many states claim a concern for the wellbeing of all children in addition to an intention to obey the mandate to protect children from harm and to become their guardian, protector, and provider of basic care when their parents cannot. In addition to the mandate to investigate, prosecute, and rehabilitate young people who are accused of delinquencies, juvenile justice statutes often include language permitting or encouraging development of programs to decrease the chances that young people will enter the justice system. Although the missions of both systems may include developmental language, the financial resources to translate language into action are usually insufficient.

Children who are placed in substitute care are rarely consulted about their views. Interviews with adolescents living in foster care in Cook County, Illinois, indicated that they had little information about the circumstances involved in changes in their care, and many had little warning of a change (Johnson, Yoken, and Voss, 1988).

Most young people are not voluntary participants in child welfare or juvenile justice organizations. Entry comes on the heels of a crisis, and the response often generates eddies of additional crises. Most young people and their families experience interventions from either system as highly disruptive.

The likelihood that a child removed from the family home will also be removed from neighborhood friendships, and organizational connections to adults and peers in schools, primary supports, and workplaces is of particular interest from a youth development perspective. In instances when young people eventually return to the neighborhood, they do so after quite modest efforts to help them reconnect socially. Their return is often as disruptive and isolating as was their departure.

Neither the congressional "independent living" initiatives that began in the mid-1980s nor other efforts to keep older foster children in school have assured adequate preparation for independence or adequate connections to essential services (Barth, 1997; Cook, 1997; Courtney, Piliavin, and Grogan-Kaylor, 1995; Courtney et al., 1998). The services considered "essential" seldom attend to the role of community connections—friends, neighbors, school personnel, or primary supports—in sustaining young people whose families have not met their needs. The stability of these connections is even more important to children in the care of the child welfare system.

By the 1990s, the number of young people in government-supervised and -funded substitute care or in correctional facilities had increased to record levels (Goerge, Wulczyn, and Harden, 1994). In 1993, Congress authorized new funds for family support and family preservation programs, although the level of funding was below what was spent on prevention and rehabilitation programs five years earlier (Wulczyn, 1998). Children and youth nine years or older made up nearly half the caseloads; more than a fourth were 13 years old or older (U.S. Department of Health and Human Services, Children's Bureau, 1994). Older children are often the most troubled children in the child welfare system, and their difficulties are often exacerbated by multiple placements and disruption of connections to families, peers, schools, or community activities (Courter, 1995; Festinger, 1986).

However, public sentiment about young delinquents (as well as adult criminals) has turned harsh, and rehabilitation efforts that are not dramatically successful are often judged failures. An interesting example is an Illinois program—Unified Delinquency Intervention Services (UDIS)—an alternative sentencing program that worked with young offenders in community settings in group homes, foster homes, or their own homes. A well-conceived evaluation found that the rates of recidivism were no greater for UDIS youth than for incarcerated offenders (Murray, Thomson, and Israel, 1978). Rather than seeing this result as positive, it was concluded that UDIS was a failure despite the fact that the UDIS participants had many more opportunities than incarcerated youth to commit offenses.

A particularly interesting example of a youth service program, Youth as Resources (YAR), is a primary support program that operates in many U.S. communities and has been incorporated effectively into youth correctional facilities. YAR establishes boards composed of youth and adult members who critically evaluate service proposals and fund selected projects. In designing, proposing, funding, and implementing service projects, youth are given opportunities to make decisions, give and receive critical feedback, and take responsibility for meeting community needs. Although projects are funded for particular periods, many continue long after funding has ended.

The Adolescent Mother's Resource Home Program

The Adolescent Mother's Resource Home Program of the Children's Home and Aid Society of Illinois involves adolescent mothers as equal participants in the development of their own service contract. A contract is developed in which the teen mother outlines what steps she agrees to take toward achieving her goals. Each member of her support system—her family, her social worker, her foster parents, the baby's father, or even a supportive neighbor—similarly outlines how he or she will help. The contract also includes a 30-day notice clause for any principal party, including the teen mother, to terminate the contract. According to Sheila Merry, the program's founder, allowing the young mothers to have legitimate control over their lives made it possible for them not to have to take it in illegitimate ways. When young mothers are given a meaningful role in planning for their own lives, while they still may not make all the ideal choices, they are able to stop fighting against the people with the potential to help them and can begin to struggle with the issues that may be getting in the way of creating the life they want for themselves and their children. When young people feel respected, they are far more likely to live up to that respect.

Organizational Structure and Dynamics

Organizational size. Public entities like schools, child welfare services, and juvenile justice programs are mandated to provide services to all children who are sent to them. Where populations are dense, these systems are large, complex bureaucracies that serve very large numbers of children. Although some services have been privatized, the magnitude of the caseloads and the expense of creating management systems to support the range of tasks required of either child welfare or juvenile justice programming mean that most of the private organizations providing these services are driven by economies of scale to be fairly large. As with schools, the magnitude alone challenges the capacity of these systems to be responsive to individual circumstances, interests, and needs.

Autonomy. Problem-focused service systems are guided by a variety of factors well beyond the control of the social worker or probation officer who actually works with individual children. These factors often constrain opportunities that might be available to promote youth development. First, legislation establishes mandated services and limits their powers. In some cases, the legislation guiding these systems is highly prescriptive—from ordering how long young people should receive services to determining what issues need to be discussed at certain kinds of meetings or hearings. This legislation is then interpreted by individual judges, who often have quite different perspectives on how legal mandates should be implemented. Service providers are required to follow regulations controlling everything from how large a bedroom must be to what procedures must be followed if a young person is truant from school. Although individual case managers are charged with identifying and providing appropriate services to young people and their families, their decisions are subject to review at many stages and must be consistent with the full range of laws and regulations. The decisions of private agency case managers, for example, may be reviewed by their own supervisors, higher officials within their organization, the public agency's review process, perhaps a variety of attorneys or laypeople ranging from prosecutors, public defenders, guardians ad litem, and judges, and, ultimately, the press. Thus, caseworkers often feel very little sense of personal authority over the children for whom they have responsibility. In these circumstances, allowing young people any meaningful control over their own lives would introduce an element of risk that staff or their supervisors may consider intolerable.

These constraints are further exacerbated by the introduction of managed care into the domains of child welfare and juvenile justice. In attempting to shift incentive structures, managed care introduces the notion that higher costs of services to one youth must be offset by more limited costs of services to another. The result is the need for much closer control and monitoring of institutional resources, often creating more "hoops" through which access is gained to more expensive services. Again, these efforts move decision making away from the individual who is in direct contact with the youth or family to be served.

The National Association of Young People in Care

In England, the National Association of Young People in Care (NAYPIC) has numerous local chapters within many of the local authorities' social service departments. These chapters are open to any young person currently or formerly in public care. Through regular meetings, young people come together to share concerns, enjoy activities, and explore avenues to affect the system of services that affects their lives. The local chapters also contribute to setting the national agenda for NAYPIC, an agenda that is articulated at an annual nationwide conference. The group works in a variety of ways to bring the voice of young people to the debate regarding child welfare services—through meetings, theater presentations, and advocacy. NAYPIC collaborated with the National Children's Bureau to publish a book titled *Who Cares? Young People in Care Speak Out,* which describes the experience of being in care.

Even if case managers recognize the developmental importance of such involvement, their lack of autonomy can undermine the capacity to engage young people in plans that could significantly influence their lives. The high level of bureaucratization further limits the flexibility of individual case managers to alter services to meet the unique needs of the individual youth they are charged to serve.

Professionalism. Since the 1960s, there has been a deprofessionalization of public child welfare and juvenile justice services. This shift has been triggered by financial constraints and by deliberate design. There has been a growing belief that families and youth can identify with case managers who share backgrounds and life experiences. More recently, the demand for case managers has grown substantially, and the supply of professionally trained workers willing to work in public service systems has not kept up with demand.

Although professional training and standards sometimes place barriers between staff and young people, the extraordinarily complex nature of the challenges faced by case managers in child welfare and juvenile justice may make such training essential to navigating these complex systems successfully and to addressing the varied problems of the families served.

Relationship building. Although many young people develop close, lasting relationships with case managers, institutional staff, or foster parents, the child welfare and juvenile justice systems often undermine the capacity of young people to form and maintain relationships. First, both systems predicate many of their services on removing young people from their homes and communities, often with little commitment to maintaining ties with their existing support systems. Young people are forced to leave family, friends, school, and any involvement in primary supports. Too often, they then move among placements or facilities and experience repeated disruptions in relationships with both adults and peers.

Most relationships developed with adults are directly related to specific interventions. Whether it is a relationship with a foster parent, a counselor, or a child care worker, these relationships are tied to a specific placement or intervention strategy, and they are not generally expected to continue beyond the period of intervention. Similarly, movement among placements undermines a young person's willingness to risk relationship building with either adults or peers.

The specialized child welfare and juvenile justice services we have considered are probably the least responsive of the three sectors to the active involvement of adolescents in planning for and about their lives. Although casework planning generally operates with the expectation that adolescents will be involved in the development of their case plans, substantial barriers undermine the ability of young people to influence decision making. A 1988 study found that children who are involved in the child welfare system rarely have an opportunity to express their views regarding their own placements. Children reported that they were informed about changes in placements anywhere from less than a day to more than a week prior to a move. In most cases, they reported being told little about the reason for the changes and did not participate in the decision to move (Johnson et al., 1988).

Few child welfare or juvenile justice organizations involve young people in program development, planning, or implementation. Young people in these sectors are much more likely to be viewed as individuals whose behavior needs to be controlled than as individuals whose input could be valuable in developing intervention strategies.

DISCUSSION

We have drawn attention to the three human service sectors that interact with young people on a regular basis through organizations that have responsibility to educate them; to provide social, cultural, and recreational opportunities during their leisure time; and to protect or rehabilitate them when they encounter problems. We have categorized these organizations as schools, primary support organizations and problem-focused services. In this section, we review our analysis and its implications for promoting youth development in organizations that serve youth, concluding with a discussion of the potential role of neighborhoods as the relevant social context. We suggest that a youth development perspective may benefit from having not only a focus but a locus.

Ambivalence about Youth

Ambivalence about youth's status in relation to adult status represents a central tension in organizations that attempt to be responsive to young people. That tension is important because it influences how competing external expectations are balanced in decisions about programs and services that aim to be responsive to young people. Youth was defined as a developmental stage in the course of the social transformations that followed industrialization (Keniston, 1974). The current era brings another transformation: the more easily young people can access information electronically without adult gatekeepers, the more the relative status of youth and adults will need renegotiation in each of the contexts in which they interact. The biosocial gap is a new challenge to provide opportunities that fully engage young people's physical and cognitive powers while they prepare for full adult responsibilities.

In this chapter, we chose to focus on the most challenging aspects of youth development practice—the involvement of youth in significant roles within the organizations that serve them—because those aspects go to the heart of adult ambivalence about youth and are a major source of organizational resistance to fully embracing a youth development perspective. Involving youth in ways that respect their ideas, foster their initiative, and include them in decisions of organizational significance can promote self-worth, a sense of control over their lives, and a sense of competence. Youth-involving strategies hold more promise to promote broad youth development than does a service approach alone. We suspect that this is because involving youth means the organization has confronted its ambivalence about youth's status.

Learning from History

Discussions about youth programs in any of the human services sector organizations seldom credit historic influences with shaping present organizational policies and practices. Nor is there much awareness of the historic parallels among organizations within and across the three human services sectors. Rather, each sector tends to operate as if the others are irrelevant to its own missions and practices.

Rooted in late-nineteenth-century concerns about population growth, urbanization, immigration, erosion of the core culture, and dangers posed by youth, each of the three human services sectors developed in response to a particular circumstance without significant interaction or integration. This is of current interest as several government and foundation initiatives have fostered service integration and coordination of separate service systems. Persistent efforts to end fragmentation in children's services suggest that the time may be ripe for reawakening a sense of common history on the assumption that ignoring history will assure its repetition (Sarason, 1971). Some efforts to integrate services for young children are based on a broadened concept of primary health care. The integrative theme for adolescents may be exploring what it means to promote youth development across the human services sectors and within the context of neighborhoods.

Organizational Structures and Dynamics

We considered a limited number of organizational characteristics that have relevance for the responsiveness of schools, primary supports, and problem-focused services to the development of youth. We would like to draw several parallels and distinctions among them and then ask if there is enough common ground on which to build a youth development agenda.

The histories, missions, and legal mandates of problem-focused services are the most specific and narrow because of the legal responsibilities entailed in protecting children from harm and protecting society from their antisocial behavior. Schools also have legally binding mandates to provide free and appropriate public education to all children. In most states, families are mandated to school their children between the ages of 7 and 16. Although not all organizations that provide educational or problem-focused services are government funded, all are regulated by government, often at several levels, as well as by boards that respond to local concerns. By contrast, primary support organizations tend to have few legally binding mandates.

Although their missions vary significantly, organizations in all three sectors are engaged in protection, education, and socialization of young people. All seem to have greater potential than they fulfill to contribute to the development of the children, youth, and families they serve. It is important to note that parents almost never have raised children in isolation from adults affiliated with extended family, faith communities, neighborhoods, guilds, and so forth. Formal organizations have replaced these informal mechanisms now that most women as well as men are in the labor force, and families have become smaller, less stable, and more scattered. It has taken a century to establish many of the organizations and institutions that stand between individual families and the mass anonymous society. It is time for them to update their missions.

Organizational size is featured in all studies of effective schools and in most discussions of problem-focused service systems. Schools within schools and advisory or homeroom groups within large high schools are among the accommodations made in recognition of the need for more intimate groupings of young people. Problem-focused service bureaucracies often contract with smaller organizations, and those organizations operate in units of varying sizes. Although these arrangements in schools and problem-focused organizations may reduce the sense of alienation young people feel, there is often less satisfaction with these arrangements than might be expected. Being in a small group at the bottom of a hierarchical pyramid is still being invisible and disenfranchised in an immense bureaucracy.

Government-sponsored organizations, such as schools, child welfare services, and juvenile justice services, must respond to all the young people who present themselves. They are often forced to accommodate to changing numbers of young people well in advance of adjusting their staff size. Primary supports have greater opportunity to decide what their capacity is and to turn away additional participants. The downside for primary supports is that they are often unaware of whom they are serving in a particular community, who is left out, and what reasonable capacity and variety might be.

Autonomy and flexibility are determined by external constraints. Schools must meet standards and must do so within budgets decided outside the schools themselves. Problem-focused services often have relatively little autonomy or flexibility, and workers tend to react as if "little" means "none." There are direct and indirect threats to autonomy in both systems. The media are perhaps the greatest threat, and avoidance of negative publicity can vastly extend the constraints placed by law, tradition, board policy, or school administrators.

Primary supports vary with respect to autonomy and flexibility, but most have considerably more leeway than do schools or problem-focused services. Learning how much leeway one has comes from experience within an organization, but many primary supports have high staff turnover and limited resources. Flexibility and creativity depend upon having relevant skills, but the staff in many primary supports are poorly educated and trained, with limited opportunities to work alongside competent, skilled youth workers.

Professionalism is a mixed blessing. Organizations that are heavily influenced by credentials, hierarchies, professional organizations, and unions often take their cues from professional standards that protect jobs and reinforce the control of professions as craft guilds once did, rather than adapting their knowledge to particular circumstances. However, lack of professional knowledge, skills, and status has weakened the creativity and development-promoting potential of many services. Lack of professional training is typically associated with low status, low compensation, and high turnover. Youth workers are among the lowest-paid members of the entire work force.

Relationship building can be defeated by organizational factors and time constraints over time. The size of an organization, the continuity of relationships over time, the number of young people staff can get to know, and the level of training and mentoring that is provided to help staff all can make a difference. To engage in developmentally appropriate relationships within flexible boundaries, staff need the skills to set consistent and reasonable limits and to resolve conflicts peacefully. They also need some awareness of their own tendencies to be ambivalent about youth.

Opportunities for active youth involvement in organizations is an aspect of a youth development perspective that is difficult for many organizations to embrace or to achieve. However, we think it is a useful lens through which to view the possibilities and the perils of fostering such a perspective in organizations that serve youth. There are many examples and models within schools, primary supports, and problem-focused service organizations to demonstrate that most types of organizations benefit from giving youth active roles (Merry, 1998). Whether youth have seats on policy boards or advise on overall operations, there are many ways in which they can be actively involved—as contributors to decisions that affect them and their interests; as contributors to an atmosphere of mutual respect, responsiveness, and responsibility; and as sources of critical, constructive feedback on programs and operations.

Neighborhood Context

Young people have always grown up observing and interacting with a wider array of social influences than those provided by their immediate families. Except for relatives who may live at some distance from them, most adolescents' informal social interactions, as well as those within organized settings, occur in or near their own neighborhoods. The character of their neighborhood and the other neighborhoods they frequent inform young people's views of the world and their place within it. Neighborhoods may offer an important locus for the promotion of youth development.

There are many reasons to promote neighborhood development in the course of promoting youth development. First, there is a convergence of evidence that the impact of educational, social, and even nutritional programs may depend on the qualities of relationships, the level of social organization and a variety of neighborhood factors. Although these are not well understood, they are drawing increasing attention (Brooks-Gunn, Duncan, and Aber, 1997; Sampson, 1992).

Second, the human and social resources of neighborhoods have eroded as the majority of able-bodied adults have taken jobs that are physically and psychologically distant from where they live and raise their families. Adult opportunities to explore a broader range of social and economic options have come at a certain cost to the implicit neighborhood structures of social support and social control on which child rearing has always depended, whether parents or politicians acknowledge it or not. There has been an erosion of the invisible "labor force" of women who formerly tended and mended the social fabric of neighborhoods in each generation. Their exodus to workplaces and the resulting need to balance marketplace and household work have reduced their time for community work. There is both the opportunity and the challenge to youth-serving organizations to step up and tend to the fraying social fabric of neighborhoods.

Third, the location of problem-focused services some distance from young people's neighborhoods has clear deleterious effects. Short visits to distant offices for counseling or other special services are not very different from occasional visits to medical centers; they are relatively infrequent, and they do not undermine the connections that are part of daily life. But major interventions in the daily lives of young people caused by foster care, incarceration, and intensive mental health treatment are so disruptive to development that it is reasonable to ask what evidence exists to support removal from the neighborhood context. Deliberate efforts can and should be made to serve young people close to home and to the organizations where they have ties. Their full reentry to the community and their investment in meeting the social norms there or anywhere may depend at least in part on respecting the constructive social connections they created.

Building a Youth Development Agenda

Organizational self-assessment. Each of the organizations described in this chapter could examine its operations jointly with its youth participants in order to assess how it is doing with respect to any of the several lists of youth development goals and practices that have been put forth by various advocates. The process of conducting the assessment could be a first step in reporting it to the relevant governing group and proposing policies to promote youth development more systematically. Although assessment is a relatively benign process, turning the results into policy proposals is potentially controversial. Most adult boards resist giving young people a voice or a vote in proceedings. Mostly they claim some version of "adults know best," but such claims tend to overstate the reality. As Andrea Schlessinger, the first student representative on the New York City School Board put it, "If we are competent to analyze Shakespeare, we can understand any policy that comes before this Board."[7]

Neighborhood niche. Organizations within neighborhoods could be encouraged to come together (and to include youth participants from each organization) to assess how they already promote youth development and how they might view their efforts in relation to sources of support and stress in the neighborhood. Although it may be easier to understand how schools and primary supports fit into the neighborhood context, if the young people of the neighborhood are the focus of discussion, the provision of problem-focused services to neighborhood youth would need to be examined as well. Current practice tends to remove young people from neighborhoods not because that is what they need (or what is needed to protect the neighborhood from them), but because the organization of problem-focused services ignores neighborhood organizations, connections young people have to them, and the potential of those connections to complement problem-focused services. A consideration of how neighborhood organizations promote youth development as a whole could reorient some of the disruptive interventions in young people's lives when they most need to maintain and to strengthen their connections to constructive activities and relationships.

Public education to address adult ambivalence about youth status. If we are correct that adult ambivalence about youth status undermines youth development efforts, promoting youth development within organizations that serve youth might be accomplished more effectively with some investment in public education about this issue. Following the model of success in the public health field in changing public awareness of preventable health problems and many behaviors related to smoking, fat intake, motor vehicle hazards, and unprotected sexual activities, the youth development movement could mount an effort to reeducate the public about the changing nature of adolescence, the biosocial gap, and the important human resource adolescents represent for community revitalization.

Additional questions for research. What would it take for exemplary practices to migrate across organizations? What parallels exist across the human services sectors that could demonstrate the "how to" for those who already accept the "why" of youth development practice? What are the relative values of funding incentives, legal mandates, and social contacts among organizational actors? What might be learned from a demonstration patterned on a public health model? What do we know about generalization and institutionalization of *new* practices?

NOTES

1   Adolescents are the focus of this chapter. *Adolescence* refers to both a biological and a social transition, the period from the onset of puberty to the completion of physical maturation and assumption of adult social status, roughly the second decade of life.

2   By *organizations,* we mean formal organizations—social structures in which people and resources are coordinated for a definite purpose—as opposed to more informal organizations like families, neighbors, and friendship networks. *Institutions* are generally well established organizations created for the promotion of a particular objective. Examples include faith communities, schools, colleges, and hospitals.
3   There are interesting parallels between the hesitancy to involve youth in organizations and the hesitancy in the United States to engage in discussions or to adopt the language of the International Convention on the Rights of the Child, which has been ratified by most of the world's nations, the United States being one of the exceptions.
4   Menarche, a girl's first menstruation, is easier to date than any biological indicator for boys' maturation and is generally used in examining secular trends in maturation.
5   Chapin Hall Center for Children at the University of Chicago includes facilities and seasonal events in its definition of primary supports. However, only primary support programs are considered in this discussion.
6   Faith communities, local nonprofit and for-profit organizations, and government-sponsored services of park districts and libraries also have long histories with probably similar themes. These histories were not easily accessible.
7   Personal communication.

REFERENCES

Ariès, P.
1962   *Centuries of Childhood.* New York: Simon and Schuster.
Barth, R.P.
1997   "Foster Family Care: Before, During and Beyond," in J.D. Berrick, R. Barth and N. Gilbert (eds.). *Child Welfare Research Review,* 2:151-160. New York: Columbia University Press.
Baumrind D.
1987   "A Developmental Perspective on Adolescent Risk Taking in Contemporary America," in E.E. Irwin (ed.). *Adolescent Social Behavior and Health: New Directions for Child Development,* pp. 93-125. San Francisco, Calif.: Jossey-Bass.
Berger, P.L., B. Berger, and H. Kellner
1973   *The Homeless Mind: Modernization and Consciousness.* New York: Random House.
Boy Scouts of America
1998   *Historical Highlights. Who Pays for Scouting?* Available on-line at http://www.bsa.scouting.org.
Brooks-Gunn, J., G.J. Duncan, and J.L. Aber (eds.)
1997   *Neighborhood Poverty: Volume 1: Context and Consequences for Children.* New York: Russell Sage Foundation.
Brown, P.
1995   *Settlement Houses Today: Their Community-Building Role.* Chicago: Chapin Hall Center for Children, University of Chicago.
Brown, P., R. Ogletree, S. Garg, and S. Robb
1995   *Strategic Analysis of the DeWitt Wallace-Reader's Digest Fund's Grantmaking in Support of the Recruitment and Development of Youth Workers.* Chicago: Chapin Hall Center for Children, University of Chicago.
Brunstetter, R.W., and L.B. Silver
1985   "Normal Adolescent Development," in H.I. Kaplan and B.J. Sadock (eds.). *Modern Synopsis of Comprehensive Textbook of Psychiatry,* fourth edition, pp. 697-700. Baltimore: Willliams and Wilkins.
Bryk, A.S., D. Kerbow, and S. Rollow
1997   "Chicago School Reform," in D. Ravitch and J.P. Vitteritti (eds.). *New Schools for a New Century: The Redesign of Urban Education,* pp. 164-200. New Haven, Conn.: Yale University Press.
Chambers, J.G.
1981   "An Analysis of School Size under a Voucher System." *Educational Evaluation and Policy Analysis,* 3(2), 29-40.
Cmiel, K.
1995   *A Home of Another Kind.* Chicago: University of Chicago Press.
Connell, J. P., M.A. Gambone, and T.J. Smith
1998   *Youth Development in Community Settings: Challenges to Our Field and Our Approach.* Rochester, N.Y.: Institute for Research and Reform in Education.

Conrad, D., and D. Hedin
1981 *National Assessment of Experiential Education: A Final Report* (Center for Youth Development and Research). St. Paul: University of Minnesota.

Cook, R.J.
1997 "Are We Helping Foster Care Youth Prepare for Their Future?" in J.D. Berrick, R. Barth, and N. Gilbert (eds.). *Child Welfare Research Review*, 2, pp. 201-218. New York: Columbia University Press.

Costello, J., J. Barden, and E. Howard
1995 *The Training of Youth Development Workers: Evidence of Impact.* Chicago: Chapin Hall Center for Children, University of Chicago.

Costello, J., and R. Ogletree
1993 *Creating a Consortium for the Education and Training of Children's Services Workers: The Need and Possible Approaches.* Chicago: Chapin Hall Center for Children, University of Chicago.

Courter, G.
1995 *I Speak for This Child: The True Stories of a Child Advocate.* New York: Crown.

Courtney, M.E., I. Piliavin, and A. Grogan-Kaylor
1995 *The Wisconsin Study of Youth Aging Out of Out-of-Home Care: A Portrait of Children about to Leave Care.* Madison: University of Wisconsin.

Courtney, M.E., I. Piliavin, A. Grogan-Kaylor, and A. Nesmith
1998 *Foster Youth Transitions to Adulthood: Outcomes 12 to 18 Months After Leaving Out-of-home Care.* Madison: University of Wisconsin.

Csikszentmihalyi, M., and R. Larson
1984 *Being Adolescent.* New York: Basic Books.

Festinger, T.
1986 *Necessary Risk.* Washington, D.C.: Child Welfare League of America.

Freidson, E.
1970 "Dominant Professions, Bureaucracy and Client Services," in Y. Hasenfeld and R.A. English (eds.). *Human Service Organizations,* pp. 428-448. Ann Arbor: University of Michigan Press.

Friedkin, N.E., and J. Necochea
1988 "School System Size and Performance: A Contingency Perspective." *Educational Evaluation and Policy Analysis,* 10(3), 237-49.

Galambos, N.L., and M.F. Ehrenberg
1997 "The Family as Health Risk and Opportunity: A Focus on Divorce and Working Families," in J. Schulenberg, J.L. Maggs and K. Kurrelmann (eds.). *Health Risks and Developmental Transitions during Adolescence,* pp. 139-60. Cambridge, England: Cambridge University Press.

Goerge, R., F. Wulczyn, and A. Harden
1994 *Foster Care Dynamics, 1983-1992: A Report from the Multistate Foster Care Data Archive.* Chicago: Chapin Hall Center for Children, University of Chicago.

Hall, G.S.
1904 *Adolescence.* New York: Appleton.

Halpern, R.
1991 *The Role of After-school Programs in the Lives of Inner-City Children.* Chicago: Chapin Hall Center for Children, University of Chicago.

Halpern, R., G. Barker, and W. Mollard
1998 *Youth Programs as Alternative Spaces to Be: A Qualitative Study of the Youth Options Unlimited (YOU) Network in Chicago's West Town.* Chicago: Chapin Hall Center for Children, University of Chicago.

Hasenfeld, Y., and R.A. English (eds.)
1974 *Human Service Organizations.* Ann Arbor: University of Michigan Press.

Heath, S.B., and A.A. Roach
1998 *The Arts in the Nonschool Hours: Strategic Opportunities for Meeting the Educational, Civic Learning, and Job-Training Goals of America's Youth.* Abbreviated notes from oral presentation prepared for the President's Committee on the Arts and Humanities.

Johnson, P., C. Yoken, and R. Voss
1988 *Foster Care Placement: The Child's Perspective.* Chicago: Chapin Hall Center for Children, University of Chicago.

Keating, D.P., and L.V. Clark
1980 "Development of Physical and Social Reasoning in Adolescence." *Developmental Psychology,* 16, 23-30.

Keniston, K.
1974 "Youth and Its Ideology," in S. Arieti (ed.), *American Handbook of Psychiatry,* Revised Edition, Vol. 1, pp. 399-427. New York: Basic Books.

Keniston, K.
1968 *Young Radicals: Notes on Committed Youth.* New York: Harcourt Brace.

Larson, R.
1994 "Youth Organizations, Hobbies and Sports as Developmental Contexts," in R.K. Silbereisen and E. Todt (eds.). *Adolescence in Context: The Interplay of Family, School, Peers and Work in Adjustment,* pp. 46-65. New York: Springer-Verlag.

Lee, V.E.
1997 "Catholic Lessons for Public Schools," in D. Ravitch and J.P. Witeritti (eds.). *New Schools for a New Century: The Redesign of Urban Education,* pp. 147-163. New Haven, Conn.: Yale University Press.

Lee, V.E., A.S. Bryk, and J.B. Smith
1993 "The Organization of Effective Secondary Schools." *Review of Research in Education,* 19, 185-186.

Levy, M.L.
1966 *Modernization and the Structure of Society.* Princeton, N.J.: Princeton University Press.

Lightfoot, S.L.
1983 *The Good High School: Portraits of Character and Culture.* New York: Basic Books.

Medrich, E.A., V.R. Roizen, V. Rubin, and S. Buckley
1992 *The Serious Business of Growing Up.* Berkeley: University of California Press.

Merry, S.M.
1998 *Beyond Home and School: The Role of Primary Supports in Youth Development.* Chicago: Chapin Hall Center for Children, University of Chicago.

Murray, C.A., D. Thomson, and C.B. Israel
1978 *UDIS: Deinstitutionalizing the Chronic Juvenile Offender.* Washington, D.C.: American Institutes for Research.

National 4-H Council
1998 *History of 4-H. 4-H Fact Sheets.* Available on-line at http://www.fourhcouncil.edu.

Newmann, F.M., and G.G. Wehlage
1995 *Successful School Restructuring.* A Report to the public and educators by the Center on Organization and Restructuring of Schools. Madison: University of Wisconsin.

Parsons, T.
1970 "How Are Clients Integrated in Service Organizations?" in W.R. Rosengren and M. Lefton (eds.). *Organizations of Service: Essays in the Sociology of Service.* Columbus, Ohio: Charles E. Merrill.

Petersen, A.C., J.B. Richmond, and N. Leffert
1993 "Societal Changes among Youth: The United States Experience." *Journal of Adolescent Health,* 14(8), 632-637.

Pittman, K.J., and M. Wright
1991 *Bridging the Gap: A Rationale for Enhancing the Role of Community Organizations in Promoting Youth Development.* Washington, D.C.: Center for Youth Development and Policy Research.

Reed, D.E., W. Permutter, and J. Gill
1997 *Juvenile Court Trends.* Chicago: Northwestern University School of Law.

Rogoff, B.
1990 *Apprenticeship in Thinking: Cognitive Development in Social Context.* New York: Oxford University Press.

Sampson, R.
1992 "Family Management and Child Development: Insights from Social Disorganization Theory," in J. McCord (ed.). *Advances in Criminological Theory,* Vol. 3. New Brunswick, N.J.: Transaction Books.

Sarason, S.B.
1971 *The Culture of the School and the Problem of Change.* Boston: Allyn & Bacon.

Schuerman, J., T. Rzepnicki, and J. Littell
1994 *Putting Families First: An Experiment in Family Preservation.* Hawthorne, N.Y.: Aldine de Gruyter.

Senderowitz, J.
1995 *Adolescent Health: Reassessing the Passage to Adulthood.* Washington, D.C.: The World Bank.

Senderowitz, J.
1992 "The Growing Biosocial Gap—A Challenge for Addressing Adolescent Fertility," in J.S. Hirsch and G. Barker (eds.). *Adolescents and Unsafe Abortion in Developing Countries.* Washington, D.C.: Center for Population Options.

Sherraden, M.
1992 *Community-Based Youth Services in International Perspective.* Washington, D.C.: Carnegie Council on Adolescent Development and William T. Grant Foundation Commission on Work, Family and Citizenship.

Sickmund, M., H.N. Snyder, and E Poe-Yamagata
1997 *Juvenile Offenders and Victims: 1997 Update on Violence.* Washington, D.C.: Office of Juvenile Justice and Delinquency.

Sprinthall, N.A., and W.A. Collins
1984 *Adolescent Psychology: A Developmental View.* Reading, Mass.: Addison-Wesley.

Tharp. R.
1993 "Institutional and Social Context of Educational Practice and Reform," in E.A. Forman, N. Minick, and C.A. Stone (eds.). *Contexts for Learning: Sociocultural Dynamics in Children's Development,* pp. 269-282. New York: Oxford University Press.

Tyack, D.B.
1974 *The One Best System: A History of American Urban Education.* Cambridge, Mass.: Harvard University Press.

U.S. Department of Health and Human Services, Children's Bureau
1994 *National Study of Protective, Preventive and Reunification Services Delivered to Children and Their Families.* Washington, D.C.: U.S. Government Printing Office.

Vygotsky, L.S.
1978 *Mind in Society: The Development of Higher Psychological Processes.* Cambridge, Mass.: Harvard University Press.

Weithorn, L.A., and S.B. Campbell
1982 "The Competency of Children and Adolescents to Make Informed Treatment Decisions." *Child Development,* 53, 1589-1598.

Whalen, S.P., and J.R. Wynn
1995 "Enhancing Primary Supports for Youth through an Infrastructure of Social Services." *Journal of Adolescent Research,* 10, 88-110.

White, R.
1959 "Motivation Reconsidered: The Concept of Competence." *Psychological Review,* 66, 297-333.

Wohlstetter, P., S.A. Mohrman, and P.J. Robertson
1997 "Successful School Based Management: A Lesson for Restructuring Urban Schools," in D. Ravitch and J P. Witeritti (eds.). *New Schools for a New Century: The Redesign of Urban Education,* pp. 201-225. New Haven, Conn.: Yale University Press.

Wulczyn, F.
1998 *Federal Fiscal Reform in Child Welfare Services.* Chicago: Chapin Hall Center for Children, University of Chicago.

Wynn, J.
1997 *Primary Supports, Schools and Other Sectors: Implications for Learning and Civic Life* (paper prepared for the Harvard Project on Schooling and Children). Chicago: Chapin Hall Center for Children, University of Chicago.

Young Men's Christian Association
1998 *The YMCA of the USA.* Available on-line at http://www.ymca.net.

Young Women's Christian Association
1998 *The YWCA of the USA.* Available on-line at http://www.ywca.org/index.

8 JUVENILE JUSTICE AND POSITIVE YOUTH DEVELOPMENT

Robert G. Schwartz

The American system of juvenile justice has existed for 100 years because of two beliefs that have remained relatively constant: (1) youth are not as culpable for their conduct as adults; and (2) youth are more capable of change and need room to grow (Zimring, 1998).

Although those two beliefs have been the bedrock of the juvenile justice system, their application goes through cyclical changes (Bernard, 1992). Sometimes the system is perceived as being too harsh, sometimes too lenient. During the 20th century it was often shaped by new ideas of the day, by theories that infused the culture at large. These have been doctrines of rehabilitation or of due process or, most recently, of accountability. Now, as we enter the millennium, "positive youth development" has found a receptive audience in the fields of youth employment, community-based services, and early adolescent initiatives. But how will it be received in the insular world of juvenile justice?

Consider Gabriel, a 14-year-old boy who lives in a drug-infested neighborhood in Steve Lopez's first novel, *Third and Indiana*. The fictional Gabriel is a brilliant artist with a photographic memory. His father has abandoned the family. To raise money, Gabriel begins serving as a lookout for a gang of drug dealers. Unlike his schoolmates, the gang recognizes Gabriel's strength:

> Gabriel, who'd always had a good memory, was an especially good lookout because he never forgot a face or a vehicle. If plainclothes cops jumped out of a car at the next intersection and threw a drug crew against a wall . . . Gabriel would wander in close enough to study the faces of the officers . . . Sometimes he drew sketches for the crew supervisor. He drew sketches of the unmarked cars, too, detailing a small dent, a missing hubcap . . . That's why he was being promoted. Gabriel was looked upon in his drug gang as something of a rising star. (Lopez, 1994, p. 58)

A boy like Gabriel is a challenge to the juvenile justice system. He represents everything that the newest version of juvenile justice is designed to punish: a drug-dealing gang member who later, for protection, carries a gun. In today's climate, he would be a candidate for transfer to the criminal court, where he would face a mandatory sentence for his use of a gun. At a minimum, he would be removed from his mother's home and placed in a residential treatment facility. Whether anyone recognizes his talent would be a matter of luck, not design.

Thus, the two questions that are the focus of this chapter apply to every Gabriel who comes in contact with the law: (1) Is there a place for positive youth development in juvenile justice, a system that exists to respond to negative behavior and is not uniformly adept at discovering talent? (2) If so, is there any chance that positive youth development will become central to the juvenile justice culture—as opposed to a characteristic of an exemplary program here or there—so that every Gabriel will be its beneficiary?

In the end, this chapter concludes that the tenets of positive youth development are more applicable in work with children who are at risk of entering the juvenile justice system than with those who are already inside the formal system itself. Diversion programs for all children are more promising than a formal juvenile justice system that is organized, staffed, funded, and regulated by law in ways that, for the most part, work in opposition to positive youth development.

However, the formal system is not hopeless. There are a few chinks in the system's seemingly sheer wall, and it is there that advocates of positive youth development must apply piton and hammer if they are to have any chance of scaling the barrier that juvenile justice represents to the field.

DEFINITION

For the purposes of this chapter, positive youth development is a medley of attitudes and activities that refer to:

- The dynamic, developmental pathway through which youth pass as they move through adolescence;
- Indicators of success *during* youth's flow along that pathway, which include "academic competence, personal contentment, interpersonal skills, social involvement and staying out of trouble" (Furstenberg, 1999, p. 225);
- Adults' attitudes about youth—that they are capable of moving along that pathway successfully, even if they stumble along the way;
- The dimensions of the activities that make the transition to adulthood most likely to succeed (described by one Public/Private Ventures [P/PV] abstract as "adult support, youth involvement, peer interaction, the developmental challenge of the activities, leadership opportunities for youth, community service opportunities and the work-learning nexus, as well as the activities' educational and cultural content" [Extended Service Schools Initiative, 1999]);
- Suppression of, or coping with, those individual or environmental traits that will impede the transition; and
- A common vision of success *at the end* of adolescence, in particular, the ability of youth "to find rewarding and remunerative employment, form a lasting

and gratifying partnership, or become contributors to their community" (Furstenberg, 1999, p. 225).

Thus, positive youth development (PYD) refers to attitudes about youth, to what youth do and achieve during and at the end of their route to adulthood, and to the informal and formal systems of support that help youth reach adulthood successfully.

Those overlapping operational definitions suggest why the juvenile justice system is not a fertile area for PYD. The areas of opportunity that do exist cluster around primary or secondary prevention; that is, they will focus either on all youth or on youth who have been identified as being "at risk" of entering the juvenile or criminal justice systems. The formal system—the system that is supposed to prevent youth from reoffending after arrest—does not in the late 1990s routinely think about children developmentally, rarely recognizes youth's strengths, does not routinely believe in youth's ability to succeed, and only spottily offers the kind of supports necessary for success. In juvenile justice, obstacles outnumber opportunities.

This chapter begins with a discussion of some assumptions about what is required for PYD to succeed in the formal juvenile justice system. It then gives an overview of the juvenile justice system, suggesting possible opportunities for the injection of some aspect of PYD into the system; discusses constraints that are inherent in the formal system; and concludes with suggestions for changes that will be necessary if PYD is to have a chance to take root and grow.

ASSUMPTIONS

Most discussions of PYD assume that it is what most parents want for their children. Indeed, for PYD to operate in the juvenile justice system—and as a gatekeeper to it—there must be someone who operates as an *ordinary devoted parent* on behalf of the child. Such a person would have the instincts to know the child's needs and strengths, know how to protect the child from harm, suppress the child's weaknesses, and organize the child's world to permit a transition to employment, partnership, and citizenship (Furstenberg, 1999). The notion of the ordinary devoted parent was conceived in the child welfare (foster care) context (Goldstein et al., 1986), but it is equally relevant to juvenile justice and its effort to absorb positive youth development into its culture.

> Parents raise their children as a labor of love and not as a professional assignment. Unlike child development experts and other professional persons concerned with child care, parents are not specialists. Their responsibility is the whole child—his every need at all times. Ordinary devoted parents [citation omitted] "accept his love, tolerate his demands and failings, share his pain and pleasure—and get satisfaction from doing so. They may be sorely tried at times, but more than anyone else they are able to

tolerate his growing pains. The child knows he is special to them, whether he is pleasing or not, well or ill, succeeding or failing. He unhesitatingly turns to them with his pleasure and miseries, confident that they will be there. He knows they are likely to see his point of view and give him the benefit of doubt before voicing critical comment. They become the brick wall he can safely kick against. Impatient or angry though they sometimes be, he recognizes that these are often signs of their concern for him. His feelings about himself reflect his parents' feeling about him. The child whose parents value him values himself. (Robertson and Robertson, 1982)

The law also recognizes that there are situations when . . . the state is justified in breaching family privacy and supervening parental autonomy. Then the . . . all-encompassing parental task is broken up and temporarily divided among specialists from law, medicine, child development . . . social work, education and other professions concerned with children . . . It is in the best interests of the child that these professionals always keep in mind that they are not the child's parents. Even though each of them may assume one or more aspects of the parental task, neither alone nor together can they replace parents. (Goldstein et al., 1986, pp. 3-5).

When the juvenile justice system replaces parents by asserting the 15th-century doctrine of *parens patriae*—i.e., the state is the ultimate parent of all of its children—it pretends that it can serve as an ordinary devoted parent. Because it cannot, to the extent that PYD is what ordinary devoted parents ensure for their children, the juvenile justice system will inevitably fall short.

THE JUVENILE JUSTICE SYSTEM[1]

The modern juvenile justice system is one of diversion, rehabilitation, punishment, and incapacitation.[2] It has had a complex history, which must be understood to appreciate the difficulties and potential pathways for PYD. The summary that follows provides a context for the modern system. It also serves as an introduction to the next section, which describes the parts of the modern system, some of which offer opportunities for PYD.

The History of Juvenile Justice in America

During much of the 20th century, public rhetoric about how to respond to juvenile crime incorrectly posited clear, either-or positions from which policy choices should be made: child or adult, punishment or rehabilitation, judicial discretion or rigorous guidelines. The reality has always been more ambiguous. Even though it is heuristically useful to divide the 20th century's juvenile court experience into opposing epochs—the benign paternalism of the first part of the century versus the get-tough policies of recent decades—the lines between these orientations are less clear.

It is also a mistake to think of the juvenile justice system as a single, self-contained unit operated by one entity (Guarino-Ghezzi and Loughran, 1991). Every state has a different mix of decision makers and services, and each divides power over juveniles in different ways. It is rare that a coherent philosophy governs the component parts (Ayers, 1997).

These caveats notwithstanding, we can nevertheless divide the juvenile justice "system" between court and corrections: on the one hand is the judicial side that determines whether a juvenile is delinquent and enters orders of detention and disposition; on the other hand is that part of the system that rehabilitates, treats, supervises, or punishes young offenders.

This chapter addresses both the formal activities of the juvenile court and the corrections component of the juvenile justice system. The judicial part of the system came second, well after decades of 19th-century experimentation with juvenile corrections. I begin, therefore, with the development of juvenile corrections policy during the 19th century. Indeed, many of the ideas that originated as a result of experimentations in corrections practices would influence the philosophy and organization of the juvenile court during the next century. As Jerome Miller has noted:

> The [focus on the] establishment of the juvenile court in 1899 obscured the fact that another revolution in juvenile justice had occurred in the early 1800s. The earlier movement had resulted in increased institutionalization of juveniles, albeit in facilities different from adult jails and prisons. (Miller, 1991, p. 5)

THE ORIGINS OF THE AMERICAN JUVENILE JUSTICE SYSTEM

Economic recessions in the early 19th century and the first wave of Irish immigrants pushed children out of work in America's new factory system during the Industrial Revolution. Concerns about poor children on the street led to the creation of institutional care for children. In New York City, in 1824, the Society for Prevention of Pauperism became the Society for the Reformation of Juvenile Delinquents and in 1825 opened the nation's first House of Refuge. Boston followed a year later, and Philadelphia in 1828. These Houses of Refuge were designed to maintain class status and prevent unrest (Krisberg and Austin, 1993; Platt, 1977).

The concept of *parens patriae* provided the legal underpinning for the Houses of Refuge many years before it also provided a legal framework for the juvenile court. In 1838, in *Ex Parte Crouse,* the Pennsylvania Supreme Court affirmed the state's accepting Mary Ann Crouse from her mother and putting her into Philadelphia's House of Refuge. Mary Ann's father brought a writ of habeas corpus, which was rejected by the State Supreme Court. In now-famous language, the court declared:

> The object of the charity is reformation, by training its inmates to industry; by imbuing their minds with principles of morality and religion; by furnishing them with means to earn a living; and, above all, by separating them from the corrupting influence of improper associates.

For the first time, *parens patriae* was applied to a poor child whose parents were still alive. By 1890, almost every state had some version of a reform school (Bernard, 1992).

In 1899, Jane Addams and her Hull House colleagues established what is generally accepted as the nation's first juvenile court. Juvenile court judges in the early part of the 20th century "were authorized to investigate the character and social background of both 'pre-delinquent' and 'delinquent' children. They examined personal motivation as well as criminal intent, seeking to identify the moral reputation of problematic children" (Platt, 1977, p. 141).

The Pennsylvania Supreme Court, in 1905, upheld Pennsylvania's version of the new juvenile court when a juvenile challenged the 1903 law's failure to provide procedural safeguards. The court asserted *parens patriae* as the rationale for its decision: the juvenile court is merely stepping into the shoes of the natural parent:

> To save a child from becoming a criminal, or from continuing in a career of crime, to end in maturer years in public punishment and disgrace, the legislature surely may provide for the salvation of such a child, if its parents or guardian be unable or unwilling to do so. (*Commonwealth v. Fisher,* 1905)

Ben Lindsey of Denver was the juvenile court judge whose practice most closely matched the rhetoric of the emerging juvenile court. Lindsey was the first to popularize "a highly personal approach to the children who came before him." The judge was like an idealized probation officer: visiting children's homes and schools, maintaining contact with employers, and becoming a confidant to the family. Lindsey saw himself as a therapeutic agent. He was the first to make the "highly personal and individualistic inquiry" that was the rhetorical hallmark of the juvenile court in the first half of the 20th century (Fox, 1997).

Judge Julian Mack, Chicago's second juvenile court judge, spoke glowingly of Lindsey in describing the idealized juvenile court:

> The problem for determination by the judge is not has this boy or girl committed a specific wrong but what is he, how has he become what he is, and what had best be done in his interest and in the interest of the state to save him from a downward career. (Mack, 1909, pp. 119-120).

The Impact of the Gault Decision

At its most idealistic, the juvenile court of the first half of the century tried to act as an ordinary devoted parent would on behalf of a child. In 1967, because the system's operation was less than ideal, the "rehabilitative" world of juvenile justice was altered forever. It was then that the United States Supreme Court injected due process into the system (*In re Gault*).

The Gault case involved a 15-year-old boy who was arrested for making calls to his next-door neighbor that the Supreme Court described as "of the irritatingly offensive, adolescent, sex variety." Gerald Gault was brought before a juvenile court judge, but he did not have notice of the charges against him, nor did he have a lawyer. The neighbor never appeared in court, but testimony was given by the arresting officer, who described what the neighbor had told him.

For an offense for which an adult could have received a fine of not more than $50 or more than two months in jail, the juvenile court committed Gerald Gault to the Arizona State Industrial School for up to six years. Gerald challenged his adjudication of delinquency, and the U.S. Supreme Court held that the Fourteenth Amendment's due process clause applied to children. This meant that at trial juveniles had a right to notice of the charges, to counsel, and to confront witnesses against them.

There was very little developmental philosophy behind the Arizona juvenile court's decision to send Gault to a training school for six years. In what sense was Gault to be rehabilitated? Except insofar as the training school would teach him a lesson and cause Gault to reflect on his life, there was certainly little if any sense in which the Arizona system conceived that the state training school would promote PYD. To the contrary, the training school looked remarkably like the early Quaker penitentiaries that sought to reform prisoners by using thick-walled cells, isolation, and a Bible (Meranze, 1996).

The Gault decision ended benign neglect of the juvenile justice system and introduced a period in which juveniles were increasingly thought to be entitled to constitutional procedural protections similar to those of adults.[3] This was one kind of "adultification" of juvenile court. During the mid-1990s, and motivated by very different concerns, a different sort of adultification occurred, one that ironically moved the juvenile court away from its rehabilitative ideal and toward a retributive model that had much in common with the philosophy of the adult criminal court. The increase in violent juvenile crime between 1989 and 1993 led almost every state to change its juvenile laws. States devised a variety of approaches to removing more juveniles from juvenile court jurisdiction, while placing them in criminal court, increasing the severity of juvenile court dispositions, and reducing the confidentiality of juvenile proceedings and records (Torbet et al., 1996).

New punitive legislative policies have led some scholars to seek a middle ground between the "old" rehabilitative model of the idealized juvenile court and the "new" model of retributive justice. In the late 1980s, Dennis Maloney called for a "balanced approach" to juvenile probation, in which it would address public safety, accountability and youth competency development (Maloney, Romig, and Armstrong, 1988). Maloney's work became part of the "restorative justice" movement of the 1990s, during which Gordon Bazemore, Mark Umbreit, and others called for a juvenile justice system in which attention would be paid to making the victim whole, involving communities in fashioning dispositions, and teaching juveniles the skills—i.e., competency development—necessary to make the transition to responsible adulthood (Bazemore and Umbreit, 1994). The balanced approach is discussed in detail in the section titled Opportunities.

Through the 20th century, the juvenile justice system sought to save children, nurture them, rehabilitate them, cure them, isolate them, and punish them. The latest synthesis of these various philosophies includes teaching youth competencies. In this regard, the modern system might serve as a platform for PYD.

MOVING THROUGH THE CONTEMPORARY JUVENILE JUSTICE "SYSTEM"

If PYD is to mean anything, it must be an inherent part of all of the decision points of the juvenile justice system—otherwise decision makers throughout the system would be implementing different philosophies, rendering the system incoherent. PYD should also affect the way the juvenile justice system makes judgments about who is no longer eligible for its benefits.

The Juvenile Justice Pipeline

It is useful to imagine the juvenile justice system as a pipeline through which water flows. Along the pipeline are diversion valves—the points of decision at which children are either diverted from the pipeline or continue through its various gates and locks. These are the points of arrest, detention, adjudication, disposition, and disposition review. One of the signal characteristics of the juvenile justice system is its diversion options across the pipeline's continuum; that is, at every point, the system uses valves to send some children home, some to other systems, and others to noninstitutional care. Another characteristic that distinguishes the juvenile justice system from the adult system is the theoretical importance the juvenile system places on a swift flow through the pipeline.[4] Both diversion and speed are important to PYD.

Each state has organized its justice system in slightly different ways, setting policies that determine which children are eligible for the juvenile justice system; which will be sent to the adult criminal justice system; which will go where, for how long, within either system; and what kinds of programs or services it offers at each stage of the process. Despite whatever differences exist across jurisdictions in policies and practices, the points of decision are essentially similar: diversion, referral, intake, detention, transfer, adjudication, disposition, and release. Each stage offers an opportunity for implementing one or more of the attributes of PYD described in the introduction to this chapter.

Diversion. As in basketball, where not every contact is a foul, on the street not every deed that can trigger a police whistle is a crime. Indeed, the period of adolescence, in particular for boys, is a time of experimentation, risk taking, and recklessness that would lead to the arrest of almost everyone if the law were applied strictly. Parents, teachers, and communities have historically taught adolescents how to behave without invoking the law. Refusing to refer a youth to the juvenile justice system is one form of diversion. (Another, available after a referral has been made, is discussed in the next section.)

Diversion is less common today than it used to be, as parents and schools develop "zero tolerance" for misdeeds committed by other people's children. For example, schools across the country have adopted "zero-tolerance" policies for misbehavior, and are today routinely expelling children and referring them to the juvenile justice system for offenses that just a few years ago would have been handled in-house. Such expulsions are inconsistent with PYD.

If parents have the resources, knowledge, and contacts, they have a chance of keeping their children from being expelled or labeled a "delinquent." A few years ago I was called by a middle-class couple who had a 16-year-old son with serious emotional problems. He fought with other kids, smoked dope, and extorted small amounts of money from younger children. But the parents were concerned and active. Thus, during the boy's troubled high school years the school district kept him in school and provided an assessment for a special education referral. When the boy's conduct got out of hand, the parents arranged for private psychiatric care. All of his conduct violated the criminal code. Many children—especially today—who behave as he did would routinely end up in the juvenile justice system, even if they only reached the front door. This boy, with the help of ordinary devoted parents, did not get to the front steps.

There are many ways to conceive of diversion. One is to tie diversion to policies and practices that support neighborhood building. To the extent that PYD occurs most easily in strong neighborhoods, it is crucial to have neighborhood groups who serve as an extended family for at-risk youth and who can provide the supervision that would be offered by the ordinary devoted parent. There are many successful examples of such neighborhood-based interventions. Robert Woodson has described the family-like support and encouragement that the House of Umoja gave gang-affected youth in West Philadelphia in the early 1970s (Woodson, 1981). Pennsylvania's State Advisory Group, which dispenses federal juvenile justice funds, has invested in community-based programs in high crime areas as part of its attack on disproportionate minority confinement (Welsh et al., 1999). While one does not want to transform indigenous groups into formal components of the justice system, juvenile probation, police, and other agents of community control can certainly develop close working ties with community-based organizations to divert youth from the formal juvenile justice system.

For many youth, diversion is a low-risk enterprise. Marvin Wolfgang's landmark longitudinal studies in Philadelphia showed that half of the children who committed delinquent acts were never heard from again (Wolfgang et al., 1972). Positive youth development is easier for an adolescent who avoids the stigma of arrest and referral.

Referral. Formal entrance into the pipeline begins with a referral to the juvenile justice system or a police arrest. Depending upon the state, a child may be too young or too old for the juvenile justice system. Children who are too young are most often diverted or sent to the branch of juvenile court that has jurisdiction over neglected and abused children. Children who are too old are tried as adults. The juvenile may also be charged with an offense that results automatically in adult prosecution.

Intake. If the child enters the juvenile justice system after being arrested, referred by a private petitioner (such as a school or next-door neighbor), or transferred from criminal court, there will be an intake decision. Should the case proceed or be diverted? If the latter, should it be an informal diversion, without further involvement by the juvenile court, or should the child be sent to a program, such as a community panel or teen court (and returned to juvenile court if he or she fails to obey a community-ordered disposition)? Some cases are diverted to other systems, such as the mental health system. Some cases are dropped entirely, as intake officers decide that this particular combination of youth and offense does not belong in the juvenile justice system.

Detention. If the intake officer (usually a juvenile probation officer) decides that the case should proceed to a hearing, the officer must decide whether the child should be sent home (with or without supervision) or should be detained, either in a maximum-security detention center or in a detention alternative. Pretrial detention has two valid purposes: reducing the risk of flight and reducing the risk of reoffending prior to trial (Institute of Judicial Administration– American Bar Association, 1996).

In the early 1990s, with support from the Office of Juvenile Justice and Delinquency Prevention, Pennsylvania's detention centers developed a model of detention service delivery. The Juvenile Detention Center Association of Pennsylvania (JDCAP) Standards go beyond a typical state regulatory framework (i.e., one that sets minimum health and safety standards) by establishing optimal standards for screening, assessment, education, health care, recreation, and other activities that can occur when youth are locked up, even for short periods of time (Juvenile Detention Centers' Association of Pennsylvania, 1993). The JDCAP Standards are an example of how proponents of PYD might approach the hundreds of thousands of juveniles who are detained each year. Juvenile detention is an opportunity for staff to learn about youth's strengths and to make recommendations to court and probation about disposition and the focus of the next intervention.

Transfer. Most persons under the age of 18 who are tried as adults are done so because of statutory exclusion of their case from the juvenile justice system. As noted earlier, state law may exclude them because of their age. In New York, for example, a 16-year-old is tried as an adult for any offense. Every state excludes some offenses from juvenile court jurisdiction if a child is of a certain age (for example, a state can decide that 15-year-olds who are charged with armed robbery will have their cases begin in adult criminal court). States usually must prove that the juvenile is "not amenable to treatment" in the juvenile justice system in the time available to that system. Recently, state legislatures have made it easier for judges to transfer (or "waive" or "certify") juveniles to criminal court if it is "in the public interest" or if "public safety" requires it (Torbet et al., 1996).

Through a lowered age limit, exclusion of offenses, and prosecutorial or judicial transfer, it is estimated that about 200,000 American youth under the age of 18 are processed as adults each year (Snyder and Sickmund, 1995). While for many this involves no more than being charged as adults before they are remanded to juvenile court, most are tried and sentenced in the adult system.

Although adequate discussion is beyond the scope of this chapter, it is worth noting that PYD is out of reach for this large number of adolescents who have been transferred to adult criminal court. They often lose their right to vote. They are often denied education when they are incarcerated, are unable to return to school if they are released, and receive inadequate physical and behavioral health care. In short, they receive little in the adult system that comports with any component of PYD.

Adjudication. If the child continues to be detained, an adjudicatory hearing (comparable to the trial in criminal court) must be held within 10 to 30 days. (While this is the general rule, in some states, juveniles charged with high-profile crimes, like murder, will have a longer time to wait until their trials.) Juveniles have no constitutional right to bail, although some states provide for bail by statute. If they are charged as adults, however, juveniles have the same right to bail as adults. Most states do not have speedy trial requirements for conducting adjudicatory hearings if the juvenile is released before trial (Butts, 1997). Slowness is inimical to PYD.

Disposition. If the juvenile admits to the offense, or if the juvenile court finds by proof beyond a reasonable doubt that the child has committed the offense, the court will proceed to disposition (comparable to sentencing in adult court).

Although juvenile dispositions historically have been aimed at providing "treatment, rehabilitation, or supervision" in a way that best serves the needs of the juvenile, the juvenile court will have a range of discretion. In some states, like Wisconsin or Pennsylvania, the juvenile court retains power over the child and has wide latitude, from ordering that a child return home under supervision—probation—to placing a child in maximum-security institutions, known as training schools, reform schools, or youth development centers. In other states, like California or Massachusetts, which use a "youth authority" model, the court will either order probation or, if placement is warranted, transfer custody of the child to the youth authority, which will then determine the level of care.

Release. Most juvenile court dispositions are for indeterminate periods of time. However, they cannot be for a longer period of time than an adult would serve for a similar crime in the criminal justice system. In states in which the juvenile court controls all aspects of the juvenile's treatment, the court will usually "review" the juvenile's case every six to nine months. In almost every instance, the review of placement focuses on whether the child is behaving or showing an improved attitude. Reviewing authorities almost never compare the youth's progress with a clear treatment plan, whether that plan is based on a medical model or on PYD.

Many juveniles in placement, particularly those with mental health needs or who have been placed inappropriately, end up being returned to juvenile court for a new disposition. Most often, those juveniles are placed in detention pending a new placement plan. These youth are like pinballs. They bounce around until someone yells "tilt." The system rarely imagines that these children, with multiple needs, are candidates for PYD.

When juveniles are released from institutions, they are placed on "aftercare probation," which is analogous to parole. A juvenile who is on probation or aftercare probation status can have that status revoked, or "violated," for new offenses or for violating the terms of probation, such as associating with gang members, missing school, or missing curfew. Despite a decade-long effort to revamp aftercare into a role that is more like that of the ordinary devoted parent, it is too often nothing more than monitoring. Aftercare is discussed more thoroughly below, in the section titled Opportunities.

Except for transfer to criminal court, each of the points of the pipeline provides occasions for PYD. Those who seek to take advantage of these openings, however, must first circumvent an abundance of obstacles that obstruct PYD.

OBSTACLES

The obstacles to introducing PYD to juvenile justice are many. While superb programs and visionary leaders exist, they are not the norm, and they operate in bureaucratic settings that make it difficult for them to succeed or be replicated (Schorr, 1997). The constraints described below make it hard for excellence to take root and thrive. Even so, in every obstacle, readers will find implied opportunities for PYD.

Constraints on PYD are exacerbated by the vexing problem of race. In the early 1990s, the Juvenile Justice and Delinquency Prevention Act required states to assess whether their juvenile justice systems disproportionately confined members of minority groups. Only one state, Vermont, found no problem. In other states, minority youth were less likely than white youth to be diverted from the juvenile justice system and more likely to be detained or placed in training schools. The general public and juvenile justice decision makers tend to ascribe negative characteristics to minority youth—in particular those who misbehave—more often than to white youth. Thus, for children of color, the following hurdles loom even higher.

Confused Mission

The formal juvenile justice system is not fertile territory for PYD because the system's goals and components are often incompatible. It is trying to control, punish, treat, supervise, incapacitate, and train youth who are entrusted to its care. Its staff are supposed to serve all of those goals, which too often work at cross-purposes to each other and to PYD.

While ordinary devoted parents are able to fill a variety of roles with their children, systems have a difficult time fulfilling missions that appear to be contradictory. Considerations of policy, practice, funding and governance make it easier to fill one role or another, but not multiple roles at the same time.

There is a pull, much written about by Barry Feld, between competing purposes of the juvenile justice system. One purpose is social welfare. The other is social control:

> When social services and social control are combined in one setting, as in juvenile court, custodial considerations quickly subordinate social welfare concerns. Historically, juvenile courts purported to resolve the tension between social welfare and social control by asserting that dispositions in a child's best interests achieved individual and public welfare simultaneously. In reality, some youth who commit crimes do not need social services, whereas others cannot be meaningfully rehabilitated. And, many more children with social service needs do not commit crimes.
>
> Juvenile courts' subordination of individual welfare to custody and control stems from its fundamentally penal focus. Delinquency jurisdiction is not based on characteristics of children for which they are not responsible and for whom intervention could mean an improvement in their lives—their lack of decent education, their lack of adequate housing, their unmet medical needs, or their family or social circumstances ... Rather, delinquency jurisdiction is based on criminal law violations ... As long as juvenile courts emphasize criminal characteristics of children least likely to elicit sympathy and ignore social conditions most likely to engender a desire to nurture and help, they reinforce punitive rather than rehabilitative impulses. Operating in a societal context that does not provide adequately for children in general, intervention in the lives of those who commit crimes inevitably serves purposes of penal social control, regardless of the court's ability to deliver social welfare. (Feld, 1993, p. 415)

While an ordinary devoted parent can resolve the contradictions in the day-to-day (indeed, hour-to-hour) course of raising a child, in the juvenile justice system, there is no person who serves in that role. And all the actors in the system—probation or community control officer, guard, sheriff, psychologist, caseworker, counselor, mentor—taken together cannot replace what ordinary devoted parents inherently know and implement. Under such circumstances, when the juvenile justice system is invoked, social control (and its sidekick, accountability) will trump social welfare (even if it is disguised as PYD).

Take this example from *The Autobiography of Benjamin Franklin:*

> I was generally a Leader among the Boys, and sometimes led them into Scrapes, of which I will mention one Instance, as it shows an early projecting public Spirit, tho' not then justly conducted. There was a Salt Marsh that bounded part of the Mill Pond, on the Edge of which at highwater, we us'd to stand to fish for Minews. By much Trampling, we had made it a mere Quagmire. My Proposal was to build a Wharf there fit for us to stand upon, and I

show'd my Comrades a large Heap of Stones which were intended for a new House near the Marsh, and which would very well suit our Purpose. Accordingly in the Evening when the Workmen were gone, I assembled a Number of my Playfellows, and working with them diligently like so many Emmets . . . we brought them all away and built our little Wharff—The next Morning the Workmen were surpriz'd at Missing the Stones; which were found in our Wharff; Enquiry was made after the Removers; we were discovered & complain'd of; several of us were corrected by our Fathers; and tho' I pleaded the Usefulness of the Work, mine convince'd me that nothing was useful which was not honest. (Franklin, 1987, p. 10)

Josiah Franklin was an ordinary devoted parent who knew his son. There was no need for involving the formal justice system. Everything that Josiah knew about 10-year-old Ben informed him that lecturing this boy at this time would be adequate to reinforce his honest instincts. How would young Franklin be handled today? Until the mid-1980s, most juvenile justice systems would have had the option of giving Franklin a lecture or finding some way to avoid a juvenile record. Today that is less likely. Prosecutors are more interested in having the theft on record (to enhance future sanctions in either the juvenile or criminal justice system). At its best, a system of "restorative justice" would require Franklin to do something to pay back the workmen, but most such restitution or community-service programs would be no better than random at figuring out how to ensure that such service improved Franklin's talents or life chances. If Franklin got bored and declined to finish the community service (as later in adolescence he ran away from his Boston apprenticeship), the formal system would surely bring him to court for an adjudication of delinquency, not necessarily because of the original offense, but because of his obstinate (delinquent) refusal to complete his community service agreement.

Jaded Staff

Many of those who work in juvenile justice, in particular those in public systems, where the job can become a sinecure, have lost their enthusiasm for their work and for the children they supervise. In many ways, these juvenile justice professionals are like teachers: some still have passion and talent; some have always been unqualified; and some once had quality and passion, but those flames have dimmed over time. Like teachers, who in order to succeed must believe that every child can learn, juvenile justice professionals must believe that every youth can succeed. That must be true whatever the juvenile justice philosophy *du jour* happens to be. For PYD to get a toehold, juvenile justice professionals must believe that every child has assets and that every child can become a productive citizen.

Unclear Measures of Success

Despite its competing goals, the juvenile justice system tends to use one measure of success, recidivism; but even that measure is not uniformly applied across jurisdictions. Some places will measure re-arrest within a particular time frame. Others will measure frequency or severity of new offenses. There is no common understanding of what this negative measure—recidivism—is measuring.

Public juvenile justice programs—training schools, detention centers, and youth-authority programs—do not measure positive outcomes. Private, usually nonprofit, agencies with whom public agencies have contracts almost never have payment tied to performance measures (unless they are negative measures, like keeping the number of escapes below a certain percentage).

There is an exception. In the early 1990s, Philadelphia deputy commissioner Jesse E. Williams, Jr., who was then in charge of the Department of Human Services' (DHS) Juvenile Justice Services, wanted to see whether he was getting value from the four dozen private agencies with which the city had contracts. Williams arranged with the Crime and Justice Research Institute (CJRI) at Temple University to develop ways of measuring whether children were better off when they left the programs than they were when they entered. CJRI created a data collection and evaluation system called the Program Development and Evaluation System (ProDES), which began collecting data in 1994. ProDES measured client and program trends, looking at changes in youth's life skills, self-esteem, behavior, and other assets that were of interest to DHS. ProDES used a pre- and post-program assessment, a follow-up assessment, and reviews of official records to see what programs were doing. This is a rare example of an evaluation system that measures positive outcomes. Unfortunately, even in Philadelphia it has its limitations. Several private agencies that serve Philadelphia youth, but that are paid by the state, refuse to participate in ProDES evaluations. The system was also not applied at the outset to youth who were on probation or in state training schools.

Historical Reliance on the Medical Model

The juvenile justice system, in its effort to save children (Platt, 1977), has tried to answer the question, "What's wrong with this child?" When cures can be found for "what is wrong," the healed boy or girl will reenter the mainstream of society. While PYD recognizes that obstacles must be suppressed or removed (e.g., a youth must learn to control anger), it places less emphasis on cure than on building upon strengths. Medical model skills—often personified in degreed professionals—that are used to cure are different from the "Yoda-like" skills of empowerment. When a youth needs a mentor, the juvenile justice system too often provides a doctor.

Thus, most of the juvenile justice system works at teaching children to avoid misbehaving. The system is less adept at teaching children to behave well. Consider the 1998 film *The Mask of Zorro,* in which the wise, erstwhile Zorro must teach a young thief and rogue (who will become the new Zorro) the charm of a gentleman and the skills of a swordsman *in addition to* demanding that the youth control his anger and impulsiveness. If the younger Zorro "wannabe" was in the juvenile justice system, he would be ready for discharge as soon as he learned to control his impulsiveness. PYD requires that he also learn charm.

Assessment for Risk

It is easier to use an assessment that will identify a specific problem and attach a descriptive label to that problem than it is to describe the ways in which a child is healthy.[5] Negative labeling pervades the child-serving field, in particular, juvenile justice. In Florida, for example, youth assessment centers have sprung up across the state as professionals screen every child after arrest. They inevitably find pathology.

In Pennsylvania, juvenile probation officers evaluate children who enter the system with an instrument called the Problem Severity Index (PSI). The PSI will find that children are skipping classes or that they have trouble relating to their parents, but they will never uncover children's talents as artists or artisans. Most modern assessments find problems, and they guarantee that children stay in coercive systems that are not congenial to PYD.

At best, negative assessment tools have a crude chance of sending a child to the kind of program that claims to be able to address the diagnosed problem, but many juvenile justice systems do not even use their negative assessment instruments that well. In too many systems, the empty bed remains the most used diagnostic arrow. Tell me where there is a vacancy, and I will tell you what the diagnosis is.

While assessments are an obstacle to PYD after adolescents have been referred to the juvenile justice system, there is promise in the primary and secondary prevention context. Pursuant to Title V of the Juvenile Justice and Delinquency Prevention Act, since the early 1990s, the Office of Juvenile Justice and Delinquency Prevention (OJJDP) has sponsored the Communities That Care (CTC) initiative. Developed by David Hawkins and Richard Catalano, the CTC grant program to states calls for self-assessments by individuals, families, schools, and communities, as part of an effort to reduce "risk factors" in each that lead to antisocial behavior. This risk-focused approach targets adolescent behaviors like drug abuse, delinquency, violence, school dropout, and teen pregnancy. It is an endeavor that requires coordinated, local efforts that will lead to targeted neighborhood activities (Hawkins and Catalano, 1992).

Communities That Care has potential, especially to the extent that PYD requires suppression of risk factors. It is certainly true that risks work together exponentially and that elimination of *any* risks will be helpful to children and families (Schorr, 1998). Indeed, early studies show that in many communities CTC has been effective in organizing adults and youth around the common task of building strong neighborhoods (General Accounting Office, 1996).

What is less well known than CTC's emphasis on risk factors is its asset-based social development strategy, which is supposed to promote healthy behaviors. Unfortunately, this strategy is not nearly as well developed conceptually as

CTC's emphasis on risk factors, and little evidence exists that CTC communities are focusing as much on healthy behaviors as they are on the easier-to-identify CTC checklist of risk factors.

Punishment, Retribution, and Incapacitation

Increasingly, legislators are infusing juvenile justice statutes with the language of the adult system. In contrast to the juvenile justice system's traditional goal of "rehabilitation," the adult criminal justice system has focused on deterrence (both of the individual and of society in general), retribution, and incapacitation (Packer, 1968). Over the last decade, almost every state that changed its juvenile justice system has added some version of those criminal justice goals to the purposes of its juvenile code (Torbet et al., 1996).

The trend was foreshadowed in the mid-1980s, when the first wave of punitive juvenile justice "reforms" was advanced by the American Legislative Exchange Council (ALEC), which published a model juvenile code based on the principle of "just deserts." The ALEC code treated juveniles as though they were adults, promoting accountability and personal responsibility as the only goals worth pursuing (Treanor and Volenik, 1987).

Some reformers proposed that a punishment model should *replace* the traditional rehabilitation model: they viewed children as being no different than adults. Others had more success in *adding* punishment to the existing juvenile justice framework. They argued again that the juvenile justice system was merely a substitute parent; since parents are motivated by love when they punish their children, punishment is, in the end, no different from rehabilitation. Such sophistry had surface appeal because the major premise was true: when parents punish their child, love is indeed a motivator. The sanction is swift, directly related in time and proportion to the offense, expected by the child, and part of a context that includes love and nurturing. In those circumstances, punishment is indeed an important part of raising a child. Unfortunately, that is not the way punishment is used by the juvenile justice system.

In the juvenile justice system, punishment can mean placement in harsh, locked institutions; shackling and handcuffing; and isolation. More benign versions, tied to treatment plans or the behavior modification program *du jour,* are erratically implemented, and the juvenile knows that the punishment is a sanction that will always appear on her or his record.

In addition, in order to promote the goals of punishment, both conservatives and liberals have proposed that juvenile justice systems be required to use "graduated sanctions." As envisioned by Representative Bill McCollum, the author of the 105th Congress's HR.3 (which was passed by the House in 1997, but which died in the Senate), there would be a justice system response for *every* alleged delinquent act, and the response would be a sanction that would increase in severity for every subsequent offense. In anticipation of HR.3's passage, at the end of 1997, Congress appropriated $250 million for the Juvenile Accountability Incentive Block Grant (JAIBG).[6] Few of the 12 authorized spending purposes of

JAIBG[7] contain elements of PYD, and the amount appropriated for JAIBG was far more than Congress had ever appropriated for juvenile justice prevention programs.

Language

One reason that punishment and graduated sanctions have found hospitable hosts in the juvenile justice system is that the language of the system has changed to reflect attitudes about children. Most state juvenile codes until recent years dealt with a range of children's issues, focusing on child abuse, neglect, status offenses, and delinquency. Everyone who was the subject of those codes was described as a "child." During the 1990s, many states changed the language. For example, in addressing delinquency, the Virginia legislature, with one push of the "search and replace" button, changed every reference to "child" in its juvenile code, replacing that benign word with "juvenile," which is more amorphous, which in turn leads more easily to punishment or transfer to the adult system.

Positive youth development does not come to mind very quickly if one is responding to offenses committed by "superpredators." But that was the language introduced to the field by respected scholars (Bennett, DiIulio, and Walters, 1996), and its impact was profound. Rhetoric about "superpredators" fueled many of the changes in state law that occurred in the mid-1990s. When Representative McCollum first introduced the bill that became HR.3, it was called the "Violent Youth Predator Act of 1996."

Reliance on Quarantine

Annie E. Casey Foundation president, Doug Nelson, once criticized the typical American foster care system for relying too heavily on three methods to save children: distance, difference, and time. Most systems have an operating philosophy that relies on moving a neglected child as far as possible from his or her parent, placing the child in a different environment, and doing it for as long as possible. In this way, it is incorrectly thought that foster children will be imbued with all the good qualities that the system has to offer. Such an approach does little to improve parental skills. It does little to change and augment neighborhood resources. It does little to enable the foster child to cope with parent and neighborhood upon his or her return from placement.

The same negative qualities characterize much of the juvenile justice system. This was described by David Altschuler who was then developing a theory of aftercare:

> The community reintegration process [which I propose] is based on a set of assumptions which fly in the face of the practice of many decades where child care institutions of various sorts were separated from mainstream socialization influences and the local

community. It was their intention first to insulate the child from these influences and then to strengthen or inculcate values conducive to law abidance and other legitimate roles. The assumptions were that (1) the youth would leave the programs appropriately immunized to survive the outside world, and (2) adjustment and progress within the programs offered some reasonably sound basis for thinking successful community reintegration would follow. (Altschuler, 1984, p. 365)

Even if the juvenile justice system reconceptualizes the quarantine rationale—rejecting the notion that youth will be able to learn skills for surviving *outside* the institution when they are *inside* it—the powerful rise of incapacitation as a goal makes it unlikely that states will reduce the use of removing youth from their communities as a major component of the juvenile justice system. It will be even harder for states to accomplish this goal when huge amounts of federal JAIBG funds make construction of new institutions increasingly affordable.

Poor Institutional Conditions

While there are many exemplary programs for delinquent youth, they do not predominate. On any day, tens of thousands of American youth are held in state training schools and detention centers. Conditions in these facilities do not inspire confidence. If PYD has a core value, it must prevent adults from harming children, especially under the guise of saving them.

Human Rights Watch has described abominable conditions in juvenile facilities in Georgia, Colorado, and Louisiana (Human Rights Watch, 1997, 1996, 1995). Take this description of a Louisiana facility:

> Here in the middle of the impoverished Mississippi Delta is a juvenile prison so rife with brutality, cronyism and neglect that many legal experts say it is the worst in the nation. The prison, the Tallulah Correctional Center for Youth, opened just four years ago where a sawmill and cotton fields once stood. Behind rows of razor wire, it houses 620 boys and young men, age 11 to 20, in stifling corrugated-iron barracks jammed with bunks.
>
> From the run-down homes and bars on the road that runs by it, Tallulah appears unexceptional, one new cookie-cutter prison among scores built in the United States this decade. But inside, inmates of the privately run prison regularly appear at the infirmary with black eyes, broken noses or jaws or perforated eardrums from beatings by the poorly paid, poorly trained guards or from fights with other boys.
>
> Meals are so meager that many boys lose weight. Clothing is so scarce that boys fight over shirts and shoes. Almost all the teachers are uncertified, instruction amounts to as little as an hour

a day, and until recently there were no books. Up to a fourth of the inmates are mentally ill or retarded, but a psychiatrist visits only one day a week. There is no therapy. Emotionally disturbed boys who cannot follow guards' orders are locked in isolation cells for weeks at a time or have their sentences arbitrarily extended.

These conditions, which are described in public documents and were recounted by inmates and prison officials during a reporter's visit to Tallulah, are extreme, a testament to Louisiana's well-documented violent history and notoriously brutal prison system.

But what has happened at Tallulah is more than just the story of one bad prison. Corrections officials say the forces that converged to create Tallulah—the incarceration of more and more mentally ill adolescents, a rush by politicians to build new prisons while neglecting education and psychiatric services, and states' handing responsibility for juvenile offenders to private companies—have caused the deterioration of juvenile prisons across the country. (Butterfield, 1998)

Thirty years ago, Jerry Miller warned us about the dangers of institutions. Institutional staff have the same problems as probation officers described in the next section (Miller, 1991). It is much easier to hire staff to be guards than to hire staff who function like ordinary devoted parents. Most institutional staff believe they have succeeded if they get through a day without incident. Family involvement or team meetings are rare. When the Juvenile Law Center sued a Pennsylvania training school in the early 1990s, we learned that the school staff, which taught youth from about 8:00 A.M. to 3:00 P.M., never talked with "custodial" staff, which had youth the rest of the time. The 3-to-11 and 11-to-7 custodial shifts rarely talked with each other, and never with the school to discuss issues that might have arisen during the evening or night. Communication—of the sort that parents might have at the end of the day about issues that arose when one was at work while the other cared for the child—is too often considered an unnatural act in institutional settings.

Institutions are also confused about their roles. Take the example of one Virginia institution, which in the mid-1990s experimented briefly—until public outcry put an end to the practice—with intense isolation for misbehaving youth. The Segregation Unit at Beaumont Juvenile Correctional Center was designed, according to its program statement, "to make the quality of life uncomfortable enough that juveniles will be motivated to work toward their objectives and return to an open cottage."

The program is astonishing. It emphasizes isolation and restrictions on mail, recreation, visitation, and education. The idea is to make youth's circumstances so wretched that they will behave in accordance with the minimum we expect of youth: do what they are told and create no problems.

Institutions across the country are mired in bad practice. While Virginia's venture into isolation-as-treatment was short-lived, and the Tallulah facility described above is an extreme version, poor conditions are commonplace. In the early 1990s, an OJJDP-commissioned study by Abt Associates found over half of the country's training schools and detention centers fell below nationally accepted standards (Parent et al., 1994). This is hardly a climate in which PYD will thrive.

Congress made a bad situation worse in 1995 when it passed the Prisoner Litigation Reform Act (PLRA). The new law was ostensibly enacted to reduce frivolous litigation by jailhouse lawyers. It did much more. PLRA made it extremely difficult for adults or juveniles to bring suits that complain of conditions of confinement. The new law ended many current consent decrees in which federal courts oversaw local efforts to improve conditions. The law prevents federal judges from entering consent decrees in institutional litigation unless there is a specific finding of constitutional violations or violation of federal law (the admission of which is the very thing consent decrees are supposed to avoid). In short, at a time when more children spend more time in overcrowded facilities, PLRA prevents juveniles, who are least able to obtain help, from complaining in federal court about institutional conditions.

Confusion of Professional Roles

To the extent that there is a single professional at the top of the pyramid of services providers and custodians of youth in the juvenile justice system, it is the juvenile probation officer. In some states juvenile probation is called "community control," suggesting the limits of the role. In those states, juvenile probation functions to supervise a juvenile until the youth is placed in the custody of a state youth authority, such as that operated in Massachusetts or California. In most communities, juvenile probation is the eyes, ears, and arm of the juvenile court. (The exceptions are few. One is New York City, in which juvenile probation is part of the executive branch.)

The juvenile probation officer has many roles, several of which are incompatible with PYD. To the extent that PYD has a chance of succeeding inside the borders of juvenile justice systems, the roles that are incompatible must be reconsidered and redefined, and those that are consistent must be nurtured.

Probation officers are both monitors and helpers. As monitors, they note infractions, have authority to take youth into custody for those infractions, report to the court on the youth's progress or lack thereof, and make recommendations for sanctions. As helpers, juvenile probation officers are supposed to counsel youth and connect them with appropriate services, education, and employment opportunities. Some communities think of juvenile probation officers as case managers, one who convenes meetings of all of the adults who are helping the youth, ensures that there are integrated service plans, and arranges for provision of services. As a case manager, the probation officer has a vision of where the youth is heading and plans for the future as well as the present.

The best juvenile probation officers indeed serve as case managers while juggling their monitor-helper roles. The problem is that it is difficult to design state-of-the-art interventions based on PYD when they must rely on the skills of the *best* juvenile probation officer. To succeed, PYD must be acceptable to, and capable of implementation by, the *average* probation officer. He or she comes with defenses.

First, although PYD envisions the probation officer as helper, it is much easier for probation officers to be monitors who note infractions than to be guides. This is not surprising. The heavy caseloads of most probation officers make helping difficult and monitoring relatively easy.

Second, there is a developing trend to arm juvenile probation officers. More than a dozen Pennsylvania counties permit juvenile probation officers to carry guns; several *require* them to be armed. When probation officers look like police, PYD faces an added challenge.

Third, juvenile probation officers consider the client to be the youth (or perhaps the juvenile court itself), rarely the family. Many consider parents to be part of the problem. They do not know how to learn what parents know about their children. (Indeed, given probation officers' monitoring role, many parents are reluctant to treat them as trusted confidants who embrace a common goal of PYD.) Once, in the early 1980s, I was addressing a meeting of juvenile probation officers about the importance of working with parents. This was a time when many human service systems were developing a family-centered, ecological approach to service delivery. When I finished my exhortation, one probation officer raised his hand, stood up and said, "I'll tell you how I work with parents. I say, 'Mom, I'm sending your kid away!'" Then, to the laughter and applause of his colleagues, he bowed and took his seat.

Fourth, many probation officers also find it difficult to work with community-based organizations that might support a culture of PYD. The system does not allow probation much time to learn about (visit, observe, build relationships with) community-based organizations. Caseloads make such activities difficult, and supervisors expect line staff to be working with individual youth. In addition, while the best probation departments assign officers to geographic districts, many are organized in different ways (such as assigning probation officers to programs or institutions, no matter where the youth come from).

Children with Disabilities

Recent studies in Illinois and Massachusetts show high percentages of delinquent youth with mental health problems (Teplin, Abram, and McClelland, 1998; Grisso and Barnum, 1998), yet children with such problems have a particularly difficult time in the juvenile justice system. There are examples of successful programs for children with serious mental health problems (e.g., Multi-Systemic Therapy in South Carolina, the Willie M. program in North Carolina, and Alternative Rehabilitative Communities in Pennsylvania), but no state system routinely screens and diagnoses children with mental health problems or has well-trained staff systemwide. The absence of attention to mental health issues, which could worsen if Medicaid managed care controls the payment of services for these children, makes it difficult for proponents of PYD. For in addition to developing strengths,

PYD entails addressing those conditions that prevent youth from maximizing their assets.

Not only do juvenile justice systems fail to act as ordinary devoted parents for children with disabilities, they impede birth parents from participating in the treatment of their children.

Some years ago, I was at a conference of parents of children with mental health problems. One angry parent rose and said, "Until my child was arrested, I was the 'majority shareholder' in his life. I held 51 percent of the stock, which meant that I had the final say, whether we were with school officials preparing an individualized education program or with mental health providers developing an individualized treatment plan. Then my son was arrested, and I became not only a minority shareholder, I was seen as part of the problem. Juvenile probation treated me as though I knew nothing about my son. Probation felt that I had no solutions to offer, that my son would be better off without me. And worse, they didn't come close to recognizing his problems or working energetically to help him overcome them."

Retooling and the Cost of Transition

The juvenile justice system exists to protect the public. Thus, there will always be aspects of it that remove children from the community, or transfer them to the adult criminal justice system, or serve to control and monitor youth's behavior. Positive youth development, to the extent that it enters the juvenile justice conceptual frame, will at the beginning arrive as an add-on to current practice rather than as a replacement for it. The system will not willingly yield the goals of control and negative labeling. For PYD to endure, however, it must be part of an overall system transformation.

To the extent that we can imagine a multiyear effort, built on the wedge opportunities described in the next section, we must be willing to pay for that effort. Changing a system requires a change in values at all levels of service delivery and decision making. It requires training. It involves adding staff with new skills even as we phase out old ways of doing business.

Most public systems do not handle multiyear transitions very well. Single-year budgeting, resistance from line staff, political turnover, and lack of leadership all contribute to doing business as usual.

There are examples of system conversions based on new values, however. These are clearest in the transformation of mental health and mental retardation systems, which were institution-based and rested on negative stereotypes of the mentally ill and mentally retarded, much as today's juvenile justice system views delinquent youth (Rothman and Rothman, 1984). There are also some examples of successful conversions of juvenile justice systems (Miller, 1991). If those examples are to be replicated, however, systems must be willing and able to pay for the costs of a multiyear, strategic transition (Conservation Company and Juvenile Law Center, 1994).

OPPORTUNITIES

Bazemore and Terry note the difficulty of injecting PYD into the modern juvenile justice system. They are right in cautioning reforms to "start small," suggesting that "the complexity of juvenile justice requires that reform efforts be carefully planned and deliberate, and that they include input form the staff as well as all other stakeholders in the system and the community" (Bazemore and Terry, 1997). I will not repeat their excellent suggestions for organizing stakeholders in order to take those small first steps. Rather, I suggest the substantive areas in which those steps might be taken.

There are, of course, examples of juvenile justice programs that implement a sound PYD philosophy. The Oregon Social Learning Center, in Eugene, has developed a successful foster care program for delinquent youth. Kaleidoscope, in Chicago, has used "wraparound"[8] services to great effect. It is beyond the scope of this chapter, however, to describe individual programs. Instead, the following sections discuss structural opportunities.

Education and Health Care

One cluster of opportunities can be implemented without regard to the incoherence of juvenile justice policy and practice. At a minimum, no matter what the philosophy or goals of the system, juvenile justice can address basic needs that any youth will need in any system. These are education and health care (the latter includes physical and behavioral health).

There are vast bodies of literature—much directed to juvenile justice—on correctional health care and correctional education (Center on Crime, Communities and Culture, 1997). Unfortunately, those responsible for serving delinquent youth often fail to meet even minimum standards. Juvenile Law Center staff see institutions that do not provide delinquent youth with basic or special education for the same number of hours as children in public schools. We see children who do not receive routine health screens and treatment. There is no excuse for these shortcomings. Education and health care are basic rights, and they ought to be viewed as prerequisites for any PYD activity.

Delivery of health care to delinquent youth—in particular, those in private residential treatment programs that are eligible for funding through the federal Medicaid program—will be affected by states converting Medicaid fee-for-service programs to managed care. Some states will include delinquent youth in their managed care coverage, and they might learn from Pennsylvania's experience. A Juvenile Law Center report on the first year of Pennsylvania's managed care program found that for children living in substitute care, the system failed to ensure continuous Medicaid coverage during the entire period of placement, to ensure prompt enrollment of eligible children, to ensure prompt selection or change of a primary care physician (PCP) when children move far from the original PCP, or to clarify who could communicate with managed care providers about the children's health care (Bush, 1998). There were other problems as well, but the cautionary note, for those who see health care as a bedrock for PYD, is that health care has been unevenly provided to delinquent youth under fee-for-service arrangements. And it can get even worse if managed care programs are not managed carefully themselves.

Education is also unevenly delivered. At least, 40 percent of institutionalized children have special education needs (Gemignani, 1994). If they were identified before entering the institution, their individualized education programs—developed with their parents and teachers who knew them well—rarely follow them to the institutional school. Parents are not encouraged to participate in the education of their children, and the distance from home to institution is usually too great, even if the parents are invited to be helpful.

Discipline inside institutional schools can border on the bizarre. Many facilities for delinquent youth will actually "suspend" juveniles for misbehavior in the institution's school, sending the child to his or her room. Some juveniles become the Brer Rabbits of their facilities ("Please, please, don't throw me into the briar patch"), daring their custodians to suspend them for in-school behavior. Keeping kids in schools in institutions should not be very difficult.

Around the country are examples, too, of delinquent youth who have difficulty returning to school after discharge from delinquency programs. While ensuring prompt reentry will be the task of aftercare probation, discussed below, reenrollment is usually a systemwide problem that can only be addressed by juvenile court and department of juvenile justice leadership negotiating with local education agencies. Protocols for prompt reentry to local schools should be mandatory.

Aftercare

Beginning in the late 1980s, the federal government invested in promoting aftercare probation services.[9] The Office of Juvenile Justice and Delinquency Prevention promoted a model for an intensive aftercare program (IAP) developed by David Altschuler and Troy Armstrong.

This program relies upon the probation officer—that is, the aftercare worker—as case manager. IAP rests on five principles: preparing youth for progressively increased responsibility and freedom in the community; facilitating youth-community interaction and involvement; working with the offender and community support systems; developing new resources to support youth in the community; and monitoring (Altschuler and Armstrong, 1992).

For some reason—most like routine system inertia—the Altschuler-Armstrong model of aftercare did not gain sufficient purchase to dominate the field. It should have. At its best, IAP is a model of reintegration that is consistent with PYD.

The reason that IAP is such a valuable wedge for PYD is that, at its best, it forces the system to imagine the youth's future *at the time the juvenile court or state youth authority fashions its first order of disposition.* It is impossible to plan for a youth's disposition, for example, unless you know where he or she is going. To which school will he or she return? Where will he or she live? With which adults will he or she need to be connected? How will the order of disposition make the answers to those questions possible?

Aftercare that begins with those questions in mind will follow the youth along a developmental pathway: through institutional care, planning with institutional staff for the future, involving family and other concerned adults, and preparing the child for school or work. Aftercare is an aggressive course of reintegrative services and supervision that should build upon a youth's strengths in a ceaseless reimagining and re-creation of the youth's future.

Aftercare should be available to all children who are placed outside their homes. In a sense, aftercare should operate as an ordinary devoted parent would for a child who is in a mental health facility, or special education program or boarding school. The ordinary devoted parent, of course, has a caseload of one, and knows how to connect the child with friends, relatives, and community institutions. Indeed, aftercare is crucial to connecting children coming out of institutions to community-based organizations that will provide the youth's next scaffold of support. Combined with independent living and the balanced approach, described below, aftercare should be a promising investment for proponents of PYD.

Title IV-E (IL): Independent Living

The federal government has for years contributed to states' expenditures on foster care, including such care for delinquent youth. The Adoption Assistance and Child Welfare Act of 1980 was designed to end foster care drift and promote permanent homes for children in the child welfare system. Because many dependent children moved in and out of the delinquency system, and because many states were quickly alert to the possibilities of refinancing their delinquency systems, federal foster care maintenance payments were soon being used for delinquent children.

The federal government pays a proportionate share of foster care (related to a state's poverty rate) pursuant to Title IV-E of the Social Security Act. In order for a child to be eligible, his or her parents must meet income guidelines for public assistance, and there must be a case plan and a judicial finding that the state made "reasonable efforts" to prevent out-of-home placement. Until 1996, Title IV-E reimbursement was only available to children placed with private, nonprofit agencies. Congress amended the law in 1996 to permit federal financial participation when the child is placed in for-profit programs.

Many states have been claiming IV-E reimbursement for delinquent youth. However, because case planning and "reasonable effort" requirements are unevenly implemented, the U.S. Department of Health and Human Services is considering eliminating such reimbursements for delinquency placements. Until that time, the case planning requirements of Title IV-E offer an opportunity to infuse PYD into the plans and services provided for youth eligible for IV-E. This is particularly true of those who are 16 or older, for whom the IV-E independent living requirements are applicable.

Title IV-E (IL) requires states to have a plan for every eligible youth, a plan that envisions how the youth will make the transition from foster care to adulthood. This requires case plans that address such issues as life skills, vocational training, and education in a way that prepares older adolescents for adulthood. The independent living initiative is an underused vehicle for PYD, but it offers promise for creative administrators.[10]

Balanced Approach

There is probably no greater wedge for PYD than that provided by the "competency development" component of the late-1990s notion of *restorative justice.* Restorative justice is an effort by juvenile justice proponents to preserve the system from attack by finding a philosophical middle ground between retributive justice, which gained in favor as states sought to "get tough" on juvenile crime, and rehabilitation, which was seen as being too "soft" on crime. By the 1990s, *rehabilitation* was used as pejoratively by critics of the juvenile justice system as *liberal* was in the political context.

In the 1980s, a form of restorative justice had been introduced by the probation staff of Dennis Maloney, in Bend, Oregon. Maloney called his intervention the "Balanced Approach" (Maloney, Romig, and Armstrong, 1988). While he originally applied it to the purposes and uses of juvenile probation, the balanced approach soon became an organizing principle for the entire juvenile justice system. It proposes that at every stage of the juvenile justice pipeline three principles should operate: accountability, public safety, and competency development. The system must hold the individual youth *accountable* (satisfying the needs of retribution). *Public safety* is the reason that the system exists (here recognizing the potential for rehabilitation, incapacitation, and deterrence). *Competency development,* which is the link to PYD, ensures that every intervention provides more than make-work or incapacitation. For example, restitution or community service that requires participation in, for example, Habitat for Humanity, in which a juvenile learns a skill and increases empathy, makes more sense than having the juvenile rake leaves along the freeway.

Many state legislatures have been attracted to the balanced approach. Beginning in the mid-1990s, several states—for example, Idaho, Illinois, Maryland, Montana, Pennsylvania, and Wisconsin—changed the purposes and languages of their juvenile codes to incorporate balanced-approach principles.

While some states have made tentative steps toward PYD in their codes,[11] few have given sufficient content in legislation to change the culture of the state system. Illinois, whose new code went into effect in January 1999, is an exception.

Illinois's new purpose clause explicitly adopts the balanced approach. After invoking public protection and accountability, it declares equipping "juvenile offenders with competencies to live responsibly and productively" as a goal. Competency is then defined as "the development of educational, vocational, social, emotional and basic life skills which enable a minor to mature into a productive member of society" (705 IL. C.S. §405/5-105).

Idaho, in addition to changing the purpose of its juvenile code, added competency development to the goals of its secure facilities (training schools). Idaho's facilities now require "training in the development of competency and life skills designed to assist the juvenile in operating effectively within and becoming a contributing member of the community . . . Prevocational education shall be provided to acquaint juvenile offenders with vocations, their requirements and opportunities" (Idaho Code §20-531).

Some states are now referring interchangeably to their restorative justice and balanced-approach programs. Pennsylvania, for example, has developed a Balanced and Restorative Justice (BARJ)[12] task force to implement the "competency development" requirements of its new juvenile code.

Gordon Bazemore, Mark Umbreit, and others have written extensively about the potential for restorative justice affecting every aspect of the juvenile justice system. At best, restorative justice is not an addition to the system, but a reformation of it:

> Restorative justice is a way of thinking, a way of behaving, and a way of measuring. Until we change the way we think about why probation [for example] exists, we can't change our behavior. We can't measure the changes until our behavior changes. (Umbreit and Carey, 1995)

Bazemore, too, recognizes the need for a paradigm shift if restorative justice is to become central to the juvenile justice system. He cautions:

> For a new paradigm to emerge, however, professionals must not only reject the old paradigm but also understand the new and embrace its implications for a distinct change in practice. In the absence of a shared understanding of core principles, and of their implications for systemic and organizational change, the competency development model can be quickly equated with one or more treatment programs or intervention techniques transformed to fit bureaucratic agendas. (Bazemore and Terry, 1997)

This warning is important. Beginning in 1997, friends working in juvenile justice residential programs reported that their agencies were repackaging existing treatment programs to call them "competency development." Such repackaging would meet contractual obligations but would do little to effect the kind of paradigm shift Bazemore and Terry advocate.

Unfortunately, most of the early state efforts to realign their juvenile justice systems with a BARJ philosophy have fallen short. It was easiest for states to begin by focusing on public safety and accountability rather than by figuring out the meaning of competency development. Thus, we have seen states building new institutions, the federal government introduce a Juvenile Accountability Incentive

Block Grant program,[13] and local investment in programs like restitution and community service, as though the latter were *identical* to competency development.

Bazemore and Umbreit's early writings were elliptical where competency development was concerned. More recently, however, Bazemore has given increased attention to competency development. His article with W. Clinton Terry in *Child Welfare* (Bazemore and Terry, 1997) is the best piece of writing to date on how the competency development leg of the balanced approach triangle can be integrated into the juvenile justice system. (For purposes of this chapter, *competency development* and *positive youth development* are interchangeable.) The Bazemore-Terry approach is illustrated by the following table from their article, which shows how competency development differs from the erstwhile medical model, which rested in individual treatment:

Intermediate Outcomes of Intervention:
Individual Treatment and Competency Development

Individual Treatment	Competency Development
Avoid negative influence of designated people, places and activities	Begin new, positive relationships and positive behavior in conventional roles; avoid placement of youth in stigmatizing treatments
Follow rules of supervision (e.g., curfew, school attendance)	Practice competent, conventional behavior
Attend and participate in treatment activities (e.g., counseling)	Active demonstration of competency through completion of productive activity (service and/or work with community benefit)
Complete all required treatment and terminate supervision	Significant increase in measurable competencies (academic, social, occupational, etc.)
Improvements in attitude and self-concept; improved family interaction; psychological integration	Improvements in self-image and public image (community acceptance) and increased bonding and community integration

The table illustrates how competency development represents a different approach, one that can be applied at any stage of the juvenile justice pipeline. In addition, as the table also points out, a well-designed competency development program can be measured and assessments of success can go well beyond traditional measures of recidivism.

Changing the Measure of Success

With tracking and evaluation tools like ProDES, described earlier, juvenile justice systems have the capacity to measure aspects of PYD. Programs will be able to learn whether they are succeeding in promoting discrete aspects of PYD, and juvenile justice administrators will be in a position to reward success.

For example, at the end of 1998, ProDES looked at system trends for the four years the system tracked youth who entered the Philadelphia juvenile justice system. With solid data, the evaluators could make a statement like the following:

> When ProDES was being developed programs were almost unanimous in stating that improved self-esteem, more pro-social values and improved school and family bonding were intermediate goals of theirs (in the sense that positive change on these was expected to have a longer-term impact on delinquent behavior). *There is no evidence yet that any of these goals are being met* [emphasis in original]. Some juveniles do improve on one or more of these dimensions while in the programs; others however do not change or even get worse. The balance among these three outcomes has fluctuated but not changed significantly during the more than four years of study. If these remain important goals, programs need to try alternative modes of intervention in the hope that they will have a more marked positive impact. (Jones and Harris, 1998, pp. 2-3)

To my knowledge, Philadelphia is the only city in the country that has the capacity to generate data that would enable evaluators to track youth's progress over time and measure aspects of PYD. This is a fruitful area to pursue. For many communities, changing what is measured will inevitably change practice.

Role of Defense Counsel

Youth in the juvenile justice system have often been ill served by their lawyers. While there are excellent examples of high-quality lawyering around the country, for the most part the juvenile defense bar has been beset by high caseloads and low expectations (Puritz et al., 1995).

Yet defense counsel can play a significant role in promoting PYD. To do so, however, requires that lawyers do more than show up for the adjudicatory hearing (trial of "guilt" or "innocence"). They must get to know their clients and the adults who care about them. They must be active participants in planning their clients' dispositions, push probation staff to think in terms of PYD and, if their clients are committed to institutions, work with institutional aftercare probation staff to ensure a transitional plan that is developmentally sound. Investment in training, and in augmenting defender offices with social workers, would create for the juvenile justice system an internal advocacy component that would promote PYD in individual cases at every stage of the juvenile justice pipeline.

In 1999, the Office of Juvenile Justice and Delinquency Prevention will provide start-up funding for the first national center designed to provide training, resources, and technical assistance exclusively to the juvenile defense bar. The OJJDP sees this project as a natural evolution of the Due Process Advocacy Project it has supported since 1993. That project, led by the Juvenile Justice Center of the American Bar Association, with support from the Youth Law Center and Juvenile Law Center, produced the first national assessment of the quality and availability of counsel for delinquent youth (Puritz et al., 1995). In 1997 and

1998, the project also hosted the first two national Juvenile Defender Leadership Summits. Those gatherings, attended by defender representatives from all 50 states, focused on building the capacity of the juvenile defense bar. They examined structural issues (e.g., caseloads) and substantive issues, such as how to improve the quality of representation at disposition, with particular emphasis on developmentally appropriate juvenile court responses.

Supporting the defense bar will be fertile territory for national and local foundations. There is an opportunity to expand upon what the OJJDP has begun and to provide regional support for juvenile defender affinity groups. Positive youth development will not become part of the juvenile justice culture unless there is an internal advocate for it in every case. The best hope for such advocacy is defense counsel.

Faith-Based Interventions

Much has been written lately about faith-based approaches to reducing delinquency (Klein, 1997), but it is unclear how those approaches will mesh with the formal juvenile justice system, let alone with PYD. It appears that ministries work best at primary and secondary prevention of delinquency (Woodson, 1998; Klein, 1997). Part of the problem is that the formal juvenile justice system is quintessentially a government function. While religious charities have provided services to delinquent youth from the dawn of the juvenile justice system, in modern times they do such work through government contracts, subject to state regulation.

It does not seem that religious charities today have any greater affinity for PYD than do lay nonprofit organizations. Indeed, Robert Woodson's early study of Philadelphia's House of Umoja demonstrated that when government intervened to fund and regulate Umoja, much of the value of its grassroots ministry was diluted (Woodson, 1981). As the Yale Law School professor Stephen Carter has observed, government funding has an impact on programs: "You run the risk of becoming a very different sort of program when you start competing for the state money. And the strings the government attaches to the money may force you to compromise your faith" (Klein, 1997).

Nevertheless, it is worth looking at the impact of religious charities that provide services to delinquent youth through government contract. Particular attention should be paid to the six attributes of PYD described early in this chapter. One should tread carefully here under any circumstances: there is always the danger that faith-based programs will impose their particular religious views on youth who are committed by juvenile courts to their care.

CONCLUSION

Each of the opportunities described in the prior section has promise. Approached strategically, even the obstacles might be sufficiently weeded out to allow PYD to grow. However, proponents of PYD should not be overoptimistic. The history of juvenile justice (Bernard, 1992) makes clear that most reforms are short-lived. A normal cycle is likely to embrace PYD, absorb some of it, and swing back to more punitive measures.

The juvenile justice system can learn from the recent history of family preservation programs in the child welfare system. Beginning in the mid-1980s, propelled by funding from the Edna McConnell Clark Foundation and then the Annie E. Casey Foundation and other national foundations, family preservation was introduced to child welfare. The idea was that a particular brand of risk management—delivered through intensive, short-term interventions by social workers with low caseloads who had access to resources—could provide supports to parents that would make removal of the child into foster care unnecessary.

As originally conceived, family preservation was based upon a particular model—Homebuilders—developed by the Behavioral Sciences Institute in Washington State. But over time, as public and private child welfare agencies tried to change their culture and preserve families, they diluted the Homebuilders model (increasing caseloads, reducing services), thereby increasing risk to children. Many caseworkers misunderstood their mandate, and left children in high-risk situations because the workers thought leaving children in the home was all that family preservation meant. Over time, children were hurt. Some died. The backlash was not merely against bad practice or misapplication of a particular model; it was against the very concept of protecting children in their own homes.

Soon foster care returned to high levels. Some intensive family preservation programs remained, but by 1997, when Congress passed the Adoption and Safe Families Act, the cycle of backlash was complete.

Positive youth development will face a similar fate unless its proponents are careful at the outset. If PYD is to be anything more than an occasional nugget in a prospector's pan, its advocates must avoid promising too much. They must not fail to address negative behavior. They must acknowledge that incapacitation, even transfer to adult court, is appropriate for some children. Risk management must be a central element of any PYD program promoted by the formal juvenile justice system. Ignoring risks will enable opponents of PYD to exploit inevitable failures, thereby turning them into celebrated cases that could lead to a backlash against PYD itself.

At the same time, advocates of PYD are fully justified in challenging the proponents of incapacitation and transfer to justify those parts of the system. Family preservation, for example, was held to far higher standards of success than foster care or residential treatment facilities. In the justice system, no one has ever evaluated prisons with the scrutiny that awaits PYD.

Positive youth development remains our best hope for creating a future that embraces the majority of our children. When I think of PYD, I reflect on one of my very first cases in the mid-1970s. It was at the height of the Philadelphia gang wars. I represented a 15-year-old boy who was charged with shooting a member of an opposing gang. The victim survived, but the district attorney sought to transfer my client to adult court.

These are the facts:

My client, John, was "drafted" into his gang, which controlled the neighborhood in which John lived. He was threatened with serious harm as the alternative. He was handed a gun and told to retaliate for a perceived offense committed by the victim against one of John's fellow gang members. John went out, shot the victim, immediately turned himself into the police, and led them to the weapon. He was badly beaten by his own gang for that infraction.

John was an "A" student who had never missed a day of school in his life. The juvenile probation and the district attorney's offices soon recognized that public safety did not require transfer to adult court after all. We moved John out of the neighborhood to his grandmother's house, enrolled him in a new school, arranged with the Catholic Church to provide after-school and evening supervision. Thus, we connected John with caring adults in a new neighborhood, built a new community of support, and permitted his academic talent to flourish.

John was adjudicated delinquent, but neither the juvenile court nor the district attorney felt the need to use John as an example by transferring him to adult court. They saw that they could hold John accountable and enable him to turn his life around.

The point is not that John was typical, because he was not. Rather, the point is that John would not have a chance today. He would be a symbol, rather than a person, and he would do adult time under almost any of the state legislative changes of the last decade. Twenty-five years ago, though, the juvenile justice system saw his potential and enabled it to be realized. John went on to college, and the justice system never heard from him again. In today's climate, that would not happen.

If PYD is to have a legitimate chance, we will have to rewind and edit much of the film of juvenile justice's recent past. If we are to have the benefit of the talent that youth like Gabriel or young Ben Franklin or John can offer society, we must toss talk of sanctions to the cutting-room floor. The field will have to return to a rhetoric of childhood, editing out X-rated language like *superpredator* and eliminating glib slogans like "adult time for adult crime." If a youth is already an adult in the public mind, then there is nowhere to develop. If PYD means anything, it is that our children who pass through adolescence are not yet adults (Grisso and Schwartz, 1999), and all of the slogans in the world will not make them so.

NOTES

1 Much of the material in this section is adapted from Steinberg and Schwartz (1999).
2 In the parlance of criminal justice, incapacitation refers to the use of physical restraint—usually confinement—that reduces the offender's capacity to commit a new offense (Packer, 1968). In the juvenile justice context, incapacitation usually refers to the removal of the juvenile from his or her home.
3 In the years after *Gault,* the Supreme Court stopped short of making juveniles' rights identical to those of adults. While juveniles could avoid double jeopardy *(Breed vs. Jones)* and could only be adjudicated delinquent by proof beyond a reasonable doubt *(In re Winship),* the court held that they

were not entitled to jury trials *(McKeiver vs. Pennsylvania)* or to have strict Fourth Amendment procedures apply in schools *(T.L.O. vs. New Jersey)*. In addition, because children are always in some form of custody, the Supreme Court approved pretrial preventive detention for the child's own good *(Schall vs. Martin)*. Juveniles also have no constitutional right to bail or speedy trial.

4. While juvenile courts still operate more quickly than criminal courts, "delays in the juvenile justice system should be viewed from the perspective of an adolescent offender. Professional standards suggest that even the longest case should be processed within 90 days. Yet, a 90-day process means that a 14-year-old offender will wait the equivalent of a summer vacation for services or sanctions. In many of the nation's juvenile courts, young offenders wait even longer" (Butts, 1997).

5. Search Institute's checklist of assets is generally not used in juvenile justice systems.

6. Public Law 105-119.

7. In order to qualify for JAIBG funds, states must certify that they have adopted or are considering (a) increased transfer of juveniles to criminal court, (b) a system of graduated sanctions, (c) a system of juvenile delinquency records for serious offenders that would treat their records similar to adult records, and (d) court-ordered parental involvement and sanctions against parents for failing to supervise their children. JAIBG funds may only be used for one of the following purposes:

   - Construction of juvenile detention or correctional facilities, including training of personnel.
   - Accountability-based sanctions programs.
   - Hiring of judges, probation officers, and defenders, and funding of pretrial services.
   - Hiring of prosecutors.
   - Funding of prosecutor-led drug, gang, and violence programs.
   - Provision of technology, equipment, and training programs for prosecutors.
   - Probation programs.
   - Gun courts.
   - Drug courts.
   - Information-sharing systems.
   - Accountability-based programs for law enforcement referrals or those that are designed to protect students and school personnel from drug, gang, and youth violence.
   - Controlled substance testing (including interventions) for juveniles in the juvenile justice system (Albert, 1998).

8. "Wraparound" refers to service providers who "do whatever it takes" to acquire or provide services that children need. Instead of trying to match a child to a program ("Does this child qualify for X, Y or Z?"), wraparound is usually offered in communities by service providers who ask, "What will it take for this child to succeed?"

9. In this chapter, "aftercare" refers to services to youth who are leaving placements to which they were committed after adjudication and disposition. Some communities, such as New York City in the late 1980s, have also developed aftercare services for youth leaving pretrial detention. The New York type of aftercare raises a unique set of issues that are not dealt with in this chapter.

10. Independent living took on greater promise in mid-December 1999, when President Bill Clinton signed into law the Foster Care Independence Act of 1999. The new law doubles federal funding for independent living. It requires states to serve youth up to 21 years old. It enables states to provide time-limited financial assistance to help those youth with living expenses. The law gives states the option of allowing youth who are 18, 19, or 20 years old to remain eligible for Medicaid.

11. Maine, for example, speaks of providing a juvenile who is in state care with "the necessary treatment, care, guidance and discipline to assist him in becoming a responsible and productive member of society" (15 M.R.S.A. §3002). Florida's system is "to provide children committed to the Department of Juvenile Justice with training in life skills, including career education" (West's F.S.A. §39.001). New Jersey calls for a "comprehensive program" that "should provide a range of services and sanctions for juveniles sufficient to protect the public through prevention; early intervention; and a range of meaningful sanctions that ensure accountability, provide training, education, treatment and, when necessary, confinement followed by community supervision that is adequate to protect the public and promote successful reintegration into the community" (N.J. Stat. § 52:17B-169).

12. It is more than a little ironic that at the same time as states implement "BARJ" initiatives, New York City has begun using a barge as a detention center to handle the overflow from its existing detention facilities. Barges are not fertile places for competency development.

13. The JAIBG structure is not helpful for restorative justice initiatives. Congress mandated that 75 percent of the new funds go directly to local units of government, thereby bypassing the state as funding source. The state was most likely to be the unit of government that insisted on a restorative justice model, and other than establishing 12 permissible uses of JAIBG money, there is nothing about the JAIBG structure that will permit states to regulate local use of funds.

REFERENCES

Albert, R.L.
1998 *Juvenile Accountability Incentive Block Grants Program.* Washington, D.C.: Office of Juvenile Justice and Delinquency Prevention.

Altschuler, D.M.
1984 "Community Reintegration in Juvenile Offender Programming," in R.A. Mathias, P. DeMuro, and R.S. Allinson (eds.). *Violent Juvenile Offenders: An Anthology.* San Francisco: National Council on Crime and Delinquency.

Altschuler, D.M., and T. Armstrong
1992 *Intensive Aftercare for High-Risk Juvenile Parolees: A Community-Care Model.* Washington, D.C.: Office of Juvenile Justice and Delinquency Prevention.

Ayers, W.
1997 *A Kind and Just Parent: The Children of Juvenile Court.* Boston: Beacon.

Bazemore, G., and W.C. Terry
1997 "Developing Delinquent Youths: A Reintegrative Model for Rehabilitation and a New Role for the Juvenile Justice System." *Child Welfare,* (76:665).

Bazemore, G., and M.S. Umbreit
1994 *Balanced and Restorative Justice.* Washington, D.C.: Office of Juvenile Justice and Delinquency Prevention.

Bennett, W.J., J.J. DiIulio, Jr., and J.P. Walters
1996 *Body Count: Moral Poverty . . . and How to Win America's War against Crime and Drugs.* New York: Simon & Schuster.

Bernard, T.J.
1992 *The Cycle of Juvenile Justice.* New York: Oxford University Press.

Bush, E.L.
1998 *HealthChoices and Children in Substitute Care: A Year in Review.* Philadelphia: Juvenile Law Center.

Butterfield, F.
1998 "Hard Time: A Special Report; Profits at a Juvenile Prison Come with a Chilling Cost." *New York Times,* July 15.

Butts, J.
1997 *Delays in Juvenile Court Processing of Delinquency Cases.* Washington, D.C.: Office of Juvenile Justice and Delinquency Prevention.

Center on Crime, Communities and Culture
1997 *Education as Crime Prevention: Providing Education to Prisoners.* New York: Open Society Institute.

Commonwealth v. Fisher, 213 Pa. 48, 62 A. 198 (1905).

Conservation Company and Juvenile Law Center
1994 *Building Bridges: Strategic Planning and Alternative Financing for System Reform.* Philadelphia: Conservation Company and Juvenile Law Center.

Extended Service Schools Initiative
1999 Research design for Public/Private Ventures. Philadelphia.

Feld, B.
1993 "Juvenile (in)justice and the Criminal Court Alternative." *Crime and Delinquency,* (39:403).

Fox, S.J.
1997 *A Contribution to the History of the American Juvenile Court to 1980.* (Draft for the National Council of Juvenile and Family Court Judges).

Franklin, B.
1987 *The Autobiography.* New York: The Library of America.

Furstenberg, F.F.
1999 *Managing to Make It: Urban Families and Adolescent Success.* Chicago: University of Chicago Press.

Gemignani, R.J.
1994 *Juvenile Correctional Education: A Time for Change.* Washington, D.C.: Office of Juvenile Justice and Delinquency Prevention.

General Accounting Office
1996 *Juvenile Justice: Status of Delinquency Prevention Programs and Description of Local Projects.* Washington, D.C. Letter Report, August 13, GAO/GGD-96-147.

Goldstein, J., A. Freud, A.J. Solnit, and S. Goldstein
1986 *In the Best Interests of the Child.* New York: The Free Press.

Grisso, T., and R. Barnum
1998 *Massachusetts Youth Screening Instrument: Preliminary Manual and Technical Report.* Worcester, Mass.: University of Massachusetts Medical School, Department of Psychiatry.
Grisso, T., and R.G. Schwartz (eds.)
2000 *Youth on Trial.* Chicago: University of Chicago Press.
Guarino-Ghezzi, S., and E.J. Loughran
1991 *Balancing Juvenile Justice.* New Brunswick, N.J.: Transaction Publishers.
Hawkins, J.D., and R.F. Catalano
1992 *Communities That Care.* San Francisco: Jossey-Bass.
Human Rights Watch
1997 *High Country Lockup: Children in Confinement in Colorado.* New York: Human Rights Watch.
Human Rights Watch
1996 *Modern Capital of Human Rights? Abuses in the State of Georgia.* New York: Human Rights Watch.
Human Rights Watch
1995 *Children in Confinement in Louisiana.* New York: Human Rights Watch.
In re Gault, 387 U.S. 1, 1967.
Institute of Judicial Administration–American Bar Association
1996 *Juvenile Justice Standards Annotated: A Balanced Approach.* Chicago: American Bar Association. [Robert E. Shepherd, Jr., Editor].
Jones, P.R., and P.W. Harris
1998 *System Trends 1994-1998.* Philadelphia: Crime and Justice Research Institute.
Juvenile Detention Centers' Association of Pennsylvania
1993 *Juvenile Detention Program Standards.* Harrisburg: Pennsylvania Commission on Crime and Delinquency.
Kent v. United States, 383 U.S. 541, 1966.
Klein, J.
1997 "In God They Trust." *New Yorker,* June 16.
Krisberg, B., and J. Austin
1993 *Reinventing Juvenile Justice.* Newbury Park, Calif.: Sage Publications.
Lopez, S.
1994 *Third and Indiana.* New York: Penguin Books.
Mack, J.
1909 "The Juvenile Court." *Harvard Law Review,* 23:104-122.
Maloney, D., D. Romig, and T. Armstrong
1988 "Juvenile Probation: The Balanced Approach." *Juvenile and Family Court Journal,* 39:1-63.
Meranze, M.
1996 *Laboratories of Virtue: Punishment, Revolution and Authority in Philadelphia, 1760-1835.* Chapel Hill: University of North Carolina Press.
Miller, J.G.
1991 *Last One over the Wall: The Massachusetts Experiment in Closing Reform Schools.* Columbus: Ohio State University Press.
Packer, H.L.
1968 *The Limits of the Criminal Sanction.* Stanford: Stanford University Press.
Parent, D.G., V. Lieter, S. Kennedy, L. Livens, D. Wentworth, and S. Wilcox
1994 *Conditions of Confinement: Juvenile Detention and Corrections Facilities.* Washington, D.C.: Office of Juvenile Justice and Delinquency Prevention.
Platt, A.M.
1977 *The Child Savers: The Invention of Delinquency* (Second Edition). Chicago: University of Chicago Press.
Puritz, P., S. Burrell, R. Schwartz, M. Soler, and L. Warboys
1995 *A Call for Justice: An Assessment of Access to Counsel and Quality of Representation in Delinquency Proceedings.* Chicago: American Bar Association.
Robertson, J., and J. Robertson
1982 *Baby in the Family.* London: Penguin Books.
Rothman, D.J., and S.M. Rothman
1984 *The Willowbrook Wars: A Decade of Struggle for Social Justice.* New York: Harper & Row.
Schorr, L.B.
1997 *Common Purpose: Strengthening Families and Neighborhoods to Rebuild America.* New York: Doubleday.
Schorr, L.B., with Schorr, D.
1988 *Within Our Reach: Breaking the Cycle of Disadvantage.* New York: Doubleday.

Snyder, H.N., and M. Sickmund
1995 *Juvenile Offenders and Victims: A National Report.* Washington, D.C.: Office of Juvenile Justice and Delinquency Prevention.

Steinberg, L., and R.G. Schwartz
1999 "Developmental Psychology Goes to Court," in T. Grisso, and R.G. Schwartz (eds.). *Youth on Trial.* Chicago: University of Chicago Press.

Teplin, L., K. Abram, and G. McClelland
1998 "Psychiatric and Substance Abuse Disorders among Juveniles in Detention: An Empirical Assessment." Paper presented at the convention of the American Psychology-Law Society, Redondo Beach, California, March.

Torbet, P., R. Gable, H. Hurst IV, I. Montgomery, L. Szymanski, and D. Thomas
1996 *State Responses to Serious and Violent Juvenile Crime.* Washington, D.C.: Office of Juvenile Justice and Delinquency Prevention.

Treanor, W.W., and A.E. Volenik
1987 *The New Right's Agenda for the States: A Legislator's Briefing Book.* Washington, D.C.: American Youth Work Center.

Umbreit, M.S., and M. Carey
1995 *Restorative Justice: Implications for Organizational Change.* Federal Probation (59:47 54).

Welsh, W.N., P.H. Jenkins, and P.W. Harris
1999 "Reducing Minority Overrepresentation in Juvenile Justice: Results of Community-Based Delinquency Prevention in Harrisburg." *Journal of Research in Crime and Delinquency,* 36:87.

Wolfgang, M.E., R.M. Figlio, and T. Sellin
1972 *Delinquency in a Birth Cohort.* Chicago: University of Chicago Press.

Woodson, R.L.
1981 *A Summons to Life: Mediating Structures and the Prevention of Youth Crime.* Cambridge, Mass.: Ballinger Publishing Company.

Woodson, Sr., R.L.
1998 *The Triumphs of Joseph: How Today's Community Healers Are Reviving Our Streets and Neighborhoods.* New York: Free Press.

Zimring, F.E.
1998 *American Youth Violence.* New York: Oxford University Press.

9 THE MORE THINGS CHANGE, THE MORE THEY STAY THE SAME: THE EVOLUTION AND DEVOLUTION OF YOUTH EMPLOYMENT PROGRAMS

Alan Zuckerman

Federal, state, local, and community-based job training programs have been evolving and devolving for more than 30 years. The Manpower Development and Training Act, passed in 1962, marked the beginning of a continuously evolving national employment and training policy labeled successively Manpower and Manpower Development in 1962, Employment and Training in 1973, Job Training in 1983, and Workforce Investment in 1998. The changes in labels reflect changes in both the awareness of their connotations (the word *manpower* was sexist; it excluded women) and the focus of national policy.

Since 1964, these policies have been charged with preparing at-risk or disconnected young people and poor adults for work. The results have been disappointing, and the level of funding has been reduced. With the passage of a new Workforce Investment Act, the federal government promises to fund states and localities to give young people the opportunity to prepare themselves for the workforce. We had better get it right this time.

The unemployment rate for youth has been more than double the adult unemployment rate for the past 35 years, and minority youth unemployment has been more than double that figure again. Today, when unemployment is at its lowest in decades, the unemployment rate for young black males is more than 30 percent nationally and more than 50 percent in urban ghettos. Yet, what are we doing about it? Instead of launching a targeted initiative to mobilize resources, Congress in 1995 slashed funding for out-of-school youth (Title II-C of the Job Training Partnership Act [JTPA]) from $610 million to $127 million. In 1998, the Appropriations Committee of the House of Representatives proposed the elimination of all funding ($871 million) for the Summer Youth Employment Program. They did agree to $250 million for a targeted Youth Opportunity Grant focused on very poor communities.

Youth, especially out-of-school, unemployed minority youth, are not a high national priority. There has been little sustained training and job-finding effort of a magnitude anywhere equal to the need. Yet it is obvious to those who have been struggling to make policies and programs effective that we need a larger investment in youth employment policies. These policies need to support comprehensive and sustained programs that provide quality services, and they need practitioners who are competent and effective. We need to build a system that does the right things for young people and does them well.

A growing body of evidence and experience strongly suggests that the incorporation of youth development principles and practices into workforce development programs causes greater positive effects on young people: they develop basic and workforce competencies, get jobs, remain in the workforce, and often continue their education and training. But, until recently, youth development principles were applied most often to 8- to 14-year-olds.

Since the mid-1990s, practitioners, researchers, and policy makers have become increasingly aware that a developmental approach to the preparation of 16- to 24-year-olds for work is critical to success. Those practitioners who incorporate youth development into workforce development programs are more effective because they:

1. Employ activities that are age and stage appropriate;
2. Create an environment that engages the interest of youth;
3. Individualize services to youth;
4. Ensure that youth benefit from ongoing support and relationships with caring adults;
5. Incorporate opportunities for youth to interact with peers;
6. Include active and self-directed learning; and
7. Provide access to long-term support and developmental activities.

Such a paradigm is in sharp contrast to the employment and training programs of the past 30 years, in which youth have been an afterthought. Youth employment programs were seen as necessary only to stop riots, civil unrest, or crime. At the same time, the development of youth employment programs and policies has been responsive to evidence, perceptions, and feelings about whether policy and programs have worked. For more than 30 years, the federal government has proposed varying job preparation and job creation policies and programs as a part of efforts to eliminate poverty, reduce the school dropout rate, minimize the human cost of job loss, and build a competitive workforce. Only portions of these efforts have focused on youth. Unfortunately, there is a general perception that youth employment efforts do not work.

Only in the late 1970s, when the Youth Employment Demonstration Projects Act (YEDPA) amended the Comprehensive Employment and Training Act, was there an attempt to develop a national youth employment policy. For the almost four decades since the passage in 1962 of the Manpower Development and Training Act, preparation of youth for work has been part of the larger, adult-focused system. Job Corps and Summer Youth Employment Programs have been sustained since 1964, but only during the YEDPA era and the period when Vice President Mondale's Task Force on Youth Employment was active, have policy makers tried to fashion a national policy and build a national youth employment system.

To understand the evolution of current policy and the significance of youth-focused programs in national employment and training policy and practice, this chapter examines the recent history of employment and training. After 36 years of experiment, the public and many elected officials believe that these programs have failed and that practitioners are frustrated by the diminishing support for their valiant efforts. As a result, investments in youth have been sporadic, not long term. Few communities have invested the resources to build and sustain institutional and staff capacity, and in periods of increased funding, we must start by building competent organizations and programs.

THE FORMATIVE YEARS

The first post–World War II manpower training program was the Area Redevelopment Act of 1961, which focused on the problems of depressed areas—urban and rural, Appalachia, Mississippi, and Harlem. The main thrust was to attract new businesses that would bring more jobs. A short-term (16-week limit) skills training program for residents of depressed areas "prepared" them for entry-level jobs in the new businesses.

In 1962, Congress passed the Manpower Development and Training Act (MDTA) in response to predictions that automation was going to replace many workers who would need to be retrained. MDTA was primarily an adult training program, but it did authorize a youth training allowance of $20 per week—less than the adult training allowance that was equal to the unemployment insurance benefit in the state. MDTA also required that youth be out of school for six months before they could be enrolled in the program to prevent young people from dropping out of school to enroll.

The mainstream MDTA programs were very basic. The State Employment Service recruited and certified that applicants were unemployed. Applicants were referred to local vocational schools or to approved MDTA courses, which took place mostly in the afternoons and evenings. Youth and adults had to meet admission requirements, which often included a high school diploma. Upon completion, the State Employment Service placed the trainees in jobs. There was no distinction between youth and adults. All training was occupation-specific and generally offered the same course of study as did vocational schools.

In the early 1960s, the Division of Experimental and Demonstration Projects had a few million dollars and a mandate to find and fund new and different approaches to preparing people to work, especially people from poor neighborhoods or with special barriers to employment. The focus was influenced by the times. The civil rights movement pushed the Department of Labor to fund programs that addressed equity issues, and training was seen as compensation for discrimination. The Ford Foundation had been funding "gray area" projects, and President

Kennedy's Committee on Juvenile Delinquency and Youth Crime was funding comprehensive social planning and programs to combat the "social dynamite" (juvenile delinquency) in our major urban areas.

The view of the Ford Foundation and the president's committee was that young people were products of their environment and that the community had to change to create opportunities for its young people. In *Youth in the Ghetto,* which evolved from a report he had produced for Harlem Youth Opportunities Unlimited (HARYOU), one of the early prototype poverty programs, Kenneth Clark described the pathologies that confronted the community, which included lack of economic opportunity. His thesis was that these pathologies had to be cured to build a healthy community in which young people could develop. The plan for the revitalization of central Harlem included a major jobs program predicated on teaching young people skills so that they could get a job.

On Manhattan's Lower East Side, Richard Cloward put his "opportunity theory" into practice at Mobilization for Youth, another community-based effort funded by the Ford Foundation and the president's committee. The opportunity theory assumed that young people's behavior was rational and that, if they were offered real opportunities to support themselves and live productively, they would be motivated to prepare themselves to move into the economic and social mainstream.

Both Mobilization for Youth and HARYOU received MDTA funding as experimental and demonstration (E&D) projects. Other E&D youth projects also included Community Progress Inc. (CPI) in New Haven and the Job Opportunities in the Business Sector (JOBS) project run by the YMCA in Chicago. These early experiments resulted in the development of more comprehensive approaches to preparing young people for work.

1. Adaptation of the diagnostic and vocational rehabilitation model that was used to train physically and mentally disabled persons. E&D projects adapted the diagnostic techniques of vocational rehabilitation to the needs of "disadvantaged young people" in manpower programs. For example, an early E&D project run by the Jewish Vocational Service in Philadelphia adapted the diagnostic techniques of sheltered workshops to the needs of high school dropouts with low levels of literacy. The early comprehensive models began with extensive testing to identify deficiencies of "clients" and then prescribed a broad range of needed services to correct those deficiencies, including basic education, GED preparation, health services, and legal services. The job developer was invented during this period, and group counseling became the norm for many E&D projects.

2. Paid work experience. CPI in New Haven created "work crews" to give young people a real work experience in the program. Crew chiefs supervised groups of young people who were working on community projects. The crews learned basic work skills—taking direction, punching time clocks, working in teams while they were building playgrounds, cleaning vacant lots and painting public facilities. The work crew assignments also served as temporary jobs while young people waited for placement in jobs in the private sector. The work crews later were the model for the Neighborhood Youth Corps and its Summer Youth Employment Program—part of the later "poverty program."

3. On-the-job training and increased employer involvement administered

by intermediaries. The National Urban League and Mobilization for Youth ran the first experiments with on-the-job training (OJT) for young people. Many job-related skills were not offered in vocational schools, and it was difficult to simulate work skill training in a school setting. OJT enabled intermediaries to work with employers to design training at the workplace. Employers' wages were offset by payments to compensate them for lower productivity. Upon completion of training, young people were hired at the prevailing wage. In addition to placing young people in jobs, OJT proved itself a valuable mechanism for involving employers in the design and delivery of training for young people.

4. Focus on the special needs of poor urban youth. The E&D programs working with the President's Committee on Juvenile Delinquency programs and civil rights organizations focused on the special needs of poor and urban young people in ways that evolved into the poverty program. MDTA had not focused on the needs of these young people because they often did not meet the education or experience requirements of vocational schools. The JOBS program in Chicago recruited young people from the street gangs and used its resources—including a YMCA-operated community college, funds provided by the E&D program, and its extensive network of employers—which prescribed a comprehensive set of services to prepare its clients for jobs. JOBS and other urban programs exposed the broad range of deficits of many urban youth. Many young people had serious health problems. Legal problems made them difficult to employ. Transportation was a major obstacle. It was becoming clear that a special long-term comprehensive effort was needed to have an impact on these youth.

5. Community-based services. Evidence was growing that it was vital that services be offered in the neighborhoods where young people lived; the early Ford Foundation projects were among the first community-based organizations (CBOs). They mobilized community leaders and employers to correct the social and economic injustices that were a part of life in urban ghettos. The growth and visibility of the civil rights movement were also a force for the development of neighborhood and community-based services. E&D projects were funded in public housing agencies, youth-serving agencies, civil rights organizations, and neighborhood organizations. One of the more controversial agencies was the Woodlawn Organization (TWO), a neighborhood agency organized around the confrontational style of Saul Alinsky. TWO picketed the suburban homes of slum landlords to inform their neighbors of housing violations. Stores that discriminated in hiring were boycotted.

6. Confronting discrimination in the workplace. Organizations like the Opportunities Industrialization Centers (OICs) in Philadelphia (a response to a successful consumer boycott of employers that discriminated against African Americans) were created to attack discrimination in the workplace and to prepare minority youth and adults for jobs when employers changed their hiring practices. OICs were committed to serving the "whole person" and developed a comprehensive model of service. Community-based organizations, like OIC, were established in many localities, replicated by community leadership in other cities, and funded by the federal government to combat discrimination by employers and agencies that too often excluded people on the basis of their race or ethnicity.

7. Comprehensive programs to prepare youth with diverse needs for jobs.
The design of the JOBS program of the Chicago YMCA was unique. It recruited more than 1,000 youth through gang workers, who worked with youth in the streets. They made a commitment to help each young person get a job or return to school. JOBS' definition of a comprehensive program was one that helped youth surmount all barriers. They assigned each young person a "coach" (a combination group counselor and case manager) to oversee her or his development. The system worked well because JOBS had access to a broad range of services, including legal, health, housing, and a community college. This was unusual at the time, and its success demonstrated the need for a broad range of education, social services, and guidance and support services if youth were to become prepared for work and life.

Youth development was not part of the practice or the rhetoric of these programs, and youth were not thought of as resources. However, these early E&D programs, based mostly on overcoming barriers and reducing deficits, did show that long-term treatment was needed and that preparation for employment had to involve the community and address the educational, health, housing, family, and other needs of young people. The connection of work and basic education was evident, and GED preparation was introduced as a part of the youth employment program.

There was already some evidence that developmental approaches produced better results. One developmental approach was OIC's commitment to developing the whole person. OIC created a feeder concept that prepared youth and adults for vocational training and jobs. The Reverend Leon H. Sullivan, OIC's founder, said, "We screen people *into* programs." OIC tested trainees once they were enrolled and used test results to help trainees focus on what they needed to learn in order to get a job. Motivation of trainees was key at OIC, which taught minority history to all trainees in order to instill pride and raise awareness of the significant accomplishments of minorities, especially African Americans. What is commonplace today was a new approach then, especially for manpower programs.

Although these were major changes in manpower development practice, they were based on a diagnostic treatment model. Change was beginning, but young people were enrolled in adult programs and treated as recipients of services: the professionals "knew" what was best for young people and other clients. Counseling, especially group counseling, was another innovation in manpower programs that focused on youth, like JOBS in Chicago. Groups of young people shared experiences with an adult and each other. Peer support and guidance was intentional. Counselors focused on helping youth overcome barriers and develop skills and attitudes that would lead to jobs.

The decade of the 1960s was a time of rapid and profound change. In 1964, President Lyndon Johnson launched the "War on Poverty," and the Congress passed the Economic Opportunity Act (EOA). The concept of the Community Action Agency was based on the experience of the Ford Foundation and the President's Committee on Juvenile Delinquency. An equally important, though less controversial part of the legislation was the authorization and funding of major Manpower programs focused on the special needs of youth. The Job Corps was created by the EOA as was the Neighborhood Youth Corps, the first Summer Youth Employment Program, which created summer jobs for poor teenagers. In addition, manpower became a significant part of the plans that community action agencies developed to combat poverty, especially in urban areas.

The first Job Corps center was opened at a closed military base (Camp Kilmer) in New Jersey. The design of Job Corps was based on a number of critical assumptions. The first was that there were some young people who would benefit from education and training programs offered in a residential setting outside their community. It was felt that some communities were so destructive that these young people should be moved away from home, trained in a military setting and then placed in jobs. The second major assumption was that big business could and would be the best resource for administering this training. Job Corps has been offering residential, and some nonresidential, job training for more than 30 years. With an average stay of more than seven months, Job Corps offers comprehensive services that include basic education and vocational training. The residential setting enables Job Corps to provide developmental opportunities that include leadership through youth government, advisory committees, alumni, and clubs. The initial Job Corps model was deficit-based, but in recent years, *youth development* has been added to Job Corps. Evaluations have consistently shown that Job Corps works. It has a significant positive impact on graduates, and the return on the investment pays off for young people and taxpayers.

In response to urban unrest and civil disturbance, a major summer jobs program was created in the summer of 1965. While it was characterized by the media as "anti-riot insurance," it was promoted in communities as work experience. It was a chance for poor young people, both in and out of school, to get a job (often their first job), do useful work in the community, and learn how to work. In addition, it increased the income of low-income youth and their families. Initially, work experience was community-based and included elements that today would be called community service. Young people were the muscle to build vest-pocket parks and mini-playgrounds. They assisted teachers in Head Start programs and were the arms and legs in poverty program offices. They learned good work habits, and crew chiefs and supervisors helped them respond to the expectations of the workplace.

THE COORDINATION AND CONTROL PERIOD

The community action agencies were responsible for planning and community involvement under the Economic Opportunity Act. The federal government funded local communities to bypass state governments that were perceived to discriminate against cities or rural areas with large minority populations. They received formula grants, set priorities for services, and selected service providers, which were most often community-based organizations. Jobs were always high on the list of priority services, but effective Manpower programs required sophisticated designs; coordination among many, often competing, agencies; and time, in order to increase the education and vocational skills of youth (and adults). Too often, community-based Manpower programs developed sophisticated plans, but lacked the resources and competence to implement those plans. The result was frustration for service providers, employers, and trainees. This was compounded by the inability of community-based organizations to coordinate services with better-funded state and local public agencies, especially the employment service and vocational education.

The inevitable conflicts and competition of the mid-1960s led to the age of coordination that preoccupied Manpower policies from the late 1960s through the 1970s. Debate and conflict about who should develop plans, which agencies should provide services, and accountability for outcomes continued to characterize the national policy debate of the 1980s and 1990s.

In 1966, the President's Commission on Manpower (PCOM) created tripartite teams representing the Office of Economic Opportunity (OEO), Department of Labor (DOL) and Office of Education (OE) to conduct a field study of Manpower programs in 19 cities. Its mission was to study and catalog all the programs and plans in each city, with a special focus on identifying instances of overlap and duplication. The commission was also charged with recommending ways to improve coordination of Manpower services.

The thesis was that coordination would lead to efficiency and better programs. Commission teams engaged in a systematic analysis of federal programs in major urban areas, a process that was both illuminating and frustrating. In examining intergovernmental relationships and planning, we found very little communication, programs that were run by one agency with no regard for cooperation or joint planning and operations, competition among agencies, some suspicion, and even hostility. In short, there were no systems. In some cases, the PCOM study brought local agencies together for the first time.

The work of the tripartite teams of the commission evolved into the Concentrated Employment Program (CEP), an attempt to coordinate and plan a focused approach to local Manpower planning in the 19 cities that had been studied. Soon after CEP was initiated, two rural CEPs were created in eastern Kentucky and northern Minnesota, recognizing the needs of rural areas and the power of Carl Perkins (D-Kentucky), chairman of the House Education and Labor Committee, and Vice President Hubert H. Humphrey.

The assumption of CEP was that prescribing services would respond to the needs of individuals. Coordination and joint planning were the goals. The objective was to prepare youth and adults for jobs, and programs were measured by the number of jobs they got for unemployed people. Coordination was accomplished by negotiating treaties among competing agencies; but comprehensive services were rare and there was no focus on developing youth as resources. Elimination of duplication of services was minimized, but that did not mean that individuals received all the services they needed or that they received them when or where they were needed.

The competition among agencies at the national level—OEO, DOL, and vocational education—increased. There was considerable debate about which federal agency should take the lead. At the local level, there was competition between the public agencies and community-based organizations. Funding mechanisms and state and local plans received more attention than did the types of services offered, the quality of those services, and the competence of the agencies and people that provided services. There was always concern about the problems of "disadvantaged" youth, but contracts with youth-serving agencies that focused on the special needs of youth with multiple barriers to employment were the exception, not the rule. Only a few youth-serving agencies were strong advocates for youth and had the capacity to provide the comprehensive services needed to prepare young people for employment.

The first phase of the consolidation era ended with the passage of the Comprehensive Employment and Training Act (CETA) of 1973. At the time, CETA was enacted as the first "block grant" that gave states and local "prime sponsors" funds by formula that they could decide, within federal guidelines, how to allocate. Decisions about whom to serve, how to serve them, and who should deliver the services were made at the state and local level. State and local planning bodies were established with broad representation to oversee the planning process. Governors and local elected officials appointed the planning bodies and staffed the prime sponsors. The U.S. Department of Labor approved all plans and was responsible for oversight. CETA also marked the end of the term "Manpower Programs," which was replaced by "Employment and Training Programs."

With few exceptions, programs for youth remained the same. The status quo was preserved by institutional inertia and resistance to change. Youth services were mostly work experience for in-school youth in the summer, and more comprehensive out-of-school youth programs that included employability development, individual referral to vocational training, OJT, and public service employment. The recession of the early 1970s and high levels of unemployment prompted a major new initiative to create jobs providing public services, and some young people were hired for these jobs.

CETA focused on getting youth and adults prepared to work. Both in-school and out-of-school youth were encouraged to stay in school or to go back to school, but these initiatives were fairly short term and focused on work experience and development of entry-level skills. There were three premises for work experience: (1) work is a valuable learning opportunity; (2) economically disadvantaged youth need to earn wages; and (3) work keeps young people busy and out of trouble. Some exceptional programs developed jobs as places to learn, and some training programs were coupled with basic education, English as a second language, and GED preparation. But most of the services were short term. Developmental opportunities were limited to work-related skills.

In work experience programs, follow-up, supportive services, or developmental opportunities were rare. For most youth, the opportunity to earn some money, buy clothes, and help their families were the most important benefits. For poor families, this income was very important. The Neighborhood Youth Corps' first priority was the same: the regulations required that 70 percent of all funds be expended on wages and 15 percent on administration, leaving only 15 percent for education, counseling, transportation, and supportive services. No extensive evaluations of work experience were conducted, and there were many news stories about "make work" or other poor practices.

Work experience programs have always been faced with the difficult choice between improving the quality of services and increasing the number of people served. Do you hire fewer people and provide more extensive services or serve more people and give less service? Nowhere is this choice more evident than in out-of-school programs. Dropouts are always less educated, often from poorer families, and in need of more intensive services for a longer period of time. Work experience, or a job without education and other services, is not enough for a dropout who reads below the eighth-grade level, has an unstable home and is confronted with choices between a job and drugs, violence, or other self-destructive behaviors. It is no surprise that the gains were modest.

CETA also made a significant investment in training for young people using institutional skills training, OJT, and the Job Corps. Skills training and OJT trained both youth and adults, while the Job Corps was and still is a youth-focused training program. Skills training has a positive impact on youth: those who complete the training get jobs with modest earnings gains. Entrance requirements vary with the occupation, so, unless training is coupled with remediation, disadvantaged youth with multiple barriers are often excluded. From 1964 to 1974, fewer than 40 percent of skills training participants in MDTA and CETA were under age 22, and approximately one-third of the OJT participants were under age 22. OJT has good postprogram placement numbers.

Center for Employment Training (CET), a community-based comprehensive job training program located in San Jose, California, has shown extraordinary placement and earnings gains for disadvantaged youth and adults. The focus is on skills training in classrooms that resemble work sites. All learning is focused on job- and work-related skills and competencies. CET also offers extensive remediation and English as a second language, which are related to the occupation and combined with counseling, job placement, and long-term follow-up. CET created a comprehensive developmental model with a counselor, a job developer, and an educational instructor qualified to teach bilingual education assigned to each skill area. Vocational instructors are recruited from industry. The impact on youth and adults in San Jose is remarkable: wages are much higher than the norm. Employers have supported CET for more than 25 years by donating equipment and hiring its graduates.

Job Corps has also been offering comprehensive training, basic education, and a range of supportive services. It is run by the Office of Job Corps, U.S. Department of Labor, and continues to contract mostly with for-profit training corporations to run Job Corps centers. Job Corps serves young people exclusively, most of whom have not completed high school. Job Corps evaluations have documented its ability to place young people in jobs and to significantly increase earnings. The cost of Job Corps is high, more than $15,000 per trainee, which reflects the comprehensive nature of its services and the higher cost of residential training. Residential programs like Job Corps are able to take poor youth out of their communities and help them learn the vocational and people skills needed to succeed on the job.

Youth development was not an intentional part of the program design in the CETA days. Training and work experience were the predominant forms of preparation for work. Some examples of informal youth development practices are found in comprehensive training programs like Job Corps, CET, and OIC. A relationship with an adult is one part of long-term skills training, either institutional or on-the-job training. Supervisors, counselors, and instructors often become guides (caring adults) who help young people learn about work and life. Many of the more comprehensive programs develop long-term relationships with graduates. Job developers and counselors maintain contacts after placement and often respond to phone calls and visits when young people lose jobs and need to talk about next steps. These developmental approaches are informal, based on personal relationships. They are not planned services available to all trainees; they simply happen and are responsible for the success of effective training programs.

THE YOUTH DEMONSTRATION ERA

In 1977, Congress enacted an amendment to CETA, the Youth Employment Demonstration Projects Act (YEDPA), that made youth employment a major focus of the act. It created federal youth employment initiatives that were designed and controlled by the U.S. Department of Labor and were more categorical. It also added three new acronyms to the alphabet soup of job training: YACC (Young Adult Conservation Corps), YCCIP (Youth Community Conservation Improvement Program), and YIEPP (Youth Incentive Entitlement Pilot Projects). These three programs underscored the belief of policy makers that job creation was the answer: each demonstration experimented with creating jobs in different sectors. YIEPP was the most expensive; it tested the hypothesis that guaranteeing a job to disadvantaged high school students would be an incentive to keep them in school. YACC provided up to 12 months of employment in useful conservation work for 16- to 23-year-olds, administered by the Departments of Agriculture and Interior. YCCIP provided out-of-school youth with supervised jobs on community projects.

CETA continued to provide training through formula grants to the prime sponsors, but most of the job-creation efforts were relatively short term and not tied to education, training, or other developmental activities. With the exception of Job Corps, none of the major youth employment policies promoted comprehensive practices. Training was generally short term, and although it led to a job, it was one dimensional and only developed job skills. Work experience provided young people with work and some "employability" skills.

In 1979, the federal government invested almost $6 billion in work experience and training of youth. (For comparison, in 1997, the federal appropriation for youth employment programs under JTPA was $2 billion, including Job Corps.) Significant amounts of money were spent on research to find out what worked. Robert Taggart, the former administrator of the Department of Labor's Youth Office, summed up the experience in *A Fisherman's Guide*. To paraphrase his conclusions:

1. Work and work experience alone do not improve labor market success.

2. Training must be long enough in duration that participants can achieve measurable and certifiable competencies.
3. An employability plan must provide opportunities for individuals to develop at their own pace depending on their motivation, interests, and abilities.
4. There must be an opportunity for all youth to participate, but resources will never be adequate and should be invested in those who put forth the effort to benefit.
5. The impact of programs must be measured for long-term gains rather than immediate job placement or minimal increases in earnings.
6. There must be an increase in long-term training outcomes.
7. The economy must create more jobs, and unemployed youth must be trained to compete for those jobs.

In spite of the significant investment in training young people under CETA and YEDPA, the effects were marginal. Most of the programs were based on a diagnostic and treatment model, but the large financial investment created pressures for short-term outcomes and pushed CETA and YEDPA into large-scale interventions that batch-fed youth into systems.

The primary focus of CETA, including YEDPA, was to create jobs and provide work experience. Training was a smaller part of the investment, and youth development was not planned or intentional in either the policies or the programs, though some providers incorporated youth development principles in their practice. Counselors helped young people identify their strengths and build on them; instructors developed personal relationships with a few of their trainees and sometimes maintained long-term contact, functioning as the "caring adults" now recognized as important; supervisors and older coworkers filled this role in OJT and work experience, and at Job Corps centers, some resident advisers, teachers, and counselors developed personal relationships with youth that were sustained when young people needed advice; vocational exploration was a part of some summer and year-round youth programs; open entry-open exit training programs enabled youth to proceed at their own pace and tailor their skill development to their personal interests; and self-paced instructional programs like the Comprehensive Competencies Program offered individualized basic skill development that empowered young people to guide their own development.

Unfortunately, most of the evidence concerning effective practices is based on the writings and memories of practitioners, funders, and researchers. There was a considerable investment in intermediaries like Public/Private Ventures (P/PV), the Manpower Demonstration Research Corporation, and YouthWork. They conducted and researched major demonstrations. But the formal long-term evaluations focused on outcomes and did not examine methods, techniques, materials, or youth employment practices. The impact of programs was measured as a whole and did not attempt to determine if some methods had a greater effect on young people with certain characteristics. The quality of programs was not examined in enough detail to determine if the impact or lack thereof was the result of the program design or the quality of the staff, facilities, or materials. The distinction is very important if the goal is to improve the quality of training and other initiatives.

THE 1980S: LESS MONEY, LESS TIME, LESS IMPACT

The election of President Reagan and a Republican-controlled Senate in 1980 resulted in severe cuts for federal job training programs. CETA was labeled "a four-letter word" and targeted for extinction. In 1981, funding for public service employment was terminated. The expiration of CETA in 1982 led to its replacement by the Job Training Partnership Act (JTPA). The total federal job training budget was slashed from almost $10 billion in 1980 to $3.6 billion in 1982—the first JTPA appropriation.

A more astonishing fact was that these cuts were made at a time when unemployment hovered around 9 percent. For 20 years, job training funding had increased during periods of high unemployment. Clearly, there was dissatisfaction with the job training system.

Job creation was the main target of the budget cutters, and its funding was eliminated in 1981. The Department of Labor's new leadership, Secretary of Labor Raymond Donovan and Assistant Secretary Albert Angrisani, had little use for the job training programs of CETA and were determined to change them radically. Budget cuts were politically popular and social programs were in disrepute. CETA was a major target for budget cutters.

JTPA emerged as a bipartisan bill that incorporated many compromises. It was a second-generation block grant scheme whereby states were given much of the authority that had been vested in the federal government under CETA. Businesses were given greatly increased authority at the local level, with a requirement that the majority of members of the local JTPA planning and oversight councils, the Private Industry Council (PIC), be business representatives. The other major change was the incorporation of performance standards with national targets. These standards for placement rates, participant earnings, and training costs were written into law and would drive JTPA services.

JTPA prohibited funds for public service employment, but continued training programs for adults and youth, including training for older persons. It also continued federal responsibilities for Job Corps, migrants, Native Americans, and veterans. Job Corps and the Summer Youth Employment Program were both targeted for elimination or major budget reductions, but were saved by a massive campaign that generated letters and phone calls from state and local elected officials, employers and business representatives, former participants, and current trainees. Both the Summer Youth Employment Program and Job Corps were continued as a result of this demonstration of public support.

JTPA administrators acted as though the previous 20-year experience had been a failure. They did not look to the experience of CETA and its preceding legislation for guidance. JTPA was based on the belief that state and local decision making were better than federal decision making and that business knew best what priorities and programs would be most effective.

In retrospect, the results were not surprising. There was a great deal of evidence that local authorities were "creaming," that is, selecting trainees who were most likely to succeed. Creaming was rationalized by sound management principles: limited funds should be expended in the most efficient manner; more people can be served if training is shorter, less comprehensive, and cheaper. The consequences of creaming are that JTPA did not serve "those most in need" in spite of a legislative requirement. JTPA applicants tended to have high school diplomas and some work experience.

Service providers were offered performance contracts that paid them based on outcomes rather than on the cost of services. Again there was evidence that service providers also creamed. They recruited and accepted trainees they could train within budget and place in jobs at the required wage rate. If they exceeded standards they made money, and, if they fell short, they could put their organization into bankruptcy. Creaming was good business for some service providers, and they learned that they could generate more income by recruiting people who were easily trained and placed in jobs.

A symptom of the emphasis on quick and inexpensive training was the rapid expansion of "job search assistance." One-third of JTPA services were for job search, an inexpensive way of getting placements that required participants to have skills that meet employer requirements. According to Sar Levitan and Frank Gallo's calculations in their book, *A Second Chance,* JTPA relied less on community-based organizations like OIC and SER-Jobs for Progress than did CETA. There was also an increase in the use of for-profit training schools. JTPA was less appealing to CBOs that were committed to serving "hard-to-serve youth and adults" because performance contracting forced them to enroll more job-ready people for less money with fewer services.

A 1994 long-term study of JTPA done by Abt Associates found discouraging results. There were no significant positive effects for out-of-school youth from classroom training, OJT, job search, or other services. This evaluation did not describe services in detail and had no data to assess the design of programs or the quality of services. Its documentation of poor performance was disputed by service providers and the JTPA system. Responding to this study, Congress cut the federal appropriation for Out-of-School Youth Programs (Title II-C) of JTPA by 80 percent.

Another significant study is Public/Private Ventures' research on its Summer Training and Education Program (STEP), *Anatomy of a Demonstration,* which had shown significant short-term academic gains from a summer employment program with intensive academic components. But these gains did not lead to improved school performance, higher grades, or higher graduation rates. The conclusion is that enriched summer programs alone do not have a significant long-range impact. To state the obvious, short-term programs cannot undo a lifetime of underachievement and discouragement, but they can be important tools in a long-term development plan for young people.

However, youth development outcomes are not being tracked by the JTPA system because they are not valued, understood, or included in the program mix of youth-serving agencies. As evidence, the U.S. Department of Labor's JTPA statistics from program year 1996 show that services were provided to 76,700 JTPA Title III-C youth in five categories of service: basic skills training, occupational skills training (non-OJT), OJT, work experience internships, and other skills training. The data do not report any services that might be called youth development; indeed, it is impossible to tell from any reported data what the nature of the services was.

THE CONFLUENCE OF YOUTH DEVELOPMENT AND YOUTH EMPLOYMENT POLICIES AND PROGRAMS

It is not surprising that youth development is missing from out-of-school youth programs. The employment and training system has only included youth development in exceptional experiments or programs operated by organizations that were primarily youth-serving agencies for whom youth development was included in all services to young people. It is not surprising that youth development is not a priority because employment and training is generally a short-term intervention and has focused almost exclusively on basic education and vocational training, with jobs and returning to school considered acceptable outcomes.

The roots of manpower programs were in the employment service and vocational education, not in youth development. Given this narrow view of the needs of youth, it is understandable that the focus of "objective" assessment is on education, skills, and welfare dependence. In contrast, effective youth programs develop the resources of youth and understand the principles of youth development. The challenge is to make these long-term services and relationships intentional planned components of youth employment programs.

In January 1995, the chief economist of the U.S. Department of Labor published *What's Working (and What's Not): A Summary of Research on the Economic Impacts of Employment and Training Programs.* The report summarized existing research and reiterated the findings of the Abt study that the JTPA youth program outcomes were discouraging. The unfortunate outcome of this was an 80 percent cut in appropriations for the JTPA Out-of-School Youth Program. Young people, especially those most in need, were being punished because they were getting inadequate services.

The National Youth Employment Coalition (NYEC), in response to the report, convened a working group of its members and other experts in youth employment and youth development and prepared a set of recommendations. One of the report's conclusions characterized youth employment programs as "islands of excellence in a sea of mediocrity."

Not satisfied with a set of recommendations, NYEC set out to develop criteria for effective youth employment and development programs by establishing a working group of youth employment and youth development practitioners, researchers, policy makers, advocates, and employer representatives. It is called PEPNet, the Promising and Effective Practices Network. From that initial meeting and subsequent conference calls and small meetings, criteria emerged in four broad areas: workforce development, youth development, quality management, and evidence of success. Effective programs are those that meet each of these criteria. They can do it in different ways, but they must show how what they do meets those criteria.

PEPNet demands outcomes and requires that initiatives document the impact they have on young people. Workforce development outcomes must include the development of skills, knowledge, and competencies that lead to jobs and careers. Youth development competencies are based on a well-conceived and well-implemented approach to youth development, including high expectations, caring relationships with adults, and holistic service strategies that build responsibility and identity and view youth as resources. Quality management is exemplified by engaged, qualified leadership and staff who collect and use information and data to continuously improve the program. Evidence of success requires that credible information be collected, documented, and presented.

These criteria have been incorporated into a self-assessment instrument designed to assist youth employment initiatives in looking at their services to youth objectively. Initiatives that believe they meet the criteria of PEPNet are encouraged to fill out an application and apply for recognition. Applications are reviewed by peer panels to select those that meet the criteria.

In four years, there have been 170 applications, 51 of which have been selected as PEPNet award recipients. These initiatives form a network of effective programs. In *Lessons Learned,* published by the National Youth Employment Coalition, these effective programs have been indexed so that interested programs can learn about the more than 1,000 practices, methods, and techniques employed by effective programs to make a difference in the lives of young people. PEPNet goes beyond the development of models, by identifying specific practices that can be adapted by other programs to improve their services to young people. Each of the 51 initiatives has met a set of rigorous criteria and has documented the impact of their methods. We intend to expand the examples and build on the experience of youth development programs that work with youngsters under 14 and have not considered employment as a developmental activity.

WHERE ARE WE HEADED?

In 1998, Congress passed the Workforce Investment Act (WIA) to replace JTPA. WIA gives more authority to the states and continues the role of business in planning workforce programs at the local level. One WIA title gives localities the authority for planning and separates the youth employment plan from the adult plan. Summer youth employment no longer has a separate authorization, and localities will decide whether to invest in summer or year-round programs. There is also authorization for youth opportunity grants, which will mean a new national investment of $250 million in a youth program focused on small urban neighborhoods and rural areas.

The new workforce investment system seems an excellent opportunity to bring new ideas and new approaches to policy and practice. The fact that most of our old approaches have had minimal benefit for young people, especially out-of-school youth, is reason enough to try a new approach. The legislation is an opportunity to make youth employment a higher priority. This may also be the last chance for a major federal investment in youth employment.

Incorporating youth development principles into youth employment policy, programs, and practice will not be simple. There is limited experience and expertise and little collaboration among agencies and professionals working in youth development, education, and employment. Most youth development agencies work with younger children (14 and below) and begin to lose contact with young people over the age of 14. Youth development does not have much experience with preparation of youth for jobs. The education community, with the exception of vocational education, cooperative education, and school-to-work, views work with suspicion. Both educators and youth development professionals point to studies that conclude that work interferes with education and can lead to destructive behavior, including drug and alcohol abuse. The youth employment field has its own provincialism. Only a relatively small number of exceptional programs recognize that a young person's stage of development is critical and that young people must be engaged in preparing for their future with the support of caring, competent adults.

The youth development principles explicit in NYEC's PEPNet criteria are consistent with the principles described in the Levitan Youth Policy Networks's *A Generation of Challenge:*

1. Each young person needs to feel that at least one adult has a strong stake in her or his labor market success.
2. Programs must be connected to employers; placement with one of these employers is possible and initial placement is one step in a continuing long-term relationship with a program that will advance the young person's employment and earnings.
3. Each young person must feel at each step the need to improve education and credentials.
4. Program support will be there for a long time.
5. Effective connections are maintained between the programs and providers of support services.
6. The program emphasizes civic involvement and service.
7. Motivational techniques—including financial incentives, peer support, and leadership opportunities—are used.

Such approaches to connecting workforce development and youth development vary, but support for the concepts is growing. However, most workforce professionals are not aware of their value. Most are unexposed, and those who have heard of youth development are not prepared to incorporate the concepts or principles in either policy or practice. Including youth development in workforce investment programs will require a massive national technical assistance and training effort.

The challenge for those who understand the importance of youth development principles for workforce development is to mount a major education and awareness campaign for an audience that does not know the value of this information. The scope of the education campaign is vast because the devolution in the new Workforce Investment Act requires that we reach out to the 50 states, the territories, and 500 to 600 localities. Awareness, training, and technical assistance must reach beyond state and local policy makers and planners. Success requires that we build new and improved deliverers of services that will need competent staff, skilled managers, and knowledgeable governing boards.

Service providers, especially traditional providers like vocational schools and community colleges, must learn that young people need more than education. They need environments where they plan for their own development and believe that adults—teachers, counselors, supervisors, and employers—are there to support them, help them solve problems, and prepare them for jobs that can lead to rewarding lives. That means continuing support as young people develop, make mistakes, and try again and again.

If we are serious about the development of our young people, we must invest in the institutions that serve them by ensuring that the facilities and equipment meet the standards of employers, and that teachers and staff are trained to do their difficult jobs and know that if they do well they will have a career. Outreach workers, counselors, coaches, teachers, job developers, and youth workers are skilled and very important to the effectiveness of programs. They need to be valued and rewarded and encouraged to make a career of youth employment development.

At the same time, we must demonstrate the value of youth development principles to skeptical policy makers and practitioners. Policy makers must be shown that youth development prepares all young people, especially out-of-school youth, more effectively for the workforce, and they must understand that long-term programs that cost more are more cost-effective because they produce better outcomes for young people and employers. Policies must support, encourage, and reward effective practice. Do we really want to entrust the education of our young people to the lowest bidder?

In conclusion, I want to make a plea for the importance of improving the methods, materials, and practices used in youth employment programs. NYEC members and supporters have been working for almost four years to identify, select, recognize, and catalog the practices of effective youth employment and development initiatives. The exemplary programs are all over the country and take many different approaches to preparing youth for the workforce. We know that these programs are effective because they can document their impact on the lives of young people. Do they have studies to document their impact? Some do. Others have management reports, counselor reports, and other evidence that are the products of quality management.

These exemplary programs have something more valuable to practitioners and policy makers than does the most rigorous study. They have experience. They have developed methods and materials in the real world, working with youth every day. This is the information that service providers need to improve the way they serve youth, that planners need when they make decisions about funding a service provider, and that policy makers must pay attention to when they write poli-

The More Things Change, the More They Stay the Same

cies or create the rules and regulations that will govern the workforce investment system. If those policies do not encourage the best practices, they are inadequate.

For 35 years, young people have been trying to change their lives with inadequate resources, little support, and no respect. Quick fixes do not work. Now is the time to test new approaches that show promise. Youth employment must take a long-term (multiyear) developmental approach to the preparation of young people for employment and for life. Youth employment policy and practice must support sound positive youth development principles. All youth must be viewed as resources that have potential to contribute to our society, not as a set of problems that need to be fixed. Education, training, and other services should recognize and build on each individual's age and stage of development. Young people should be engaged in their own development and the development of programs and policies that are designed to help them. Services and support must continue after youth are placed on a job.

Finally, young people must have access to programs of the highest possible quality. If basic education is part of the program, young people should learn to read, write, and compute better. If workplace skills are being taught, they must achieve high levels of competence. If the object of the program is to place young people in jobs, they should get a job, and if they lose that job, they should receive help finding the next job.

The Workforce Investment Act (WIA) includes language that encourages a more long-term approach to developing young people as a resource. The success of WIA requires a commitment to develop service providers of the highest quality; to do this will require the development of well-trained staff and well-run organizations.

An action-research agenda is needed to improve the capacity of youth employment policies and programs. This agenda should include:

1. Development of systems and capacity to recognize and use work as a developmental tool. There must be an intentional link between work and education and other developmental activities. These approaches assist young people as they gain work-related competencies, basic and advanced education, problem-solving skills, skills working in groups, and other skills that will prepare them for life.
2. Development of youth employment and development approaches that recognize and respond to the needs of youth who are at different stages of development.
3. Experimentation with sound asset-based approaches that build on the experience of working with youth under 16 to older youth (16 to 24) who are preparing for work and family.
4. Adaptation of leadership skills learned in youth clubs to help older youth lead in the workplace, a labor union, or in their community.
5. Incorporation by education of developmental approaches, by

linking school and work, engaging youth as active learners, and demonstrating the practical implications of knowledge.

The primary lesson of the past 30 years is that young people benefit most from programs that integrate the principles of youth development into a workforce development framework. Jobs and work should be viewed as developmental and should be integrated with education. Youth development techniques must be adapted to meet the needs of older adolescents. Work and community service must be organized as developmental activities.

Youth development agencies and workforce development agencies are separated by institutional, philosophical, and methodological differences. Young people benefit when these differences are bridged and services are integrated and focused on the needs of each youth. Getting a job is a stage of development, and young people must be taught to use work to develop their skills and competencies. Youth development agencies must view work in positive developmental terms. The goal is a broad range of integrated age- and stage-appropriate activities.

Clearly, we need an educational campaign that underscores the importance of youth development and demonstrates the impact that derives from the incorporation of youth development principles. The principal purpose of this campaign is to raise the awareness of workforce investment boards, governors, and elected officials so that they will set realistic developmental outcomes for youth development and employment programs.

NOTE

This chapter is drawn from my personal experience working with the federal, state, local, and community-based employment and training programs since 1962. The observations are based on my experience with youth employment policies and practices for more than 37 years. I also read a number of valuable source materials by researchers, policy analysts, and social scientists.

REFERENCES

Clark, Kenneth B.
1964 *Youth in the Ghetto: A Study of the Consequences of Powerlessness and a Blueprint for Change.* New York: Harlem Youth Opportunities Unlimited, Inc.
Levitan, Sar A., and Frank Gallo
1988 *A Second Chance: Training for Jobs.* Kalamazoo, Mich.: W.E. Upjohn Institute for Employment Research.
Levitan Youth Policy Network
1997 *A Generation of Challenge: Pathways to Success for Urban Youth.* Baltimore: Sar Levitan Center for Social Policy Studies, Johns Hopkins University.
National Youth Employment Coalition
1999 *Lessons Learned 1999.* Washington, D.C.: National Youth Employment Coalition.
Taggart, Robert
1981 *A Fisherman's Guide: An Assessment of Training and Remediation Strategies.* Kalamazoo, Mich.: W.E. Upjohn Institute for Employment Research.
U.S. Department of Labor
1995 *What's Working (and What's Not): A Summary of Research on the Economic Impacts of Employment and Training Programs.* Washington, D.C.: U.S. Department of Labor.

U.S. Department of Labor
1992 *Dilemmas in Youth Employment Programming: Findings from the Youth Research and Technical Assistance Project.* Washington, D.C.: U.S. Department of Labor.

Walker, Gary, and Frances Vilella-Velez
1992 *Anatomy of a Demonstration: STEP from Pilot through Replication and Postprogram Impacts.* Philadelphia: Public/Private Ventures.

10 YOUTH DEVELOPMENT IN COMMUNITY SETTINGS: CHALLENGES TO OUR FIELD AND OUR APPROACH

James P. Connell, Michelle Alberti Gambone, and Thomas J. Smith

BACKGROUND AND OVERVIEW

Youth policy in the United States historically has been characterized by a fragmented set of programs with no center. No single entity addresses youth issues holistically at the national level. The recent outbreak of youth homicides has brought renewed attention to juvenile crime; national reports on increased drug use have led to political finger pointing and new commissions; and ongoing debates about public education in economically disadvantaged communities have generated what most think are simplistic funding and management fixes.

Finding coherent ways to better support the development of youth (and particularly the 10- to 18-year-old population with which we are concerned) is rarely the object of urgent public concern. The 1997 President's Summit for America's Future is an exception to the public's more typical out-of-sight, out-of-mind orientation to youth.

Youth Development: A Brief History

Fortunately, the past decade has seen some progress as researchers and practitioners have focused more attention on the concept of "youth development." At its inception, youth development was neither a field nor an approach. It was a concept and a movement united around two central axioms.

Axiom 1: Program thinking fails as a basis for policy thinking. This point was painfully supported in the late 1980s and early 1990s by substantial research findings that past approaches to specific youth problems have produced weak, transient, or no results. These publicly funded approaches centered on "interventions" that assumed the problem lay with a deficit in the young person. The intervention sought to provide youth with skills or knowledge that would correct the deficiency. Such approaches failed to take into account the complexity of young people's lives or the environment in which they still had to function. The pattern of disappointing results seemed to suggest that policy expectations needed to be rethought (and lowered) and that "social engineering" had its limits.

Axiom 2: Developmental thinking should organize youth policy in general and youth interventions and settings in particular. Converging evidence and findings from the adolescent development field, youth resiliency studies and applied social research provided a credible platform for the movement. The work of the Center for Youth Development and Policy Research in articulating the issues and advocating a new approach to youth issues helped create wider policy awareness. Applied research findings, particularly the work of Public/Private Ventures and Search Institute, brought new substance and credibility to a set of ideas that were already intuitively appealing.

At the center of this thinking was the idea that young people are assets in the making—their development dependent on a range of supports and opportunities coming from family, community, and the other institutions that touch them. When supports and opportunities are plentiful, young people can and do thrive; when their environments are deficient or depleted, youth tend not to grow and progress.

In our view, the potential of these important insights has not been fulfilled as the youth development movement has evolved into a *field* of practice—where work with youth actually takes place—and into an *approach* to practice—understanding how youth development occurs and what happens to youth when it does occur.

In this chapter, we explore two major issues: first, how do current views of youth development as a field and as an approach inhibit its capacity to serve as a catalyst and practical guide, particularly to comprehensive community-based initiatives for youth; and, second, how can youth development be recast to be more helpful to these emerging initiatives, to existing youth development programs and organizations, and to youth policy at all levels?

Too Narrow a Field, Too Broad an Approach

Our basic premise is that, as a *field* of practice, youth development is defined so narrowly that it excludes key settings in which youth develop. At the same time, we have allowed youth development as an *approach* to practice to remain far too broad. We have not agreed on, much less communicated effectively, non-negotiables or standards that would establish the approach's parameters and make it useful as a guide to practice. Those of us involved in youth development need to define what the implications of a youth development approach will be for practice and the benefits that should accrue to youth and communities if the youth development approach "takes." We will lay out each of these two problems in turn.

The youth development field as it is now defined is largely identified with two types of settings:

- Activities offered by community-based organizations serving youth during gap periods (before and after school, evenings, weekends, and summers);[1] and
- Add-on or insertion programs in schools and other institutional settings.

Indeed, the youth development *field* is defined more by what it is not than by what it is. For the most part, we are not talking about internal family interactions or intermittent encounters between youth and adults or their peers in and outside a youth's home and neighborhood. We are not talking about most of the time youth are involved with such public institutions as schools, juvenile justice, and health services.

Considering youth development as an *approach,* we go to the other extreme and have trouble saying what it is not. The inclusionary impulse has produced a mind-boggling melange of principles, outcomes, assets, inputs, supports, opportunities, risks, and competencies, much of which is only loosely tied to what actually happens in the daily lives of youth.

And What Have We Wrought?

The good news about our movement thus far is twofold:

- We have brought justifiable and needed attention to youth-serving organizations that have long taken a developmental approach, even if they did not call it that. These organizations have exemplified, and continue to exemplify, practices that many agree constitute good things for young people.
- We have helped policy makers and program designers focus on the many positive attributes of young people. The notion that youth have assets, not problems to be fixed, and that their development is what policies and programs should seek to support has penetrated the discourse of some local, state, and federal initiatives.

The bad news is that we have created expectations that we can produce a myriad of positive skills and psychological traits in young people outside the influences of families, schools, or neighborhoods. As we sought to shift the discourse around youth from fixing problems to supporting development, we also unintentionally created an expectation that youth-serving organizations can provide on their own—without the involvement of families, neighbors, schools, and other institutions—experiences that are necessary and sufficient for youth to reach a healthy, productive adulthood.

Taking the Next Steps

How do we extract ourselves from this conundrum? We propose three interrelated steps:

- First, articulate a compelling and unifying statement of:
  a. What the basic supports and opportunities are that all youth need to grow up healthy—the nonnegotiables of the youth development approach; and
  b. What these nonnegotiables can realistically be expected to yield when in place within and across settings where youth spend time.
- Second, formulate a set of community strategies that, when implemented, will close the gap from existing levels of these supports and opportunities to what is needed to achieve our goals for youth.
- Third, offer ways to mobilize and build the capacities of all stakeholders who live with and work on behalf of youth to embrace and then implement these community strategies.

ADOPTING A UNIFYING FRAMEWORK

The framework presented in Figure 1 is our attempt to take these steps.[2] It builds on three main sources: existing frameworks that are currently influential in shaping the field's thinking; academic theory and research on adolescent development; and the lessons we have learned either directly or indirectly from the following initiatives:

FIGURE 1
Community Action Framework for Youth Development

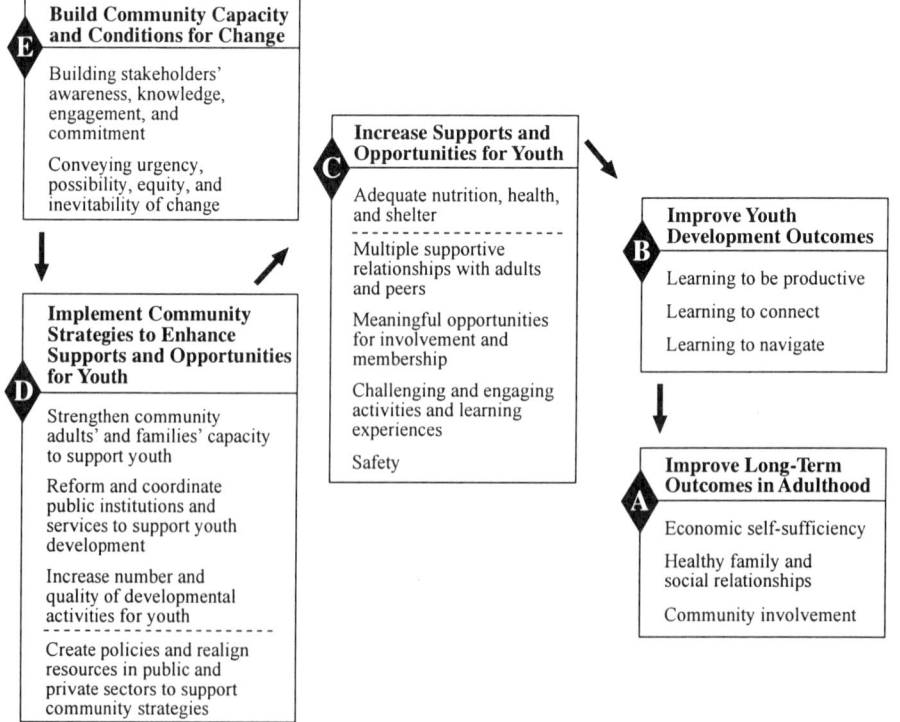

Youth Development in Community Settings

- Center for Youth Development and Policy Research's Youth Development Mobilization;
- Community Network for Youth Development's San Francisco Beacons Initiative and Youth Development Learning Network;
- Development Research and Programs Inc.'s Communities That Care;
- Institute for Research and Reform in Education's First Things First;
- National Urban League's Community Youth Development Mobilization Initiative;
- Public/Private Venture's Community Change for Youth Development; and
- Search Institute's 40 Developmental Assets.

An initial explication of the evidence—from research, practical experience, and common sense—for the framework's validity is available upon request. As it stands, the framework is meant to be a practical guide for investors, planners, practitioners, and evaluators involved in community-based youth development initiatives.

The framework (see Figure 1) seeks to address five questions:

1. What are our basic long-term goals for youth? (Box A)
2. What are the critical developmental milestones or markers that tell us young people are on their way to getting there? (Box B)
3. What do young people need to achieve these developmental milestones? (Box C)
4. What must change in key community settings to provide enough of these supports and opportunities to all youth that need them? (Box D)
5. How do we create the conditions and capacity in communities to make these changes possible and probable? (Box E)

What Outcomes Should a Community Realistically Expect from Implementing a Youth Development Approach?

According to the framework, the long-term goals of community-based youth development initiatives are to improve the long-term life chances of young people:

- To become economically self-sufficient;
- To be healthy and have good family and social relationships; and
- To contribute to their community.

Some commonsense indicators of these long-term outcomes are:

- For economic self-sufficiency, all youth should expect as adults to be able to support themselves and their families and have some discretionary resources beyond those required to put food on the table and a roof over their heads.

They should have a decent job and the education or access to enough education to improve or change jobs.
- For healthy family and social relationships, young people should grow up to be physically and mentally healthy, be good caregivers for their children, and have positive and dependable family and friendship networks.
- Contributions to community could come in many forms, but we hope that our young people will aim to do more than simply be taxpayers and law abiders—to contribute at a threshold level to their community, however they define that community.

By highlighting these "positive" indicators, we do not mean to exclude "negative" markers of outcomes in these three areas. Meaningful decreases in welfare rolls, behavior-based physical and mental health problems, child abuse and neglect, and incidence of violent crimes are also important markers of these same three long-term outcomes.

What Developmental Outcomes Are Most Likely to Lead to Adult Success?

Our review of the relevant literature suggests that the likelihood of these three goals being achieved increases dramatically if youth accomplish certain things as they move from childhood through adolescence:

- They must learn to be productive—to do well in school, develop positive outside interests, and acquire basic life skills.
- They must learn to connect—to adults in their families and community, to their peers in positive and supportive ways, and to something larger than themselves, be it religious or civic.
- They must learn to navigate—to chart and follow a safe course. This third task takes multiple forms:

  - They must learn to navigate among changing conditions in their multiple worlds—their peer groups, families, schools, social groups, and neighborhoods, each of which may require different ways of behaving and, in some cases, even different languages.
  - They must learn to navigate the developmental transitions from being taken care of to taking care of others, and from just learning about their world to assuming responsibility for their role in it.
  - They must find ways to navigate around the lures of unhealthy and dangerous behaviors (premature sexual activity, substance use, and other high-risk activities) and experiences of unfair treatment, rejection, and failure—challenges that all youth face but that are much more prevalent for children living in economically disadvantaged circumstances.

Research and common sense tell us that if young people can achieve these outcomes, their prospects as adults improve dramatically; and, if they do not, success as defined by the three long-term outcomes in this framework will be difficult to achieve.

These three outcomes and, more importantly, their respective indicators reflect both a narrowing and an expanding of other frameworks' content in order to better guide community action. For example, we do not include *personality* characteristics and other *internal traits,* many of which are included in other developmental frameworks. But we do incorporate avoidance of negative behavior and educational outcomes as youth development outcomes.

This approach recognizes that we need to plan for, and monitor, interim steps along the developmental path toward the long-term outcomes we seek for youth. We want to prioritize outcomes shown to predict success in adulthood. We have tried to keep the list short, focused on behavioral accomplishments rather than internal traits and abilities, and feasible for all youth, but still sufficient to give them a strong foundation for a successful adulthood. Some of the ways we measure developmental progress for younger children meet these criteria. For example, we look at their ability to wash and dress themselves, to play cooperatively with other children, to deal with minor peer conflicts or difficulties without adult intervention, and to engage in reading and learning numbers as indicators of their readiness to move on to more complex social roles and cognitive activities. We need to do the same for older youth.

Measured this way, the goals of learning to be productive, to connect, and to navigate lend themselves to observable, understandable, and defensible thresholds that all youth can and should achieve. For example, setting the goal that all youth in this community will finish school and know enough to get a decent job or go to college establishes a clear threshold. Trying to make sure that all youth will have high enough self-esteem does not. Similarly, tracking whether youth have a set of friends that they and their parents trust is more informative and accessible than assessing whether they have enough empathy and compassion. Finding out whether youth treat diverse peers and adults respectfully, manage to avoid serious involvement with drugs and alcohol, and do not overreact to minor rejections by their peers seems clearer and more compelling than whether they are good enough problem solvers.

Having diverse stakeholders know what youth development outcomes actually look like and agree on what constitutes "good enough" are important early tasks for any community-based youth initiative or program.

What Supports and Opportunities Must Communities Provide for Youth?

The framework asserts that, for youth to learn to be productive, connected, and able to navigate, they have to experience a set of supports and opportunities that are the critical building blocks of development across all of the settings in which they spend their time. Research points to five key experiences we expect young people need to have in order to achieve our goals for them.

1. Adequate nutrition, health and shelter. This first developmental need stands alone among the supports and opportunities as a necessary *precondition* for youth to benefit from the others. When a young person is hungry, ill, or inadequately sheltered, it is very difficult to experience gains from even the most enriched social or intellectual environment. While every setting or organization may not be relevant to, or capable of, providing for these needs, they must be addressed if we expect young people to grow.

2. Multiple supportive relationships with adults and peers. Perhaps the most consistent and robust finding on human development is that the experience of support from the people in one's environment, from infancy on, has broad impacts on later functioning across multiple domains. Relationships with both adults and peers are the source of the emotional support, guidance, and instrumental help that are critical to young people's capacity to feel connected to others, navigate day-to-day life, and engage in productive activities. In supportive relationships with adults and peers, youth experience high, clear, and fair expectations, a sense of boundaries, respect, and the sense of another person giving of themselves.

3. Challenging and engaging activities and learning experiences. Youth, especially adolescents, need to experience a sense of growth and progress in developing skills and abilities. Whether in school, sports, the arts, or a job, young people are engaged by—and benefit from—activities in which they experience an increasing sense of competence and productivity. Conversely, they are bored by activities that do not challenge them in some way. Often in adolescence, this "boredom" can lead to participation in high-risk activities because healthier life options do not offer the appropriate blend of challenge and sense of accomplishment.

4. Meaningful opportunities for involvement and membership. As young people move into adolescence, they need ample opportunity to try on the adult roles for which they are preparing. They need to make age-appropriate decisions for themselves and others: deciding what activities to participate in, choosing responsible alternatives, and taking part in setting classroom, team, and organization policies. They also need to have others depend on them through formal and informal roles, including peer leader, team captain, council member, or organizational representative. In order to develop a sense of connectedness and productivity, and to begin making decisions from a perspective that is less egocentric, young people also need to experience a sense of belonging. Specifically, they need to participate in groups of interconnected members, such as their families, clubs, teams, religious groups, theater groups, and other organizations that afford youth opportunities to take on responsibilities. They also need to experience themselves as individuals who have something of value to contribute to their different communities. When healthy opportunities to belong are not found in their environments, young people will create less healthy versions, such as cliques and gangs.

5. Physical and emotional safety. Finally, young people need to experience physical and emotional safety in their daily lives. With these supports, young people are able to confidently explore their full range of options for becoming productive and connected; and, when they experience challenges to navigate, they can focus their full attention on meeting these challenges. The absence of these supports has profound effects on youth's options and decisions: they become distracted from opportunities to be productive in school and other settings; some will choose to belong to gangs or carry weapons as a means of providing for their own safety if it is not provided for them; and, if youth feel consistently rejected, discriminated against, or under physical threat, adults' arguments for avoiding the highest-risk behaviors become much less compelling.

In sum, this framework suggests that the presence of these five supports and opportunities across key community settings will result in dramatic and sustainable improvements in young people's productivity, connectedness, ability to navigate, and, in the longer term, their success as adults.

Conversely, if these investments in youth are *not* made, we will continue to see a growing proportion of our young people move into adulthood, at best, ill-equipped to achieve the goals we have for them and, at worst, dangerous to themselves and others.

The presence of these supports and opportunities then become the nonnegotiables of the youth development approach. They are the lens through which a community should first examine its ecology to identify the resources available in the lives of its young people. They are the guideposts that communities can use to plan and assess these supports and their efforts to enrich and realign resources; then communities can be confident that when these supports and opportunities are available for all youth, across settings, from ages 10 to 18, their developmental outcomes will improve dramatically. These are also the standards of practice to which individual organizations and programs working with youth should commit themselves, and against which they should document their accomplishments.

What Strategies Can Communities Pursue?

We suggest three strategies that communities can implement to increase supports and opportunities for youth across the major settings in which they spend time: family and neighborhood, schools and other public institutions, and gap period settings. A fourth community strategy calls for policy and resource realignments to support the first three strategies. As can be seen in Figure 1 (Box D), these strategies include and go beyond the current identification of the youth development field with "gap" activities. Applying a youth development approach to this wider range of settings is essential if we are to achieve meaningful change in a broad and diverse population of youth at the community level.

We will briefly describe and present a rationale for including these strategies in a youth development framework and then grapple with some of the challenges to doing so.

What must a community do to deliver the goods?

1. Strengthen the capacities of community adults (parents, families, primary caregivers, neighbors, and employers) to provide these supports and opportunities. History, research, and common sense tell us we cannot "program" or "service" young people into healthy development. Providing specific programs and high-quality youth services are key strategies for optimizing youth development outcomes; but without caregivers, neighbors, and employers of young people providing the supports and opportunities at home, in their neighborhoods, and where they work, our impact on the lives of a community's youth will be minimal.

Any honest community effort to increase supports and opportunities in the everyday lives of youth will and should inevitably bump up against the sensitive question of how to deal with families and family issues. In one sense, the case for including families in youth development approaches is clear: the family is the single most critical source of support, encouragement, moral development, love, and sustenance for a young person.

However, governments have limited their interventions in the families of youth on the principle that, since children are under the jurisdiction of their parents, the "state" should not interfere but rather should play a protective or supportive role. Until recently, the state would intervene in family life only in instances of demonstrable and egregious failure to meet the basic needs of youth, resulting in foster care, child protection, and juvenile justice activities, or in the case of certifiable need, through the welfare system. However, in recent years, there has been increasing recognition that public policy and institutions have a role to play in supporting parents as they work to raise their children. This is evidenced in the creation of community-based family support centers; a growing investment in developmental child care programs like Early Start and Head Start; and an increase in child-rearing programs and interventions for parents in high-risk categories (such as teen parents).

Nevertheless, most supportive interventions and policies have, to date, focused on the parents of young children in the hope that early intervention would prevent problems and make it unnecessary to "interfere" later. However, parents of adolescents are in as much need of support as are the parents of young children, especially in disadvantaged communities where networks and resources for children from 10 to 18 are particularly thin. The youth development field has not directly involved families of youth and has not yet found a rationale or mode to do so comfortably and coherently. The reluctance to address the issue head-on is understandable. But that reluctance also circumscribes the impact our field and our approach can have and the issues to which we can give voice.

To be effective, community efforts to improve youth outcomes will need to address some of the key needs of parents and families that have been shown to be directly related to how their children fare in the short and long term. These strategies will need to address the quality of parenting, other sources of child care, and the connections among parents and others who care for their children. This framework includes the following indicators that community action strategies have succeeded in strengthening the capacity of adults to "raise their youth."

Parents and families:

- Have access to strong support networks among other families with youth;
- Know about, and have affordable and reliable access to, alternative care and positive activities for their youth;
- Have effective communication networks with other adults who care for, or

Youth Development in Community Settings

who can provide needed service for, their youth, e.g., child-care workers, counselors, and teachers; and
- Are knowledgeable about effective parenting practices.

Optimizing adult support of youth will also have to involve neighbors (many of whom are themselves parents), as well as employers of youth. Communities will need to understand and then build on youth's often casual but sometimes crucial contacts with neighbors and on their early work experiences to increase the supports and opportunities available to youth. Therefore, the following are critical features in this framework for neighbors and employers:

Neighbors:

- Know and initiate constructive interactions with youth living in their community; and
- Communicate openly and constructively with each other, with parents of youth, and with other adults responsible for youth.

Employers of youth:

- Structure work for youth as closely as possible to youth development principles.

Community-based youth development initiatives will not achieve thresholds of supports and opportunities adequate to produce meaningful change in young people's lives unless specific programs and broad, community-wide strategies help caregivers, neighbors, and employers support youth.

2. Reform and integrate the large institutions and systems that affect young people. Reforming and coordinating public institutions have proved formidable challenges, which the field has usually sidestepped. The most glaring example is public education. Outside the home, schools are the main environment for young people. Long before youth development became a widely accepted concept, schools were widely urged to change, to become more responsive and effective. "School reform" is still a central topic in most large cities. Yet public education is an immense and densely packed sector—at times defensive and at times quite justified in being so. It also has a thicket of peripheral organizations working to serve, improve, and reform it, and its core activities have remained outside the scope of youth development efforts. Because public education has seemed too tough a nut to crack, youth development has avoided taking it on.

Some major educational reform efforts are using the supports and opportunities included in this framework—or conditions closely related to them—as guideposts to rethink and redo how schools work.[3]

Based on research, practice, and common sense, the following are indicators of schools supportive of youth development:

- Students interact with adults in small groups (< 15) during core instruction, over extended periods of time, during the school day, and across multiple years;

- Teaching methods reflect established best practices for maximum student engagement and learning;
- School policies and practices ensure collective responsibility for education professionals and provide opportunities for parents and other community adults to monitor and contribute to student success; and
- Schools and other institutions are linked in ways that maximize (1) continuity and consistency across settings and (2) ease and quality of communication with youth and their caregivers.

Reluctance to take on institutional issues extends beyond schools. Juvenile justice as a system, and as it is practiced in communities, bears directly on the lives of many young people—young people whose development is most seriously devoid of support and opportunities, and who are least likely to gain access to traditional, youth-serving organizations that currently define our field of practice. Other public institutions and policies touch youth through separated funding streams that originate at federal and state levels—welfare, housing, drug and alcohol treatment, child care—and end up in many communities being unorganized, unstrategic, and underfunded. Seldom do these institutions build from a coherent recognition of what needs to be done to support youth. They respond most of all to the dictates of funders and must constantly order their work and priorities to keep their funding, even when inadequate. Past efforts to achieve "service integration," whether at national, state, or local levels, have generally had discouraging results. The few incentives to work together that might be tried are heavily outweighed by funding dependency, inflexible rules, and institutional habits and culture long in the making.

Based on experience and research on effective community-based services, the following are indicators of public institutions (parks and recreation, juvenile justice, law enforcement, housing, welfare, social services, transportation) supportive of youth development:

- Such institutions locate services for youth and their families in the community;
- They have cooperative relationships with each other and with families of youth;
- They are accessible, affordable, and reliable; and
- They employ individuals who are equipped, empowered, and expected to (1) respond to community needs, and be accessible and respectful to community youth and families; and (2) establish the practices necessary to provide supports and opportunities to youth in direct contact with their systems.

The supports and opportunities described in the framework extend the idea of appropriate standards to all these institutions that serve youth. Once these non-negotiables for youth are embraced, these institutions can take on the next challenge: working together to provide supports and opportunities for their "shared" clients.

3. Increase the number and quality of developmental activities available for young people before and after school, on weekends and holidays, and over

Youth Development in Community Settings

the summer. Here is where our traditional definition of the youth development field fits into this unifying framework. Stronger and more widespread supports for youth outside their homes, schools, social service, and work experiences are essential to optimize youth development outcomes.

Key to this third strategy will be a full assessment of the supports and opportunities available in gap periods to all youth and particularly to youth who are hard to reach. Also key will be the capacity of the organizations currently providing these activities to absorb expanded responsibilities for youth different from those currently served.

Given what we know from research on these gap periods, areas of programming and community-based activities need to be strengthened and made more accessible. We also must realize that adding new programming and activities is not enough. As with the strategies for strengthening community adults' and public institutions' capacities to support youth, standards for the quality of these activities are needed to provide designers, operators, and consumers of the programs and activities with ways of knowing that what is going on there, at minimum, does no harm and, at best, maximizes the supports and opportunities young people get.

Wherever free-time activities and programs are located—in schools, youth organizations, recreations centers, churches, or parks—research is converging on a set of organizational features that translate into high levels of developmental support and opportunities for youth participants. The following are characteristics of quality gap period activities (before and after school, weekends, holidays, and summer).

Organizations are structured to provide:

- Effective adult/youth ratios;
- Safe, reliable, and accessible activities and spaces; and
- Continuity of care within and between activities.

Organizational policies include:

- Ongoing, results-based staff and organizational improvement process;
- Flexibility in allocating available resources; and
- Engagement of staff in local community.

Organizational activities include:

- Range of diverse, interesting, skill-building activities;
- High, clear, fair standards; and
- Youth involvement in organizational decision making.

4. Realign policies and resources in the public and private sectors in ways that support the implementation of the strategies described above. The youth development field, even as it is currently defined, has recognized that without policy supports from the municipal, state, and federal governments, it will remain marginalized in its efforts to affect youth development outcomes. Our framework broadens the field's purview to incorporate family supports, neighborhood revitalization and institutional reform, as well as expanded youth development programming and activities. Common sense, if not scientific research, makes it clear that public policies will have to be realigned if this expanded set of strategies is to have any chance of being implemented. Policy should support thoughtful, innovative, and rigorous proposals by community stakeholders for providing supports and opportunities to youth in all settings in which they grow up. These proposals can include recommendations for policy realignments at the state and federal levels to support the proposed community strategies.

Results-free resource allocations of the past haunt current efforts to marshal resources for new initiatives. Therefore, policy makers will need evidence early on that existing resources are being realigned to begin implementing these three sets of community strategies.

It seems clear that implementing all three strategies—and doing each better—is crucial. The price for our communities and our country will be high if we continue to promise meaningful change in the life chances of young people—particularly for youth living in economically disadvantaged areas—and fail to tackle this full range of strategies. First, if we continue to tinker around the edges of these young people's lives, community-level outcomes for youth will not meaningfully improve. This "failure" will only deepen the cynicism of investors in youth development, including among the participants themselves, and make future investments more difficult to obtain. Second, if our experience from repeated efforts to reform urban schools through programmatic (versus core and systemic) interventions and compensatory (versus preventive) activities is a reliable predictor, the final fallout of this "big goals, little intervention" approach will be further entrenchment of "blame the victim" scenarios in some professional, community, and policy quarters.

While calling for all of the above, we have to continue doing each of the above, but doing these things better. The framework provides similar expectations for the smallest, most targeted program as it does for larger, more heavily funded programs: provide the supports and opportunities to your youth. These ideas can be a useful lens through which all practitioners can critically view and then improve their own practices. At the same time, the framework encourages small and focused players in our field to look outside their immediate purview and find ways to connect their work to other community settings and stakeholders that touch their youth's lives.

Bringing the Community Together

By definition, realignment of political, economic, and human resources toward new and better youth development practices means that some old practices and policies will have to go. For adults living and working with youth, for public institutions, and for community-based organizations that serve youth and their families, making these choices and living with their personal and political consequences will not be an easy task. Therefore, these choices and their associated risks cannot be delegated or assigned to any single community stakeholder group.

Youth Development in Community Settings 305

Communities will need mobilization efforts to create conditions that encourage *all* stakeholders to put their oars in the water and pull together. In this framework (Figure 1, Box E), we have identified four conditions that mobilization efforts should seek to achieve to launch and sustain implementation of the community strategies (Figure 1, Box D).

First, there must be a sense of urgency among all stakeholders, a feeling that something they care about is very wrong and must be made right. Second, stakeholders must believe that these changes are achievable. Success stories have to be told and believed, and credible evidence of the efficacy of these strategies must be made available in compelling ways. Third, people asked to risk their comfort with the status quo have to see others doing the same; they have to sense equity in the pain and gain of change. When school reform means that teachers change what they do but no one else does, it does not work.

Finally, before individual and institutional stakeholders put themselves on the line, they will have to believe that business as usual can, in fact, be changed. The decline in supports and opportunities available to youth in many economically threatened communities over the past 50 years has been clear and dramatic. At times, it appears inexorable. Conversely, intentional programmatic investments to enrich these supports and opportunities over this same period have been intermittent, erratic in approach, and ephemeral in impact. With this backdrop, the new generation of community initiatives needs a collective sense by all stakeholders that "this is the big one," that this too will not pass, or the energy necessary to implement these bold and high-stakes strategies will not be there.

Creating these conditions is a tall order, but we believe that activities focused on building stakeholders' awareness, knowledge, engagement, and commitment to the story this framework tells can work. For example, stakeholders who see the gap between where youth are and where they need to be can create a sense of urgency. Stakeholders who interact with youth and adults in other communities like theirs, where their concerted efforts are closing this gap, gain a sense of possibility that this can also happen in their community. Achieving a sense of equity requires stakeholders across existing power relationships to engage in honest discussions about what they can do individually and collectively to implement these community strategies, the risks involved in doing so, and the supports that will be needed from each other to pull it off. Finally, change of this kind becomes inevitable only when key stakeholders—those who control political and financial resources in the community and those who have immediate and persistent impact on the lives of youth—jointly agree that the risk/reward ratio makes business as usual the more painful option.

SUPPORTING COMMUNITY ACTION

We believe the framework outlined above provides a structure within which both broad and highly focused community-based youth development initiatives can be located or created, and then critically examined. From our initial discussions of this framework with other national and local youth development organizations, and from our ongoing work with this framework in several community initiatives, some pressing needs have emerged.

The following are suggestions for how funders, technical assistance providers, and evaluators of community-based initiatives could help support effective community action on behalf of youth.

Funders could:

- Adopt a community approach that recognizes young people's need to receive supports and opportunities across all of the settings where they spend time, not just in programs or gap activities;
- Assist communities by investing in activities (and technical assistance) that equip and empower community stakeholders to use this community approach effectively;
- Provide funding for technical assistance to help communities develop local intermediaries or strengthen existing ones that can act as managers or conveners, and monitor these initiatives; and
- Invest in communities' assessments of their readiness for change, and whether and how well the community strategies are currently being implemented.

Technical assistance providers could:

- Assess and strengthen their capacity to assist community stakeholders in using this approach, specifically to support the stakeholders in mobilizing around this framework and in planning and implementing the community strategies; and
- Create strategic and cooperative partnerships with complementary intermediaries in order to offer the full range of assistance that communities will need to take this approach to supporting their youth.

Evaluators of community-based initiatives could:

- Provide communities with a range of assessment strategies for tracking progress across the framework elements. This requires both organizing existing tools and developing new ones.

These suggestions are meant to strengthen the field's capacity to support community-based efforts to implement the community action strategies included in this framework. They assume that our field is ready to adopt such a framework as a guide for its collective work on behalf of youth. This is a risky assumption. Within this project, participants debated, and did not resolve, whether it was a good idea to adopt such a framework for our work as investors, technical assistance providers, and researchers-evaluators.

In this chapter, we are calling for the field to move beyond the current state of "dueling frameworks." We think we need an overarching structure within which all of us can find our place—within which we can each articulate what we can contribute to making meaningful change and learning from it, on the ground, in diverse communities. We believe this reflective process will help us identify gaps in our network of support for community-based youth development initiatives. It will also permit and pressure us, as a field and as individual entities, to become more collectively responsible for the outcomes that we, and our community partners, seek for young people.

NOTES

1. A number of proponents of youth development have been trying for some time to have the field more broadly conceived and supported. However, for the most part, resource allocation to "youth development activities" has been primarily channeled through youth organizations.
2. For other publications related to this framework, contact Community Action for Youth Project, 308 Glendale Drive, Toms River, NJ 08753, or e-mail jnirre@aol.com.
3. First Things First, the school reform framework of the Institute for Research and Reform in Education, makes explicit links between changes in school structures and classroom practices, youth experience of supports and opportunities, and ultimately improved youth development outcomes.

INDEX

Aber, Larry, 52
Ability, areas of, 94, 174
Abt Associates, 251, 282, 283
Academic competency, 6
Academy for Educational Development (AED), xi, 25, 53, 144
Addams, Jane, 236
Adjudication, in juvenile court, 241
Adolescence, use of term, 68-69, 225n1
Adolescent Mother's Resource Home Program, 217-18
Adolescents, 68, 113-14, 122
Adolescents at Risk (Dryfoos), 46n7
Adoption and Safe Families Act, 262
Adoption Assistance and Child Welfare Act (1980), 256
Adulthood, preparing youth for, 3-5, 6-7, 66, 196, 293, 296-97
Adultification, of juvenile court, 237
Adults, youth relationships with, 212-14, 298
Advocates and advocacy, 13, 21, 22-23, 26, 30, 48n23, 51, 187
AED. *See* Academy for Educational Development
AFDC. *See* Aid to Families with Dependent Children
African American youth, 209, 273, 274
After-School Corporation, 100, 120
After-school programming, x, 83, 84-85, 118-21, 123
Aftercare, and juvenile justice, 255-56, 264n9
Aid to Families with Dependent Children (AFDC), 47n11, 79
Alan Guttmacher Institute, 48n16
Alternative Rehabilitative Communities (Pa.), 252
Altschuler, David, 248-49, 255
American Legislative Exchange Council (ALEC), 247
American Youth Policy Forum, 46n1
America's Children, 47-48n16, 156. *See also* Key National Indicators of Well-Being
America's Disconnected Youth (Besharov), 47n11
America's Promise, 7, 18, 46-47n8, 47n10, 83
Amundson, Daniel R., 61-62
Anatomy of a Demonstration, 282
Angrisani, Albert, 281
Annie E. Casey Foundation, 26, 117, 156, 158, 248, 262
Antisocial behavior, 246
Area Redevelopment Act (1961), 271
Arenas of action, xi, 51-53, 187. *See also* Youth development, agenda
Armstrong, Troy, 255
Assessment. *See* Measurements and measuring

Assets, developmental, 179, 295
At-risk behaviors, 24, 61-62, 171, 233, 239. *See also* Behaviors; High-risk behaviors
Aubrun, Axel, 64-65, 67-71, 73
Autonomy, of organizations, 201-3, 210-11, 218-19, 222-23

Baden-Powell, Robert S., 207
Balanced and Restorative Justice (BARJ), 258, 264n12
Bales, Susan Nall, xi, 52
BARJ. *See* Balanced and Restorative Justice
Bazemore, Gordon, 238, 254, 258, 259
Beacon Schools, 91
Beacons case study (New York City, N.Y.), 39-46, 119
Beacons Initiative and Youth Development Learning Network (San Francisco, Calif.), 295
Beaumont Juvenile Correctional Center (Va.), 250-51
Behavioral Sciences Institute, 262
Behaviors, 9, 22-23, 82, 246. *See also* At-risk behaviors; High-risk behaviors
Benson, Peter L., 25, 53
Benton Foundation, 20, 21, 52
Berkeley Media Studies Group (BMSG), 62-64
Besharov, D., 47n11
Best Practices in Youth Development, 183
"Beyonds," 9-11, 15, 35, 39, 40-42
BGCA. *See* Boys & Girls Clubs of America
Big Brothers/Big Sisters of America, 47n15, 83, 84, 88, 100, 124n5
Biosocial gap, 193-94, 221
BMSG. *See* Berkeley Media Studies Group
Bostrom, Meg, 57-58, 64, 66, 67-68
Boy Scouts of America, 96, 138, 207-8, 210
Boys & Girls Clubs of America (BGCA), 4, 47n15, 78, 83, 84, 85, 88, 96, 100, 138
Boy's Life magazine, 210
Brookline High School (Boston, Mass.), 202-3
Budgets and budgeting. *See* Funds and funding
Business, as support system, 187
Business Adventure program, 209

Campaign for Kids, 20
Carnegie Commission. *See* Carnegie Council on Adolescent Development
Carnegie Corporation, 83
Carnegie Council on Adolescent Development, 3, 4, 5, 12, 93, 98, 100, 105-9, 115, 137
Carter, Stephen, 261
Catalano, Richard, 48n19, 246

Catholic schools, 203
Causality, 12-13, 167, 172
CAYP. *See* Community Action for Youth Project
CCYD. *See* Community Change for Youth Development
Center for Children in Poverty, 52
Center for Employment Training (CET), 278-79
Center for Youth Development, 7, 21, 48n17
Center for Youth Development and Policy Research (CYDPR), xi, 53, 91, 93, 106, 109, 111, 117, 122, 123, 173, 183, 292, 295
CET. *See* Center for Employment Training
CETA. *See* Comprehensive Employment and Training Act
Chapin Hall Center for Children, xi, 25, 144, 188, 226n5
Character, as task of adolescence, 6-7
Charles Steward Mott Foundation, 83, 118
Chicago Youth Agency Partnership, 48n20
Child-care subsidies, 197
Child Trends, Inc., 156
Child welfare, 214-15, 216, 233, 262
Children and Youth Funding Report, 107
Children's Defense Fund, 107
Children's Trust Fund, 111
Churches, 78. *See also* Faith community
Civic competency, 7
Civil rights movement, 273
Clark, Kenneth, 272
Clinton, Bill, 264n10
Cloward, Richard, 272
Collaboration, and policy, 89
Committee on Juvenile Delinquency and Youth Crime, 271-72
Communication professionals, 20
Communities, 8-9, 22, 35, 36-38, 47n14, 96-97, 136, 140-41, 142, 145, 151, 184-85, 187, 189, 273. *See also* Neighborhoods
Communities That Care (CTC), 48n19, 246-47, 295
Community Action for Youth Project (CAYP), xi, 189, 307n2
Community-based youth-serving organizations (CBOs), 187. *See also* Communities; Organizations
Community Change for Youth Development (CCYD), 46-47n8, 47n10, 295
Community Network(s) for Youth Development, 30, 48n20, 48n21, 295
Community Progress Inc. (CPI), 272
Community Youth Development Mobilization Initiative, 295
Competence/competency, 6-7, 46n3, 66, 212-13, 257-59. *See also* Academic competency; Civic competency
Comprehensive Competencies Program, 280
Comprehensive Employment and Training Act (CETA), 270, 277-82
Comprehensive Services for Youth Act, 116
Concentrated Employment Program (CEP), 276

Confidence, as task of adolescence, 6-7
Connect for Kids, 20
Connections, as task of adolescence, 6-7
Connell, James P., 1, 6, 16-17, 18, 189, 195
Conrad, D., 137
Contributions, as task of adolescence, 6-7
Costello, Joan, 25, 29, 136, 188
Costs. *See* Funds and funding
Crime and Justice Research Institute (CJRI), 245
Crouse, Mary Ann, 235-36
Csikszentmihalyi, M., 194
CTC. *See* Communities That Care
Cultures, as support system, 187
CYDPR. *See* Center for Youth Development and Policy Research

D. Bonnet Associates, 111
Darwinism, 79
Data collection, 178-85
David and Lucile Packard Foundation, 52, 55
Defense counsel, and juvenile justice, 260-61
Delinquent, use of term, 239
Department of Health and Human Services (DHHS), 256
Department of Human Services (DHS), 245
Detention, and juvenile justice, 240
Deterrence, and juvenile justice, 247
Development, and prevention, 23-24, 172-73. *See also* Early childhood care and development; Economic development; Families and family support/development; Youth development; Zone of proximal development
Development Research and Programs Inc., 295
Developmental assets, 179, 295
DeWitt Wallace-Reader's Digest Fund, 83, 140
Disabilities, youth with, 252-53, 272
Discrimination, in workplace, 273
Disposition, in juvenile court, 241
Diversion programs, and juvenile justice, 232, 238-39
Donovan, Raymond, 281
Dorfman, Lori, 52, 63
Drugs, use by youth, 82
Dryfoos, Joy, 46n7, 93, 105-9, 116
Due Process Advocacy Project, 260
Dynarski, Mark, 171

Early childhood care and development, 22
Early Start, 300
Earls, F. C., 141
Economic development, 22
Economic Opportunity Act (EOA), 274-75
Edelman, Marian Wright, 13
Edna McConnell Clark Foundation, 262
Education, x, 63-64, 100, 187, 254-55. *See also* Schools and schooling
El Puente youth program (New York City), 211
Elliott, Delbert, 46n6
Employers, use of youth development principles, 301

Index

Employment of youth. *See* Youth employment
Environments, and behavior, 9
Evaluations, 24, 150, 306. *See also* Measurements and measuring
Evidence base, 17, 24-26, 43
Ewing Marian Kauffman Foundation, x
Expenditures. *See* Funds and funding
Expenditures for Children (Sugarman), 107
Extended Service Schools Initiative, 232

Faith community, 187, 261. *See also* Churches
Families and family support/development, 22, 48n18, 96-97, 102, 187, 300-301. *See also* Parents
Family and Youth Services Bureau, 108
Federal Interagency Forum on Child and Family Statistics, 47n16, 178
Feld, Barry, 242-43
Ferber, Thaddeus, 2
Fight Crime: Invest in Kids, 21
Finance Project, 93, 107, 109
Finances and financing. *See* Funds and funding
First Things First, 295, 307n3
Fisherman's Guide, A (Taggart), 279-80
Ford Foundation, 271-72, 274
Forgotten Half, The (Grant Commission), 3-4
Forum for Youth Investment, xi, 2, 48n24
Foster Care Independence Act (1999), 264n10
4-H clubs/movement, 85, 96, 110, 138, 207, 208, 210
Frame analysis, strategic, 56-57
FrameWorks Institute, 52, 56, 68
Franklin, Benjamin, 243-44, 263
Franklin, Josiah, 244
Freidson, E., 204, 212
Funds and funding, 53, 91-133, 306. *See also* Philanthropy

Gallo, Frank, 282
Gallup polls, 57
Gambone & Associates, 189
Gambone, Michelle Alberti, 1, 6, 16-17, 18, 189
Gault court case/decision (*In re Gault*), 237-38
Gault, Gerald, 237-38
Generation of Challenge, A, 285
Gilliam, Franklin D., Jr., 52, 71-72
Girl Scouts of America, 96, 100, 138
Girls Incorporated, 83
Gleason, Philip, 171
Goals, broadening, 5-7, 8, 34, 38
Good High School, The (Lightfoot), 205
Government-sponsored organizations, 222. *See also* Organizations
Governments, and youth development, 102-3, 106
Grady, Joseph, 64-65, 67-71, 73
Grant Foundation Commission on Work, Family and Citizenship, 3-4, 5, 12
Grassroots citizen constituencies, 21
Greatest Generation, The (Brokaw), 70
Green Book, 107
Guided Tour of Youth Development, A, 181-82

Hahn, Andrew, 52
Hall, G. Stanley, 193
Halpern, R., 139
Hampton Coalition for Youth, 48n20
Harlem Youth Opportunities Unlimited (HARYOU), 272
Hawkins, David, 48n19, 246
Head Start, 79, 275, 300
Health care, 29, 187, 252-53, 254-55, 298
Healthy Communities • Healthy Youth, 48n17
Heath, S. B., 212, 213
Hedin, D., 137
Heintz-Knowles, Katharine, 60-61
Hero youth model, inadvisability of, 71-72
High-risk behaviors, 18-19, 24. *See also* At-risk behaviors; Behaviors
Historical context, 188, 191-97, 199-200, 207-8, 214-18, 221, 222, 234-35, 245-46, 271-72, 291-92
Homebuilders, as model of family preservation, 262
House of Umoja (Philadelphia, Pa.), 261
Houses of Refuge, 235
Hull House, 236
Human Rights Watch, 249
Humphrey, Hubert H., 276

Identity, aspects of, 94, 174
Incapacitation, and juvenile justice, 247-48, 262, 263n2
Independent living, 216, 256-57, 264n10
Indiana Youth Institute, 48n20
Indicators, of youth development, 26, 117, 170, 301-2
Individualism, 79
Infrastructure(s), 16, 17, 29-31, 32, 33, 37-38, 46
Inputs, 35, 36-37, 146, 148
Institute for Research and Reform in Education, 189, 295, 307n3
Institutions, 226n2. *See also* Organizations
Intake, and juvenile justice, 240
Intermediaries, 30, 38, 124
International Convention on the Rights of the Child, 226n3
International Youth Foundation (IYF-US), xi, 2, 6, 7, 42
Internet, 114
Interventions, 9, 239, 259, 261, 291-92
Investments, 102, 104-5
Irby, Merita, 2, 149
Iyengar, Shanto, 56, 71
IYF-US. *See* International Youth Foundation (IYF-US)

JAIBG. *See* Juvenile Accountability Incentive Block Grant
Jewish Vocational Service (Philadelphia, Pa.), 272
JLC. *See* Juvenile Law Center
Job Corps, 79, 271, 274-75, 278, 279, 280, 281
Job Opportunities in the Business Sector (JOBS), 272, 273, 274

Index

Job Training Partnership Act (JTPA), 79, 269, 279-84 *passim*
JOBS. *See* Job Opportunities in the Business Sector
John F. Kennedy High School (Bronx, N.Y.), 201
Johnson, Lyndon, 170, 274
JOV. See Juvenile Offenders and Victims
JTPA. *See* Job Training Partnership Act
Justice, juvenile. *See* Juvenile justice
Juvenile Accountability Incentive Block Grant (JAIBG), 247-48, 249, 258-59, 264n7, 264n13
Juvenile Defender Leadership Summits, 261
Juvenile Detention Center Association of Pennsylvania (JDCAP), 240
Juvenile justice, x, 4-5, 21, 187, 188, 215
Juvenile Justice and Delinquency Prevention Act (1974), 215, 242, 246
Juvenile Justice Center, 260
Juvenile Justice Project, 260
Juvenile Law Center (JLC), xi, 188, 250, 254, 260
Juvenile Offenders and Victims (JOV), 156, 166-67

Kaleidoscope (Chicago, Ill.), 254
Kellogg Youth Initiative Partnerships (KYIP), 179-81, 183
Kennedy, John F., 271-72
Key National Indicators of Well-Being (KNIWB), 156, 160-63. *See also America's Children*
Kids Count data/*Kids Count Data Book(s)*, 26, 48n17, 117, 156, 158-60, 162, 163, 177
Kids These Days, 180
KNIWB. See Key National Indicators of Well-Being
Kunkel, Dale, 62
KYIP Youth Survey. *See* Kellogg Youth Initiative Partnerships

Labeling, moving beyond, 10, 11, 41
Ladewig, H., 138
Lakoff, George, 52
Larson, R., 194
Law. *See* Juvenile justice
Leadership, and funding, 121
Leffert, N., 137
Lessons Learned, 284
Levitan, Sar, 282, 285
Libraries, as support system, 29, 187
Lichter, Linda S., 61-62
Lichter, S. Robert, 61-62
Lightfoot, Sara Lawrence, 201, 205
Lilly Endowment, 32, 36
Lindsey, Ben, 236
Little Leagues, 84
Lopez, Steve, 231

MacDonald, Gary B., 26, 53
Mack, Julian, 236
Maloney, Dennis, 237-38, 257
Manpower Demonstration Research Corporation, 280
Manpower Development and Training Act (1962), 269-78 *passim*

Maryland Advocates for Children and Youth, 103
Mastruzzi, Bob, 201
Mathematics, and academic progress, 168
Matter of Time, A, 93, 98-99, 115, 137
Maturation, 226n4
McCarthy, Bob, 202
McCollum, Bill, 247, 248
MDTA. *See* Manpower Development and Training Act
Measurements and measuring, 26-27, 53, 150, 155-86, 245, 259-60. *See also* Research
Media, 60-65, 82, 275. *See also* Berkeley Media Studies Group
Mental hardships, 82
Mental health, 252-53
Mentoring, x, 83, 84-85
Merry, Sheila, 217
Midnight Basketball, 24
Miller, Jerome, 235, 250
Milton Academy (New England), 205
Minnesota Youth Development [Web] Page, 114
Mobilization for Youth, 272, 273
Mondale, Walter, 271
Money. *See* Funds and funding
Moore, Mark, 14-15
Mott Foundation. *See* Charles Stewart Mott Foundation
Multi-Systemic Therapy (S.C.), 252
Murphy, Richard, 18, 21, 53
Museums, as support system, 29, 187

NAEP. *See National Assessment of Educational Progress*
National Assessment of Educational Progress (NAEP), 156, 168-69
National Association of Child Advocates, 109
National Association of Young People in Care, 219
National Center for Education Statistics, 96, 124n2
National Children's Bureau, 214, 219
National Collaboration for Youth, 21
National Education Longitudinal Study, 138
National 4-H Council, 208
National League of Cities (NLC), 51, 112
National Longitudinal Study of Adolescent Health, 141
National Network for Youth, 21, 47n14
National Urban League, 34, 83, 94, 273, 295
National Youth Employment Coalition (NYEC), xi, 48n19, 189, 283-86
Neighborhood Youth Corps, 272, 275, 277
Neighborhoods, 17, 31-33, 46, 102, 187, 223-25, 239, 246. *See also* Communities
Nelson, Doug, 248
Networks for Youth Development, 42, 181-82, 183
New Expressions (monthly newspaper), 211
New York City Beacons. *See* Beacons case study
Newman, Robert P., 18, 53
Newmann, F. M., 204-5
NLC. *See* National League of Cities
NYEC. *See* National Youth Employment Coalition (NYEC)

Index

Office of Economic Opportunity (OEO), 276
Office of Juvenile Justice and Delinquency
 Prevention (OJJDP), 215, 246, 251, 255, 260, 261
OICs. *See* Opportunities Industrialization Centers
OJJDP. *See* Office of Juvenile Justice and Delinquency Prevention
OJT. *See* On-the-job training
On-the-job training (OJT), 272-73, 277-83 *passim*
Open Society Institute, 83, 120
Opportunities Industrialization Centers (OICs), 273, 274, 279
Options, increased, 5, 7-8, 38
Oregon Social Learning Center, 254
Organizations, and youth development, 136, 137-39, 142, 145, 181-84, 188, 191-229, 226n2, 303. *See also* specific organizations
Out-of-School Youth Programs, 282
Outcomes
 behavioral and psychological, 6-7
 of community youth development, 295-96
 developmental, 117, 147-48, 296-97
 as desired positive results, 94, 174
 and employment, 282-83
 of intervention and juvenile justice, 259
 long-term, 147-48
 measuring, 156
 monitoring, 36-37
 movement, 80
 short-term, 6, 147-48
 and successful adulthood, 296-97
Outward Bound (Minn.), 212-13

P/PV. *See* Public/Private Ventures
Pacific Research Institute for Public Policy, 104, 107
Packard Foundation. *See* David and Lucile Packard Foundation
Paradigm shift, 5-16, 32-33
Parens patriae, 234, 235-36
Parents, 34-36, 43, 300-301. *See also* Families/family
Parks, as support system, 187
Paternalism, 235
Peer courts, and juvenile justice, 215
Peers, relationships with, 298
PEPNet. *See* Promising and Effective Practices Network
Perceptions, vs. reality, 57-60
Perceptual barriers, to positive youth development, 17, 19-20, 52, 55-75, 156
Perkins, Carl, 276
Pertschuk, Michael, 52
Philanthropy, 43, 51, 83-84, 103, 120, 187
Pilot programs, 10, 11, 41
Pittman, Karen, 2, 149, 172, 195, 208-9, 210, 212
Policy, and developmental needs, 51, 79-80, 85-90, 185, 187
Policy climate, and youth development, 52-53, 77-90
Policy makers, 8-9, 12, 117

Positive youth development (PYD), 188
Powell, Colin, 83, 91
Power of Public Ideas, The (Reich), 12, 13, 14
Practice, as arena of action, 51, 187
President's Commission on Manpower (PCOM), 276
President's Committee on Juvenile Delinquency, 273, 274
President's Summit for America's Future (1997), 18, 80, 83, 291
Prevention, 9, 11, 40, 23-24, 143, 170, 172-73
Price, Hugh, 34, 83, 94
Priority One: Put Kids First, 103
Prisoner Litigation Reform Act (PLRA), 251
Private Industry Council (PIC), 281
Probation officers, 251-52
Problem-focused services. *See* Services
Problem Severity Index (PSI), 246
ProDES. *See* Program Development and Evaluation System
Professionals and professionalism, 10, 11, 21, 25-28, 41, 203-6, 211-12, 219, 223
Program Development and Evaluation System (ProDES), 245, 259-60
Programs, 5, 9, 12-13, 34, 91, 135-37, 142, 145, 189. *See also* Pilot programs; specific programs
Promising and Effective Practices Network (PEPNet), 283-85
Puberty, 226n4
Public Agenda, 19, 20, 35, 81, 180-81
Public idea(s), 5-16, 32-46
Public opinion, 19-20, 43, 51, 187
Public policy. *See* Policy
Public/Private Ventures (P/PV), x, xi, 25, 46-47n8, 47n15, 52-53, 83, 88, 124nn3, 4, 144, 232, 280, 282, 292, 295
Public safety, and juvenile justice, 257
Punishment, and juvenile justice, 247-48
PYD. *See* Positive youth development

Quick fixes, beyond, 9, 11, 40
Quinn, J., 137, 138

Raley, Gordon, 52
Raudenbush, S. W., 141
Reading, and academic progress, 168-69
Reagan, Ronald, 281
Reality checks, 34
Recipients, young people as, 10, 11, 41
Recreation, as support system, 29, 187
Referral, and juvenile justice system, 239-40
Reform efforts, 23
Reframing Youth Issues, 56
Rehabilitation, and juvenile justice, 257
Reich, Robert, 1, 12, 13, 79
Religion. *See* Faith community
Research, 25, 51, 57-68, 136-42, 187, 225. *See also* Measurements and measuring
Resources, 36-37, 176
Restorative justice, 257-58

Retribution, and juvenile justice, 247-48
Risk, assessment for, 246-47
Risky behaviors. *See* At-risk behaviors; Behaviors; High-risk behaviors
Roach, A. A., 212, 213
Rodriguez, Richard, 73
Role definition, and policy, 89
Ruth, A., 58

Safe and Sound Campaign/Safe and Sound Community Promises, 21, 47n13, 119-20
Safe environment(s)/places, 8, 139
Safe Passage (Dryfoos), 93
Safe Passages Movement, 116
Safe Streets, Safe Cities, 41
Safety, personal, 298-99
Safety, public, 257
Saito, Rebecca N., 25, 53
Sampson, R. J., 141
Scales, P. C., 137
Schlessinger, Andrea, 225
School reform, 301, 307n3
School shootings, media coverage of, 82
Schools and schooling
    autonomy of, 201-3, 222-23
    beyond, 9-10, 11, 40-41
    Catholic, 203
    history of, 199-200
    organizational structure and dynamics of, 200-206, 222-23
    professionalism in, 203-6
    as public institution devoted to development, 12, 43, 198-99
    relationship-building capacity, 206
    segregation by age and ability, 203
    size of, 200-201, 222
    as support system, 29, 187, 198-206
    and youth development, 43, 96-97, 301-2
    See also After-school programming; Education
Schwartz, Robert G., 29, 188
Science, academic progress, 168
Scientific foundations, of youth development, 53, 135-54
Sconyers, Nancy, 124n11
Scouting for Boys (Baden-Powell), 207
Scouting Life magazine, 210
Search Institute, xi, 21, 25, 48n17, 53, 144, 179, 264n5, 292, 295
Second Chance, A (Levitan and Gallo), 282
Segregation, by age and ability, in schools, 203
Self-esteem, 138
Self-sufficiency, 66, 295
Self-worth, 196
Services, 9, 11, 40, 95, 214-20, 222-23, 224, 302
Settings and systems. *See* Systems and settings
Shelter, 298
Shinke, Steven, 47n15
Sierra Club for Youth, concept of, 21
SMART Moves, 138
Smith, Stephanie M., 18, 53

Smith, Thomas J., 1, 6, 16-17, 18, 189
Social control, and juvenile justice, 243
Social Development Research Group, 137
Social engineering, 292
Social integration, 212
Social Security Act (1935), 214, 256
Social services, as support system, 187
Social welfare, and juvenile justice, 243
Socialization, 222
Socializing systems, 136, 140, 142, 145
Society for Prevention of Pauperism, 235
Society for the Reformation of Juvenile Delinquents, 235
Soros, George, 83
Spielberger, Julie, 25, 29, 136, 188
State Employment Service, 271
Stereotypes, 65-68
Strategic frame analysis, 56-57
Strategies, redefining, 8-11
Substance abuse prevention, 36
Sugarman, Jule M., 107
Sullivan, Leon H., 274
Summer Training and Education Program, 282
Summer Youth Employment Program(s), 269, 271, 272, 275, 281
Support for Youth, 124n3
Supports and support systems, 151
    autonomy and flexibility of, 210-11, 223
    developmental, 175-76
    history of, 207-8
    organizational structure and dynamics of, 208-14, 222-23
    primary supports, 206-14
    professionalism of, 211-12
    public and private, strengthening, 17, 28-29
    voluntary participation in, 209-10
    and youth development, 95, 297-99
Sustainability, 29-31, 43, 120-21, 123
Systems and settings, xi, 36-37, 187-89. *See also* Socializing systems; Supports and support systems

Taggart, Robert, 279
Tallulah Correctional Center for Youth (Miss.), 249-50
Tannen, Deborah, 56
Task Force on Youth Employment, 271
Taxes, dedicated tax for children, 103, 130-33
Technical assistance providers, 306
Teen Outreach Program, 47n15, 100
Teenager(s), use of word, 68
Terry, W. Clinton, 254, 258, 259
Third and Indiana (Lopez), 231-32
Thomas, J. K., 138
Time, 98-100, 123
TIMMS study, 48n16
Toles, Mark, 25, 29, 136, 188
Transfer, in juvenile justice system, 240-41, 262
Transition, in juvenile justice system, 253
Treatment, 170, 259

Index

Trends in the Well-Being of America's Children and Youth, 156, 164-66
Turning Points, 3
21st Century Learning Centers Program, 4, 118

Umbreit, Mark, 238, 258, 259
Unified Delinquency Intervention Services (UDIS), 217
United Way, 103, 111, 210
Uniting Congregations for Youth Development, 140
Urban Strategies Council, 48n20

Valdivieso, Rafael, 26, 53
Violence, coverage in media, 61-62, 63-64
Violent Youth Predator Act (1996), 248
Vocal constituencies, 17, 20-21
Vocational rehabilitation and training, 272, 277
Volunteerism, 181, 209-10
Voyageur Outward Bound (Minn.), 212-13
Vygotsky, L. S., 196, 204, 210

W. K. Kellogg Foundation, 179, 183
W. T. Grant Foundation, 52, 55
Walker, Gary, x, 23, 35, 52-53
War on Poverty, 79, 274
Web pages. *See* Internet
Wehlage, G. G., 204-5
What's Working (and What's Not), 283
White House Conference on Children (1909), 214
White House Conference on Teenagers, 67
Who Cares?, 219
WIA. *See* Workforce Investment Act
Williams, George, 207
Williams, Jesse E., Jr., 245
Willie M. program (N.C.), 252
Wolfgang, Marvin, 239
Woodlawn Organization (TWO), 273
Woodruff, K., 63
Woodson, Robert, 239, 261
Workforce Investment Act (WIA), 284, 286, 287
World Wide Web. *See* Internet
Wright, M., 195, 208-9, 210, 212
Writing, and academic progress, 169
Wynn, Joan, 25, 29, 136, 137, 188, 209

YDDP/YDD Project. *See* Youth Development Directions Project
YEDPA. *See* Youth Employment Demonstration Projects Act
YMCA/YWCA, 83, 85, 138, 207, 210, 272, 273, 274
York County Youth Development Center, 114
Young Adult Conservation Corps (YACC), 279
Young Americans Act, 108
Young Men's Christian Association. *See* YMCA/YWCA
Young Women's Christian Association. *See* YMCA/YWCA

Youniss, J., 58
Youth, definitions and use of term, 68, 221
Youth as Resources (YAR), 217
Youth Communications (Chicago, Ill.), 211
Youth Community Conservation Improvement Program (YCCIP), 279
Youth development
   as academic discipline, 25
   agenda, 44-46, 149-51, 224-25
   as approach, 292-93
   consensus on, lack of, 114, 122
   defined, 94-96, 173-76
   as field of practice, 292-93
   framework, 1-2, 56-57, 294-305, 306
   history, 291-92
   from idea to moral imperative, vii-xii
   ideal, for all youth, 96-97
   lack of consensus on, 114
   movement, 194-96, 292-93
   positive, 232-33
   practice(s), 221, 304
   promotion of, 2, 3-50
   term, use of, vii, ix, 5, 135
   See also Positive youth development; Programs
Youth Development Block Grant, 108
Youth Development Community Block Grant, 4, 116
Youth Development Directions Project (YDDP), x-xi
Youth Development Funders Group, x
Youth Development Institute, 7, 8, 42, 48n20, 181
Youth Development Mobilization, 295
Youth employment, 187-89
Youth Employment Demonstration Projects Act (YEDPA), 270, 279, 280
Youth in the Ghetto, 272
Youth Incentive Entitlement Pilot Project (YIEPP), 279
Youth Initiative Project (YIP), 209
Youth Law Center, 260
Youth Opportunity Grant, 269
Youth Risk Behavior Surveillance (YRBS), 156, 157-58
YouthWork, 280
YouthBudget, 103, 111-12, 118, *129*
YouthBuild, 4
YouthMapping, 48n17
YouthNet of Greater Kansas City, 48n20
YouthPlaces, 119-20
YRBS. See Youth Risk Behavior Surveillance (YRBS), 156, 157-58
YWCA. *See* YMCA/YWCA

Zero tolerance, 239
Zone of proximal development, 196, 204, 210
Zuckerman, Alan, 29, 189